ILLINOIS CENTRAL COLLEGE
PS3523.I58Z6 1990
STACKS
City of discontent /

A12900 745551

PS 3523 .I58 Z6 1990

Harris, Mark, 1922-

City of discontent

78778

WITHDRAWN

Illinois Central College
Learning Resources Center

WITHDRAWN

CITY OF DISCONTENT

An interpretive biography of Vachel Lind-say, being also the story of Springfield, Illinois, USA, and of the love of the poet for that city, that state and that nation.

Mark Harris

SECOND CHANCE PRESS
SAG HARBOR, NEW YORK

I.C.C. LIBRARY

78778

PS
3523
I58
Z6
1990

In this, the City of my Discontent,
Sometimes there comes a whisper from the grass,
"Romance, Romance—is here. No Hindu town
Is quite so strange. No Citadel of Brass
By Sinbad found, held half such love and hate;
No picture-palace in a picture-book
Such webs of Friendship, Beauty, Greed and Fate!"
—Vachel Lindsay, "Springfield Magical"

For Josephine
Who Advised, Subsidized,
And Was Patient

Copyright © 1952,1980 by Mark Harris

All rights reserved
including the right of reproduction
in whole or part in any form

Library of Congress Catalogue Card Number: 89-062512
ISBN: 0-933256-75-2

Originally published by Bobbs-Merrill

First republication 1990 by
SECOND CHANCE PRESS
RD2, Sag Harbor, New York

INTRODUCTION

IN SIMPLE SHELTERED 1945, in quest of a girl to marry and a book to write, I discovered in Springfield, Illinois, not only the girl but also the poet Vachel Lindsay, married both, and have lived ever since in a polygamous awe arising from the repeated discovery that when I reach the truth of one or the other I am nevertheless as distant as ever: all roads lead not to finite horizons but merely to new turnings. I was twenty-three, if not too young to marry certainly too young to acknowledge any deficiency in myself likely to prevent me from promptly grasping every aspect of every motivation of a poet who was by that year fourteen years dead, whose geographical origin, educational training, and religious background were significantly different from my own, whose literary production was mature and extensive although my own had scarcely begun, and whose disposition, perhaps as the very result of that production, had led him to a despair I had not the least preparation to share. It was the year the bomb fell upon Hiroshima, a city in which I have since lived with my wife and the children of our Springfield union, and the year I undertook, with all the passion of a dedicated Know Nothing, a biography of the poet.

My passion was attacked but never subdued by the poet's sister, Olive Wakefield, of Springfield, her objections being that my mind was too young and unformed. These objections my young and unformed mind discounted as the peccadillo of a lady whose own mind had necessarily been weakened by long missionary years in China. My publisher, for different and less valid reasons, roughly ordered me to abandon the project, and I suffered, as a consequence, an affliction of spirit which settled in my lungs and left me almost dead in a Catholic hospital in Springfield. Luckily, I was rescued by nuns equipped with needles loaded with a new, war-born drug called penicillin, and by a devout lay nurse who in the moment of most extreme crisis actually restored warmth to my body by leaping upon me with her own; it was an act of mercy performed for my salvation in spite of the fact that my fevered tongue had contin-

uously declared to her my contempt for her Church. Whether I
was aware of it or not (these things take time) I was now better prepared than before—my mind less young, beginning to be
formed—to seize hints of love, faith, charity, and hope.

Once more upon my feet, still far short of full strength or
full understanding, I resumed my work. Over and over I read
the books of Vachel Lindsay, traced his route through life upon
calendars, index-cards, and maps of the United States, accumulated mountains of correspondence, and visited persons who
had known him in Springfield and elsewhere. It was my first
excuse to place myself in the presence of men of artistic promi-
nence—Louis Untermeyer and Langston Hughes in New York,
Percy Grainger and John Sloan in New Mexico, and others,
each of whom was indulgent, and all of whom warned me
against haste.

For me, the most memorable of these interviews was with
Edgar Lee Masters, who had already written a biography of
Lindsay, and who was puzzled why anyone should attempt an
improvement upon it. We met in the lobby of the Hotel Irving
in New York on a fine autumn day. His face brightened as we
shook hands, but he soon grew sullen and withdrawn, as one
does who knows too much. He was well, but anxious to die.
He stared briefly with wonder at an object nearly sixty years
his junior, soon shifting his gaze to some memory upon the
wall behind me, and the conversation proceeded, as his wife
had warned me it would, principally between her and me. At
the end of about twenty minutes she gently suggested that
we had talked long enough. Masters agreed, and rose, adding
only, "Vachel was the greatest of us all." It was the thought
he meant me to carry away.

My book was subsequently published, not in haste, but perhaps too soon. On the other hand, how could I have put it
indefinitely off? A writer must discharge his mistakes and
go on to others; if they loom to embarrass him so much the
better: he can revisit them with the added advantage of having
followed Lindsay upon the dangerous path of literary en-
deavor. On the day it was published I stood upon a street in
Minneapolis, in the company of the poet Allen Tate, admiring
my brilliant production in a bookshop window and trying to
persuade Mr. Tate that if he would only read it (first buying
it) he would learn what the life of a poet is like. Like Mrs.
Wakefield before him, he appeared to be under the impression
I was unready, and we passed on, he to the post-office in flapping galoshes, and I into the future *via* Hiroshima.

INTRODUCTION

I have carried about the world and down the years a great many books which, in one place or another, I have abandoned, but the shelf of Lindsay's books, and my own contribution to his history, have remained intact. In fancy and in fact they have altered. My interlinear and marginal notations in Lindsay's books, and in the Masters biography, have begun to fade, and my own volume, like some aged, wasting, distant cousin occupies a sentimental place in the house without contributing to the family's present style.

The life of Vachel Lindsay is so incredible in its details, and so rare an example of the extinct passion to mingle poetry with a programmatic national and religious purpose that we are compelled in the name of our own sane preservation to doubt that he actually lived it. We may comfort ourselves in recoil by charging that his effort was inspired by a vast illusion whose outcome could have been nothing less than his eventual despair. Thus we fortify ourselves with the conviction that he was the author of his downfall, and we relieve ourselves of the obligation to question whether the illusion was, in fact, illusion; or whether, even if it was, it was not the best of all illusions, especially for a poet.

Lindsay died in 1931, harvested. Done in. Had. He was fifty-two. My marginal notations for 1945 tell me exactly why—"society did it . . . look what society did to him!"—although I am now less inclined to press the case. In the end, every poet dies when his work is done, society his perennial exasperation, but never his killer. All poets are mad, or, to be gentler, estranged, alienated, perceiving too much, feeling too much, ranging too far, lingering too long at the poles of exaltation and morbidity. Not to explore life all the way is not to be a poet, and one must draw what consolation he can from the thought that the alternatives must be rather dull.

In Lindsay's case "success" took at first the happy form of ready publication. Thus his work is available to our solitude. It would have been well had he retained his own.

Unfortunately he was tempted—self-tempted—into a program of platform recitals, exhilarating at first, whose missionary character committed him beyond return.

His touring soon effectively displaced his writing as a way of life. As early as 1922 he complained "how utterly impossible it has become for me to live a private life . . . I am like a newspaper or the front-door rug for everybody to use." He planned to say "good-by to all such schemes by July 1, 1923." He felt himself "on the tantalizing verge of converting the

INTRODUCTION

General Public." In 1922 he declared that all America was "blocked in": within three years he would "do Australia, New Zealand and South Africa . . . the edges of the English speaking world."

In November, 1924, he vowed, from Spokane, "I am here for all time so far as I know, and haven't the least notion of lecturing or traveling." But it was not to be. Seven years later he was still circling America on the railroad.

Why did he not retreat to his room in his house in Springfield?

Possibly he found unbearable the prospect of closeting himself for long creative periods bereft of the companionship of the optimism which had for a lifetime sustained him. In an age of carnage, the death of agrarian hope, the repudiation of Wilson, America's rejection of the League of Nations, the cynicism of Prohibition, the incoherence of Harding and Coolidge, and the underlying vulgarity which these symptoms express, harbingers of hope must sound alarmingly detached from reality. That is to say that his work, then, was done.

I suppose no writer ever quite tells himself this, and I do not mean to say that Lindsay coldly knew it and therefore died. A fighting man fights on. There are at least a dozen writers now dashing about the United States whose significant work was long ago done, their fame made and their money spent, whose gracelessness depresses us all. Lindsay's symptoms of his late years, so strange and special to me in 1945, now appear to me the familiar, commonplace sorrows of writers to whom American society, in its shameless moneylust, offers no climate for a second chance.

He who had once marched with Booth on a dollar a day could not now live on ten thousand a year. Masters suggests that his situation could have been eased by the solitude a pension would have assured:

> Springfield was then full of millionaires, not to mention Chicago, some of whom had made their money by exploiting and stealing the resources of the State; and others by operating mills of hate and false reports, ignorance, and calumny. They had thriven on the fame that Lindsay had brought to Illinois, while ignoring him, or libelling him. Money is all, practically and in the Marxian sense. Resolutions of respect, speeches, prayers, and even funeral wreaths are much cheaper than pensions, and make so much more noise!

So it may be. We are left to our speculations.

CONTENTS

Book I—CHILD

CHAPTER ONE

1

SPRINGFIELD ILLINOIS. 1879. Twenty thousand persons. Abraham Lincoln is fourteen years dead.

Burr Davis runs an inn on the road from the east, and because he knows a good thing when he sees it he offers something special: a dollar a night for bed and breakfast, and for another dollar a head he carries folks by carriage from his inn to the house Lincoln owned and lived in at Eighth and Jackson. Already he realizes that overland traffic is giving way to the railroads: soon he will conduct excursions from the depot, and afterward he will abandon his inn altogether and concentrate on hauling people for a look at the place where Lincoln lived. He will make a good living.

There is something about the city: people are beginning to sense it, beginning to feel the outpushing of its contours, feeling as a girl-child fourteen feels new growth and change, suddenly conscious of herself, realizing all at once that she is an object of attention.

Clem Reddy is toothless and dry, and he can remember, or claims to remember, when he came as a boy to a prairie village where wild weeds grew as high as the cabins, and in time so many folks came up from Tennessee and Kentucky and across from Virginia and Indiana that he cannot, as once he could, call all people by their given names.

Burr Davis tells the professor down from Chicago that the best person to see is Clem Reddy. "Now relax and think," the professor says, and the men at the square crowd around, and Clem sits back in the November sun and runs his tongue across his smooth gums and tries to think.

"Well, now you ask," he says, "in the beginning there *was* a man, but as far as his name goes I can't rightly say," and after many sessions with Clem, after a long time, the professor pieces it together: in the beginning there was a man, and his name was Hunter Kelly, and as far as is known he came up from Carolina and cleared ground for himself. He was an Irish Catholic, and he was reading St. Augustine's *City of God* and he thought he would build such a city in the Illinois country.

"Twasn't no Catholic," Clem says a little heatedly. "He was a Swedenborg the way I heard it."

"Is it possible you forget?" The professor knows how the accumulation of myth and the decline of memory tend to distort fact.

15

"No," says Clem, "it ain't possible."

"Did you know Lincoln?"

Ole Hibben steps forward. "I knowed him," he says. (Ole is a preacher. There were twenty-three preachers in Springfield when Lincoln ran for President, and twenty of them preached against Lincoln, and Ole is one of the twenty. He is a big-shouldered man, and the professor, confronting Ole, speaks with an earnest caution: yesterday, on the square, there was a stranger on horseback, traveling from Peoria to St. Louis, and he stopped to rest his horse. "There was an atheist in Peoria . . ." the stranger began, and Ole had brought his right arm up from where it was at rest in his belt, and he slapped the stranger a whipcrack slap on the side of the face, and the stranger toppled backward as much from surprise as from hurt, and from the ground he finished: "They run him out." "Good thing," said Ole.) "He lacked religion," says Ole Hibben of Abe Lincoln.

Yet there are some who declare that with their own eyes they saw Lincoln upon his knees in church, and the professor fears that the only certainty likely to emerge from the pursuit of facts is the fact of there being no certainty. He asks Ole Hibben his name, his age, and how long he has been a resident of Springfield.

And the professor will take a suitcase full of notes back with him to Chicago and try to make a straight story of the jumble of things that Clem Reddy and Ole Hibben and the men and women of Springfield tell him:

There was a man called Hunter Kelly (some say "Elisha Kelly") and he was either a Swedenborgian disciple of Johnny Appleseed or an Irish Catholic; there was Sangamon Phalanx and it set itself up as the agency of Utopia in forty-five with a membership of fifty (or in fifty with a membership of forty-five), and Peter Cartwright came in twenty-four or twenty-eight or thereabouts, and he could preach forty-eight hours and never sit down. "A joyous battlefield against the devil and rival sects." He ran against Lincoln for Congress in forty-six, and he lost.

Dates. A city's history, for the professor, is dates, the establishment of pivots. 1837, the capital is moved from Vandalia to Springfield. He hangs history conveniently on hooks.

2

Dr. Lindsay sniffs distastefully. He does not like the smell of tobacco that swirls about the girl. Her brothers and her father chew tobacco all day long, and the doctor knows it and submits to the inevitability of it and leads the girl upstairs to the room where birth is about to take place.

"Scorpio," she says.

"What is Scorpio?" His voice is deep and gruff, but it is gentle.

"Scorpios is different."

"Yes?" he says, but he does not believe in the signs any more than he believes, as her brothers and her father do, that the juice of tobacco is both healer and precaution. He believes in signs, but they are signs of a different sort, not superstition. (Bob Ingersoll, the Peoria agnostic, would call it superstition.) The doctor calls it faith, faith in the Campbellite God, the stern faith of a stern church. *There is a fullness of joy, a fullness of glory and a fullness of blessedness of which no living man however enlightened ever formed or entertained one adequate conception,* says Alexander Campbell, and this is strength for the doctor each time he reads it or hears it spoken. "Wash your hands," he tells the girl. He pours steaming water from a large pan into a smaller one.

"It's hot," she says.

"That's right. Go ahead, wash them," and she does, and he rubs his black beard and watches her. She feels that she is being punished, and she does not know why, and she washes her hands, reluctantly, half-knowing it is a good and necessary thing to do, and he half-thinks it is really not necessary, but it is the new way of doing things and he is scientist as well as religionist. At the worst there is no harm in it. He explores his beard again and orders the girl to enter the room and tend the mother. "When the time comes I'll be downstairs," he says.

"I'll come a-running," says she. She seats herself in a chair beside the mother. She takes an assortment of charms from her apron pocket and arranges them in her lap. In her hand she clutches a metal disk upon which raised letters appear. The disk was given to her by a feed salesman who explained its twofold purpose: it would bring good fortune and it would help her to remember the name of the feed company.

Dr. Lindsay has done all that he can do. Downstairs he places a kettle of water on the hot stove. He will have tea. He seats himself at the kitchen table and waits for the water to heat. He is nervous. He is not so nervous as when his first child came, but he is nervous nevertheless: more babies die than live, and almost as many mothers die as live. He paces. He walks into the parlor, and here, in the air, there is the passing suggestion of the odor of tobacco introduced into the house by the girl, and he wishes he had, just for now, just this once, a square of tobacco into which he might clamp his teeth. It would relieve the tension.

He returns to the kitchen, and he prepares strong tea. It tastes weak. *Scorpio,* she had said. *Scorpios is different,* and he smiles, and then the smile disappears, and, like the coming and the going of a silver line of lightning, his mind grasps a truth: it is not the question of the health of the mother-wife that worries him (she is Rush County Indiana people, and they are a hardy people) nor the question of the survival of the child. It is larger, a question of conflict and confusion in terms of the child-to-be, a question of the sign of Scorpio and the strong hold of an old-time religion, and these ranged in turn against a fast-changing world (who knows how many atheists there are in Peoria, and Peoria just up the line?), and then the line of lightning is gone, and the girl is calling from the stairway.

3

In the Illinois country wild turkey run (in ten years they will be extinct) and the tame deer lope free (in a year they will be dead) and the corn grows wild (in fifteen years there will not be a stalk of corn that does not belong to someone) and the secret of life is survival, protection and survival, and the wild turkey hen keeps her young beneath her wing, and the tame wild deer keeps its half-developed fawn a long time in its protective shadow.

Mama is Rush County Indiana and Papa is Gallatin County Kentucky, and both are bred strong in a pioneer tradition, and, even so, time hurls its spears and wounds them. In full flower they re-create themselves, and for each new life created they pay in strength and gain in wisdom. But they are no longer pioneers. They have found their frontier.

Mama and Papa (the new son will call them Mama and Papa all his life) are as far west as they will ever be. They retrench and plant themselves solid. They will not return to the older East, but they will not remove to the newer West. They have come to stay and suffer time's wounds, and the wounds are many:

There are six children. The first is Olive, black-haired, dark-eyed and plump, and now there is Nicholas Vachel under the sign of Scorpio, and Mama explains that the *a* in Vachel is broad like the first *a* in Abraham, whether the Biblical Abraham or the Springfield

Abraham is not known (she is devoted to both) and Vachel will insist that the name rhymes with Rachel, not with satchel. He will have more imagination than Mama, which is saying a good deal, for she has a wild polite imagination.

After Vachel there is tragedy, Isabel, Esther, Endora (called Dodo), diphtheria, scarlet fever, milk poison, swift, swift, swift, the plunging spears. The babies are the first to lie in the Lindsay plot in Oak Ridge. They sleep a few steps from the knoll where Lincoln lies in a tomb that is simple at first but improved with time until it is oversized, gaudy and tasteless.

There is a sixth child, a girl, and she is optimistically named Joy, and she lives, and the three living children are held close in protective embrace, for Mama and Papa have felt three times the keen pain of loss, and those who live they nourish and guard and guide and hope to build strong.

4

Summer day. Dry day. He moves down the street and crosses over and no one can see that beneath his shirt is a box of matches. They are sulphurous and good to smell. The smell has always tempted him. Dust rises on the dry street. He kicks the dust as he goes, and a man shouts at him—"Say boy don't rile the dust like that"—and the boy runs a little, but even for a small boy it is hot, too hot to run, and he slows to a walk again and resumes his kicking of the dust. He imagines that he is Papa's team beating down a dusty road on an urgent call.

At road-end is a stile, and he climbs it and straddles the topmost timber and turns to see how far he has come. He has come a frightening distance and he thinks he hears Mama's call, a little shrill, somehow a little more anxious than usual, and he listens, but it is not she. He stands atop the stile. He is a famous discoverer discovering Egypt (Mama has introduced him to the wonders of Rawlinson's *History of Egypt*) and the haystacks in the field are pyramids. He descends the stile.

Two farmers in the field stand talking, their faces partly hidden by the shadow of their wide-brim straw hats. They are talking of the heat and how the hay is dry, and they wonder to each other how the almanac could be so wrong about the rain. They see Vachel cross the field.

"Seems like we get more closer to the sun every year," one farmer says. He smiles as much of a smile as he can allow himself. It has been a summer of much heat. It was a winter of much snow and a spring of much rain, and they thought it would be a good summer. Every year they think it will be a good summer. And then the earth moves close to the sun and the melted snows and the spring rains seem to have been but pleasant dreams, and now the ground is thirsting to the roots of the trees. They have sprinkled it as generously as they dare with well water. But people and animals must have water before crops, and by August the animals lick dry muzzles with dry tongues, and by the end of August the farmer himself drinks sparingly. "Then if it's a good crop the prices is down." They cannot understand it, and they stand looking at the brown-green field as they have stood every afternoon this week, and at the dry blue sky. "Well if it burns then I go into the mine for the winter," the farmer says, and at the moment the cool mine with dripping walls, the cool mine that is always damp, looks good to him. "Then when you're down you remember how you was standing out here like this in the heat."

Vachel reaches the end of the long row of haystacks. His heart pounds hard, and he kneels and reaches inside his shirt for the matches, and he takes one and carefully closes the box and puts the box back inside his shirt. He twists until his hand can conveniently reach his shoe, and he rubs the green tip of the match against his sole, but it does not light. He has seen Papa light matches a hundred times with a quick motion along the bottom of his shoe or on his pants or simply with a fingernail. It is not so easy as it looks. The match snaps in two and he takes another from the box and replaces the box inside his shirt, but still the match will not ignite, and he takes the box again and sets it beside him, and a third time and a fourth time the matches refuse to fire, and the boy is patient. He has great patience.

Then it happens. For no good reason it happens. He rubs the match against the sole of his shoe, and it flares, and he is startled, and the match flies from his hand and ignites the others in the box, and before he knows what has happened the skirt of the stack is burning, and brown smoke rises and two men advance across the field toward him. "Get away get away," the farmer shouts, but Vachel cannot move, and now they are upon him and one farmer pushes him backward and the other stamps upon the burning hay. Then they tear down the stack with a pitchfork and spread the hay and study it, and then they build the stack again, and then one farmer takes Vachel by the hand and leads him home and shows Mama and Papa the blackened matches in the blackened box. Papa reads the label on the box through the char and says thank you to the farmer and offers him money, but the farmer will not take any money. He departs.

They talk about him. They often talk about him, and they think he is not listening, but he is. He listens very carefully to every word, even though his eyes are on *History of Egypt*.

Mama is gentle. Papa is firm. It is Mama he runs to when things go wrong. Papa is frequently busy in his study or out on calls or catching up on his sleep. It is Mama who first put the picture books into his hands. Papa approves of books, but he says a boy must start learning to be a man; Papa says it is a hard world and a boy must first of all know how to be a man. (Papa sees Vachel a doctor someday. He dreams of the day when he will say well Vachel you're ready now you take the rounds north of Capitol and I'll take them south. He sees the young doctor riding away in his own carriage, the medicines scattered in tight-capped bottles on the floor, two dollars for white folks and free to colored folks and medicine for everyone lest people think the young doctor does not know his business.)

It is Mama who kept him in golden curls, and Papa who finally won out one Christmas when Grandpa Lindsay came and felt of Vachel's head because the old man's eyes were strangely blind and he could only see (they said) with his hands, and with his hands he saw that Vachel wore curls, and he stormed about demanding that a boy be made to look like a boy, and Mama said no, but Papa said yes, and Grandpa Lindsay roared yes yes off with them off with them, and off they came, and Papa won a small victory then.

Now Papa says, "It's time he was acting and doing like a man," and his voice is like firm thunder.

"He's just a baby." Her voice is low and soft.

"No baby. No baby at all. If he's big enough to get a fire started on Jeff Hatten's place he's big enough to take the consequences. I don't like it any more than you. But I got to do it."

"Wait awhile. We'll talk about it some more. Act in haste . . ."

"No waiting." He knows that if he waits he will not do what he must do.

"Oh Papa," Mama says, and Vachel hears in her voice that she has weakened, and he knows that something is about to happen and whatever it is it is bad. Papa wishes to argue further. He has justified his position to Mama, but he has not justified it entirely to himself. He is a sensitive man and thoroughly aware that fire has a curious attraction for children. He has spread goose grease on the burned flesh of a hundred inquisitive children, and he dimly remembers committing similar mischief himself as a child.

But the thing must be done and done now, and he takes Vachel by the hand as the farmer took the hand this afternoon. Vachel looks over his shoulder once at Mama. She has a sad, hurt look on her face. He goes to the barn with Papa. Papa takes a knife from his pocket and stands with it open, and for a long time he studies the old harness that hangs on nails on the wall. "Vachel," he says, "we must have respect for other people's property. Suppose Mister Hatten wasn't in his field today. How would you feel if you burned out his hay?" Papa does not seem to expect an answer. He slices a length of leather from the old harness and folds his knife and puts it back into his pocket. "How do you suppose I'd feel if a boy came and burned this barn down? Or burned the house down? We must have respect for other people's property."

"Papa I'm sorry and I will never do it again."

Papa looks pleased, and Vachel thinks that now he will lay aside the strip of leather and not do what he has planned to do. "Take off your shirt. A boy has got to learn neighborliness and respect for other people's property." Papa says it as if it were a commandment *Thou shalt not set fire to property.* "One little match could burn all Springfield down." *Thou shalt not burn the town down.* And Papa does what he came to the barn to do, and Tom and Charlie whinny and beat the sides of their stalls with their hooves. "You wouldn't want people to think you're not a proper boy. If you are always a proper boy life will be good to you." Papa knows this is good advice. It is his way of protecting his child. He helps Vachel into his shirt, repeating the advice *If you are always a proper boy life will be good to all proper boys you must be a proper boy,* and they go inside to Papa's study and Papa spreads cool goose grease on Vachel's back, and they go to supper.

Tonight, in bed, he lies on his stomach, but he cannot sleep on his stomach and after a time he turns onto his side and he wishes he could lie on his back but his back stings and he wishes he were dead, and tonight he will lie on his side, facing the open window and feeling the breeze from the north on his cheek. He tries to sleep.

But he does not sleep. It is the first night of his life that he cannot sleep (there will be sleepless nights before the last night of all) and he does not know why. Perhaps it is the noise: across the street, in the Governor's yard, there are voices, the hoarse laughter of men and the tinkling laughter of women and muffled conversation and the slow rise of voices sounding unnatural. He does not know that the people are drinking on the lawn. All he knows is that it sounds as if people are tickling people, and he smiles, thinking how Papa sometimes traps him on the bed and tickles him and makes him laugh that way. Smiling, he starts off to sleep, and when he awakens again it is still dark outside, but there are no noises, no voices. Yet something keeps him awake; it is the thin pin point of light that shoots down through the trees from the dome of the Statehouse. He slips out of bed, and in so doing feels a sharp ugly pain in his back, and for an instant he scowls and wonders what it is, and then he remembers. He stands beside his bed and straightens, and winces, and once he is straight the pain subsides, and he goes to the window and draws the shade and looks back at his pillow and sees that now it is in darkness. He returns to his bed, and this time he sleeps, and by morning he has all but forgotten the small events of evening and night.

By morning the light of the Statehouse dome is out. It is extinguished by a politician from Jefferson County (he gets twelve dollars a week for the job and lives well.)

The bottles are cleared from the Governor's lawn by a politician from Effingham County. (He also gets twelve dollars a week.)

By seven o'clock a Negro woman named Rebecca has risen and dressed and cleaned her house and prepared breakfast for her husband who works as a shoveler for the Illinois Central and taken her babies to a neighbor woman and tramped cross-town to the Lindsay home and lighted the stove and made coffee. (Papa pays her three dollars a week, which is all he can afford and all she expects.)

By eight o'clock Mama and Papa are up and dressed and Papa has fed his horses and he stands for five minutes with Mama and

Rebecca in the yard, admiring the morning. In the morning Mama and Papa and Rebecca like to stand on the dew-wet green and enjoy a few minutes of cool day before the sun roars hot across the plain. Then Papa waters his horses and the women enter the house, and Joy comes downstairs with her shoes in her hands, and everybody is too busy to lace them for her, and Olive comes and laces the baby's shoes, and Vachel comes and takes the Bible from the mantel and sets it by Papa's place, and at eight-fifteen all but Rebecca sit at table. Papa reads aloud for five minutes from the Bible, and then he calls Rebecca, and she comes, and they all kneel, and Papa prays that God will keep them safe today. Then Mama and Rebecca hurry to the kitchen and come back with a steaming platter. Rebecca withdraws, and they eat. "I wonder," says Papa, "will Vachel get into trouble today."

"I don't think so," says Mama. She is still in pain from yesterday.

"No sir," says Vachel.

"What's trouble?" says Joy.

"Maybe he would like to go with me today," says Papa. He looks at Vachel, and Vachel looks down at his cereal.

"Perhaps another time," says Mama, and Papa does not press the point. He had his victory yesterday. Today is Mama's turn. Still, he wishes Vachel would go and see for himself what the doctor's life is like. Papa wipes his mouth with a napkin and rises and goes to his study for his satchel and then turns and comes out again and slams the door behind him. Mama helps him into his coat. He goes to the telephone table and looks at his memo pad (there are two pads; one is Mama's) and tears several sheets from it and sticks them into his pocket, and then the back door slams behind him and in a moment there is the creak of harness, and then the carriage drive-shaft sound and the snap of a whip and the drumming of hooves on the road. "Tom Charlie," he roars. He is off. Dust rises behind him, and in the kitchen Rebecca relaxes perceptibly and Mama moves to the telephone, saying aloud "Wednesday."

She takes a pencil from her hair. (She puts it there the first thing every morning, and except on rare formal occasions she is never more than arm's length from her pencil.) She jots names on her memo pad. "Rebecca," she says, "Every Wednesday this afternoon. Olive will walk with the baby twice around the Governor's square."

"Not a baby," says Joy.

"How many for Every Wednesday?" says Rebecca.

"I'll know soon." She grips her pencil in her mouth and cranks the telephone. There are not many telephones in Springfield yet but of course a doctor must have one. She places the pencil in her hair. "Good morning Frannie," she says. "I want Mrs. Williams. Then after Mrs. Williams Mrs. Logan. Are you taking it down? Mrs. Williams Mrs. Logan Mrs. Church Mrs. Day Mrs. Reverend Lomax."

"Isn't it too bad about the Reverend?" says Frannie.

"Isn't it," says Mama. "That's five to start with. No, Frannie, I was talking to Rebecca. You heard me, Rebecca?"

"Five to start," says Rebecca.

"Some people says they don't think it's right for me to walk the baby alone," says Olive. "They say I'm too young."

"Mrs. Williams? Mrs. Lindsay. Every Wednesday today. My house." Mrs. Williams talks. Mama cups her hand over the mouthpiece and turns to Olive. "Never worry what people say. Yes, Mrs. Williams. That will be fine. Two. No, I hadn't heard. I want to hear all about it. This afternoon." She reaches into her hair again for her pencil, draws a swift, sure line through Mrs. Williams and puts the pencil back in her hair. "Go ahead now Olive. No Frannie I was saying something to Olive."

"Did Papa say if I could go?" says Vachel.

"Mrs. Logan don't answer," says Frannie.

"She's hanging wash. We'll go back to her. I didn't speak to Papa. It will be all right. Mrs. Church? Mrs. Lindsay. Every Wednesday today."

"I'll be careful."

"Straight there and straight back," Mama says. "No loitering on the way. At two. Yes I did. I must hear about it—this afternoon. Not yet, she's hanging wash."

By ten o'clock Mama has organized the day. Mama is an organizer. (Vachel will predict: "Mama will die with the telephone in her hand.")

At ten o'clock Vachel walks up the wooden steps of the Springfield public library. It is a modern, up-to-date library with almost a thousand volumes, and under *L* are five volumes about Abraham Lincoln, and Miss Gloria Fisk the librarian has begun to wonder whether it might not be feasible to set the Lincoln books apart, perhaps on a small table all their own. She is absorbed in thought. She has a love for books, a certain feel for them, and every morning she takes a soft rag from her desk drawer and spends ten minutes dusting all the books on all the shelves of the library. She is proud of her shelves and proud of her library. The city pays her six dollars a week to tend the volumes, and like all people who work for the public she tries to be nice to everyone without altogether losing her dignity, and unlike many people who work for the public she is conscientious. She tries to build a library for the future. (Someday the city will house thousands upon thousands of volumes in a cement building called Lincoln Library and there will be scores of Lincoln books in special sections, and the library will hire people who go about doing nothing all day but shelving and dusting books as Miss Fisk is now doing.)

She turns when Vachel enters. He has come from bright sunshine into the semidarkness of the library, and at first he does not see her. He pushes his blond hair back from his forehead and stands a moment until his eyes adjust to the lesser light, and then he sees her and smiles. The last thing Mama told him was to smile and be pleasant to Miss Fisk.

Miss Fisk does not smile. She tries to be nice to everyone, but she does not smile except in unusual circumstances. In particular, she never smiles at children. He walks toward her desk and stands before it, and when she finishes dusting the books she sits at her desk. "Now what can I do for you, Vachel? How do you like these?"

"I didn't," he says.

"Didn't?" she says. "All children love Rollo."

"Well, I didn't."

"I cannot understand," she says, and she cannot. Rollo and Grimm and Louisa Alcott and Elsie are for children (she will not stock Nick Carter) and all children are supposed to love them, and she cannot understand why Vachel does not.

"I want to try Dante," he says.

"Dear me," she says.

"Can I?"

"No. You may not."

"Mama says . . ."

"I can give you only the books on the children's shelf."

"Well golly."

"What kind of language is that?"

"No kind," he says.

She is perplexed. She is always perplexed by Vachel and by Mama and by the new things that are happening in books and the new language children are using. She is always perplexed by the new; she feels that the old world is slipping away, and she is right. "It's not proper," she says, but she goes to the shelves and takes Dante down and hands him to Vachel and writes on a sheet of paper *Dante, Vachel Lindsay (younger)*, and Vachel signs his name and thanks her and turns and goes to the door and opens it and moves out into the sunlight and starts down the steps, and halfway down he stops and opens the big book and gasps, and slowly he lowers himself until his rear end touches the step, and he sits and goes through the book from picture to picture, and each is more vivid and more horrible than the one before, and at each he gasps, and Miss Fisk stands at the open door behind him and tells him he had best start home or his mama will worry, and he rises and moves forward slowly down the street, turning the pages of the book and gasping as he goes.

At eleven o'clock he is home, and he shows Mama the book and she studies it with him. The study must be hasty at best, for Every Wednesday meets at two and there is much to do before then, yet she knows it will all be done in good time (the ladies are always late). She does not gasp when she sees the pictures. She owns two copies of Dante, and although they do not have pictures she has seen Dante's world vividly in her mind's eye. "Pictures can do a good deal for a book," she observes thoughtfully.

"Miss Fisk didn't want me to have it."

"No?"

"Not at first."

"I don't see anything wrong. Just as long as you take it back when it's due." She sees nothing wrong in a boy's reading Dante, and she has been considering taking the whole matter up with Every Wednesday, the whole matter of books and what Christian people shall and shall not read and at what age children are old enough to air smaller children. These things have troubled her. (In the end they boil down to one question, *what would Christ do?* In Maryland her family held council and asked itself what would Christ do and freed its slaves and moved west, and all things boil down in her organizing, simplifying mind to that, everything to that, and once she has decided what He would do she defends whatever it is she is defending with grimness and tenacity. She will die defending and expounding, with a telephone in her hand and a pencil in her hair and Christ in her heart.)

Mama closes the book and hands it to Vachel and he goes upstairs and opens it on his table and reads and understands a little. He is captured. The world dissolves.

At noon Papa stops to water his horses at the trough at the square. He always stops at the square at noon and he is never quite comfortable among the cruder men of the city. He feels that he intrudes. He does. There is something in the nature of intrusion when a busy man stops among idle men. Papa is not a strictly democratic man or a man who mixes well in any company. He hopes that all people will like him (not for business reasons; he has as much business as he can handle) and consider him a part of them in his own special, skillful, important way.

"Seen your boy," Ole Hibben says.

"I hope he was behaving himself," says Papa. He looks almost but not quite into Ole's eyes. He is fonder than he once was of Ole Hibben. He used to treat Ole regularly for bruised knuckles and, later, for blackened eyes and cuts about the mouth and nose, and he felt that Ole was too quick with his fists. But Ole seems to have quieted some and Papa likes him better now. Ole is a preacher, not a Campbellite preacher but a preacher nevertheless, and Papa would rather a man preach even in the hit-or-miss way Ole preaches than not preach at all.

"Seen him comin out a the library," Ole says. Papa looks to his horses. "Never had much use for books myself," says Ole. He has read one book in his life, and that one many times.

"The one you read is good enough," says Papa.

"I guess," Ole says, and Papa hears that his horses have stopped drinking, and he turns their heads toward home, and when he turns off the square he is somehow uneasy about something, not knowing what, thinking maybe he has forgotten an instrument somewhere or missed a call or forgotten to do something Mama asked him to do. All the way home he is troubled.

He stops his horses in the shade beside the house, and Vachel by his window hears Papa draw up, and he shouts from the window *hi papa*, standing and waving, and Papa hears Vachel slam a book shut, and he sees him disappear from the window, and he pictures the boy dashing downstairs, and Papa knows what it is that makes him uneasy: it is the boy. The boy is different.

5

Jeff Hatten owns a brown gelding marked like its sire with a white breast and white at its ankles, and from the beginning he knows he will have trouble with that horse. "It's one a those things," he says, "but I ain't beat yet," but the truth is that Jeff is beaten from the beginning as far as that horse goes.

It is a beautiful horse. It comes when Jeff calls. Jeff Hatten who is bitter as the farmers are bitter up and down the dry Sangamon Valley says half-joking "That horse got more sense than most people I know," and anyone who knows anything about horses in Springfield (it used to be that everyone knew horses, but now there are some who do not) says it is everything Jeff says it is. Jeff calls him Tough. (One day Jeff was standing with Bret Newcombe showing Bret the horse, and he said "This horse'll be tough but as soon as I get him broke right he will be the best horse you ever seen," and then Jeff tried to get a bit in the horse's mouth, and the horse was tough, and he called him Tough.)

He will not let Jeff get the bit in his mouth. The first time Jeff tried Tough came together fast with his jaws and it was all Jeff could do to get his hand out without losing fingers, and the second time Jeff tried he wore leather mittens and Tough went through the mittens like a plow through soft spring earth. Jeff is beginning to think there is something ornery about the horse, and he is beginning to worry that after all he put into the horse it will turn out unusable, and he was counting on Tough for next year. And the thing that hurts is that people don't say "Hello Jeff" any more on the square. They say "Well Jeff how are you comin with that horse?"

Jeff says he will get the horse broke to the bit or know the reason why, and he is twice wrong, for he will never get the bit into Tough's mouth and he will never know the reason why any more than anyone knows why the horse behaves himself for two hundred years and then suddenly won't take a bit in his mouth. Jeff says that on Saturday afternoon he will get the bit in Tough's mouth and anyone who wants to watch him do it is welcome.

On Saturday afternoon people come down Fifth Street headed for Jeff's, and Papa and Vachel follow the crowd. Papa goes end-around the stile at Jeff's line. Vachel climbs over. Two hundred people are gathered in a circle about Jeff and his horse. Tough is not nervous. He stands in the center of the circle of people and smells the grass and fans flies with his tail in a slow, easy way, and Jeff comes with ropes and a bit and drops the bit behind him. Tough stands docile and people think it will be easy.

Bret Newcombe comes with a stake and a shovel and digs a hole four feet deep in the ground and plants the stake, and Jeff ties the docile horse close to the stake, and Tough is peaceful, as if he has been ten years before the plow.

Then Jeff goes for the bit, and Tough knows it and he locks his jaws fast, and Papa watches with interest the muscles that work at the side of Tough's head, and the people shout advice to Jeff and a young man overcome by excitement leaps forward and beats Tough on the rump with Bret's shovel, and Vachel breathes hard and watches and gasps as he gasped at the pictures in Dante and becomes rigid and tense with excitement and he feels that he must shout as the people are shouting and cheering for Jeff, and he shouts one shrill, piercing, shrieking boy-scream that is halfway between his baby voice and the new voice developing low in his chest, *hold, Tough, hold,* and the cry is too much; the cry undoes Jeff. Jeff relaxes. He is beaten. He will try again in private, with only Bret watching, but he will always lose to the horse, and finally sadly he will sell the horse. Papa looks at Vachel in a puzzled way.

The boy is different. Papa senses it in the beginning and does not know what it is he senses. It is like a pain that at first is hardly noticed, a small pain, and it is not worth the effort to think about when it began or how, and for a long time it is no more than a dull, nagging pain, and sometimes for days or weeks there is no pain at all. And then it comes back. Each time it comes it comes harder and brings a heavier worry with it, and then it is gone again. It is a mystery where it comes from and where it goes. (*Seen him comin out a the library,* Ole Hibben says.) It is a small pain and Papa hardly feels it. He is not even sure it is a pain at all except that there is something about the way Ole says it. (*Vachel reads Dante,* Miss Fisk tells Papa.) She touches her hand to her forehead where it hurts every night probably eyes there ought to be an eye man in Springfield take these as directed on the label get more sleep and read less what does she mean *Vachel reads Dante* what is she trying to say if anything.

But Papa is careful not to let the thing build up big in his mind.

He knows too many people who let a thing build up in their minds until it unstrings them. There are a lot of people in Springfield with nothing wrong with them except what's in their minds. (*Why hell, Jeff Hatten tells Papa, I never even heard the boy. It was that goddam horse done me in.*) And Papa thinks maybe it is all in his mind, and for a while he forgets it, and every so often it recurs like a forgotten pain.

Yet Vachel is different, and Papa is right. Papa's pain has a real source. (He gives Vachel a disassembled skeleton to rebuild, and Vachel spraddles on the parlor floor and draws pictures instead of rejointing the bones.) Papa is sometimes hurt, and Mama says if the pictures Vachel draws are Christian pictures expressing Christian thoughts then she approves his drawing. Mama says God created the world in six geological ages (Papa calls them days) and she says that when God has an idea He wishes men to have He puts them into a mortal's head as He put them into Jesus' head, and Vachel thinks maybe God has put an idea into his head that will come out in the drawing. He feels a need to draw as some boys feel a need to heave rocks or to go behind the barn together and talk the thing they talk behind the barn.

6

In October a thing develops between Vachel and Papa. All of a sudden he feels something between himself and Papa. Partly it is feeling sorry for Papa, but it is something more.

Papa is a Democrat, and in Springfield in October it can be a lonesome thing to be a Democrat. Even in his own house Papa is alone. Mama is not permitted to vote, but she is a Republican, and Vachel tells Papa, "I have decided I'm a Democrat," and Papa laughs and says, "You don't have to be a Democrat just to make me feel good, son," and he messes Vachel's hair. His hand feels good to Vachel.

On Election Day Papa votes for Grover Cleveland for President and for John Peter Altgeld for Governor in the basement of the First Congregational Church across the street (the street is bricktop now) and he clatters back home in high hat and holiday boots and tells Mama he has voted. She says nothing. She thinks she ought to be permitted to vote.

In the evening Papa and Vachel go down to the *Journal* office and stand in the crowd behind Lester Grady, listening to the buzz of

Lester's machine. Lester bends at his table, adjusting and readjusting his earphones. He scratches figures on a long sheet of paper.

Then he removes his earphones and goes to the bulletin board set up for the occasion, and he tacks the long paper to the board, and Papa elbows through the crowd and when he is close enough he reads, and he comes away looking glum. Cleveland leads. Altgeld leads. "Well Papa that's good," says Vachel. "It's the cities," Papa says.

Lester says there will be another report in thirty minutes, and the men move off in little groups and stand talking on the square (the Leland tavern is closed tonight) and Vachel stands among the boys and tells them Cleveland and Altgeld and all the Democrats will win, and one boy calls him rebel, rebel bastard, and the others take up the chant and they circle the square aimlessly, chanting *rebel bastard rebel bastard* until the men make them stop. Jim Fessenden says "Where'n hell do they learn such language them little bastards?" and Papa talks quietly on the courthouse steps with two men who admit they are Democrats.

Later, after the returns are in, the Republicans will march, winding about the square and up Capitol Avenue to the Statehouse. Governor Fifer will greet them on the Statehouse lawn and shake their hands one by one. He went home this morning to vote, but he will be back by midnight. By midnight it will all be over.

At ten o'clock the returning Governor stops in Decatur. Cleveland leads. Altgeld leads. "It's the cities. Wait'll the farm vote rolls in," he says, and he shakes hands all around. Between Decatur and Springfield he is thoughtful and silent. He is even slightly worried. It is not Cleveland who worries him. Cleveland was President once before and he may be so again, but the Governor does not care who is President. It is Altgeld who worries him.

At eleven o'clock, in Springfield, he skirts the square, not wishing to be seen and somehow not in a talking handshaking mood.

It is quieter at the square than it was an hour ago. In Papa there is something almost like hope: the farm vote is coming in and the Democratic lead is being whittled away, but it is whittled not slashed, and after the eleven-o'clock report Papa says to Vachel that it will not be so bad after all. "We'll make a better run than I expected," Papa says, and Vachel is afraid Papa will send him home to bed but Papa seems not to have noticed how late it is. "Keep walking," Papa says, "it'll keep you awake," and Vachel walks around and around the square among the clusters of men. The men talk in low voices the way men talk at a funeral, and the moon goes down behind the Statehouse dome.

At midnight the men still stand talking, and there is no parade and no sign of the makings of a parade and no Governor handshaking on the lawn. The night turns cold and Vachel shivers. There are few boys left on the square to run with: the boys have been sent home the way men always send boys home when something unpleasant seems about to happen. The light in the capitol dome burns steady and Vachel squints at it with eyes full of sleep, half-wishing Papa would send him home to bed. But Papa seems to have forgotten, and at one o'clock Cleveland and Altgeld are reported holding firm. And at half past one. And at two.

At two o'clock a politician from the Governor's home county who has never as far as anyone knows done anything at all for his twelve dollars a week telephones the Governor from the desk of the Leland Hotel and tells him the news, and the Governor hangs up and gets ready for bed and wonders what is happening to the good world he knows. And he knows that he should have known all along that something was happening, changing. Now, possibly, it is too late, and the last thing he does before going to sleep is to reflect upon the fact that in four years he will be fifty-six, and he wonders if that is too old.

At two o'clock John Jones second cook at the Leland fresh from his warm bed slips shivering into his clothes. He is not fully awake. He never comes fully awake until he has started the fires and had coffee. He leaves his house and walks down Washington Street, turning the corner at Sixth, and at the square he sees the men. He stops short. He always stops short when he sees groups of white men at night, but in the instant of hesitation all becomes clear and he starts forward again, and at the square some of the men turn and say *evenin John* and he says *mornin mornin*. As he passes the *Journal* he sees Lester Grady adjusting his earphones for the two-thirty report. John sticks his head in the door and tells Lester he will have coffee in fifteen minutes and Lester says "Sounds sweet to me John." "How's it going?" John asks. "Not good," says Lester, and John Jones repeats—"Fifteen minutes"—not saying so but feeling somehow glad, not knowing much about politics but somehow feeling that what is happening is good.

There is little relative change in the two-thirty figure. It could go on changing like that all night and still not dump Altgeld or Cleveland. Altgeld is virtually in. Downstate had rain and the farmers did not vote as heavy as expected, and the men drift through the dark Leland lobby back to the kitchen for coffee, talking about how a little thing like rain can change the way of things. "Well John they done us in," Jim Fessenden says.

"The goddam rain," Jeff Hatten says. "Three months ago I could of used the rain." (Jeff voted for Altgeld, but he tells no one.)

Vachel stands by Papa and wraps his hands around the warm coffee cup. He cannot remember ever being so sleepy.

At three the men remain where they are. Lester goes alone to take the report and comes back in and the men see by his face that there is no change, and Vachel hoists himself onto the meat block and sleeps, and when he awakens it is still dark but almost light and there is noise and he is in Papa's arms. Papa is laughing. Vachel makes Papa put him down. He is thirteen years old and he will not be carried. He runs beside Papa down the street and into the carriage, and all about him are noise and light and men waving torches and drinking coffee from a bottle, but Papa does not drink, and the parade begins up Capitol Avenue.

It is not a big parade but it is bigger than anyone would have thought a Democratic parade could be in Springfield. The parade passes the mansion and the Governor lifts his window shade and sees the people and knows who they are and lowers his shade and thinks: it was the tariff and Altgeld rode in on the tariff. The Democrats promise to lower the tariff (Cleveland will not live by the promise), but the Governor is wrong; it was not the tariff. It is something else. Few men—Papa and a few others—know any more than Vachel what a tariff is. They vote like they vote because of something more than tariff. Vachel would have voted Democratic if he had been able to vote, and it would have been partly feeling sorry for Papa, yet something more than just being sorry for Papa, yet nothing to do with the tariff.

7

In the morning the politician from Jefferson County neglects to extinguish 'the light in the capitol dome. He will soon be going home.

The politician from Effingham County comes by habit to the Statehouse lawn but the lawn is clean, and he wonders what he will do now. He thinks maybe he will go to Chicago and work in as a Democrat or maybe go home and farm but farming is hard work after so many years of doing next to nothing for twelve dollars a week. He did not deliver Effingham the way it should have been delivered and there is really no sense in going home. Maybe in four years . . .

Illinois. 1892-1896. Four million people or thereabouts and the rising population shifting fast from farm to town and town to city, and something in the air from Chicago Illinois to Cairo Illinois and up and down the Mississippi and the Illinois and in the valleys of the Sangamon and the Spoon.

Chicago has grown too big for itself. The Chicago River is choked with garbage. Its waters lie motionless, black, and Chicago smells of river rot and death in the packing houses, and factory smoke forms a blanket between Chicago and the low-lying clouds, and there are children in the factories. Men called anarchists sit waiting for death in a Chicago jail for something called the Haymarket riot.

Yet in the air there is the good clean smell of protest and revolt that will blossom and make Illinois heroes of Illinois men.

There is black soot over Illinois. It poisons the pores and clings moist and germinous to everything in every city from Chicago to Cairo. Folks speak of King Coal and he powers factories and railroads and river boats, and he takes men's lives. John Llewellyn Lewis an Iowa mule boss will come with three brothers to Springfield.

There are the dry farms of Illinois and the farmer ruled by something called prices, and he does not understand. Ninety-three a good year for corn, oats, tame hay and winter wheat, but somewhere far away the bottom drops out of things and it has not been so bad for farmers since before Andrew Jackson, and it will be that way again and again and again, but it is this year, this ninety-three that crushes the farmer. He does not read history and he does not worry about the far future, but for now, for the immediate future, he looks for a way out of things and becomes a part of the spirit of unrest from Chicago to Cairo.

Papa piles the corn high beside the barn. The farmers come every day with wagons piled high and they pay their debts with corn, and the merchants are cheated as Papa is cheated. But they take the corn.

"Sonofabitchin thing you works your ass to the bone and back in New York they cuts the price from under," Jeff Hatten says, pointing to the east. He voted for Cleveland and he wonders why, and Papa rakes the corn together beside the barn, and after he has given away all he can give away and after he and Mama and Vachel and Olive and Joy and Rebecca have eaten all the corn they can eat in all the forms Mama invents there is nothing to do but to burn the corn. All over Illinois the corn goes up in smoke. Papa burns the corn and Vachel watches and draws pictures of the smoke. He likes to draw. (He tells Susan Wilcox that if he were an orphan with no responsibilities he would be an artist.) It is the summer that he draws and reads Milton (Miss Fisk thinks him unready for Milton) and secretly writes poems in the style of Poe (Miss Fisk will positively not let him read Whitman) and tastes of Swinburne and Tennyson, Lanier, Blake, Keats and Ruskin, and he hears like Keats melodies unheard in the rising smoke, and he tries to write the melody but he cannot, and he tries to draw the melody but he cannot. He will not stop trying. (The one thing he writes that anyone understands is a letter to the *Journal*. He says that if he had a million dollars he would change it into dimes and scatter it on the Statehouse lawn and invite everyone to come and take his share.)

It is the summer of the fair at Chicago. It is not so big a success as was hoped, because of the corn, and Papa cannot really afford to go, but he has promised Vachel all summer that they will go, and they go in September to the great international exposition. The word is new to Illinois—international—and the fair is mostly tinsel painted to look like gold and bad fried food and in a far corner a beautiful woman whose stomach people come from everywhere to see. Yet it is something more. It is culture (culture is new to Illinois) and Vachel sees great paintings that he has seen only in picture books. He hears Harriet Monroe recite. It is culture and wonder, great paintings and a fifty-foot whale, Harriet Monroe and a desk George Washington once sat at, and on the midway Vachel sees a live Turk in a fez and is mightily impressed. He sees African dancers. The world opens up a little and comes to Illinois and the farmers who waited in long lines for hours to see the lady's stomach bare and milk-white and luscious see also a painting, a live Turk, and they feel that they are wiser than they were.

(There is music at the fair, but Vachel has no ear for music. In school he sings Marching Through Georgia and Battle Hymn of the Republic, and in Sunday school he sings Blest Be the Tie That

Binds Our Hearts in Jesus' Love and Softly and Tenderly Jesus Is Calling, and Miss Wilhelmina Forbes who is young and pretty and likes to laugh and sing says there is something wrong with the singing. "One by one," she says, and one by one they sing. Vachel sings: *the bird with a broken pinion can never rise as high again,* and she stops him. "I've found it," she says. "Now! Now everybody sing but Vachel.")

8

Susan Wilcox is a schoolmarm. She does not like the word. It is a patronizing word. But she is not paid for liking things or not liking things, and she must hold her job because the alternative is getting married, and she goes about her business in her own way and behaves herself (Wilhelmina Forbes lost her job for holding hands on Christmas Day with Abraham Ott) and speaks softly and holds her own counsel.

She is a tall woman, and the smaller one is the taller she appears, and the more austere. She is considered a good teacher because she has an austere look about her (Fred Haney teaches in Springfield because he is quick with his fists) and a teacher must be austere or at least look austere or be quick with his fists, for children must be fired with fear or they will not learn. But she is not austere. She is not even certain that it is good for a teacher to be austere, but she goes about Springfield looking stern and severe and smiling when she feels she ought to smile and dressing as she ought to dress and discussing politics with no one and saying what she feels she ought to say when spoken to. Sometimes the things she says are not precisely the proper things to say, for sometimes her heresies rise in her throat, but few people have the idea she is saying anything she ought not to say. She is a woman and a schoolteacher and past the age of indiscretion. She wears black or brown or on special occasions dark blue and in summer white that is in no sense a frivolous white and no rings on her fingers or bright combs in her hair.

She has made up her mind how she must live her life. She reads books, and they are dangerous books, but she reads them in private. Fred Haney, who reports to the Brewery on school affairs, and the Brewery itself which hires and fires teachers and librarians and other public servants, would not know that the books are heretical if they saw them. She lives her life as she has decided it must be lived, in a secret way, and if heresies drop in a classroom in a purely accidental way and strike a young ear and pollute a young mind it is none of her doing. Inside, she is aflame.

She does not sleep well. At first, when sleeplessness afflicted her, she went to Dr. Lindsay and he gave her pills wrapped in brown paper, and she took one pill every night before going to bed, and after a while one pill was not enough, so she took two, and when two pills were no longer enough she went back to the doctor and told him so, and he said, "Ever try reading before bed?" She said, "I always read before bed," and he rubbed his beard, thinking. "That's what does it," he said. "Reading puts some to sleep and keeps others awake," and she gave up reading before bed and slept like a child, and finally enough was enough. She prefers reading to sleeping.

Generally she reads for four hours before sleeping. Promptly at midnight she turns down her light and lies awake in bed, motionless, and in an hour the tenseness in her body disappears and she sinks into sleep, and five hours later she wakes and turns up her light. In winter she reads in bed. In summer she reads at her desk, and sometimes, when a spirit moves her, instead of reading she writes.

Usually she writes poetry. It is poetry for her alone, satisfying in a small way the discontent within her, the love for beauty and order and creation, and nobody sees it but her as no one will see until after the deed is done the fierce flame she will nourish from the flame within herself.

It is September. At six o'clock Susan awakes and lies in bed with her eyes closed and hears through the open window the huffing of switch engines and the coupling of railroad cars and now and then angry steam whistles. The sounds do not bother her. Five years ago the railroad in the vastness of its inefficiency maddened her (Springfield is not on a main line and every train that comes through must be broken down and redistributed) but it no longer bothers her. This morning she hears the noises but faintly, and she rises and looks once at the morning and sits at her desk with a copy of Hamlin Garland's *Main-Travelled Roads*. She reads.

Today is the first day of the new school year. In the past the day was rich with meaning, but today she is not even altogether sure what year of her tenure it is, whether the eleventh or the twelfth. It is not like Septembers of the past when the beginning of each school year was a time of excitement and challenge.

She reads on, and the morning birds come awake and fill the tree outside her window with a clamor she does not hear and the dark sky turns pale blue and the more she reads the more alive the day becomes. (Garland is saying that life on the midwest farm is not all golden butter and flaky biscuits.) Susan thinks it is a good thing to say. She has seen the farmers' boys herded to school to learn things seemingly useless. (*I will not lie even to be a patriot,* says the truthful Garland.) And by the time the sun is high she is alive again, Susan again, and this is the first day of school and the time of new challenge.

She closes the book. She dresses in brown. She boils eggs and makes coffee and picks up the book and reads while she eats. When she finishes her breakfast she goes to her desk and takes three long yellow pencils saying International Exposition Chicago 1893 and three silver pen points and puts them in her brown purse. She takes a watch from her purse and winds it and puts it back. She washes her dishes and makes her bed and puts the ice card in the window, all in five minutes, by habit, as if she last did it yesterday, not three months ago. At the door she turns and looks around at her room and sees the ice card in the window and goes back and takes *Main-Travelled Roads* from the table and a plain brown book jacket from the closet shelf. She wraps the book in the plain brown jacket and stands it in the bookcase and goes forth.

There are the things that come from books. (Aunt Leona, visiting at Christmas, traces in a book she brings the way people trace with their finger the breed line of a spaniel back to a champion bitch the line of the family back to 1642. Vachel studies the book and sees far out on a limb of the tree the far far uncle named Hatchet. "Yes," says Aunt Leona, and she smiles. "We have an Indian in our line." And Vachel thinks all afternoon about Hatchet, and at supper he declares: "Then if we have one Indian we must have millions." Aunt Leona says children should be seen and not heard.)

Books are a part of the thing in the Illinois air in the brief time of Altgeld.

From his window Vachel sees Governor Altgeld walking in the yard in the early morning or just after supper, carrying a book and marking his place with a finger, and Vachel would like to go talk with him and see what he is reading. Sometimes Brand Whitlock walks with him. Whitlock is an odd man for a Governor to keep

close to him. Brand Whitlock does not control a single precinct in
the state of Illinois and he does not buy drinks for the crowd at the
Leland and he does not get girls for the newspapermen, and he goes
about telling people he is a Democrat with a small *d*. Brand Whitlock knows what is happening in Illinois and he keeps a sharp eye
on the books people stand on their shelves.

Vachel watches from the window. The morning after the Governor pardons the surviving anarchists he walks as usual in the yard,
but he carries no book, and the day after he refuses to send troops
to fight the striking Pullman Company union (Cleveland will send
them) he walks in the yard with Brand Whitlock and they talk of
the books they will read when their four years are over.

Altgeld must go and Whitlock with him, and the Governors of
Illinois will restore potted plants to the window sills that John Peter
Altgeld has desecrated with books.

The books speak of things that may sometime be. Miss Fisk keeps
four copies of *Looking Backward* in the library and they are always
out, and people are reading *Progress and Poverty* by Henry George
*I would take that million dollars and change it into dimes and scat-
ter it on the Statehouse lawn and everyone may come and take his
share* and Garland on the midwest farm and the shocking truth of
Maggie a girl of the streets and George Ade the skeptic and Ingersoll who disbelieves and Mark Twain just across the line in Hannibal Missouri, and old disgraces are re-explored. (Elija Lovejoy
was lynched at Alton Illinois for printing Abolition tracts and
Joseph Smith was lynched at Carthage for preaching a Mormon
Zion. The last words of August Spies the Haymarket anarchist are
widely and secretly printed and widely but openly read: "Now these
are my ideas," said Spies. "If you think you can crush out these ideas
that are gaining ground more and more every day by sending us to
the gallows—I say if death is the penalty for proclaiming the truth
then I will proudly and defiantly pay the price. Call your hang-
man.") Lincoln is examined anew in Illinois. The muckrakers are
poised in Chicago, and Markham has buried in a trunk a poem he
will soon unbury because somehow now is the ripe time. Brand Whitlock is full of hope and not at all sure the people will turn his beloved Altgeld out. Whitlock is young.

Vachel loves Altgeld and he does not know why. After Altgeld
pardons the anarchists Vachel looks the word up in the dictionary
—anarchy—and he does not believe in anarchy because he believes

in government; and he cannot quite feel sympathy for the men who strike against the Pullman Car Company because the Pullman Company sends the circus to Springfield every summer and it's free. Yet he sketches Altgeld walking stoop-shouldered in the yard and somehow sees him swooping like an eagle and changing the face of Illinois.

It comes down to Vachel and to four million people shifting fast from farm to town and town to city, down through the books people read clear down to the people who do not or cannot read books, down and around, infecting the fertile air and the ready minds of simple farmers and virgin schoolmarms and children like Vachel.

Youth no longer stunted and starved says Henry George. *Age no longer harried by avarice, the child at play with the tiger, the man with the muckrake drinking in the glory of the stars.*

All right says Huck Finn across the line in Hannibal *then I'll GO to hell* and he guides his raft and the slave Nigger Jim down the river to Cairo and freedom.

Susan Wilcox teaches English and science, how to read and write and speak, how to see. She carries a long white sheet of paper in her hand, and she glances at it quickly as she comes into the room. When she enters there is silence, for everyone knows Susan Wilcox, by reputation stern and severe. She begins, reading from the paper, *Henry Arrance* no answer and she looks up and repeats *Henry Arrance?* and a small boy raises his hand *I seen Henry at the circus and he is running away in the circus* draw a straight line with a new silver pen point through the name *Joshua Bell here Lila Berkins here,* and below the window a train whistle shrieks and sends white clouds of smoke against the panes. The whistle dies. There is talk of a new school building. Someday, perhaps. *Abraham Buxton here* old man Buxton a big hardware man might not be amiss to remember *Eugene Catlett* no answer *Eugene Catlett?* big boy needs a shave grows red in the face in the rear row *Eugene answer me* his papa farms east of town and does well enough farm boys slowest to answer and it is now or never *Eugene, please answer me.*

"Who laughed? You laughed. I saw you. See me after class. Now, Eugene," very patiently, easy easy, "speak up. Never be afraid to speak up," and he has never been so frightened before, but at last he speaks *here Crystal Davis here* her papa the livery man Burr Davis *Elmer Eck here John Ford here Marybelle Ford here Patri-*

cia Gleason here, "I spoke to your mama and she said you would come to school after all. I am glad," *Shirley Haber here Roy Ide here John Jones Junior here* brown boy *Patrick Kelly here,* "Patrick I saw your father on the street." "Papa's working for the union now." "That must be interesting work," the train moving away a bit now *Nicholas Lindsay here* his hand goes up try always to notice their hands. "Please call me Vachel," very well call them whatever they want to be called it's their names *Olive Lindsay here* her mama kept her out of school a year so the brother could catch up maybe a good idea maybe not so good *Phylis Macaulay here.* "Does anyone know of a famous poet named Macaulay?" one hand the doctor's boy. "Thomas Babington Macaulay," in an unhesitating boy voice very interesting very interesting *Bret Newcombe Junior here John Nutting here* look up in surprise as if to say what is so funny if there is a joke tell us all the joke. "We do not laugh at people's names," *Bertha Oakes here Fred Packard here* dear me another but just say it like any other in a firm strong voice papa a miner could change it might speak to him of changing it someday firm and strong *Lulubelle Pigg here Thomas Pruitt here Hart Reddeker here* no Robinsons? there are always Robinsons *Joseph Rockwell here.* Down the line, down the line, learning their names and their faces *Abraham Tolley here Richard Zimmer here.*

"Well," says she (she will teach them never to begin a sentence with *well*) "we have a nice class here." She looks into each face. Some avert their eyes. "Of course there is some hard work ahead, but none of us is afraid of hard work." Why do they look away? Patricia Gleason is pregnant and she thinks the whole world stares at her, and she looks away, and Patrick Kelly's papa tells him you are a miner's son but as good as any, and he does not look away, and John Jones Junior son of the Leland second cook is told by his papa when white folks look at you look away.

The class assumes a pattern. Some will defeat the habit of looking away and some will avert their eyes as long as they live, and some will burn with things to say and wave their hands in the air from early morning until midafternoon, and some will not speak except when she pries their tongues loose and some will resent her and a few will love her and cling to her words and dream of her at night and wish, when it is all over, that they could go on with her forever. She knows, in a general way, what lies ahead.

"Now about the noise from the trains," she says. "For some mysterious reason the high school was built very close to the railroad. When the noise becomes too great we simply stop and wait until it dies down," and they will learn to do that, but for a while they will try to shout above the railroad and she will watch their lips move in silence, but after a while they will learn. "Soon we will have the new building," she says.

Susan assigns, for a certain Monday, a drawing of the genus Violaceae, and Vachel brings his drawing on Monday and passes it down the row with the rest, and it is not a violet or anything that looks like a violet. To be sure, it started as a violet, as a sketch of Altgeld started as Altgeld and turned into an eagle, and Susan studies the alleged violet on Monday night and brings it again to school on Tuesday and asks him to explain, and that is what he wants to do. He is bursting to stand and explain. "As anyone can see," says he, "it is not a violet. It started out to be but it turned into something else if you hold it upside down. Right side up it is nothing, but upside down it is the soul of a spider," and the class laughs, but really, to him, it *looks* like the soul of a spider and he is sorry no one sees it.

"Exactly what," says Susan, "is the soul of a spider?"

"Why, Mammon," says he. "Mammon."

"Tomorrow I shall expect a genus Violaceae from you. No monkey business. Are we agreed?" and Vachel nods yes and takes his seat and does not know what makes him do such things. Tuesday night, in ten minutes, he sketches a violet. He will return to the spider.

9

In the spring ground is broken for the new high-school building. The foundations are planted, and by fall the skeleton has shape, and Susan comes and stands by the building and peers into its vast empty belly. Far away the trains screech and blow their whistles and clang their bells. Here it is quiet.

In winter work stops on the building. Winter, like most Springfield winters, is bitter cold and the wind sweeps endlessly out of nowhere down the river valley and the sky is seldom full blue: the sky is almost always gray-brown clouds during the short days. Sometimes in the late afternoon Susan comes and stands for five minutes with her back to the wind, and she runs her eyes along the

steel girders stretched from wall to wall. Long icicles hang solid
from the girders and lengthen as the winter draws on until they almost reach the ground.

Sometimes in the late winter afternoon Vachel comes. He has an
odd habit of meeting her at times when she is alone, of forgetting
his books and returning for them and meeting her in the darkening
classroom, of overtaking her on the street in the early evening, of
coming upon her by accident beside the new schoolhouse, and she
is flattered. Today he comes and stands beside her and says something into the wind. She cannot hear what he says, but it does not
seem to matter either to her or to him. She moves off, bending
slightly in the face of the wind, and he follows and walks beside her,
and at her doorway she says "Thank you Vachel for accompanying
me." She takes her keys from her purse and opens the door, and
warm air rushes out and he says "The pleasure was all mine" and
catches in the warm air the smell of Susan, and she closes the door
behind her, waving a last time. He crosses the street and stands
in the wind and her light goes up and he sees the top of her head
above the bookcase by the window, and he turns and walks down
the street feeling as always that he has left unsaid what he wanted
to say.

Yet it is said. Over the weeks and the months it is spoken in the
way all friendship that is almost something more than friendship is
spoken, and she understands the thing it is he feels for her though
the words are carried away by the wind or unsaid altogether. "You
are my best friend," says he.

"Now Vachel," she says.

"Yes you are," he says, and in March he carries her umbrella
overhead for her and him and they walk past the place where the
school will be, and she asks him quite casually, "In June—how
would you like to make the dedication speech in June?" and he
halts in his tracks and the umbrella falls.

"Me?" says he. "Do you suppose I could? I'll faint," and she
walks ahead a few steps in the rain and then turns. "The umbrella
please Vachel. The umbrella."

In April there is a roof on the schoolhouse and glass in the windows, and in May it is announced that the Governor himself will

speak at the dedication. The mayor will speak, and the three members of the building committee, and one student, and the cornerstone will be laid and the flag raised.

In May Vachel works on his speech and reads it aloud in his room and sees before him upturned agreeing admiring faces and feels the June sun as it will beat down on the platform and the red white and blue bunting.

He copies it a final time in the big round hand that will always be big and round and generous until Vachel himself broken and useless goes under, changing a word here, changing *sin* to *misdirection* and taking out the quote by Washington and substituting one by Jefferson, and knowing as he goes that Susan will like the way he has thought the thing through, and knowing now for sure that writing is hard, hard work as Susan says.

He knows that she will like it. She will say *oh Vachel this is grand* and she will rush about showing it to people saying *Vachel wrote it you know Vachel my very best friend.* Then there will be the day itself and the people on wooden benches and camp-meeting chairs all listening to him.

So what do I do? Susan thinks. So what do I do do I tear it up and make him start over or let him speak it and take the blame myself or tell him straight out why he cannot speak it because Papa must make a living in Springfield and Vachel himself must someday live with Springfield. He is not Bryan who can come one day and leave the next.

She reads the speech again. It is the third time, and she reads hopefully, thinking she might find something she did not see before, something more traditional, more polite, but there is nothing either in the lines or between the lines.

She reads the speech a fourth time and marks lightly in pencil words and phrases that must come out, and when she is finished the manuscript is ribbed with light lines and there is nothing left that makes continuous sense, nothing she can save except a few sentences here and there, and she folds the speech (she will return it to him Monday and he will put it on the closet shelf) and wonders further what do I do.

The thing has happened before to Susan, and it will happen again. It happens for the first time to Vachel. He takes the speech from

Susan, and after school he goes home and upstairs and drops his books upon his table and lies down on his back on his bed and crosses one leg over the other and whistles softly and reads the speech again. It is a good speech Susan said so herself and that is what matters what Susan says, and if he must give another speech saying properer things if there be such a word then he will give it because Susan knows best.

He gets up from his bed and goes to his table and unthreads the red white and blue threaded binding and spreads the papers on the table and takes a pair of scissors and cuts away all the things Susan drew light lines through, and when he is done he has the nucleus of a different speech, and it seems unfair somehow. But it will be just this once and next year he will be in college, and in college far from home people say whatever they want to say, and then when he comes home he will be able to lead his own life and say whatever he wants to say whenever he wants to say it. He rereads the salvaged passages, arranging them on his table in a tentative way, and there is nothing much left, nothing but jumping-off points. He takes a sheet of paper and jots down things that might be helpful. He goes to the bookshelf for the Washington quote he had discarded, and then there is something from Hamilton that he might be able to use, and in no time at all he will have a new speech and the matter will be done with, and he cannot get out of his memory the way Susan looked when she was telling him, the sad way she looked as if something were terribly wrong, something more than the speech.

Vachel himself is not hurt. For a moment he was pained, and then the pain fled, and now he rewrites the speech the way Susan says it must be written. He puts the discarded papers on the shelf with the drawing of the soul of the spider. And he knows that the time will soon come when he will be able to say exactly what he wants to say as long as it is thought through honestly. He weaves the new version of the patriotic speech about Washington and Hamilton and ties it together again with the red white and blue thread, and he is not hurt at all, or at least he does not have the feeling of being hurt. At sixteen he is bruised a dozen times a day and never notices.

In June he delivers his address. The mayor speaks first (the Governor is out of town), followed by the three members of the building committee, followed by Vachel.

10

It is a time of oratory and William Jennings Bryan up from Salem Illinois is the greatest by far, greater than Webster who is much too intellectual and greater than Debs who is after all a Socialist, and a man can go a skeptic and a cynic or a downright disbeliever to a Bryan speech and come away knowing there is truth in the world and God in the world. He will speak outdoors or indoors for twenty people or fifty thousand (there were fifty thousand in Chicago) and the guarantee is that once he is heard he is remembered forever because there has never been anyone like him, not Lincoln or Douglas or anyone, and there will never be anyone quite like him again. There will be smarter men and wiser men and foxier men, but there will never be Bryan again.

Bryan is the West, born in Illinois, to Congress from Nebraska, the enemy of gold (in the Democratic cartoons the banker East stands grossly fat, and small children drip between his fingers into pits of flaming gold) and the friend of the farmer the cowboy the hog caller the friend of everyone west of the Alleghenies, and the enemy of all the rich (all the rich live east of the Alleghenies), silver Democrat with a voice like ten thousand trumpets. He will lead the people two by two out of the ark of gold, into the silver ark, and the people follow because he promises change, and a man cannot remember after a Bryan speech very much of what he says except that it is wonderful and beautiful like angel music, change change change. Cleveland promised change, but there is none, and the promise of Bryan is change itself and the world will be new because Bryan says it will be new, and a man can hear it close up or a quarter mile away because Bryan has lungs like that. People faint, fall dead away, fall from their horses, swallow their teeth, and he comes like rain in August to the dry West on a silver horse like Abraham like Christ Himself like a new Bible.

Long before dawn it begins. It can hardly be heard because it is only now and then a wagon rattling in from the north from Lincoln or Pekin or Bloomington down Tenth Street to Capitol and west on Capitol to the Statehouse, and now and then a wagon from the east from Decatur south from Centralia west from Jacksonville, and when they come in from the west they swing around the Statehouse and stop, and the children are hushed to silence in the cabins of the wagons but they do not sleep. Then there is nothing in the sky but the last brightest stars and the wagons are head to tail on the road, and in front of the Statehouse the men pull their wagons together hub to hub to make room, and the lanterns are extinguished on the tails of the wagons and the sun is not yet up and already there has been one fist fight and one death from apoplexy and one lost child weeping in the street.

The early-morning sun is touched with warmth. The day will be hot unless there is rain, but it does not look like rain. The clouds on the horizon are only clouds of dust, and the dusty wagons roll into Springfield and come in double columns down Tenth from the north and up Tenth from the south and in from the east on Capitol, and they meet on Capitol and come three abreast to the Statehouse and join in bewildering confusion the wagons and carts and men on horseback and men afoot who swing around the Statehouse from the west. The crowd is packed dense. It fans out and spills into the side streets off Capitol and backs up on Capitol all the way to Fifth and a Texan and a Kansan roll on the ground and when they are pulled apart the Texan has a knife wound in his cheek and someone runs for Papa and he leaves in the middle of breakfast to cleanse and patch the wound, and he cannot get home all day through the tight-packed people. "So this is how the millennium comes," says Mama, staring after Papa out the window, and this is how it comes, in bloodshed and shouting and screaming and fainting and runaway horses and trampled children and God knows how many people steaming in the sun. It is the kind of crowd that comes any day to a hanging or any other sort of crucifixion, only bigger.

And different. There is something different today, and Vachel feels it. He leaves soon after Papa and works his way down Fifth Street along the fringes of the crowd and then by foot to the Statehouse lawn and slowly and painfully across the green carpet that will not be green tomorrow, and he climbs a tree and works his way deep into the branches where no one can see, and he cries and remains hidden until the crying is done with. He is ashamed to cry. Papa would be puzzled to see him cry and him sixteen and going to college in the fall, but Vachel cannot help himself.

Now and then a shout goes up, "There he is!" But it is not he. He is somewhere in the mansion standing with Altgeld looking out at the crowd, and now and then a chant begins *Bryan Bryan sixteen to one sixteen to one,* rising from some corner of the peopled streets and catching on and spreading until it is a roar and then dying all at once until the next time. Vachel wishes they would not do it. He tries to shout with the people but his voice is blocked. There is a tightness in his throat and a weakness in his body and he thinks that maybe he is sick, but he is not sick; he is only overcome by the thought of so many people pressed together on the day of delivery and change, and he is about to come down from the tree when the crying starts again, the happy crying that comes from knowing that all Illinois and all the West see the very thing he sees and feel the same need he feels to be saved and delivered and free forever.

Bryan is not so sure. He has never been sure of anything except the existence of God and the need for someone to rise and do God's work in Washington, a Jackson or a Lincoln to lead the people against slavery and gold. He stands at a window with Altgeld and squints through a slit in the blind, and then he looks away and for an instant feels guilt as any man must feel guilt who has assured the people he knows the route through the wilderness, for suppose he should lose his way or suppose it turns out that he did not know the way in the first place. He is full of the thousand doubts that never plague lesser men.

"We ought to start," says Altgeld. "It'll take time to get through."

"Yes John," says Bryan, but he does not move. He holds a glass of cold water in his hand, and he looks into his glass. "You never doubt," says he.

"It's time to start," says Altgeld, and he takes Bryan's glass from his hand and helps him into his coat, and outside the people are singing John Brown's Body and Marching Through Georgia, some of them remembering the last time they won a great victory, some of them too young to remember.

"Do they know what it's all about?" says Bryan.

"Maybe. Some do. They feel it even if they don't know. How in hell can they know what goes on?" and he takes Bryan's arm and steers him to the door. At the door the troopers surround them and someone opens the door and the noise and the singing thunder through and the troopers clear the way across the lawn and the singing stops when the people see Bryan. In a moment it is known everywhere that Bryan has appeared and a roar begins and shrill whistling and the pounding of drums and the explosion of firecrackers and the imitative echoes of five-cent noisemakers. The troopers lock arms and clear the way to the carriage that will bear Bryan, and a farmer crashes the troopers' wedge to touch Bryan and a trooper swings his stick and the man falls to the ground and Bryan shouts to the trooper—Don't!—but his voice is lost, and Altgeld follows, stepping over the fallen man, and he presses forward behind Bryan and they dare not stop for one prone man or the thousands will be kept waiting and there is not the time now to stop or doubt. Bryan is hoisted into the carriage and Altgeld climbs in behind him and the horses plunge forward and the crowd gives way, and the people see Bryan now, high in the carriage, and the cheering is, if possible, louder than before.

They reach the wooden platform in front of the Statehouse and the wordless shouting takes form *no cross of gold no cross of gold* and overhead William McKinley made of burlap hangs and is set afire and Bryan sees and wonders if McKinley were here would they hang him and burn him. Altgeld takes him by the arm to the center of the platform and they raise their locked arms, and in five minutes the shouting ceases, dying slowly until quiet bombards the ear. Altgeld says "William Jennings Bryan," that is all, nothing more, and after ten minutes more there is quiet enough, and Bryan speaks, and that is the wonder of it all, that voice, the hypnotist voice that maybe in any other time would have been less than magic but now, in this time in this place before this angry seeking hopeful people, it is a call to glory and plenty.

The sound of his own voice reassures him, and though there are doubts they are gone in this moment. A respectful, worshipful silence falls, and part of the wonder is that he does not shout, he speaks, and yet the voice floats a quarter mile. Behind him Altgeld has taken a seat and crossed his legs. He closes his eyes against the high, hot sun. He listens to Bryan. Boy Bryan they call him.

"We are Crusaders, we silver Democrats," and it is time for cheering again, and the awed silence breaks, and when the cheering stops Bryan goes on. "We believe that the man who is employed for wages is as much a businessman as his employer. The farmer who goes forth in the morning and toils all day—who begins in the spring and toils all summer—he is as much a businessman as the man who sits on the board of trade and bets upon the price of grain." Loud cheers, louder than before. "Ah my friends who rear their children near to Nature's heart where they can mingle their voices with the voices of the birds, we are fighting in the defense of our homes, our families and posterity." (Altgeld covers his ears; the din is great, the sun is hot, and his head aches.) "I stand with Jefferson. The banks must go out of the governing business. We will win, we struggling masses. We will win over the idle holders of idle capital. We will not legislate to make the rich prosperous and hope that prosperity will leak down to those below. No! No! We will legislate to make the masses prosperous," and the cheering rolls in waves toward Bryan and will not ebb. He relaxes. He turns and looks at Altgeld and smiles and the Governor smiles back and shakes his fist at Bryan in a victory salute and the people see the salute and renew themselves *Altgeld Altgeld Bryan Bryan sixteen to one no cross of gold sixteen to one no cross of gold,* and Altgeld supposes that somehow this is how revolution is launched, that somehow Bryan is necessary six hundred Bryan speeches twenty-seven states eighteen thousand miles Boy Bryan tireless.

"Burn down your cities and leave our farms, and your large cities will spring up again as if by magic. But destroy our farms and the grass will grow in every street in every city of the country, and upon that issue we expect to carry every state in the union," and the cheering breaks out again redoubled and Bryan goes on and the sun is hot on Altgeld's head (what issue? what issue? he thinks what was it Boy Bryan just said make every man a businessman and see where we end will not every man want to be Pullman himself?) "We do not need to fear a Robespierre. No tyrant will rise from the people. What we need is an Andrew Jackson to stand as Jackson stood against the encroachment of organized wealth." Altgeld crosses and recrosses his legs and the afternoon sun lowers behind him and he grows stiff give them Jefferson and Jackson sweet Boy Bryan and how do we carry every state in the union they are strong they are strong Mister Pullman is strong burn down his ugly city he will build you an uglier one.

Now silence. The famous words are coming, the words the people came to hear, up from Texas east from Kansas from everywhere in Illinois, and Bryan is working around to the words saying anything anything at all because it does not much matter what he says so long as he says the words, and he says to them "You shall not press down upon the brow of" but the people do not hear. They cheer before he has fairly begun. He will stand all day uttering the sentence until it is heard. It is the sentence he came to pronounce and he will stand all day and all night if he must with the words on his tongue. "You shall not press down upon the brow of labor" and they will not wait: it is too big, and they have waited days and come long miles to hear it and they will not hear it all in a rush.

Then at last they agree to hear it, and they are silent, and now he will say it and then they will surge toward Bryan and tear at his clothing and tonight they will march and Bryan will be led quietly out of a rear door of the mansion to the depot, and they will wait at the front door all night waiting for Bryan and in the morning wind home in long caravans and tell folks they saw Bryan and heard him say the words (and in November thinks Altgeld they will vote the elephant not the Democratic chicken here is a dollar vote the elephant or the bank will close let me show you how for the elephant waves the dollar owns the bank and the Democrats are words and heart and men like Bryan and me John Altgeld threw Cleveland in the street and we are words but not the dollars) and now they are quiet, waiting for the words.

"You shall not press down upon labor this crown of thorns, you shall not crucify mankind upon a cross of gold."

11

Whatever it is that was in the air is dead. Vachel knows it. He knows even before November that it is dead, or if it is not dead it is at least lying very still with a slow pulse and a faint heart. It is almost dead whatever it was in the air from Chicago to Cairo and on the Mississippi and the Illinois and in the valleys of the Sangamon and the Spoon. Quite suddenly Vachel knows that there is something large and invisible and formidable that says Bryan must not win and Altgeld must be turned out. It is the thing that gives the land McKinley in November and a quick happy war with Spain to take people's minds off things.

Vachel does not know what it is. Maybe it will come to him sometime in a great moment as this much knowledge comes all of a sudden, bursting into his brain out of nowhere, shaped in the unremembered past.

It is a good thing to know, and he can never say he was not taught (*if you are always a proper boy life will be good to you everybody sing but Vachel carry the tune or be silent write the proper speech or you may not speak wrap the rebel book in plain brown paper so the iceman won't see rebel bastard rebel bastard)* and maybe he will be wise and remember the lesson.

Something large and invisible and formidable, and babyhood is over and the easy dream is dead. He will study medicine as Papa wishes one does the thing Papa says because there are rules written large. One does not go on for long making patriotic speeches that are not quite patriotic or he sits alone weeping like Bryan in November, bitter and alone like Altgeld in November. One must learn to smile and sail cheerfully with the patriot fleet to the quick happy war.

CHAPTER TWO

1

A MAN lies dead on a marble table.

The first time Vachel saw a dead man naked on a marble table he swallowed hard and shut his eyes and steadied himself against a young man who a moment later fainted away, but now it is nothing, nothing at all. He has seen so many dead men that he has lost count. Dr. Page in his years at Hiram College has seen so many dead men that they are all one to him, and the students are all one, and this year and every year the first time they meet death cold and naked face to face a few will totter in their tracks and one or two will fall to the floor.

By this time, he thinks, they should be able to tell with one swift glance at the man on the table what caused his hemorrhage. "Lindsay, cause of death?"

"Really sir I haven't the vaguest idea," and the doctor takes it from there and asks Ross Butler and Ross Butler always knows, and Vachel prepares to concentrate on the answer Ross Butler gives, but by the time Ross Butler gives it he is lost again. Concentrate concentrate concentrate he tells himself, and sometimes he thinks it is no use at all he cannot concentrate.

The hands and forearms of the man on the table are dark. Above the elbows the arms whiten, and his chest is white except for the V at the neckline, and below the point of the V there is an incision and Vachel read last night in a materia medica what such an incision is called. There was a diagram with numbers and arrows and he studied it very carefully. He tries to call the diagram to mind because maybe Dr. Page will ask what do you call this incision why was it made. He thinks it would be a good idea to be able to answer Dr. Page once in a while because the doctor is a good and sincere and earnest fellow and materia medica such a nice sound like Il Penseroso hence vain deluding joys the brood of folly without father bred or is that L'Allegro. No. L'Allegro goes hence loathed a thing over the *e* hence loathed melancholy he has been reading too much

Milton lately and not enough materia medica. "This incision," the good doctor says, pointing with his baton (there is a name for the stick he points with and Vachel should know because he missed it on the first-week quiz, but he does not know, and in his mind it is a baton). Ridiculous, he thinks, it is not a baton. "Who can name it? Lindsay?"

"Really sir. No sir."

"I didn't expect so," the doctor says, smiling. "A human or animal body, in this case the specimen we are now considering . . ." considering considering when I consider how my light is spent. Concentrate!

The *V* at the neckline means the man wore his shirt open at the neck, and Vachel sees him now, upright and alive in his open-neck shirt, working in the sun, maybe bending over his garden somewhere in a nice part of town. No, if he planted a garden in a nice part of town he would not need to sell himself to a laboratory. On his left foot it is tattooed deliver this body to such and such and they paid him for his body. To a laboratory. Not to a quiet grave but here to be sliced up and incinerated maybe a gardener working for somebody else in a nice part of town and getting over to the nice part of town every day in the summertime and maybe in the winter going somewhere in the sunny South to garden. It is almost as good to work in someone else's garden as your own. A month ago a week ago perhaps with the tattooed foot in someone's garden in a nice part of town rubbing dirt from his hands at quitting time drinking a long silver drink of well water and then going home to a part of town not so nice. Yet even if his own part of town was not so nice, Vachel thinks, perhaps the gardener home from work was greeted at his door by a plump good woman and there was the smell of good if not fancy food from within. "You might at least answer me," says Dr. Page. "I'm sorry sir. Terribly sorry," and he supposes that being sorry redeems him. It is all he can say *I'm sorry sir terribly sorry* (it is the time at Hiram that students overwork the word *terribly* and professors of the English language recoil but soon fall into the habit themselves) and he sees himself not far in the future dosing someone with whosit when he should be administering whatsit and he sees the patient dying in the night and the next day he will say he is sorry terribly sorry. He dreams the dream at night and emerges sweating from the dream and lies awake in the dark. God save the sick from me, he prays, and he turns over and closes his

eyes and dreams the same dream once more. "In the case of a specimen which has been for a period of time in this condition, should
we wish to examine the blood what should be done? Lindsay, what
should be done?"

"Exercise it," says Vachel.

"Quite right," says Dr. Page, and he takes a shining knife from
a drawer of the marble table and slits the skin deftly, swiftly, like a
warm knife through a Christmas pie, and it is really not so difficult
after all; all it takes is a little concentration, and Vachel is proud
of himself for answering the question.

He watches intently as the professor goes to work with expe-
rienced hands. Vachel supposes that once he gets the feel of the
thing it will come easy. One learns by experience what to do and
where to cut, and how. "Practice, interminable practice," Dr. Page
is always saying, and in time one has the feel of the knife the way
one has the feel of a pencil or any other everyday instrument, the
way the people in Shakespeare go for daggers all the time and
plunge them into the exact mortal parts unless of course the action
calls for only a wound as when Antony only half-stabs himself and
does not die until the next act, and why does Hamlet spare Claudius at his prayers it is not logical really. Hamlet is somehow
greater all in all than Antony and it would be interesting to figure
out why. Virgil Green is Hamlet in Chicago and that would be something to see maybe next summer if it runs that long you would think
they would run the plays longer.

"Lindsay?" Very patiently, very understandingly, a tired professor with a bloody knife in his hand, standing over a marble table
on which a dead man lies but not coming down with the knife at
all it is not logical. Very softly, "Lindsay?"

No answer.

(Back in his freshman year, long before they had reached the
autopsy stage, even before they had touched upon the femur bone,
Vachel lay on his back in the Hiram infirmary while Miss Curtis
who was even then so competent and up on everything that it made
him sick cut the stitches from the long gash on his chin and said in
her knowing way, "Vachel, there are some things in life that we are
suited for, and there are some things we should never attempt," and
he should have seen then how right she was. She taped a dry band-
age on his healed wound.

(It had been an unhappy experience, even humiliating, and yet it was the honor of the freshman class and so forth and he could not well refuse. "Where do you play?" they asked. "Quarterback," he said. He was unlearned in the art of football, but he had observed that the quarterback invariably appeared to be less involved than the other members of the team, and he thought he could bluff his way through by remaining far behind what seemed to be the central point of the controversy. For one minute and thirty seconds he did so, at which point a sophomore named Tolliver, intent upon glorifying his class at the expense of the freshmen, tore through the defense and proceeded at great speed toward Vachel. Vachel's first impulse was to turn and run, or at least to step aside and allow Tolliver the right of way. He recalled swiftly Falstaff's wise scornful words upon the subject of honor. Tolliver was large and determined (he weighed one hundred and ninety pounds; Vachel weighed one-fifty) and Vachel was suddenly and inexplicably equally determined Falstaff or no Falstaff, and in a moment of foolish bravery he attempted to tackle Tolliver. Vachel an instant later was flat on his back on the unresisting ground, and a great many freshmen in pursuit of Tolliver and a great many sophomores in defense of Tolliver ran across Vachel's face in the dark seconds that followed.

(At the infirmary Miss Curtis stemmed the flow of blood and Dr. Page sewed sixteen stitches in Vachel's chin, and Miss Curtis said for the first time, "Vachel, there are some things in life we are suited for, and some things we should never attempt," and he should have known then how right she was.)

Yet it is not as if he wants to be a doctor any more than he wants to be a quarterback, and he tells them at home the first summer that he flunked trigonometry, physics and chemistry, that he almost passed botany and biology and indeed passed astronomy, Latin and rhetoric altogether. "The first year is always the hardest," says Mama, and Papa says nothing. He goes into his study and closes his door behind him and does not come out for two hours, and when he comes he looks as any man looks who knows all at once that the thing he dreamed of all his life is not about to happen. People say all year to Papa, "What of the boy?" and Papa says he is doing fine, just fine.

"Things will be better the farther you progress," Mama says.

"People expect you to do well," says Papa. "You have the brain for it, son," and he is determined to do better in the second year because Mama and Papa expect it and deserve it and all Springfield expects it because that is the way the doctor planned it from the beginning. Meanwhile he shows them in Springfield a lengthwise scar across his chin, and he laughs as he points to it and explains what happened. "It was really terribly funny," he says.

Looking back at it twenty years later, looking back on Hiram after it no longer matters, it will be funny.

But now it is not really so funny, and at the end of the summer he goes back by train to Hiram, and all through the trip he plans to do better this year. It is a very serious matter and not in the least bit funny, and the future hangs in the balance, his future, and Papa's and Mama's, and somehow Springfield's, too, and he never knew until now, seeing Springfield at a distance, how much he loves that place and the good people friendly on the streets and it would be something, something good and something noble, to go back to them with skilled hands and tape their wounds and ease their aches and mend their bones and soften their pains and say like Papa pay me when you have it no hurry and write their names in a black notebook and when they pay cross the names out and when they die before paying cross their names out and do as Christ would do and walk among the sick like Saint Francis among the lepers, like Whitman among the wounded. It is not funny. It is something that can be wonderful, and he will try this second year to do better at Hiram.

Hiram College Ohio. 1897-1900. Four hundred townspeople and three hundred students side by side in delicate relationship.

James Garfield was once president of the Eclectics Club and later became President of the United States, and the townspeople know there must be something in book learning after all though they are not quite sure what. Ben Tillington, a townsman, runs the book exchange, and books cross and recross his counter year in and year out and he can look at a book and tell by the condition of its cover how much it will bring. He knows books by their price. He is innocent of their value. Gray's *Anatomy* four dollars Pipkin's *Muscular Theory* three-fifty Johnson & Johnson *The Circulatory System* six dollars Goldstein's *Eyes Ears Nose and Throat* four-fifty the life of Garfield three-fifty Tom Jefferson fifty cents Tom Paine a quarter.

The Eclectics Club. The Natural History Club. Intramural football.

Tuition sixteen dollars and well worth it. Eli Zollars who was once a preacher in Springfield Illinois is the President of Hiram College and he directs a sectarian Protestant school that is, above all, Christian rather than sectarian and anyone may enroll who has the tuition and if he (or she) does not have it he may pay it back sometime in later life. They always come back sooner or later and pay the bill. The Civics Club. The Club for the Study of Other Peoples. The Spider Web, a publication. (Vachel is represented in The Spider Web by thirty-five illustrations and twenty prose selections, and the book is given away free. Ben Tillington who runs the book exchange wonders why anybody would get up a book and then not sell it, and he takes a few Spider Webs and stores them away, and much later, many years later, people write to him or come through Hiram and stop at his shop and buy up old copies, the ones with the Lindsay in them. "Damnedest thing I ever seen.")

Hiram Hill, where young men and young ladies sometimes hold hands, where the holding of hands is, for some, the first time, the first intimacy, the first suggestion of a warmth between persons, quite unlike the warmth of the sun or the warmth of fire or the warmth of things that are simply warm, a warmth that is sun and fire and an unnamed thing beyond all warmth and fire, an act of innocence which some of the young men and young ladies on Hiram Hill learn to call by the name of love.

"But what is love?" says someone in the darkness. "We must define our terms," for it is the year of life when all are intent on defining terms, and love is thereupon defined as love of country, love of God, love of the world, but never as the act of holding hands. All are young, and all are of time's newest generation, and all are hopeful. The holding of hands will be remembered. Likewise, the noble definitions of love will be remembered and cherished even if, for practical reasons, they will be discarded by all but the few who will carry with them the notion of love as the love of the world transcending the holding of hands.

And sometimes on Hiram Hill a small circle of young men and young ladies and someone reading aloud because the custom is that those who are creative shall be listened to. Like all of Hiram's customs it is a nice custom, and there is something civilized about Hiram, something most students do not feel until a long time afterward when they go home to the barren towns whence they came, home to Cleveland, Akron or Columbus where people do not read to one another or study other peoples very much or work together on books and give them away free or do any of the things the three hundred students do at Hiram when they are young and the world is all books and being terribly happy and terribly thrilled and terribly creative.

The seniors begin to worry a little and ask themselves what happens when all this is over, but not for some years will they know. But then they will know, and some of them in a fuzzy hasty way (there will be time for only fuzzy hasty thinking) will realize that this is what is permanent, this is all there is. The rest is nonsense and only this is worth the trouble, the books, the readings aloud on Hiram Hill, the tender and frantic putting together of the Spider Web late at night, and the innocent holding of hands.

2

Helen Curtis is pleased. If she has said to him once she has said a dozen times, "Vachel it's not terribly hard you know," and he does things now the way Helen does them, methodically, and she is terribly pleased.

Last June when he was not quite sure he would ever be a doctor he had gone down to Ben Tillington's and traded his four fat texts for half a shelf of books that Ben had tried a long time to get rid of Blake Ruskin a Bible a book of folk songs some Swinburne some Poe and the Tom Paine that Ben cannot sell for a quarter but is nevertheless reluctant to part with because it is very old and may someday be worth something. Now, in September, charged with resolution, Vachel gathers his books from the floor and from the corners of his room and goes down to Ben's and leans across the counter. "Say Ben," says he, "I've changed my mind. I want my textbooks back," and Ben says he can give only three texts back. "Not the Johnson," says he, and Vachel makes the trade, paying six dollars cash for Johnson & Johnson and losing on the deal the way he will always lose on every money deal he ever makes. But now, at this time of his life, it does not matter much because Papa sends money every month.

Outside Ben's shop he meets Helen Curtis, and that is where it begins with Helen, such as it is. She is tiny and full of energy, and Vachel carries her suitcase for her and tells her how he is full of good intentions this year. He had planned not to tell anyone. He had planned just to do it, to go ahead on his own and let them see for themselves the new reformed Vachel, but he knows she will be pleased, and she is.

In the evening they have a soda at The Haven and they talk about what they did all summer and what is ahead of them in the year to come. "There comes a time when a man just settles down and assumes his responsibilities," says Vachel. "I guess my time has come."

"I thought about you this summer," she says.

"You did?"

"I was thinking how lucky you are, your papa being a doctor."

"What's yours?" Vachel asks.

"Nothing," she says.

"He must be something." Vachel's straw makes empty noises at the bottom of his glass. He orders another soda.

"Not a doctor," she says. He is not a doctor and therefore he is nothing. There is only one calling in life she respects.

"Tomorrow it begins," he says. He wishes he had a few more days to think about his resolutions before putting them into practice.

"You ought to work out a schedule," she says. "One day this, another that. That's the only way."

"Oh I am," he says. He takes a piece of paper from his pocket and shows her. "I wrote it on the train and it's a little jumpy." He reads: "Eight to noon, classes. Noon to one, lunch. One to three, classes. Three to five, study. Five to six, supper. Six to nine, study. Nine to eleven, read. Eleven, bed."

"Read what?"

"Books. Things."

"Well yes," she says. She takes the paper from him. "From three to five we can study together." She is very bold and Vachel never knew a bold girl before, and somehow it is decided. She pays for her own soda. Vachel protests but she pays it just the same, and he walks with her to her dormitory. "After lights out," she says, "I cover my window with a blanket. You'd be surprised how it blocks the light. You can get a lot extra done that way."

"Well anyway not tonight," he says.

"Why not?"

"Well classes haven't even *begun*," he says.

"No matter," she says, and in the darkness she squeezes his hand. It is a quick motion, and before he is fully aware that her hand is on his it is withdrawn. She squeezes his hand the way a doctor squeezes the hand of an ailing patient who will, in time, recover, and then she is gone, and he thinks it will be a long time until tomorrow when they study together.

He walks alone through the night, and the hand that she touched is warm. He lifts it to his face, and the hand has a fragrance both sweet and oversweet, first one and then the other. He cannot decide

which, even as he is indecisive about Helen herself who is both
sweet and something else, both gentle-sweet and strong, driven and
driver, strong, as Mama is strong, her eyes upon a fixed and rigid
place which one might call Goal. Yet the touch of her hand was
good, and he thinks that he might touch her hand again sometime
and know again that goodness. He erects in his mind a time and a
place and the appropriate words, and he creates the moment of the
touching of hands.

Would he dare? He wonders if he would dare. It was, after all,
her hand that reached for his. She is a bold girl, bold and unafraid,
and he has decided that women, like men, should be bold and fear-
less in a world that needs above all things the quality of courage.
He will have courage. He will touch her hand.

The grades go up. Not much, but some. Enough to carry him
across the line that seems to him somewhat arbitrary between something called passing and something called failure, and at Thanksgiving there is something to give thanks for, and on the first of December a little something extra in the regular envelope from Papa.
Papa does not write letters. He is not a man of words. It is Mama
who deals in words. At Christmastime there is a longer letter than
usual from her. Vachel does not go home for Christmas. He remains
at Hiram, close to the books, because even though his grades go up
the knowledge gathered lodges precarious in his brain and seems
likely at any moment to slip away, down through his shoes to be
lost in the snow, out the window, up the chimney, and he must stay
close to the books. He allows himself the luxury of the *Journal* in
the morning and a sweet hot chocolate at The Haven at night, and
the letters from Mama to be read and reread and the generous
bonus from Papa at Christmas, but not so comforting as Mama's
letters. Mama seems to understand that this is not for him, these
books, and one day in the mail three lines from Mama, quoting
Browning. (She has never been entirely sure that Browning is
wholly Christian.) But the lines seem right: *Grow old along with
me. The best is yet to be, The last of life for which the first was
made,* and Vachel smiles, knowing Mama's reservations about
Browning. He pastes the sheet of paper on a piece of stiff cardboard
and puts it on the window sill to dry, and the words that follow beat
all morning in his brain, *Trust God see all nor be afraid,* over and
over, trust God trust God all of the morning.

The year turns and Hiram refills, and it was terribly good to get home and it is terribly good to be back, and on the third day of January classes resume. It is as if there had never been vacation at all, except that there is snow on the ground and there was no snow before, but all else is the same, the familiar feel and weight of the books and the same unique chocolate smell of The Haven and the same climb up the Hill and the same smell in Chemistry and the same lecture that Dr. Page gives at the beginning of every new year. "Practice, interminable practice." And some of the boys still terribly fond of the same girls despite Christmas at home and all the chance there was to find out that the girl one had back home was the one who *really* meant something, especially at Christmas when all was love, and the boys who still like the same girls despite Christmas are assumed to feel something deeper than just plain liking. There is a distinction between liking and something else, like the fine line between passing and failing, and Vachel is assumed to like Helen in a way that is more than just liking. "He didn't even go home at Christmas imagine," and there was something terribly noble in that, not even going home at Christmas, and let him deny it but he meets her at three at the library every afternoon and they sit with their heads close together and sometimes, turning a page, both reaching for the corner of the page at the same instant, their hands touch.

Spring will tell. In the spring if they go to the Hill together in the afternoon it will mean beyond all doubt that there is something more than liking between them. It will mean that the line has been crossed.

At six o'clock in the morning in January her alarm rings and she moves her arm quickly downward to the clock that stands beside her bed. Her clock is the first to ring in the dormitory and there have been complaints that she rises too early and Mrs. Brinker the preceptress has told her often that a young lady needs sleep if she is to be beautiful, but Helen Curtis does not particularly care to be beautiful. Mrs. Brinker knows that Helen stretches a blanket across her window at night and studies until midnight or later, and the preceptress speaks to Dr. Zollars about it and Dr. Zollars says he will speak to Helen, but he never does.

Helen takes the blanket from the window and wraps it about her and walks briskly but not quite in a straight line down the dark dormitory hall to the sinks, and she washes her face in cold water because cold water wakes her up better than warm, and warm water takes time to rise through the pipes and she cannot spare the time because by seven o'clock she must do all the things to herself and her room that other girls spend all evening doing.

She fumbles beneath the blanket. The small pocket of her gown, originally intended to hold only a tiny, preferably lacy sweet-smelling handkerchief, contains a piece of paper, and wrapped in the paper are pills. She withdraws the paper and takes a pill and bites it in half and wraps the pills again and puts them back into her pocket, next to her warm body, and she swallows the half-pill and follows it down with cold water from the spigot. The pill helps to keep her awake, the pill and the cold water against her face and the cold room and the violent determination that is within her and the shame of a father who was never anything in life, just a workingman, and the shame of being a woman in a world that belongs to men.

Between six o'clock and seven she is busy, and from time to time she glances at her clock. Somehow the hour of seven is important. She would be miserable if she thought anyone knew that seven o'clock is important, somehow, to her.

At seven o'clock Vachel's alarm rings and blends with his dream, and if he were a swearing man he would swear because he hates clocks. But he rises because if he lies late he will fall behind in the race and once he falls behind he will be behind for good, and everything depends on getting out of the warm bed and pressing the stem of the clock to silence it, pressing gently because after all the clock is a machine and does not understand violence. It does no good to smash clocks; he smashed one in his freshman year and nobody suffered but him. He could not put it together again and he had to buy a new one. "Simon Legree!" he says. It is as much of an oath as he will allow himself, and he presses the stem gently and reaches under his covers for his clothes. He keeps them warm that way. He hates cold clothes against his body, just as he hates clocks.

But the clock rules him. At seven-twenty he passes through the door of the dining hall and brings warm food to his mouth, not knowing quite what he is eating except that it is warm and if he does not eat it his belly will yowl in midmorning, and after he has eaten he crosses the campus to chapel, keeping well behind the crowd.

At fifteen minutes of eight Helen meets him. "Wake up," she says. "It's a new day."

"So it's a new day," says he, feeling and knowing, but not saying, that Monday is like Tuesday is like Wednesday, as January is twin to February, and March arrives in the image of both.

But at the end of March the snows melt and the days grow longer and the boys and the girls on the Hill drink the spring and Dr. Page warns as he warns every year on the first day that looks like permanent spring, "Practice, interminable practice. Spring, summer, winter and fall. I warn you," and then in his best dramatic voice: "In spring a young man's fancy lightly turns to thoughts of love or words to that effect, but I warn you against the spring." He throws open the classroom window the way he throws it open every year on almost exactly the same day and in exactly the same way, with a warning motion.

At three o'clock on the afternoon of the first day of spring Helen waits in front of the library as usual, and each time someone approaches it looks like Vachel, but it is not Vachel. She walks to the infirmary but he is not there. She goes to his rooming house and asks for him, and Mrs. Richie shouts upstairs for Vachel and someone replies that he left an hour ago. "For where?" says Helen, and Mrs. Richie shouts *where?* and the answer comes *he did not say,* and Helen tries The Haven and he is not there.

He is not in front of the chapel at fifteen before eight on the following morning, nor at the library at three, and Helen starts for home, and everywhere she thinks she sees Vachel, and her eyes deceive her; it is not he. At least he could have told me, she thinks, at least he could have told me was the very least he could have done. In her room she lies on her bed and cries.

But it is merely the spring, and three days only. On the first day he walked almost as far as Southington, and on the second day into Southington itself, and the third day beyond Southington as far as Champion Heights along the dusty country road, and somehow he felt free, and he sang to himself and whistled and heaved rocks and shouted for Bryan, remembering when Bryan came to Springfield and Altgeld greeted him and the two giants stood together on the platform and shook hands and it seemed then that change, colossal change, was about to occur, and that was long ago and Mark Hanna smashed Bryan with a fistful of gold. Vachel spits on Mark Hanna's Ohio and shouts four times for Bryan, *Bryan Bryan Bryan Bryan,* four times, four echoes, eight distinct and individual senses of freedom.

On the fourth day at fifteen of eight he meets Helen. She does not speak. They enter the chapel together, and afterward, in class, Dr. Page says "We are honored," looking at Vachel, and Vachel does not reply, does not smile, does not even resent.

At three o'clock at the library Helen, now trusting herself to speak, tells him grimly, "We lost three days. Three whole days do you know what that means?" "We'll get them back," he says, but it is not so easy. Sixty pages in Gray forty-eight in Pipkin forty-five in Goldstein thirty-six in Johnson & Johnson like running from a snake in a bad dream when the legs will not move, running and running and always overtaken, and finally the only way to do is to jump the chapter on the femur bone and pray it does not pop up on a quiz and trust God that nobody in Springfield ever breaks a femur bone because it cannot be set by bluff, and in April one whole blooming quiz about nothing but the femur bone, and the only consolation is that the whole thing is averages. It is yet possible to get through knowing nothing at all about the femur bone.

It is a race, and for a while he was up there somewhere with the crowd, well behind the leaders but nevertheless in the crowd where his name was not conspicuous, and now he runs a little behind the crowd, precariously along the thin line that separates the passing from the failing, now this way and now that. In May he regains the ground he lost, and Dr. Page winks at him one day after class. (Dr. Page did it once himself, once in the spring, and he always winks at the ones who stumble but see the light and get back on the track because once he too was young and heard something call to him, and for six months, six whole months, he went scooting about defying life, and then he returned and was meek and faced the reality of the thing, and now he winks at Vachel.)

Vachel clings, and in June the grades are posted and he is somewhere among the crowd, not up with Helen and the geniuses and yet not down below the thin line, just somewhere in the crowd with boys and girls who jump a chapter now and then and worry about it, but not too much.

(And spring has come and gone. On spring afternoons he had gone with Helen Curtis to Hiram Hill, and they had selected a tree that threw its shade upon the surrounding grass, and the tree and its shade had become, for this season of the year, *their* tree, *their* shade, and he had spread for her an issue of an unread Springfield

Journal, and she had sat upon it, and he beside her explored with her the books for which he had no taste. Sometimes, furtively, he read those items of the *Journal* that were visible, lamenting that the news from home lay, for the most part, crushed and concealed between the girl and the earth. They exchanged questions concerning the texts, and she found it all rewarding and exciting. "The basic things," she said. "The basic stuff."

(And he thought that he might one day have the courage to take her hand in his, for he liked her and remembered the fragrance of his hand after the first touch of hers, and he knew that if he were to take her hand she would permit that liberty, for although she is very learned she is also tender. He remembers how, tenderly, she had bandaged his torn chin. And although she is stern and stiff and proper in the presence of the texts he has seen her unbend and relax during those hours of the week she methodically sets aside for unbending and relaxing. She seems to be, in many ways, Woman as Vachel imagines Woman will be in the perfect age, Woman of brain and Woman of beauty, the equal Woman.)

Now, after the coming and going of spring they are together at a time of parting, and such a time, even if it is only a summer's parting, is always a sad time for men and women when they are very young.

"It's late," says Vachel.

"It's always late," she says. "It's never on time. It's always late," and they step together onto the tracks and contemplate the expanse of empty rail, as if the study of distance will hasten arrival. Then they leave the tracks and stand together on the platform beside the suitcase which Vachel, overestimating his own powers and underestimating the heat of the day, had offered to carry the four miles between Hiram and the college station. "A very big suitcase for such a little girl," he had said after the first mile and again after the second. He cannot now very clearly recall what he had said between times, although he remembers that it had reference to the sadness of parting, and he makes reference now, again, to the heaviness of the suitcase and the sadness of parting, and boldly he takes her hand, and they stand together, hand in hand.

"Try to read this summer," she says. "It'll do you good. If you need any particular book write me."

He plans to read. He does not plan to read the books she has in mind, however. "There are two suns," he says. "A sun on each

track," and he points with his free hand, and she laughs indifferently, and then in the distance brown smoke mushrooms above
the treetops and a moment later the train is visible, and she says
again, "Read. Whatever you do, read."

"I'll be a good boy," he says, and still he holds her hand, and
now the silent train becomes audible, and hand in hand they retreat from the tracks, and then, quite suddenly, she withdraws her
hand from his and turns and faces him.

"Be serious," she says, "because you're never the least bit serious. What's going to become of you! You must be serious." Then
her tone is soft, softer than he has ever known it. "Suppose this
were the last time. I'm glad it's not because it worries my mind that
someday there'll be a last time and we'll be saying good-by for the
last time. Did you ever think of that? Please think about it this
summer and you and me. Do you love me? Don't you love me?" and
the huffing train slows and stops, and the students converge, pressing forward toward the train, enveloping Vachel and Helen, forcing
them forward, and even if he knew how to answer her there would
not now be the time or the space. He helps her aboard, handing her
suitcase up to her, and then, quickly, he turns, retreating, not looking back, freeing himself from the confining pressure of the happy,
the homebound, freeing himself and not looking back.

Behind him the train makes fretful noises, and then it is in motion. Tonight another train will carry him toward Springfield, home,
away. Away from what? At least away from here.

He turns once, and he sees the train, and it occurs to him that
each split second represents a widening distance between him and
her and between the two hands that so recently embraced. And
sadly and guiltily he knows that the widening distance is also, for
him, a kind of freedom, at least for now, because he has as yet no
goal, no destination, as she has a Goal, as she has a course as neatly
laid as the tracks upon which she now rides. She knows where she
is going and when she will arrive, and he in turn knows nothing.
He knows only that he is in search of something that has as yet,
for him, no size, no shape, no substance, that he must press the
search, that he must go in search, and that he must go alone.

3

It is a hot Springfield summer, a long summer, and there is nowhere a retreat from the heat, and the tiny parks that hardly de-

serve the name parks are too crowded with people trying to get off the streets onto something green, even the tiny areas of green called parks, and water is at a premium (let them drink beer) because nobody, least of all the Brewery, has ever thought to plan a city instead of letting it grow wild like a jungle.

Ice, first come first served, and an old lady pushing along on old thin legs to the icehouse and carriages passing her along the way, and she shifts her bucket from hand to hand as she goes, and when she gets there somebody very generous drops a five-pound cake of ice into her bucket and she is thankful for that. It melts before she is home, and on her wall at home are the words sewed in white against a sky-blue felt background and bordered in red and framed, Be Thankful For Small Things, and she dies of the heat that night and Dr. Lindsay, a man of few words, writes cryptically on her certificate, Exhaustion.

Vachel wakes promptly at seven every morning and remembers that this is Springfield, not Hiram. He goes back to sleep. He does not sleep well because he knows he should be up and doing. He had thought he might spend this summer doing some of the things he really wants to do. He has been working on a drawing of Lucifer (Lucifer, later called Satan, was expelled from Heaven) but the work has been only five minutes now and five minutes again sometime later and usually in secret with the heavy weight of guilt on his wrist because he ought to be out with Papa doing the rounds. Yet he ought to be working on his drawing, too, because maybe after this summer there will never be time to do another. He compromises between the two looming duties by staying in bed; it seems to be the safest thing to do.

Vachel avoids Papa, and when they meet at table he will not look into Papa's eyes. Papa says nothing, but he is waiting, and Vachel feels him waiting and knows that he cannot stall and stay in bed forever, and finally one day in July he takes a deep breath and tells Papa, "Very well. Today," knowing it is the end of everything, the crossing of the Rubicon, the decision of Hamlet, and Lucifer will lie half-drawn on the table upstairs, Lucifer who sang well but nevertheless displeased the angels.

Papa always starts his rounds downtown. "Downtown mostly it's cardiac," Papa says, playing his whip lightly against the horses. "Enlarged heart. Overwork. Exhaustion. Nothing you can name exactly. Just too much strain on the heart. Dirt. Filth. Coal dust.

Like any machine, just too much to pull, too much for the system."

"Tuberculosis?"

"Sure, tuberculosis. Not much you can do about it. Climate. Too low. Damp. Downtown'll take up most of the time. Roughly, two blocks either side of the tracks. You'll see."

Downtown, two dollars for white folks and colored folks free and nothing much Papa can do for the people in the shacks beside the railroad. "Mostly a matter of making them comfortable. Sedatives. Sedatives are cheap. Also, comfort their mind," and then in a widening circle Papa moves, and Vachel beside him in the buggy the way Papa dreamed it would someday be. A long time ago Papa dreamed it. "Things change as you move away from the railroad," Papa says.

"Interesting," says Vachel.

"Very," says Papa. "Cardiac still. Not so frequent. Not so bad. Chance to do something about it. A little cash on hand. Drugs. Rest," and the people with faith in Papa, knowing that he knows best and will cure them, more faith in Papa than he has in himself. He knows inside himself that there is nothing he can do, really, nothing but keep the parts moving a longer time than they might otherwise move, but basically nothing.

"Worry overworks the heart, too," says Vachel.

"That's what they say. Maybe so." Meanwhile the drugs, rest and hopeful words, and at noon they stop at the square and water the horses and then move on again in the widening circle to houses that are neater and airier, the common cold, the flu, cardiac and tuberculosis less frequent and the stops farther apart, and then still farther out, one stop, two stops, and the lawns are green and it is a long walk to the house. High blood pressure. Anxiety. Overweight. Little green wonder-working pills made of flour and salt to be swallowed with water. "One every two hours," says Papa, and a fat bill to pay for the day's work because Papa too must pay his bills, and the ride home, Vachel high on the seat beside Papa, and Papa proud, and behind them the people with faith in Papa, and tomorrow more of the same, and office hours from three to five and Vachel not so sure, not sure at all that this is what he wants to do.

But all summer he does it, riding with Papa and learning the secrets. Six days a week the widening circle, beginning downtown and winding about the city and stopping where sickness is, and the circles somehow remind Vachel of Dante's circles, and in some way or other there must be escape from this because the circles have no end. No circle has beginning or end and the bodies break down because they are pushed too hard, and the stresses and strains are too many, and Papa does not really know the cures and not even the new young Springfield doctors with their new drugs and new instruments know the cures.

Perhaps, Vachel thinks, there is no cure. Perhaps it is like Dante's Hell and the sickness goes on forever and ever and Papa can ease the pain here today but it develops next door tomorrow, and the more the young doctors know the more strange sicknesses there are with more new names for them and more new pills and never the cure way down at the roots, down in the coalpits, down by the railroad, down in the hundred places where the evils begin, out at the Brewery and on the floor of Sangamon County Trust ("I was doing fine and the fever was gone and the note came and the fever came back. That was Tuesday."), in the Statehouse and in the Governor's mansion, and finally, having run the circle full, the new young doctors will compound pills of flour and salt with a little green color mixed in, the same pill that Papa now compounds, now that his step is no longer so brisk and his hope no longer so high as it was when he was young and knew all the answers and thought whatever was wrong with the world could be cured with medicine.

4

The year the century turns at Hiram College Ohio is the year of the jolly circumstance. The word *terribly* is still in vogue, but it is giving way to *jolly circumstance*. Whatever one wishes to describe he may describe as jolly, jolly meaning good or jolly meaning bad, and in extraordinary situations a thing may be a terribly jolly circumstance, and even among professors (in private) a circumstance is frequently jolly, and how or where it began is an inscrutable mystery. It simply exists and there is nothing anyone can do about it and indeed nothing anyone wants to do about it because it is convenient. It says anything anyone wants it to say.

In September the race begins again, and from the beginning it is lost and Vachel knows it and Helen knows it.

On the first of November Vachel is in chapel in the morning, but he is up front, not in the rear with Helen with Pipkin across his knees, and his arms are innocent of books because he traded his books to Ben Tillington for an annotated *Hamlet* and a life of Daniel Boone, losing on the deal but doing the best he could in the face of Ben's insistence that business is bad (it is always bad to hear Ben tell it).

A jolly circumstance, Helen thinks, terribly jolly, terribly damn jolly like death. For she loves him, and there were times when he seemed to love her, when he held her hand and then, as suddenly as he had taken it, released it, and it was as if, in releasing it, he was unbinding himself, unchaining himself, fleeing, and she asked him in so many ways so many times did he love her and he said he loved her and loved everyone and that was nonsense because nobody can love everybody. You have got to love some person, and it can only be one. Fleeing from what? From me? Why from me? Why flee from me? And yet he flees from her to himself, takes flight from the substantial books and loses himself in mere storybooks, legends, make-believe. As if I were a captor, she thinks, and he a captive, as if I were not good for him keeping him in line and all as if I could not make a man of him and settle him down and make him not restless not always thinking on things outside the field and bring him down out of the air onto solid ground and teach him to do the things a man can do and not impossible things no man can do. There are some things in life a man can do and some things a man should never attempt.

Every morning the *Journal* and every evening The Haven with the Spider Web gang, and twenty prose sketches that are terribly funny at the time, although afterward he cannot recall what it was that was so funny, but at the time each and every one is funny, and one by one he brings them to The Haven at night and reads them aloud, and they are jolly circumstances, and the drawings are equally praised, and the creative people who will no longer be creative when their time at Hiram is done think Vachel is the sharpest of them all, and he is.

Now and then Vachel goes to class and sits hopefully, listening, or stands hopefully watching, and the knife dissects the body, and the hope is never realized. He hopes that all of a sudden Pipkin will take on meaning and Goldstein will come alive and Gray will somewhere see the sections of the body as something whole and Johnson

& Johnson will stop comparing human beings to trees and rats and locomotives and elements of the earth because people are something more. Vachel knows that people are something more. People are a thing, a god, a spirit, a dream, something nobody can diagram, and he knows it and feels it the way he felt something, not knowing what, the day Bryan came with words to set folks free. But it never comes alive, and his mind wanders, and Dr. Page stands with his knife upraised and Vachel sees through the mist that it is not logical.

His alarm clock winds down and lies flat on its face, and one night Greg Slaughter, sitting on Vachel's desk and explaining, at least to himself, why Hamlet does not kill Claudius at prayers, knocks the alarm clock to the floor. The crystal shatters with a satisfying sound.

And there are moments now and again between one absorption and the next when Vachel brings himself up sharp and feels a cold pain in his belly and knows he has done wrong. He has deserted Papa and Helen and Dr. Page and all Springfield, and he wonders what will ever become of him in the future that cannot be always spent here with his books and his drawing board.

And there is Shakespeare again and again and new discoveries each time and Dante and Milton and the drawing of Lucifer that never emerges exactly as Vachel sees Lucifer in his mind, and a long poem on Lucifer to illustrate the picture, but never as Vachel wants it, and he dabbles a little with the drawing of Mammon the soul of the spider, and on the first of February an envelope comes from Papa. Greg Slaughter is in the room when it comes. Inside the envelope are three one-dollar bills. "That's all?" says Greg, and Vachel shakes the envelope upside down.

"All," he says.

And in the spring he leaves, and years and years later, the Hiram scar faint but still visible across his chin, the lines that Mama quoted from Browning still pasted to a piece of cardboard in his pocket, and the boys and girls gone home, the Hiram degree will be his, and he will remember the anguish of this first spring of the great new century and the time he felt fear and guilt but nevertheless did what he had to do because he was not so simple as a locomotive, the young man who after three years became a sophomore, the jolly circumstance.

CHAPTER THREE

1

IT IS ONLY half a room. It does not matter because Vachel, who plans to be the biggest man of his size in Chicago in three years, knows that a man can be big in half a room or no room at all. (Saint Francis had no room of his own when he went down among the lepers and Daniel Boone coming west on the Great Valley Road sitting cross-kneed among the Indians had only the sky overhead, told his men "Plow! Don't plunder" and Johnny Appleseed moving west sleeping in the open planting trees as he went had no room at all not even half a room.) The comforts of life are not important to Vachel. He looks upon himself as a pioneer.

He comes late to Chicago. The Indians have been expelled from Fort Dearborn, pushed west who knows where somewhere west of Chicago, and in his second year in Chicago he has but half a room. It is quite enough, and he is glad to have it. "Five dollars a month and don't try to Jew me down," the landlady says, and he winces because he does not like the expression. Last year, his first year in Chicago, he read Mark Twain concerning the Jews, and he has decided Yahweh is as good a god as the others, and he has met Jews at the Institute as Christian as anyone else, and she is about to lower the rent to three-fifty, seeing him wince, but before she can speak he says he will take it.

The room in the big house on Kenwood Avenue has a partition down the middle, and everything on Vachel's side is his. "Once upon a time," the landlady says, "this house belonged to the Diggenses. The whole street clear to Fiftieth was people of refinement. And then it all came to this and now the street is low-class riffraff. Once upon a time into this house came people of the better classes and dances and balls and all sorts of things."

Now the old house is but an echo of days that were, and instead of the Diggenses and the guests of the Diggenses there are the Vachels, and all of them in their secret hearts plan to be the biggest men and women in Chicago in three years or thereabouts, and meanwhile they live in half-rooms and it does not matter now because the comforts do not matter now.

Half the room is Vachel's. Half the radiator is his, and half the window, and half the light that shines bleakly from the ceiling above the partition, and half the sliding door that Vachel pulls open clumsily on leaving because the handle is out of sight and out of reach beyond the intervening partition. Everywhere in the house are signs the landlady posted turn out lights do not talk in loud voices after ten o'clock turn off the water no checks cashed no musical instruments no phonographs no loitering in the toilet. It would be nice if his room were as large as his room at home or as private as his room at Hiram, but it is not important, really.

Crimmins, on the other side of the partition, is an agreeable sort of fellow. He is seventeen years old from Fort Wayne Indiana and he works at Marshall Field's department store. "I got a notion," says Crimmins, "that I could get to be a big man at Fieldses," and he looks up to Vachel because Vachel has been to college and is an artist. "At the Institute do they really have naked girls you could paint?" says Crimmins. He has heard that such things go on at the Institute, but he cannot believe it. "I got a notion I could draw if I wanted to," he says, and he borrows paper and crayon from Vachel and draws a house with green grass and a blue sky and a golden sun and a friendly tree that throws no shadow. "That's good," says Vachel, "except that the tree ought to have a shadow and the sky should come down somewhere and meet the grass. You've got to think when you draw."

"I got a notion I can fix that easy enough," says Crimmins, and he fixes it.

"It's still not right," says Vachel. "My feeling about drawing is this: it must *say* something. Now, what do I mean by say something?" He is not sure, and Crimmins laughs his fine, hearty laugh that Vachel likes to hear. When Crimmins laughs he shakes all over. "It is not easy to explain," says Vachel. He has been explaining it or trying to explain it for one whole year to the people at the Institute, and it is clear in his mind but when he explains it aloud it is not so clear to him and less clear to the people who listen.

"Well the hell with it," says Crimmins.

(The first year at the Art Institute there were the big questions, *what is art?* and *who is an artist?* and many more questions and nobody in Chicago who could answer them, and the more they were discussed the farther away the answers seemed, but it was fun.

(The first year Vachel had a whole room to himself on South Paulina, and plenty of time to himself, and he filled six notebooks with his own answers, slowly and carefully, long days and long nights, and he began to feel that the answers were coming.

(At the Institute after classes they sat about tables and drank coffee and talked a great deal about the things they had been talking about all day, and sometimes out of all the hours of talk one sentence, one phrase, remained and made good sense to Vachel and brought him closer to the answers to the big questions. It did not seem unlikely, then, that in three years he would have what he wanted and be the biggest man of his size in Chicago.

(That first year when they were not talking they were painting Myra Tompkins' hands and feet. Myra is from a place near Louisville Kentucky and she worked at Marshall Field's department store when she was not painting at the Institute or sitting barefoot on a high chair with her hands straight out before her. She has beautiful hands and beautiful feet, and the hardest thing for young artists is painting hands and feet. Myra is an artist, but she poses for fifty cents an hour with five minutes of rest each thirty minutes because, says she, she needs the money. Vachel could not understand why she should need money. He assumed that her papa sent her money and paid her tuition like Papa sent him money and paid his tuition, but Vachel did not yet know as much about the world as he thought he knew sitting about the tables at the Institute talking about what art is and who is an artist and what art and artists should mean and say.

(He tried very hard to draw Myra's hands and feet. For almost a year he drew them, and still they did not look human. But he improved. It is a matter of time. An artist is not made in a year.)

After the first year it happens. The envelope comes from Papa with the money, and also, for the first time in a long time, a note, and Vachel is glad Papa is speaking to him again because he loves Papa and frequently Papa seems to love him, and Mama said all along that Papa would forgive. But the note is not good. There will be less money hereafter, and in the evening, sitting at table after class and admiring Myra's hands and listening with his mind only half on the subject to something about possibilities in primitivism he knows for the first time that art has something to do with money and money has something to do with art. Not much, but something. "My papa cut off my money" (gaily).

"What's money?" someone says.

"My papa never sends me as much as a card," says Myra. "Have you ever thought of working?" She leans her elbows on the table and clasps her beautiful hands beneath her chin.

"I've been working all along."

"I mean for money."

"No. Not for money," and everybody laughs because they know, and he is first learning, that money and art have something to do with each other.

Myra does not laugh. Vachel is young and just learning about life and art, and there is something about him that is innocent and clean and serious, something she came from near Louisville to find and has not found.

"I certainly hate the idea," says Vachel.

There is a month yet before the money will be reduced, and he does not blame Papa. Papa is not getting any younger, and one eye is going bad, and Vachel knows something is bound to happen and change things for him before the month is up because he is getting close to some of the answers and drawing Myra's hands and feet with remarkable skill at last, and something always comes along to pull people out of tight spots.

But the first week goes by and nothing happens, and nothing the second week, and after the third week he moves from the house on South Paulina into the house on Kenwood. "It's only half a room," says Myra. "I suppose you've been used to something better. The landlady is cranky. But there's a lot of young people in the house," and he moves from the whole room into the half-room and it is not bad at all, and a considerable saving, and Crimmins is a fine fellow with a big laugh, and the comforts of life are not important, really.

Myra lives down the hall and has beautiful hands and beautiful feet, and these are the things that count. (One night at the Institute he shows them what he thinks: he takes a dollar bill and folds it once and with quick fingers tears the bill down the middle and then unfolds it and holds the bill up and shows them the pretty design. "Vachel!" says Myra. "Don't Vachel me," says he, but she reaches

out quickly and captures the mutilated bill, and afterward, in
Vachel's room, laughing low because it is after ten o'clock, she
pastes the bill together with her beautiful hands.)

In the beginning when she was fresh in Chicago from near Louisville Kentucky there were the big questions what was art and what
was meaning and who were truly great, and Crimmins, who fancied
himself a big man at Marshall Field's, came home breathless one
night and burst in upon her and told her there was a job for her if
she wanted it. He felt big and important, and he did not tell her
that the truth of the matter was that anyone with two arms and
two legs and white skin could get a job at Field's.

For a while it was not so bad that it could not have been worse
except that she stood on her feet all day and at night was too tired
to go to the Institute. At night she came home and lay on her bed
with her feet propped higher than her head. She worked ten hours
a day six days a week for sixteen dollars a week less breakage and
spoilage, and there was no time to devote to art and no time to go
to the Institute and sit around listening to artist talk, no time for
anything except lying with her feet propped higher than her head.

After six months she had another idea. It was an old idea but she
thought it was new, being fresh up from near Louisville. She had
read about such things in books but it had never seemed real.

It was a good idea, all things considered. At least she did not have
to stand on her feet looking at ugly things all day and trying to
persuade people to buy them, and it was quick and it left her time
to pose at the Institute and talk artist talk, and it paid, and sometimes when the mood was right it could even be fun and give her
a sense of doing some good for someone else, and she never knew
their names or asked, and they never knew hers. All they knew
about each other was what she knew, the warmth of flesh and the
clash of bodies and then sometimes soon and sometimes late and
sometimes perfectly a fall as if from a great height, and a kind of
shame, and thankfulness that the room was dark, and the passing
of money from hand to hand, and the striking of a match and the
quick look at the money in the flickering light.

And why should she not? It is quicker and cleaner and as honest
as standing sixty hours at Field's. She is still an artist, and the big
questions still concern her, and she has not sold herself like the

whores in Chicago who sell themselves to magazines and newspapers and advertising agencies, pimps and perverts, men who had
once been men and women who had once been women, selling their
art as if it were simply the body, as if it were a thing that can be
revived each night.

At least she has not sold her art. At least there is sometimes
pleasure in selling what she sells, and at least there is good in it
for someone else. At least the big questions still concern her.

The hunger is not like the hunger at Hiram, where there was
something missing in his life and he was not sure what, and it is
not like the summer in Springfield, riding high beside Papa and feeling something within him rebelling, not like that at all. The hunger
is very real like the hunger in Dante and the hungry people and the
fruit on the vines just out of reach in Dante's Hell, and maybe,
thinks Vachel, he is being punished for breaking free, as Dante's
people were punished for gluttony. Yet he had considered it all
beforehand and asked himself what would Christ do and done as he
thought Christ would do. Christ did what seemed to Him right at
the time and they hung Him up by his fists.

"Ten dollars a week would do me," says Vachel.

"I got a notion you could get it at Fieldses," Crimmins says.

"No," says Myra. "Not Field's."

"After a while it goes up," Crimmins says. "It's like this: they
want people to stay. After a while it goes up. Take me. First I was
hardly anything because I was unskilled, and then it goes up."

"We'll see," says Vachel, sounding to himself like Mama saying
we'll see, but knowing that sooner or later it will come to pass, and
Myra does not like Field's because after Field's, after the long day
and the weary legs and the utter disgust one has no choice but to
go on forever at Field's or to sell his art like a whore in the market
place, and she does not want either to happen to Vachel. She does
not want to see the cleanness and the innocence despoiled. "It's all
a trap," she says, and she laughs, and Crimmins laughs a big Indiana laugh because he too knows it is a trap, everyone trapped
except him, and Vachel laughs because he always laughs with
Crimmins.

"I got a notion you could work awhile and save up," says Crimmins. He would like to see Vachel down at Field's. He would like

to ride downtown and back on the trolley every day with Vachel because they have good laughs together, and because he is sorry for Vachel and likes him so much.

"I've been thinking along those lines," Vachel says.

"I've got a hot iron inside," says Myra.

"Good," says Vachel, and Myra goes out of the room and stands in the hall, and Vachel takes his drying clothes from the radiator (all except his trousers, which he wears) and then he removes his washable trousers fifty cents and he empties the pockets and lays the contents on his bed, and he hands his clothes out the door, stretching grotesquely around the partition, and Myra's hands come toward him in suspension out of the dark and take his clothes.

"The manuscripts, too," she says. They have been ironed once already and it hardly seems worth while to Vachel to iron them again. "Some other time," he says.

"Now."

"Well I'm out of postage anyway," he says.

"Come on come on," she says.

"Well, stay where you are," and she stands in the dark in the narrow hall and smiles to herself, the innocent the innocent, she thinks, feeling very old and wise and worldly, and Vachel pads barefoot across his half-room and gathers up his manuscripts and squirms between the partition and the door and hands the papers to Myra, and she goes down the hall.

"Girls girls girls," says Crimmins. "But she's a nice girl. I'll say that for her." Crimmins squeezes sideways past the partition into his own half of the room. "I'm going to bed," he says.

"If the light bothers you . . ."

"No, it never bothers me. When I sleep I sleep."

"Just thought I'd ask."

"Vachel," says Crimmins, "you suppose the old lady'd let us take this herky-jerky down?" He raps his knuckles against the partition.

"Maybe sometime," says Vachel.

"What you doing?"

"Reading."

"What you reading?"

"A book."

"Sometime I am positively going to read a book," says Crimmins, and he pretends to fall asleep, and Vachel reads his Blake (it is overdue at the Institute), and Myra comes down the hall and raps softly on his door. "Your junk," she says. "Good night. I'll just drop it."

"Thanks," says he. "Night."

"Night," she says, and her footsteps die as she moves away, and Vachel hears her door close behind her, and Blake is saying that what any artist needs is multitude, solitude, and plenitude, and somehow Vachel finds Blake replacing Poe, Blake saying things that are closer to Vachel, things about the stomach that he cannot find in Poe, Blake moving ahead of Poe, and Tennyson giving way to Tolstoi, and Ruskin even though a Socialist moving up with Blake and Tolstoi, and Christ Himself becoming for Vachel somebody secular, a roadside socialist ("The moneylenders," says Myra. "Remember?") and it is probably all nonsense and Susan Wilcox would say he is not thinking it through, but being hungry changes things. He feels he ought to turn the light out because Crimmins is not sleeping just says he is sleeping and Myra a nice girl except she sometimes swears and people especially girls oughtn't to swear, and he turns out his light and sleeps with his knees up close to his belly because the hunger is eased that way.

(There were two drawings looking more like Blake than anything Vachel had ever done. Nobody understood them, not even Myra who is quick to grasp things. Even the more religious people at the Institute did not understand the drawings, and the drawings went thirteen times to New York and came back each time in the familiar envelope with Vachel's own big round writing on the front. One night Myra ironed the drawings and they looked crisp and new as if they had never been anywhere much less thirteen times to New York and back, and Vachel took them himself in the rain to Christian Century and the man promised to look at them sometime when he was not busy. "We always look at everything," he said.)

Now, in the morning, on top of the freshly pressed clothes outside his door, is an envelope from Christian Century with Vachel's name spelled Vachell Lindsey, and a two-dollar check inside.

Crimmins is gone or he would tell Crimmins. He slips into his clothes and races down the hall and pounds on Myra's door, but there is no answer, and he runs downstairs and telephones Christian Century and thanks them and tells them he has many more drawings and will bring them over today, and the man says there is no great rush. But there is a great rush. He runs outdoors.

When the trolley comes to a dead stop in front of him he remembers that he spent his last nickel for the telephone call. He waves the trolley on, and he walks all the way to the Art Institute and shows everyone the check and then cashes it and pays for his overdue Blake and buys a large breakfast which settles heavy on his empty stomach, and all of a sudden the world is a different place. He buys drawing paper and rides home on the trolley car with almost a dollar in his pocket, and it is as if the president or governor or chief or whatever it is of the United States mint opened the doors and said "Help yourself, Vachel," the way Vachel sometimes dreams it, or Marshall Field himself unlocked his big safe and motioned Vachel to enter and help himself the way Vachel sometimes dreams it on nights when he has not had supper.

It is the beginning, and Vachel does not know it but for now it is also the end because the drawings are not very clear to anyone but him, and the poems that explain the drawings are sometimes clearer but still not entirely clear, and for a long time he will not sell another thing.

All day he draws. The small sale means a great deal, and he is easier in his mind than he has been for a long time.

In the evening, with Myra and Crimmins, he sees E. H. Sothern and Virginia Harned in *Hamlet,* and Crimmins groans in disgust when Hamlet fails to stab Claudius when the stabbing is easy. Quietly Crimmins leaves his seat and disappears on an adventure of his own, and Vachel, in the dark theater, sits transfixed at the alternate wonder of the play and the wonder of the man who wrote it, the man who, in writing it, demonstrated that peculiar ability of the human being, as opposed to the beast, to transcend time and place and prove for the benefit of all skeptical centuries that man is not beast but god. It is this vision of transcendence that has lately captured Vachel's imagination, that has developed from the evenings about the tables at the Institute. It is the sophisticated explanation of what he meant when he said to Crimmins once that drawing must say, must *say.*

Afterward, after the swordplay and the poisoned drinks and the final good night to the sweet prince he goes with Myra from the dark theater into the dark city, and it is as if they are actors in a play, first in the dark city and then up the dark stairway of the shabby old house that was once a proud house and that now, in a late scene of the tragedy, has become a forlorn house. At her door they say good night, and she thanks him for the lovely evening, and he announces, "Exit Myra," and strides down the hallway with a sword at his side.

The light is on in his room. Crimmins is abed, awake.

"Enter Vachel," says Vachel. "Where did you disappear to?"

"I was itchy," says Crimmins. "I couldn't sit still."

"I trust you're unitched," says Vachel, and Crimmins does not reply, although indeed his adventure unitched him, and he says to Vachel crisply, as if for a long time he has known the line: "What Hamlet should of had was a wife."

Vachel laughs. In his own half of the half-room he sits on the bed with his back against the wall, his legs stretched straight before him.

"That's what you need," says Crimmins. "You need a wife."

"Maybe someday I'll have a wife."

"You need to have the real troubles of life. You got no troubles. You make up your own troubles. There was a man near home that farmed alone. He had more troubles than anybody else. He lived all alone and had no troubles except what he could think up. That's what come of living alone."

There is a pause, and Vachel studies the pause, considering the fact that pauses in real speech are longer than the pauses of drama. He wonders if the fact ever bothered Shakespeare.

"In the end he went mad and they carried him off to the public home. If he had of had a wife it would of been different. He begun to see spirits of trouble everywhere. He seen troubles where there were no troubles at all. Like in the play. She would keep a man neat and fed and his mind on the things of life."

"Exit Crimmins. That's a long speech."

"That's a sample of what I'm driving at. Your mind is not on life. She would steady you. She would calm you and keep you steady. You would not be tangled up with troubles and spirits that you can't even see. His old man was done in by the uncle, and it was all clear, and he should of done him in right there and got back at him and not of gone about considering it so much that in the end he got done in himself. My old man says they were spirits and I believe him." His voice is lower and softer, and sleep comes upon him.

There are stars in the window. They twinkle. Susan Wilcox says that if a star does not twinkle it is a planet. Suppose Hamlet had taken a wife? Suppose he had taken the fair Ophelia? Would he

have slept such sleeps as Crimmins sleeps? People are always telling other people how to order their lives. Papa says medicine, and
Helen said medicine. Crimmins says find a fair Ophelia. Everybody wants to play Polonius. Words words words. Polonius wound
up dead for spying on Hamlet from behind the curtain. In a way
it served him right.

Yet he thought he was doing what was best for Denmark. They
always do what they think is best. They always mean well, and they
always know, deep in themselves, that there is something rotten,
but they insist you cannot change it and make it not rotten, and
they try to prove that you're better off taking care of yourself and
not worrying about Denmark, setting up your own practice in your
own house with your own Ophelia and that way it will all come out
all right in the end. Except that Denmark will still be rotten.

But there has been a murder, and there is a ghost abroad. Who
made the murderer murderer? Whose ghost? Can I believe in the
ghost? Some ghosts are real and some are not, and if I settle down
and tend the sick and love the wife who then will walk the battlements? I must walk the battlements, and I will walk them, and I
will talk with the ghost, and if there is somewhere a fair Ophelia
who will walk them with me I will take her hand in mine and we
will walk them together. But she must go my way with me, because
I cannot go hers, because it is somehow ordained that I pursue the
mystery that is Denmark. I am the servant of the holy ghost. It is
in the stars that Susan says are planets unless they twinkle.

Then all of a sudden the two dollars gone and the twenty Papa
sends him down the drain in less than a month and a dollar Crimmins lends him and two from Myra all of it gone and the new drawings back from New York and not another sale in Chicago, and he
is back where he was before the two dollars ever came from Christian Century, and the hunger is not so easy to bear the second time
around. Now even Sidney Lanier the Georgia poet (they sang
Marching Through Georgia in school and they sang it again when
Bryan came and Georgia is a place to go marching through and to
hate and detest because they burn blacks there and hate Abe Lincoln), even Lanier he moves up ahead of Poe because he wrote
about this thing, this money thing, and just when things are coming
easier it all must cease because of the hunger the second time
around. The lines begin to cross. The view changes. The soul of the

spider becomes the big thing, not the rhythms of Poe or the romance of Tennyson, not West against East, not Springfield singing the bloody song about the time they burned Atlanta to the ground, but the thing he drew long ago as a child, not knowing what he was drawing except that it was the soul of a spider and he called it Mammon.

2

Crimmins is not the important person he said he was. He pushes a handcart in the toy department and his cart is no bigger than Vachel's or anyone else's, and Marshall Field does not know Crimmins from a hole in the ground and nobody knows anybody because the rules forbid talking. A man whom Vachel calls Caesar sits high on a crate of boxes in the middle of the room and folds his arms and scowls and now and then shouts across the vast room *hurry it up hurry it up.* Except on nights when Caesar drinks from a bottle and cannot see what is happening below, Vachel hurries. If he does not hurry the handcart behind him to which is attached a man will ram him and bruise the hardening muscles in the backs of his legs. He hurries.

At night he sleeps with his legs straight out. The hunger is gone. He eats. At least he eats. "You see," says Crimmins, "it could be worse. I got a notion you like to eat."

Caesar is drunk, and he cannot see the men below. He shouts *hurry hurry* in a thick voice.

Below, at the end of the row, Vachel tears open the boxes one by one and removes the toys.

Then he winds the toys tight, the singing albums and the jumping jacks and the crying dolls and the fire engine that clangs and whines and the horses rotating their legs in front of the engines and the church with bells in its steeple and the cash registers that ring.

He leaves no slack in the springs. He stands the toys on the empty boxes, all in a row, a parade of toys, and then he goes swiftly down the row and releases the springs, and the singing albums sing and the jumping jacks jump and the crying dolls cry and the fire engines clang and whine and the horses run and the church bells ring and the cash registers open and close, ringing, and the noise is abundant.

The next moments are clear. They will always be clear, as some moments will stay fixed in his memory all of his life, Papa reaching for the harness on the wall of the barn, Susan looking sad and telling him the speech must be rewritten, Dr. Page poised with a bloody knife, Bryan and Altgeld shaking hands, the first time he saw the pictures in Dante, Jeff Hatten's gelding resisting the bit, this moment of triumphant clamor, and Crimmins standing paralyzed with his mouth wide open and his eyes bulging, and Caesar climbing down from the boxes, unsteady, uncertain, framing with wet lips silent, vile words.

3

The Big Towns. Chicago. New York. The zero years of the new century. The quick happy war with Spain is over.

Somebody shoots McKinley dead and Theodore Roosevelt is President.

Something that afterward will be packaged in the books between The Nineties and The New Freedom, a zero time.

John Peter Altgeld is dead. Henry George is dead.

But Bryan is back on his feet. He goes about the country reading the Markham poem, and of all the outlandish things, a poem! The defenses stiffen, and a hundred whores are hired to write answers to the poem. *How will it be with kingdoms and with kings, with those who shaped him to the thing he is, when this dumb Terror shall reply to God after the silence of the centuries?*

Can anyone recall a line penned in answer by the hired whore?

Bryan. Debs. Jane Addams in Chicago. Jacob Riis in New York. The muckrakers.

Chicago. The artists center about the Institute, and everybody or almost everybody is considering New York.

New York is even bigger than Chicago. Bigger than anywhere. In New York the artists live on Twenty-third Street and up around Columbus Circle. Greenwich Village is as yet undiscovered. *Babes in Toyland* plays on forever at the Colonial Music Hall.

Robert Henri at the Chase School, and the young artists who paint what they see paint for Henri and nobody else, and they do not sell their paintings, not now in the zero years. They are too far ahead of their time. John Sloan. Davies. Glackens. Luks. Lawson. Prendergast. Shinn. The Ash Can School. The Apostles of Ugliness. They paint what they see: Union Square, prostitutes, the jobless, side streets, taverns, Hell's Kitchen, pushcarts. "McSorley's Bar." "Sixth Avenue and Thirteenth Street." "Sunset, West Twenty-third Street."

Why don't the painters stick to painting and leave politics alone?

Somebody named Dreiser and a book called *Sister Carrie*. He is ordered to clean it up. He will not, and the publisher will not publish his book, and Dreiser goes back to his six-day job, and he falls ill, and it is thought that now that he is ill and broke he will do as he is told. But he has no price.

Twain, Howells and Moody join the anti-imperialists.

Why don't the writers stick to writing and leave politics alone?

Something that afterward will be packaged nameless in the books between The Nineties and The Literary Revival, because it can have no name, because all it is is a time between times when the young men and the young women who will not be whores are hard at work framing the questions.

Vachel is the practical type. He knows or thinks he knows everything the Art Institute can teach him in Chicago; he learns what he wants to learn, and for the rest it is hokum because the idea of painting is not necessarily to paint the way they painted in the Renaissance but to paint the way he Vachel Lindsay wants to paint, to paint like nobody ever painted before, and so he gets money from Papa and goes to New York and bunks with George Richards on the top floor of a house on Fifty-seventh Street just off Columbus Circle. It is a practical place to live: it is just down the street from the Chase School around the corner from the Pig and the Goose two minutes west of Central Park five minutes' walk from the Colonial Music Hall. The room itself is practical: the big windows face north, and it is important to an artist that his windows face north, and in the ceiling is a trap door leading to the attic, and when Vachel has no money for his rent he goes into the attic to live, and when he has money he comes down again, and there are not many landlords like Mike Didakis who will give a man an attic rent-free. George Richards offers to pay Vachel's rent when the need arises, but Vachel says no. It is gratifying, however, when George offers, because this is what Vachel comes to New York to find, this feeling of oneness among the artists.

Up and down Fifty-seventh Street just off the Circle the young artists and writers live in small rooms with big windows, and there is a knowledge along that street that it is the only city block of its kind on the continent except maybe down on Twenty-third where the artists congregate about John Sloan or maybe in the neighborhood of Robert Henri's studio above the stable on Fortieth. At the most there are maybe three streets in the city where artists feel at

home. "Art is a wandering gypsy," says Henri. He constantly reminds the artists at the Chase School that art has no home and no
nation, and they go back to their easels freshly aware that art is
a lonesome gypsy looking for a place to live and be loved.

Yet when people paint for Henri they paint things that people
can understand, even people who live far from the one or two or
maybe three streets in the world where art is at home, and he says
that is how art will find a home, by looking for it, and Vachel learns
a lot from Henri. "Art should *say*," says Robert Henri standing tall
and slender and grim before his classes, and Vachel knew that much
a long time ago in Chicago.

Henri is a mild man, but when he is angry he raises his voice
slightly and clips his words, and when he is angry he is usually
angry with someone to whom art is only an exercise in form and
color, meaningless, and he says, clipping his words and losing a syllable here and there, as if he were making a speech, "The artist is
not one who floats affably in his own culture. The artist is the blazer
of trails, my friends," and if an artist does not wish to blaze trails he
had best get out from underfoot or go somewhere where Henri
won't have to look at him every day.

He never makes an artist of Vachel. He never loses patience
with Vachel. He never scolds. He hangs Vachel on the line with the
rest, with the artists who are striving to say, and he sits a long time
forward on his elbows staring at Vachel's drawings, twisting his
head one way and then another, squinting his eyes and frowning
and biting his lip, and then he goes home and thinks about Vachel's
work and comes back in the morning and tries again, and always
there is something missing, yet something there that is saying.

There is something that Vachel calls the soul of a spider, and
after the first year something larger called a map of the universe,
the spider still prominent, and Henri thinks God it is trying to say
something that it never quite says. And something called The Heroes
of Time, but the heroes are clumsy figures, and for an instant Henri
is tempted to say as he says to many young artists *where do you live
do you need fare to get home?* but he does not say it to Vachel because there is something more here than clumsy figures.

Vachel stands waiting. "Let me think about it," says Henri, *there
is something here I know damn well there is something but where
the hell is it where?* "Suppose you paraphrase it for me," he says.

Vachel points with a ruler. "Over here . . ."

"Tomorrow," says Henri. "Why not try writing it?"

"It's all written," says Vachel. "A poem, however."

"Well, bring it in," says Henri, and after the room is cleared he sits before the portraits of the heroes of time. *That would be Buddha and over there Abraham or possibly Moses and the man with the sword Alexander and the man with the bird on his shoulder Saint Francis and Socrates with the cup in his hand well hell that much is easy easy enough.* But what does it say? he asks aloud of the empty room *well the kid not so much a kid twenty-five six he is driving at something be damned if I know something big something floating around in his mind. Dante! Sure. Should have thought of it before leaves one two five figures there big as hell the kid fusing a whole universe of idea but it gets away from him keeps slipping away maybe he tries for too much.* Then he turns out the lights and locks the door behind him, and on the way home he remembers the kid said something about a poem writes better poems than he paints pictures. Henri, walking, sees the painting again, a mass of color and cumbersome figures and every rule of painting lying scattered and broken at the foot of the easel. ("I don't believe in rules or schools," Henri is always saying.) But there are, after all, *some* rules and the kid breaks them all. He scowls down at his feet: it is bad; it is bad painting; the kid gets it down better on paper than he does on canvas; kid writes the *damnedest* poems.

On the afternoon of the following day George Mather Richards who bunks with Vachel in the room on Fifty-seventh Street drops into the Pig and the Goose for coffee. George is a hard-working painter who does bread-and-butter painting before lunch and who paints to satisfy his own soul and nobody else's in the afternoon until the sun goes down behind Jersey. For a while he lived alone and looked around in the slow careful way he does everything for someone to live with him and cut the expense in half and at the same time make a noise around the place because George by himself is a silent fellow, and then he met Vachel one day in the Pig and the Goose at the table he sits at now on this cloudy afternoon.

Vachel says afterward that George is a veritable Niagara of silence, and he never knew anyone could stay so silent so long and just listen and look without opening his yap and throwing something out for the general education.

George knows many artists along the street, and he knows that often when they talk they talk to hide themselves, and here is a kid from somewhere way out west drifts into town and pours himself empty because he thinks everyone is honest and will therefore believe, because he has nothing to hide and thinks nobody else has anything to hide, because he thinks that all the wrongs of the world can be set right by simple honesty, because he will give you his last dime if he has one or jump off Brooklyn Bridge if he thinks it will do anyone any good. And one does not believe in people like Vachel, but it is not a thing to be believed or disbelieved or proved or disproved. It is a thing that is in all men, and in some it flowers and in most it dies before it ever really lives. It is born in every naked child. And when George meets Vachel Vachel is still a trusting, honest, naked child, and George likes him and they bunk together.

George stirs his coffee and lifts his cup to his lips. The door of the Pig and the Goose opens and Robert Henri, with an armful of books, sees George and sits across from him, and George tilts his head and studies the titles of the books, and a waitress without asking brings Henri a cup of tea with lemon. "How's it go?" says Henri to George.

"Fair."

"Rotten weather," says Henri, and he squeezes his lemon into his tea. He looks down into the mixture. "I had a long talk with Vachel this morning." He pauses and stirs. He waits a full minute, but George does not answer. George can outwait anyone. He feels it is a good way to learn. "I told him. I felt I had to tell him. It seemed to me to be the right thing." George's coffee cools, but he is no longer interested in his coffee. "Maybe it was right and maybe it was wrong," says Henri. "You know, George, everybody has a certain genius. Who's to tell anybody what to do? Vachel has a genius. There's something almost Blakeish in his work. But there's something that doesn't catch fire if you know what I mean."

"I know what you mean," says George, and he leaves his coffee and rises and goes out into the street, and Henri opens a book and reads and sips his tea.

In the park, far in the park, George sits on a cold bench and looks straight ahead, and something in him lies heavy and gray like the solid clouds overhead. Vachel will be crushed. It is monstrous and unfair and tragic, and the big city hangs above George, oppressive and gray and cold and ugly and mocking, and in the big city the thing that Vachel represents to him is the thing that is crushed. Of all things in the city of stone it is Vachel who must be crushed. It is unfair.

George hesitates to go back to the room. He is afraid to look Vachel in the face because he is ashamed, but he gets up from the bench and walks along the path and out of the park and down Fifty-seventh, and he climbs the stairs to the room and pauses an instant with his hand on the doorknob. Then he takes a deep breath and turns the knob and enters, afraid to see what he will see, and angry, and ashamed to be a part of the solid rock structure that crushes Vachel and the likes of Vachel.

And Vachel sits cross-legged on the bed with his drawing board on his knees, sketching as if nothing has happened, as if the greatest man in art in the greatest city in the world had not told him the blunt truth straight out and asked him in the subtlest way possible did he need railroad fare to get back home, and George exhales the deep breath and sits on the bed beside Vachel and leans back against the wall and supposes he should have known all along that nobody and nothing can crush Vachel. It is not that easy. It can be done, but it will be hard to do and it will take a long time.

"Where you been?" says Vachel. "What's new?"

"Nothing," says George. "I ran into Henri." He swings his feet to the floor and walks across the room to his easel. He takes a package of cigarettes from the tray of his easel and slides one out and sticks it in the corner of his mouth. It hangs there and he forgets to light it. He stands staring at the blank canvas on the easel.

"I suppose Henri told you," says Vachel. "Of course he could be wrong. Even Henri. There's matches right there in front of you, George. I mean—it's not as if he said I was a total loss. Not a *total* loss. He says himself I draw like Blake."

"He said there's something almost Blakeish," says George who is a careful listener.

"Maybe so. You're probably right. Still and all, George, a man has to be practical about things like this and suppose I were to throw it all overboard and go back home after all this time and tell them I'm not an artist. Then they'd say who says so. After all that time in the big cities you've *got* to be an artist after all your papa poured down the drain for you, and I'd say well that's what Robert Henri advises, and they never heard of Henri, so what do you mean by coming home after all these years and giving it all up just because so-and-so that we never even *heard* of advises. It wouldn't be practical. George, why don't you light your cigarette? George, what does a man get out of smoking anyhow?"

"Smoke," says George, reaching for the matches and scraping one listlessly along the side of the box. "Practical?" (When he came —when Vachel came—he went down to the *World* and told them he was an artist, and he expected them to sit up and take notice, and the man whose face the way Vachel told it was half eyeshade and half cigar leaned forward across his desk and told Vachel he was five years late, that newspaper artists went out when half tone came in, and where had he been these five years, and Vachel told him he had been around but that he didn't read the newspapers much, only the Springfield *Journal*. "On the whole," said Vachel, "newspapers are pretty sad, but I thought you might have some work to tide me over," and the man tilted his cigar upward in his mouth saying "On your way smart aleck," and Vachel went puzzled down into the street and over to the *American* and told them he was a poet and expected them to sit up and take notice. "Well I tell you," said the man at the *American*, "we pay twenty cents an inch for poetry. Poets ain't of too much use to us. Most of the poetry we want we can bat out ourselves. But we'll take it four to six inches single space, slope it off in the last stanza so's we can cut it if we want," and Vachel went home and measured six inches and proceeded to write. He spent a long time—maybe three days—trying to say what he had to say in six inches. But it was hard work. Saint Francis would not fit into six inches, nor would Andrew Jackson or Abraham Lincoln or any of the people Vachel wanted to write about. "Especially when you've got to slope them off at the end," said Vachel. "Forget it," said George.)

"In a practical way," says Vachel, "I consider this period of my life a period of building. From twenty to thirty you might call a period of development. From thirty to forty you might have a period of leisure, soaking up all the things you've learned and gathering them together within yourself and preparing your attack. Then you're ready to begin. From forty to fifty a period of scholarly work. From fifty to sixty a man might be in a stage of further development. This seems to me the time that God takes care of a man. From sixty to seventy a man has a lot of wisdom gathered up and he ought to be a prophet and seer and advise the younger generation. Wisdom. From seventy to eighty-five a man is ready to take part in public affairs in a wise way. After eighty-five it's strictly up to the individual. For myself, I intend to live to be one hundred and five years of age. If a man takes proper care of himself he ought to live that long at least. How old do you think you would like to get to be?"

"I figure on another year or two," says George, and Vachel laughs. "Come on, George. Be practical." (Vachel is practical. When he saw that he could not write poetry by the inch he moved into the attic and remained there awhile. Walking in the park one day he met a man who asked him had he ever thought of the possibilities of gas-tubing, and Vachel said to tell the truth he never had, and the man said gas-tubing was the coming thing, and he said he admired Vachel's honesty and would rather hire an honest man however ignorant of gas-tubing than an expert who was a liar, and he hired Vachel, and every week Vachel was paid fourteen dollars and he moved down out of the attic. But he quit the job because it was not practical. "Figure it this way," he said at the Pig and the Goose one night, and everybody listened. "You can go around gas-tubing until your beard is as long as Methuselah's, but you do not have time to write poems or draw pictures. Then when you've gas-tubed the whole blasted city what do you have? But write a poem like Dante wrote or a *Hamlet* or be Homer or even Markham or Swinburne and you've done something really practical. Take Dante. There isn't a shred of plumbing left from Dante's time or from Homer's either. Nothing. Nothing remains. The buildings collapse and Rome falls and all the great structures except a very few, and all the forts and wigwams and ships and canals and dams and dikes and plumbing fall to pieces, and all that is left is the poetry and maybe a few pictures here and there, and some old buildings rather drafty by now. But mostly the poetry, the word. All that is left is the word. The only practical thing to do in the world is to write or to paint," and George thinks perhaps Vachel is right. A man lives one life and aims his creation at immortality, but the nearest he comes is a tombstone, and in time the tombstone is consumed, and Vachel has a point. "I'm just being practical," Vachel said, and everyone laughed, but the laugh was reserved because what Vachel said was true and everyone knew it and everyone was afraid to state it because no matter how true it was it was not practical. "So how do you pay your bills?" somebody said.)

4

One by one they buckle and go under. Up and down the street the rooms are emptied and refilled, and the faces along the street grow older and suddenly are gone, and young faces replace them, and the familiar faces across the tables at the Pig and the Goose are new faces soon.

Charlie Peter Paul who did the murals at the Pig and the Goose drops in now and then and sits at his old table in the corner. He did the murals (yellow boy and the night-black girl and the fire-red man and the milk-white lady and the melted chain at their feet) and he drops in now and then to look at his work, and then he does not drop in at all, and someone notices and says where is Charlie Peter Paul I have not seen him in a long time, and no one has seen him and no one knows where he went, whether he went home to Wilmington or where. That is the last time but one that anybody mentions him in the Pig and the Goose because the people who remember him are few. It was a long time ago, two years or more, and that is a long time along this particular street; it is not like a street where solid people live, and their children after them. It is a street of young faces, always young faces except for a few.

The last time anyone ever mentions Charlie who did the mural is when George and Vachel agree to do a new one. They paint with long slow strokes over the old mural until the wall is white, and Vachel is sad to see the bright-colored people die under his brush because he knew them well and loved them. When he and George have free time they paint Vachel's heroes on the wall, and Vachel is in charge of bright colors and significant facts and historical allusions, and George does hands that look like hands and feet that look like feet, and Vachel eats well at the Pig and the Goose all winter. As long as they remain in the neighborhood the mural will remain on the walls, and afterward someone will paint out Dante and Moses and Buddha and eat well all of one winter or summer or whenever, but they do not talk about that time or think about it now or even believe that it will ever come to be. They do not plan to buckle under or give up their art and go back home. It is never planned that way. (Sam Howland who wrote ferocious essays on the decline of capitalism at his table near the window, he never planned it that way, and he comes back now and then and sits at his old table and watches George and Vachel paint. Sam is a writer for the *World*, and he has lost a good deal of his ferocity. "You know, Vachel, what you want to do is pull a stunt. Throw a fit. Eight or ten inches in the *World* is worth more than a year of hard work. Ten years. You could throw a fit in the Colonial lobby and me just happen to be on hand and jot it all down and maybe get a picture at the same time and the world will beat a pathway to your door to quote the old poet. Artist downtown, no doubt you read about it, locked himself in his room and said he would starve, and you know what happened to him. Wasn't there two days before there was a parade to his place, and among them two heiresses and both of them set and determined to marry him. I forget his name. An heiress no less. Oh, it's cheap stuff," says Sam, "but you got to face the facts. I say it's a shame for artists to let these things slip through their fingers. It's lying around waiting and if you don't grab it somebody will," but it somehow does not appeal to Vachel or anyone else in the Pig and the Goose. Not now.)

George does not buckle or go home to Washington because he has no illusions to begin with. He paints for bread and butter half the day and for himself the other half. He is a well-balanced person and somehow a little wiser and worldlier than many of the people along the street.

And Vachel does not buckle or go home to Springfield, not the first year and not the second. He is an old-timer along the street, and looking back he will never be sure what it was that gave him courage and made him stubborn and kept him hopeful, and assured him that the best was yet to be here in Babylon where stone is piled atop stone, higher and higher, and eight or ten inches of cheapstuff in the *World* is worth ten years of hard work, and the hopeful children one by one lose hope and go home.

It is the discordant note of music that keeps Vachel in New York, a note now too high and now too low, something off-key that he hears. It is the thing that keeps him sane. (Back home in Springfield Mama organizes Via Christi, and there is only one Way of Christ and that is Mama's way. About her she gathers a knot of women who never knew for certain the sure way of Christ until Mama showed them, and Mama keeps sane this way and fights the Brewery and makes speeches for the Anti-Saloon League.) There is a good deal of Mama in Vachel. Neither he nor Mama can carry a tune. In New York he hears the discordant note above and below the dominant song. His ear is tuned that way, and the discord sounds louder than it is, for he listens hard, and he hears it on Fifty-seventh Street just off the Circle and at the Chase School where Robert Henri announces heresies and in the Pig and the Goose where the young are too young to know that their heroes singing off-key are barely heard at all, and Jacob Riis wars on the slums and there will be bigger and better slums after he is gone, and Robert Henri is all but unheard of west of Eighth Avenue.

Yet the faint rebel yell sounds to Vachel like a mighty roar, and once long ago he saw and heard Bryan and felt himself but a step away from a world the way it ought to be (it is not yet clear in his mind what it ought to be except that it ought to be beautiful, and it ought to be love, and men and women ought to be Lincoln-hearted) and he feels that the world is but a step from glory, and the only practical thing is to get behind and push or get in front and pull and someday soon the great forward step will be taken.

In New York he finds the retreats and he thinks the retreats are the city, and his hope is as high as the day he heard Bryan, and he does not go home. Every time he puts a poem into the mail, or carries it himself to Harper's or The Outlook or Current Literature or The Delineator or The Critic or Century Magazine he knows very well they will take the poem and put it on page one if possible. Maybe they will pay him for it; it is a secondary consideration. And the poem will sweep the country and change men's minds about things.

And they never do. The poems come back in the mail with sometimes a note from the editor, and Vachel is never discouraged. He puts them into new envelopes and sends them out again, and when they have been around to all the magazines he sends them to the Springfield Illinois *Journal* and someone at the *Journal* slides them one by one across a desk and into a wastebasket or tears them neatly into squares and clips the squares together clean-side up and sets them beside a telephone, a handy memo pad, and a long time afterward a sharp-eyed little girl rummaging through yellow files looking for something else will find the scraps of paper and piece them together and everyone will gasp a little the way people gasp a little in Springfield when somebody finds an old handkerchief Abraham Lincoln once blew his nose into. Vachel goes on writing poems and sending them out, and he knows that someday someone will print his poems. All of the artists know, all up and down the street, that someday somebody will print their poems and stories and hang their paintings.

Meanwhile, there are the retreats. There is the YMCA and the humpbacked young man at the desk, and old men in soft chairs, and in the distance the sound of a handball thumping against a wall, and upstairs a classroom with a blackboard, and chairs riveted to the floor, and anyone with a message may come and deliver himself to anyone who cares to pay a small fee and sign up and listen.

Vachel lectures on art. The first week he speaks of Ruskin. There are three people in his audience.

The second week there are six people, and Vachel tells them why the Paulist Fathers' Church and the Judson Memorial Baptist Church are superior to and more artistic than the Flatiron Building. It is somehow interesting, the way Vachel explains it, and the three older men, listening, wish they were young again, and the three young men become deeply interested in building artistic buildings, and Vachel enjoys himself because the more he talks the clearer things become to him, and every week the class grows larger.

He likes to talk. He stands before his class and rests a hand on his hip and leans backward slightly and closes his eyes and sees behind his eyelids the pictures and the buildings he wishes to explain. He brings large picture books to class and discusses the pictures, the meanings, the histories behind the pictures, and many things come alive that were never alive before, for Vachel and for the people in his classes. (An old Italian man sits in the front row. He does not hear well because he fell from a scaffold once, but he always liked pictures, and when he was young he thought he would like to be a painter. He always looks at pictures when he walks past a gallery, and he never knew until now what it was about the pictures. "It is the way you bring it out I like. The desperation.") The class grows big, and when there are twenty-five people Vachel thinks he might be paid a little money by the YMCA, and after a good deal of letter writing back and forth to headquarters he is paid ten dollars a week. It is good money.

It is a retreat. Afterward, out in the street with the books and the posters, he talks for a moment with the men and the boys who were kind enough to come and listen, and then they go their separate ways and in a moment are lost to his sight in the great city, and then for an instant he is aware, as always he is numbly aware, that their numbers are small, that for each who comes to listen there are two sitting lumpily in the lobby on the soft chairs, and two pounding the handball against the wall; it seemed that there were a great many when they filled the room before him, and always he leaves the retreat with regret and with the painful knowledge that there are few, very few, who feel the need for beautiful buildings and paintings. But at least there is the brief time, the hour or two hours or however long he went on, and it is for these happy hours that he remains in New York, and for midnight sarsaparilla at the Pig and the Goose or a steaming smooth hot chocolate to quiet him after the exhilaration of lecturing, and then deep sleep, and in sleep forgetfulness that there are only a few, and in the morning fresh hopefulness that the few will soon be many.

5

At Tenth Avenue and Fiftieth the wind roars in from the river and turns the corner and whips down the wide street. Vachel stands in a doorway, shielded from the wind. A girl stands beside him. Her face is white, except for the tip of her nose, which is red, and cold tears fill her eyes. She stands erect, staring straight forward across the wide street. She wears a severe blue dress, and the wind catches the hem of her dress and wraps it about her ankles, and Vachel thinks she must be cold, but she is not cold because beneath her dress she wears two sweaters and two petticoats and two pairs of long underwear, but Vachel does not know of these. Only her face and the tips of her fingers are cold. "The Lord made it brisk," she says, not turning her head toward Vachel.

"That He did," says Vachel. He is glad she talks to him. He likes to talk to people, but he has a bad habit of stepping right up and talking to people, and it always makes him unhappy when people turn their backs and will not talk, and now he no longer speaks to people until spoken to. "How much do you make in an evening?" he asks.

"It depends on the Lord." He looks down into the plate she carries. It is filled with coins, and he takes a nickel from his pocket and drops it into the plate. "God bless you," says she, and it is a warm feeling the way it is always a warm fine thing when somebody asks God's blessing for somebody else, and now the girl looks at him for the first time. Her face is very plain, and her peaked cap is too

large. Her hair is bunched beneath her hat, and Vachel wonders
what color hair she has.

"You should let your hair straggle out from under your hat."

"Oh no," she says.

"Why not?"

"The rules," says she.

In the half-light he cannot see her eyes, and he wishes he could
know their color because it is always important to him to know the
color of a person's eyes. "The Army's rules?" he says.

"The Lord's rules."

He supposes her eyes are fiery. He would draw them fiery. Like
the eyes of John Brown, flame-throwing eyes, and he would draw
her plain face beautiful. "I certainly hand it to you people," he says.
"The way you go out in all weather," and she moves the plate toward him slightly, and he drops another nickel into the plate.

"God bless you," she says, and she reaches with her cold hand
somewhere deep into the folds of her dress and brings forth a
pamphlet and hands it to Vachel. It is entitled *There's An All-See-
ing Eye Watching You,* and Vachel digs into the inside pocket of
his coat and draws forth a poem and hands it to her, and she takes
it but does not read it. She will place it later on the reading table
at the Fallen Woman Mission on Forty-second Street. "God bless
you," she says. "These are what you sell?"

"Try to sell," says he.

"For how much?"

"It varies," he says. "Last night I sold them two for five. It depends on the type of person."

"They are Christian poems," says she.

"Oh yes," he says, and she steps forward out of the doorway and
holds the poem up to the light. It flaps in the wind and she cannot
read it easily, but she distinguishes a line or two of We Who Are
Playing, and she steps back into the doorway and thrusts the poem
toward Vachel, but he does not take it. "It's a Christian poem," he
insists. "You must learn to read between the lines. It's jammed to
the eyes with Christian ideas."

"Very well," she says, and she withdraws her hand. "Will you
sing with us?"

"I'm not a very good singer. Back home I remember Miss . . ."

"We sing every night on the—which is it?—southwest corner of

Forty-second and Tenth. In an hour. I hope you sell your poems."
She shifts the plate from one hand to the other. "Which side of the
street will you be on?"

"Either side. No matter. Take your pick."

"I'll go down on the—which is it?—east side. You take the west."
She crosses the street.

It does not really matter which side of the street he takes. In the
beginning he thought it mattered about the street, but it does not
matter. They are all the same. With minor differences Third Avenue
is Tenth and the men on high stools in crowded saloons are the same
as anyone else though he thought in the beginning that Greeks and
Chinese would have more interest than other people in poetry but
they do not. He had the idea that New York Greeks knew about
Homer, and Chinese people were somehow more conscious of the
span of time and more settled down than New York people in general, but they are not. They are like other New Yorkers. They sit
on high stools in saloons and turn to look at Vachel as he walks
down the sawdust floor behind them, and then they turn away and
hope he will drift out again because he bothers them. He tries to
sell them poetry and they do not want any. They want to drink
and forget about everything else and be let alone and not have
people bother them, not Vachel or the Salvation Army or the Sisters
of Mercy or the Ezekiel Society or any of the people marching up
and down Tenth Avenue and in and out of saloons reminding people
of things like poetry and God and the soul and whatnot that they
would rather not think about.

Vachel thought the Negroes on the high stools would be interested
in poetry. He feels a kinship with Negroes: they do not entirely fit
into the scheme of things, just as he does not seem to fit into things,
and he thought they would buy his poetry, but they do not, and it
hurts him that people will not pay even two cents for poems written
in the poet's own hand and delivered in person to the shops and
saloons on the cold streets of New York.

He thinks that perhaps it is the city the cold hard unfriendly city
of stone, and he goes up and down the street looking for someone
who loves poetry well enough to buy it and read it and maybe copy
down a poem and give it to a friend or lover, but hardly anyone will.
The men turn away when he enters and turn to look after him when
he leaves, and then they look at one another; all up and down the
avenues people march with messages they feel must be delivered if

people are to be saved. (The Ezekiel Society marches on Tenth Avenue. "Blow the trumpet and warn the people," cried Ezekiel.)

There are always people abroad with messages and they always come into the saloons (as if saloons were the source of evil) and they always smile as if they are sure of triumph and speak their piece and leave, and there is always fire in their eyes, and sometimes they wear uniforms and sometimes they are ununiformed like the young man selling his poems and looking lonely and a little bit hurt because hardly anyone will buy them, and someone will save the world someday, and maybe it will be the young man, and whoever it is, good for him. Meanwhile it is warm in the saloon, and the men on high stools slosh their whisky in their cups.

Tonight is not so bad as some other nights have been. On the first block he does not sell, but between Forty-ninth and Forty-eighth he sells twelve cents' worth of poetry to a Negro man very dark and flat-nosed, and the man wants to buy him a drink but Vachel does not accept it because he is not a drinking man. Besides, he wants to move on; he has the feeling that this is to be a lucky night, and he wants to be at Forty-second Street in an hour. He skips the next block altogether, not stopping; he is about to pause and try a florist but the florist is busy with a customer and Vachel knows it is a waste of time to try to sell to a man when he has a customer. People do not give a damn about poetry when they are selling to a customer. Vachel crosses Forty-seventh, and in the middle of the block he pushes through the swinging doors of a place called Ed's, and the men at the bar turn to look at him. He stands by the door and announces, "I have poetry for sale."

"How much?" someone says.

"Two poems," says he.

"Money," says the man. "How much money?"

"Two cents per poem," says Vachel.

"Too much," says the man, and there is laughter. "I can get me a whole goddam *American* for a penny."

"The extra penny is because you see the poet himself," says Vachel.

"Let's see," says the man, and Vachel hands him one copy of each poem that he carries, and the man studies them a moment before passing judgment. " 'Taint no goddam good," he says. "Besides, you never writ them."

"Yes I did," says Vachel.

"Well you're a liar."

"No sir," says Vachel, and the man turns back to his drink, and Vachel retrieves the poems and goes again into the street. He still feels lucky. He is not hurt because he is not easily hurt.

Across the street, walking purposefully, erect and white-faced, the Salvation Army lass marches from saloon to saloon. Vachel calls to her, and she does not hear. "Miss," he calls, but she does not hear, and he crosses the street and follows her. She enters a saloon, and he peers through the window, and she stands with her tambourine outstretched. She stands very still between two drinking men. They pretend not to notice her. She does not move. She is doing God's work and she will not be moved until the men drop something onto the tambourine, and at long last one man reaches slowly into his pocket and brings forth a coin and looks at it and then digs into his pocket for another, smaller. The girl raises her eyes to his and stares at him, and he changes his mind and drops the first coin, the larger, onto the tambourine, and her lips move *God bless you* and she turns slightly toward the second man. He gives her a coin hastily, without looking at her, looking only onto the tambourine and wishing he had the money that is there.

Vachel recrosses the street. It is his lucky night. In a way it is the luckiest night of his life (he will know later how lucky it is, and he will remember it) and he does not feel cold or lonesome or rejected and homeless as he has more and more been feeling lately. Between Ed's saloon and Forty-second Street he sells ten poems for twenty cents, handwritten poems that tomorrow will lie on sawdust floors, wet and splotched with running ink, but very good poems as a matter of fact.

The wind dies and snow begins to fall, and Vachel wonders if they will sing even in the snow, but of course they will sing. (They fought hired armies in the place General Booth calls Darkest England, and they will sing in a hailstorm or a snowstorm or in flood or pestilence or anywhere sing Praise God From Whom All Blessings Flow while the police smash their drums and confiscate their tambourines and tear up their music because they are still an Army and not yet a corporation.) Along Forty-second Street snow lies gray on the pavement and the man with the drum pounds slow and heavy to attract attention, and where people gather about him the snow turns slushy underfoot. "We will sing," says the drummer. "Everybody. Jerusalem the Golden. Number thirty-five," but Vachel does not sing because he cannot carry a tune.

They raise their voices. The drummer's voice is deep. Beside him the girl with the plain face beats her tambourine, changing hands now and then and doubling a fist quickly and raising it to her lips and blowing warm air into her hand, meanwhile beating the tambourine on her elbow. She is very plain. In the light of the street lamp Vachel can see that she is very plain and very beautiful. Beside her a second woman sits at a portable organ, and across the organ in red letters it is written How Beautiful Heaven Must Be Will You See For Yourself and Vachel smiles and wiggles his toes for warmth and opens his mouth, tempted to sing. But he closes it quickly, not wishing to spoil the music.

"Softly and Tenderly Jesus Is Calling," says the drummer, beating softer but with more intensity, and the plain girl raps tenderly her tambourine, and the organ is covered with snow and the trio sings, and then they are silent and the man at the drum reaches forward and swings the suspended kettle, and some of the people turn away. No one approaches the kettle, and finally, after a minute, Vachel steps forward and drops a dime and all his pennies into the kettle, saving his nickel for the streetcar, and after Vachel there are others. (Because it is night and the City of New York and the snow falls in large flakes and three soldiers in the cold sing of Jerusalem, and he is not alone, he is among friendly soldiers.)

"Thirty-one," says the drummer.

Are You Washed in the Blood of the Lamb?

"Yield Not To Temptation," says the drummer, later.

And after a time: "Thirty-six," says the drummer.

When the Roll Is Called Up Yonder I'll Be There!

"Will you be there?" says the drummer, reaching again for the kettle, and someone laughs behind Vachel, and he does not laugh. He replies, singing, *when the roll is called up yonder I'll be there,* and the organ lady plays the song again and the drummer drums, forgetting his kettle. (Because here are three souls in Babylon in a snowstorm, three going forth on a winter night, and Vachel hates Babylon hates whatever it is created Babylon in defiance of the Lord. He is transported and warmed and the music makes his heart pump fast and sends the blood warm through his body and chokes him the way he choked and hid in a tree the day Bryan came, makes him love these singing people the way he loved Bryan, makes him love and admire anyone who sets out to save the world goes crying to the people goes blowing the trumpet of Ezekiel, goes with a speech like Bryan or a poem like Markham, with seeds like Johnny Appleseed, with a staff and a secondhand coat like Saint Francis. No matter how they go just so long as they go. With fire eyes like John Brown. Better that they go than submit. Better that they sit here until their fingers freeze and drop off finger by finger than never to raise the hand and the voice and fight Babylon or Mammon or whatever it is. Better to die fighting and save what can be saved than to live silent and therefore give approval. It is better to die somewhere with a gospel on the lips than to let the gospel die in the living man. Like Papa says of Ole Hibben: better that he preaches, however he may preach, than that he does not preach at all.)

And he stops singing, and he drops his streetcar nickel into the kettle, and he walks home and never remembers the walk.

CHAPTER FOUR

1

NOTES ON a journey, penciled in a black notebook stuffed bulkily into a hip pocket with a bar of soap wrapped in old newspaper and a green stiff-bristled toothbrush wrapped in tissue.

Notes on a journey, penciled in letters deposited at post offices looking, at best, untrustworthy, small frame buildings in towns along the St. Johns River Florida. Palatka. East Palatka. Welaka. Enterprise. Orange City. Sometimes there is no post office at all, only a man carrying in his overalls the business of the mails, and Vachel wonders each time if the letter will be delivered. Notes on a journey, postmarked Macon, Atlanta, Asheville, Morristown New Jersey, Easton Pennsylvania, and addressed to those few souls in the wide world between Vachel and whom no distance, however great, means separation, to such brothers and sisters as George Mather Richards and Susan Wilcox.

In his pocket he carries copies of three poems, a poem on Lucifer, a poem speaking of a rather diverse contingent of heroes, and a poem entitled God Help Us To Be Brave.

He has no money. One of his rules of the road is to travel without baggage or money. He is nearly thirty years old and he has no money and not much hope of ever having money, and all that he owns he wears on his back or stuffs into his pockets. He writes in his book: "Be neat, deliberate, chaste and civil and Preach the Gospel of Beauty." He vows that he will avoid railroads and cities, and beg two meals a day.

Postmark, Palatka: "Remember, if you go a-wandering, the road will break your heart. It is sometimes like a woman, caressing and stabbing at once."

Postmark, Oil City: ". . . a sort of trap in the mountains. As a corporate soul she has no excuse . . . an ugly, confused kind of place. There are thousands like it in the United States."

And the penciled notes and the postmarked letters will, in a later time, be collected and brought together between the hard covers of a book, and the book will chart the progress of a young man almost thirty, alone and afoot, alone upon the battlements, searching for something. It will be a strange book, not a collection of tales, not a novel, but a book which will defy the librarian's definition because it will have neither beginning nor end as stories and novels have beginnings and ends and whose heroes, in the final chapter, regularly find what they are seeking and win the lover they are wooing.

"This book is dedicated to all the children of Don Quixote who see giants where most folks see windmills."

The searching young man both finds and wins and, then again, fails to find and fails to win, and the road is a woman challenging the seeking man, and she is both pain and pleasure, stabbing and caressing. She is nameless, though she might be called Love, even as the Gospel of Beauty he preaches might well be called a Gospel of Love, and the giant he sees is the intervening monster who stands between man and man.

And Vachel thought once, long ago, that the Party of William Jennings Bryan would smite the giant dead, and later he thought that the Army of the faithful, singing with the organ on the wind-blown street, would smite the giant. Now he knows, or at least suspects, that no Party and no Army can wholly affright the giant, that only the children of Don Quixote can hope to succeed.

Thus he sets out, penniless and afoot, armed with a notebook, seeking proof that Love is alive in the land. He will go a stranger to the listing huts and the whitewashed cabins and the red-brick homes of the people of that land. He will speak the speech: "I am the sole active member of the ancient brotherhood of the troubadours. It is against the rules of our order to receive money. We have the habit of asking a night's lodging in exchange for repeating verses and fairy tales."

They will scrutinize him, and at first they will disbelieve: no man goes about knocking upon doors requesting of honest householders the opportunity to prove that he is chaste and civil and that he wishes only to sing for his supper, that he is willing to sleep on the floor or in the extra bed, if any, that he would like to have breakfast in the morning, and that then he will be gone.

Yet, strangely, one house in two will take him in and feed him and listen to his verses, and on such nights the road—the woman who is the road—is the lover caressing.

In the black notebook: "As to that night, I slept in that room in the corner away from the fireplace. The pillow and comfort came from the bed of my hosts. I hoped they were not cold. I looked into the rejoicing fire. I said: 'This is what I came out into the wilderness to see. This man had nothing, and he gave me half of it, and we both had abundance.' "

Again, and yet again, there are the acts of love. The giant, however frightening, is also vulnerable, and Vachel learns to believe that these acts of love are the proof that man may someday annihilate the giant altogether and live in love on the distressed earth, for he comes a stranger and alone, and they shelter him. Of these eloquent gestures of love he keeps a careful record: "The floor was smooth and clean and white. My host had no bed. When I awoke the sun was in my eyes. He had awkwardly folded his overcoat, and put it under my head."

The notes on a journey and the letters to Susan and George—these are the blood and the bone of the book that will report the findings of a young man who nominates himself a committee of one and goes in pursuit of evidence tending to prove that Love exists and is discoverable.

The book will not appear for a decade. He must first become known. Unknown, he is not worth the risk. When, at length, it is published, it will be greeted indifferently on the grounds that it is not quite a book at all since it has no beginning, no end, no hero, and Love, after all, is but a word. Thus the good book will be quite overlooked in the press of things, at least until the time arrives when men will know, as Vachel learns to know, that Parties and Armies are futile, and brave concepts like Wisdom and Courage but branches of the stout tree whose root and principal trunk are Love.

Penniless and afoot he begins his journey. Penniless and afoot he will return to Springfield. He will be richer for having dared to woo the woman of the road, for having dared to love though love be out of fashion. All in all it will prove to be a profitable journey: out of the sights and sounds, out of the wilderness of impression, out of disjointed notes and letters, out of deep indignation deepened along the way will come the report, the protest, the notes on a journey.

2

There is just enough cash in his pants to take him as far as Sanford. The river ends at Sanford and Vachel disembarks and walks

a dozen unsteady steps, getting the feel of land again. It is afternoon, and he wonders where he will sleep tonight. Never before has
he wondered in the afternoon about a thing like that. He tells himself, forget it, but it cannot be forgotten; it is a big thing and it
blocks all else from his mind, and yet it is only afternoon, and a
long time until dark. He never knew before how big it is—where
one will sleep tonight, what happens to a man in an unfamiliar place
after the city has locked its doors and turned out its lights and gone
to bed. It was never a thing to think about until now, and he does
not like to think about it. He thinks he will walk away from it. He
begins to walk through Sanford and then, coming upon the post
office, he goes inside and stands at the table against the wall. He
tears a sheet of paper from his notebook and writes *Dear Susan* and
he reaches into his pocket to make sure he will have money for
stamps because if he does not mail letters right away he forgets
them. *Dear Susan.* He thinks of Susan Wilcox. She will understand.
She will remember how it was from the very beginning when he was
a child and could not sing or write like the rest or see things as all
other children saw them she will not think less of him that he writes
from somewhere far away restless and wandering without a return
address without a home like other young men not think less of him
that at thirty nearly he does not amount to anything and from the
look of things never will. And partly it is her fault to begin with:
she never told him. *Dear Susan it is not true what it says in the
books, that there is no king. But you never told me.* There is a king
and his name is Mammon, and Vachel knows now, or is learning
fast, and he wonders where he will sleep tonight.

Railroad ties are awkward. They are too close together for a man-
size step and too far apart to take two at a time. He had planned
to steer clear of the railroads, but the railroads travel more directly and Vachel wants to get out of Florida in as direct a manner
as possible. He follows the Atlantic Coast Line, and sometimes he
is tempted to board a train and hasten the business of getting out
of Florida. He has been hungry and shaky ever since he arrived,
and finally he boards a train and sits in a corner and makes himself as small as possible, pretending sleep, and after a while the
conductor comes, and they chat, and all the time the train glides
north, and after a spell the conductor asks Vachel for his ticket,
and he has none. "Well then," says the conductor, "off you go," and

at the next stop off Vachel goes, and in this way, little by little, train by train, Vachel gets out of Florida. Georgia will be better.

The map shows a road through Okefenokee Swamp, but it is a gesture rather than a road, two ruts filled with motionless water, and a ridge between the ruts. Vachel walks on the ridge clear through the swamp toward Fargo. The sun is good on his back. His face and neck and arms are brown and he feels light of foot and head, and nothing lies before him but the road to be traveled, and every turn of the road is a mystery, and he is alone and happy. On the long stretches where there are no people, where the birds make song and the sun shines warm on his neck, here there is peace, new strength in his legs, new clarity of thought, and he sings a song off-key and whistles the same, and bluebirds circle above him and move with him like satellites, and now and then out of hiding a wet fat dog appears and barks at him and comes closer, and Vachel bends and holds out his hand, and at length the dog draws close and licks his hand. Vachel feels triumphant, and the dog walks brisk and businesslike beside him, and then the dog turns off and the birds are no longer overhead and a town is near. Existence becomes real again.

According to the map it is Fargo, and there are men sitting on the steps of Lumberman Inn, and the dogs at their feet uncurl themselves and bark at Vachel's approach, and the whittler looks up from his knife, and the men wonder who comes because nobody has walked the swamp road all winter. Vachel draws close to the men and they greet him with silence.

"Afternoon," says he.

"Evenin," says the whittler, grudgingly.

And they do not believe he is out for the walk, trying it out to see if it is the way to live and to learn what he can learn along the way about people and life and the soul of something he loves, a whole nation he loves and wishes to beautify. The men think him at best a tramp and at worst a revenue agent. "Neither," says Vachel. "My name is Nicholas Vachel Lindsay and I'm a rhymer and designer from Springfield Illinois," and the whittler returns to his knife, saying "Welcome. Have a seat," and whisking the step beside him with a handkerchief. "Illinois," says he.

"Yes," says Vachel.

"Well I reckon they ain't all cussed folk in Illinois. Too late now to go on. Nothin between here and Statenville and nothin but sassy folk there. Stay the night here. If we don't like you we'll hang you in the mornin."

"Fair enough," says Vachel, and as it turns out they like him and do not hang him. But something makes him uneasy in Fargo. There is something about the men that makes the few hours in Fargo long hours of a kind of sadness. ("There's bound to be a war between whites and niggers," says the whittler. "Japanese, Chinese, Italians, French, Jews and niggers is niggers. Russians, Germans, English and America is white.") A hardness mysterious beneath interesting beards and flabby faces. An ignorance. ("Let's all go into Statenville in a bunch and shoot the place up.") Vachel thinks perhaps Statenville will be a better place than Fargo, but he does not say so. He remains and eats at the big round table at the Inn, and he means to say something to these men, but he does not. They might hang him. They could do it and there would be no one to see. The silence of Fargo is different from the silence of the swamp road. It troubles Vachel, and in the morning he moves on, and the road and the sun are good again, and they restore his spirits and he whistles all the way to Statenville.

A three-pronged fork in the road just north of Valdosta, and a slow freight, and Vachel sits waiting on a rock with an old man who carries a pail. The long freight creeps by. In large letters on the side of one car it is written ILLINOIS, and the sight of the word stirs Vachel briefly. He would like to go home to where he knows the people, where he feels he belongs. "Wonder where she goes?" says Vachel. "Chicago? St. Louis? Where?"

The old man points. "Goes clear beyond Autreyville. I been there," and Vachel jots words in his notebook and the old man leans and reads. "Fine hand you got."

"If you were I which road would you take?"

"Road on the right goes to Carter. Road in the middle goes to Ray City. Road on the left to Mineola. I wouldn't take none a them."

But Vachel must take a road. He cannot remain in Valdosta. He must get away from Valdosta. (There was a long empty train at the depot and Vachel asked the agent to let him ride free and the agent said no. Vachel showed him a letter of reference from the YMCA but the agent said no again and laughed.) Now Vachel decides he will ride the train free or break his leg trying, and he rises from the rock beside the old man and runs beside the train and regrets as he runs that he is breaking his rules to stay away from cities and railroads, and somehow he cannot help himself. He adjusts his speed to the speed of the train and spies a footing and lifts himself from the ground, and for an instant he thinks he is losing his footing and he recalls word for word what the one-legged man told him in Statenville roll away backwards make like you was kickin yourself with both feet in the head, but he does not fall. He boards the train and finds a soft spot on a feed bag, and he sleeps part of the way to Macon. The rest of the time he sits upright with his hands clasped behind his head and he knows, like it or not, that his path is aimed north at a spot somewhere between New York and Springfield, and sooner or later it must direct itself one way or the other, and sooner or later he will be back where he started, in New York or Springfield, because running away leads him nowhere. There is no home anywhere, only more cities and more people, and for the most part pain.

Macon. Two strangers worth recording. A man, he knew Lanier or says he knew Lanier but at least thinks it worth while to establish the connection and that is enough for Vachel, that someone remembers Lanier even in Georgia where he lived and thinks it worth while to say so; an old lady, she once wanted to be a missionary and to go to far places and convert people and make them Christian. But then she got married and had enough trouble just keeping her own household Christian, but even so it is enough for Vachel, and worth recording, and she feeds him a good supper and likes him as she likes all young people starting out in the world. "We must preach," says she, "till our heads fall off," and the supper and the good words make Vachel stronger and he walks whistling clear to Barnesville through the night on the black road. His whistling pierces the darkness. Night sounds travel far—crickets and bullfrogs and dogs and far away the huffing of engines and the stutter of hooves on the road and a dim light in a distant house, weird shapes on the landscape against the gray-black sky, and at least at night when there is nothing to see there is little pain.

He walks through Forsyth at midnight. He does not see it. All he remembers of Forsyth is a man comes out of nowhere shines a bright light in his face, and Vachel keeps walking and the beam of light follows, and when Vachel reaches the limits of town the light dies, and for a moment the cool night walk is painful, and he tries to dismiss the incident from his mind because it is not important, but later, when dawn comes, he sits beside the road and writes about it in his black book because it is in fact important, maybe the most important thing in the world.

The darkness lifts and the sun brings into view green fields and red earth, and the flatlands stretch away before his eye, and men and women go slowly into the fields, and Vachel is glad he is not among them. He has sometimes thought there must be some reward, something about the closeness of men and earth that is uplifting, but he knows better now, and he is glad he need not spend the day bent in the fields it is too much work and unending and perhaps there is a way to abolish the routine of work the dullness and the waste of labor.

North from Atlanta, not knowing why, nor why he walks a little faster now, whether he is going away from somewhere or toward somewhere, what is pushing him or pulling him.

But he knows now, because it has happened to him before, that wherever he goes he will not stay long. There is something wrong with him. Maybe it is a gland squirting too much or too little of something. There is something wrong with him and he does not know what it is. Maybe if it is a gland it can be cut out or stopped up or pumped clean or twisted around a different way or something like that, and then wherever he finally ends up he will settle down and work like other people work and have a family and money in the bank and children and dogs and cats and work his way up in the world and amount to something.

He thinks maybe he will walk all over the United States first, however. And then Alaska and all the national parks, and after he knows North America pretty well he might try France and then Japan. He writes in his notebook: *Jerusalem Constantinople St. Petersburg Mecca Kamakura Calcutta Benares.*

In Springfield he will work for Sangamon County Trust and write on the side, perhaps, and finish up pictures he never finished, and work up to be Senator from Illinois and take things easy and live to be one hundred and five.

Maybe it is not a gland at all, but the way things are. Perhaps it is really he who is right and the rest of the people their glands and not his are downside up.

I will let you lecture on art says the minister in Asheville, *but say nothing of nudes, science, the Single Tax, labor agitation, socialism or Thoreau.*
I will try says Vachel.

But what is there to talk about except the new ideas and the old rebels and Thoreau who went to jail rather than support the war and why is it wrong to talk of Thoreau in a church?

Now son says the man in the piny woods, *answer me this. Has a nigger got a soul?* and Vachel answers him yes. *Well damn you're the first that says so. I ask everybody I meet and you're the first that says so.*

And under the falls at Tallulah Vachel sits and soaps himself and sings and throws rocks and builds a dam and washes his clothes and hangs them on a tree and lies naked in the sun while his clothing dries. It is wrong. He should be somewhere and doing something and meeting his obligations and responsibilities, and instead he is sitting under the falls and studying the way the water distorts his legs before him. He wonders why it does that, and he should go somewhere and look it up and know the scientific why, but it does not interest him, not *that* much, and all the world is at work and doing the right thing by themselves and their families. All but him.

Chain gang in the hot sun by the side of the road near Bobtown Tennessee. The ditch does not need digging, really. Soon other men bound together with chains will come and fill the ditch again. Vachel walks past the men and tries not to look at them, but he looks, and he is ashamed, and the men (all Negroes) straighten and watch him as he passes, and he looks at them, at the wet faces, and he waves, and the men wave and the guard waves and in Bobtown, ill, he stops for water. "Why shoot" says the man in the general store at Bobtown, "Chain gang don't turn MY stomach."

Yet the strong-stomached people are kind enough to listen to his poetry, to feed him and bed him. They sing their songs for him. Somebody picks at a banjo and they sing the old songs that were sung in the villages before their time, verse after verse, and the melodies raise goose-bumps on Vachel's flesh. Far into the night they sing tall tales in song of crops so high and peace so sweet and wells that never run dry, and he writes them down *Who put the hex on (name of town) When the man from (name of bank) comes with the news When the old (name of mill) shuts down for good,* and somebody ought to write all the songs down and write poetry about the people and their heroes and the names on the land.

North from Asheville. North through Tennessee.

In Flag Pond Tennessee he steals a rose. There are millions of them and he thinks one rose will never be missed and he steals it and wears it in his hat and walks with high confidence through Flag Pond as if he had bought the rose.

North into Kentucky, north and west to Louisville and not at all sure which way he wants to go.

3

Notes on a later journey.

Across the big river and west from New York. He tells himself he will never go back. He went back after the South and he gave the great city one last chance to read his poetry, and it did not read it, and now he leaves again and the city does not know that he leaves and does not miss him.

Behind him the stone city rises to the sky and never knows who comes or goes. It absorbs its people as the seas gather rain and a man is lost like a raindrop. (There were the magazines again, and poetry by the inch, and the requirements are that a poem must celebrate the blue of the sky and the red of the rose and the proper heroes or else not be printed at all. Poets must please the court or starve.)

He thinks he will go to Hiram Ohio. Those were the happy days!

He thinks that maybe he will go home first and sneak in by night and see Mama and Papa and walk around town a bit and keep in the shadows and then go away by night again. But at least he will sleep one night in his own room. Maybe he will see Susan again and talk awhile with her. He wants to see Springfield again. He has been away twelve years Hiram Chicago New York and the Southland and written a good many poems and painted a good many pictures a lot of water under and now he would like to go home.

Except that he is afraid. In twelve years he has not begun to amount to anything, never made any money or got married or learned a trade or learned to dress very well nor done anything except write poems and draw pictures and wander around the country and wire Papa for a few dollars when he was absolutely broke somewhere. And all the time Springfield was spreading out and getting to be among the hundred biggest cities in the whole United States and bringing in new industry and running its trains on time and its name in the Eastern papers, and a lot of Springfield people up in the high money brackets and paving its streets and building bigger buildings and bringing in the tourists to the finest hotels between Chicago and St. Louis, and never stopping a minute, growing and growing, and all the time he Vachel just piddling about and never amounting to anything or being a constructive citizen or taxpayer it is not easy to go home.

4

Morristown New Jersey. "The Richest Little Village In The Nation." In the late afternoon it reminds him of Springfield. He walks along the tree-shaded streets and pretends he is home. He hears children at play, and somewhere a clock strikes in a tower, and he half-closes his eyes and pretends he is home, walking down Fifth Street and greeting people he knows, and the people know him he went away for twelve years and now he is a great poet. In Springfield, behind his half-closed eyes, a great poet amounts to something and belongs to the city the way a great builder or Senator or newspaper editor belongs to the city. In Springfield young men and young women write poetry and books and paint pictures, and everyone concerns himself with Philosophy, and a man must know Ruskin's ideas on beauty before he can build so much as a shanty, and Susan Wilcox is Senator from Illinois.

In Morristown over the door of the mission is the word *charity*. Vachel has twenty-five cents but he is saving it for an emergency. He goes into the mission and signs his name on the Roll of Those Who Prayed Today, and the man behind the desk asks him, "Have you written your mother, son?"

"No," says Vachel.

"We must."

"My mama can't read," says Vachel, and the man leads him through the rear door into the yard behind the mission and gives him an ax and indicates the woodpile. "It looks about as chopped as it can get," says Vachel.

"We must chop," says the man.

"Very well. You first."

"You must chop," says the man. "You, that is."

"I thought you said we," says Vachel, and he lays a log against the pile and raises the ax above his head and brings it down hard and likes the splintering sound of the log, and the man re-enters the mission. Vachel chops awhile. But it is hard work because some of the logs are too small for further chopping. Yet a man must work for his supper, he supposes, and after twenty minutes the mission-keeper comes out and says it is time, and Vachel goes inside.

He stands in a long line of men. There are ten men ahead of him, and he is the youngest. The men cough and scratch themselves and pass a comb up the line, and the missionkeeper walks to the front of the line and opens a door, and the line moves forward, and Vachel looks at his hands and supposes they are clean enough to eat with, but it does not really matter because the room is not a dining hall at all, but a chapel and a gloomy one at that, and the men file into the pews as if they have done all this before, and the mission-keeper stands before them, the book open in his hand.

The men stand with heads bowed. In the silence of the moment before the reading Vachel is conscious of the coughing again, and of a whining which he realizes is breathing, and of a breathing that is heavy and slow like the breath of sleep, and of the sound of the man beside him scratching himself, and of the missionkeeper-preacher clearing his throat, of the door behind Vachel being closed from the outside and of the click of the door handle, and of late-afternoon sunshine filtered gloomily through the stained-glass windows. The preacher reads, and then the men sit.

"It gives me a sad feeling to see some of you men here again," says the preacher. "I see some of you here again and again by courtesy and charity of the good people of Morristown and it makes me sad because I know all of you men would not be here if it was not necessary, yet I cannot help but think that it is not necessary and some of you might find ways to help yourselfs on your own hook. The Lord helps them that helps themselfs in the words of the Scripture, and yet the Christian charity of the good people who stand ready to aid the needy in their time of need—stands—ready to help

you men now. There are the poor among us and always have been
and always will be, and yet there is no need, and I must warn you
that for the city we keep a record of you men and some of you are
coming back too often over and over again and not helping yourselfs. Now I don't say that is true of all of you, but it is true of some
of you and you know who you are. It is sinful for men not to help
themselfs when all about you is green fields and the wind and the
sun and the stars and all the good things of life and all it takes is a
little willing labor for men to help themself and not always be
trudging to the mission. There are advertisements in the newspaper.
And I quote to you the word of the Scripture," and he consults the
Scripture, but he does not find the passage he seeks. "God never
let a good man down and never will, not if he went out and wasn't
afraid to work and be a man as God created him in his image and
followed the advertisements," and afterward the line re-forms and
moves from the chapel toward the dining hall, and the men enter,
all but Vachel.

The missionkeeper plucks at Vachel's sleeve and orders him to
follow. Vachel follows the man to a small room behind the kitchen.
In the room is a large tub. "State law," says the missionkeeper.
"Tub bath and fumigation for all new men. You can get water in
the kitchen. Here's soap." He hands Vachel soap and then he takes
a bottle of white powder from the shelf and sprinkles the powder
sparingly into the tub.

"Can't it be after supper?" says Vachel.

"Hurry and you'll get in on the supper."

Vachel fills the tub with water which, if not hot, is at least not
cold, and the fumigator has a strong but not too unpleasant odor,
and Vachel goes quickly through the motions of bathing because he
is hungry for the supper, and the supper, if not elegant, is at least
edible: the milk is blue, and he is not accustomed to cereal for supper, but on the whole it is not a bad supper. He supposes it is as
good as he deserves.

An automobile. Vachel has never ridden in one. He has tried
never to be in so much of a hurry that his feet are not fast enough.
"Carry you as far as Phillipsburg," says the motorist, stopping
the car beside Vachel. "Nothin to be scared of."

But Vachel has a blister and he thinks it will be good for his blister just to sit back awhile and roll along, and then, too, to be in Phillipsburg by nightfall. He climbs up and sits on the hard seat beside the driver.

"Ever rode before?"

"No," says Vachel.

"Nothin like it," the driver shouts, peering sideways at Vachel through his goggles. "Used to take three days from Raritan to Phillipsburg. Do it in one with this machine."

"That's certainly an improvement," Vachel shouts in reply. He wishes the driver would keep his eyes on the road.

The motorist is a young man, Vachel's age. He wipes a gloved hand frequently across his goggles to keep them clear. "You ain't a preacher?" he says, turning sideways again.

"No," says Vachel.

"You put me in mind of a preacher. Bummin are you? Live in Phillipsburg do you?"

"Just moving along," says Vachel.

"Be in Phillipsburg by night."

The road jumps ahead of them and the landscape blurs before Vachel's eyes. Behind, a trail of blue-brown smoke widens and rises, and in the fields behind the fences grazing animals retreat as the car approaches.

"What sort of a place is Phillipsburg?"

"Nothin much. Bigger than Raritan. Place in Phillipsburg sells gasoline. That's why I go. Lots a pretty girls. You ain't no preacher?"

"No."

"Lots a pretty girls. Course there's some in Raritan too. Still and all I know all the girls in Raritan if you know what I mean. Aim to settle down in Phillipsburg do you?"

"No. Just moving along."

"Ought to have an automobile. Move along three times as fast. Comin things these here machines. Tell you right out, I never did like Phillipsburg much. But the road is good. Hell of a lot a foreigners. Say, you ain't a foreigner? I got nothin against foreigners but there's too many in Phillipsburg. Course it wasn't never much of a town to begin with. Ever been there?"

"Can't say that I have," shouts Vachel, and the milk he drank in Bloomsbury churns in his stomach and the noise of the automobile makes his head ache.

"Listen to her purr."

"I bet you make it in two days from Raritan."

"One day. One day there and one day back when the road is dry. Used to take three days from Raritan."

"Really an improvement."

"Course you ain't goin to find Phillipsburg much of a town when you get there."

West and north, aimed at Hiram, and then a change of mind. West and south again, and down the Susquehanna thinking maybe he will double back to Bethlehem thinking maybe he will mail a bunch of cards from there for the sake of the postmark, and then a change of mind again, and west again, and something pulling him home despite himself.

A day of rest, his blistered foot elevated bare on a rock, soaking up the sun.

West through the smoky towns and up and down the winding roads among the hills of Ohio.

West across the Ohio, across the Scioto, tempted again to steer north to Hiram, and almost but not quite turning, and thinking in Indiana that he might go visit Grandma Frazee in Orange County and read the books that line her shelves and let her feed him she will be glad to do it and rest his foot and then go home.

But he does not go to her. He reads his poems all across Indiana, and he tells the farmers he has Indiana blood in him, and they feed him, and somewhere ahead of him is the Illinois line, and he is afraid.

Across the Wabash. Across the line.

Illinois.

Illinois, and west across the flatlands, and it looks like Ohio or Indiana, except that it is Illinois, and Vachel loves it, for there is one place that belongs to every man, and that place he must love and make beautiful and by precept and example show the world that place and let other men in other places do likewise. He loves Illinois, and he does not know exactly why for it looks like Ohio or Indiana, and yet to him it shows a different face from any place he ever saw, and this is because he is its lover and every man must see his lover different and more beautiful or he is no lover at all.

From the beginning he was sick with love for people and places and names on the land and the bright hope for his country and all of the people all of the time like Lincoln said like Bryan said and Henry George and John Peter Altgeld said, and now he is home and walking the breast of Illinois, and it is like no place he has ever been and like no place he has ever seen.

Edgar County Douglas County Paris Mattoon and Fairgrange Pana and Shelbyville and all the names of all the towns along the road to Springfield, and he thinks that someday he will make a poem of the names, nothing but the names all strung together Kinmundy Murphysboro Alto-Pass and Horseshoe, and the names of all the heroes from Hunter Kelly the settler of Springfield through Abe Lincoln on down to the heroes of tomorrow now at play in the schoolyards of Illinois.

Yet in Edgar County, and a day later in Moultrie, the people are the same as everywhere: one night a farmer shelters him and listens to his poetry, and the next night he sleeps in a haystack because he is nowhere welcome. Illinois people are like the people everywhere, but the lover must have a love or he cannot be a lover, and Vachel loves Illinois as few young men anywhere love their state or village or think about it at all except to think how they can rise in life and sell something in the market place and carry off its wealth and buy it up and trade it back for more than they paid in the first place and to hell with the people starve them or hang them or shoot them down or sell them a war do whatever must be done along the way.

In the black notebook: *I will make you sorry you were not born in Springfield Illinois.*

Ten miles east of Springfield the land lies familiar. On the right hand is a house to which Vachel came once with Papa when the young doctors would not come, and on the left is a well where they drew water for the horses, and later, in the distance, the dark dome of the Statehouse projects itself like a thumbnail above the horizon. Vachel sees it, and he knows that buried beside it, too low to see, is the house, and he always knew he would come back to the house. He always said so and he always told Mama so, in all his letters, and he always told them everywhere, at Hiram, at the Institute, at the Pig and the Goose, that someday he would go home to his old room in the old house, home to Springfield. And he would set that town right when he got there.

He always said so, and often he envisioned this day of return, and somehow it was never quite like this: his foot aches. Yesterday it seemed better, but today it is worse again. He supposes it is the excitement. Whatever it is it sends long shooting pains along his leg, and the foot throbs with every step. But he does not pause. Mama will fill a tub of hot water and know just the thing for the foot, and Papa will lance the blister and in the morning the pain will be gone.

The billboards along the highway are new: FIVE MILES ABE LINCOLN HOME FIVE MILES says the sign FOUR MILES LIN- COLN TOMB and a marker beside the road, "Here Abraham Lincoln addressed a group of Rochester farmers during his first campaign for election," and beside a dried well, "Here Abraham Lincoln stopped to refresh himself while en route to Rochester to address a group of farmers during his first campaign for election (the well is exactly as Lincoln saw it)," and beside the well, nailed to the stone, is the cup from which he drank.

It is a long ten miles. Of all the miles in all the states these ten are the longest, and of all the hours of all the days these last few are the longest and the most painful. It is dusk when the country road ends. Vachel turns left off Rochester Road onto Edwards Street goes limping down Edwards toward home sees the downstairs lights half a block away and forgetting his throbbing foot breaks into a run and crosses the front lawn beeline because he has no patience for the paved walk swings open the door and shouts *Mama it's me anybody home? Papa!* and then urgently *Mama!* again, and Papa comes slowly from his study and Mama slowly from the kitchen, and neither of them run as somehow he expected they would run when he came. He sees swiftly that both of them are suddenly older, very much older. Papa's black beard is suddenly gray.

Book II—LOVER

CHAPTER ONE

1

AT SUPPER they are usually three, Papa and Mama each at an end of the table and Vachel at one side. Papa thinks they ought to take a leaf from the middle of the table, but Mama is opposed: she is hopeful that someday there will be a reunion, Olive home again with husband Paul, Joy home, or maybe Vachel will be married someday.

Olive is in China. She is a missionary, and Mama and Papa are proud of her because they are strong for missions, and Vachel is strong for them, too. He says he believes one third of everything they preach, and nobody knows now of course that someday it will be shown that China will engulf the missions, for China is the sea that salts all rivers. But they are people of faith, these Lindsay people, and they cannot know a later truth, and things look bright for China.

One night, after they have eaten, Vachel asks, "Would everybody like to hear a poem?"

"First the dishes," Mama says. Vachel helps her with the dishes. He likes to do them.

"It's still rough," he says, "but I think I can smooth it up in a day or two and send it out." He wipes the dishes quickly and stacks them away.

"Papa and I aren't critics," Mama says.

"Oh you don't have to be critics. Anyhow you *are* a critic." Leaning to kiss her he drops a handful of spoons and she makes him put them back into the water.

"We'll see," she says.

"If the average man sitting in his living room can't understand my poems then there's something wrong with them."

"With the people," Mama says.

"With the poems," says Vachel.

"Well, go get it," Mama says. "I'll finish up," and he goes upstairs and gets the poem. Papa folds his *Journal* and sets it on his knees and Mama comes and sits quietly in her chair.

125

"It's the Altgeld poem," says Vachel.

"Just read it and we'll figure out what it is," says Mama. Mama is a Republican, but she is determined to like the poem nevertheless.

"No title as yet," says Vachel.

"Might just call it To Altgeld," says Mama.

"Might," says he. He clears his throat. He reads softly *sleep softly eagle forgotten* . . . He reads the poem through.

"Mighty fine poem," says Papa. "Darn near anyone could understand it. I like those last lines," and Vachel rereads them *to live in mankind is far more than to live in a name, to live in mankind, far, far more* . . .

"An excellent poem," says Mama. "Vachel, you have a very fine gift of words. I think it comes from Grandpa Frazee."

"He was a good man," says Papa. "The more I see of what's come since the more I know. We didn't appreciate." There is nostalgia in his voice.

"Might call it Time Has Its Way," says Mama.

"I'm glad the way you feel about it. It's not so rough as I thought."

"I didn't think it was rough at all," says Mama. "Did you, Papa?"

But Papa has returned to his paper. Vachel goes up to his room. He wishes he had a typewriter. It is quite smooth as it is. He copies the poem, scarcely changing a word. He might take it down to the *Journal* except that they print only doggerel and are not likely to start printing good poetry tomorrow, and especially they are not likely to start with a poem about a Democrat. It is, he thinks, a very fine poem. He is enough of a poet to know good from bad by now, even in his own work.

He thinks he will go downstairs and read it to Mama and Papa and have them tell him again that it is good. They always like his poems, and he knows it is as much because he is the poet as because of the poem itself.

It is a very fine poem, he thinks, but there is nowhere to send it, really, because it is not the sort of poem people are printing these days. He might telephone Susan Wilcox and then go over and read it to her.

What good is a poem if no one will print it? What good is a poem if there is nobody to read it to? Sometimes he feels lonesome and alone. Sometimes he wonders why he ever came home.

Springfield Illinois. July 4, 1910.

Home is the place.

In the black notebook: *Nobody will have anything to do with me in Springfield but Willis Spaulding . . . the Liberal Democrats . . . Maydie Lee . . . the Single Taxers . . . Duncan McDonald and the Socialists . . . Rabbi Tedesche and the Jews . . . Charlie Gibbs and the Negroes . . . Susan Wilcox and the English teachers . . .*

What does he expect? Does he expect a brass band, fireworks, flags and bunting?

At courthouse square there are fireworks and a brass band and a profusion of flags and a speech by a State Senator whose repeated popularity at the polls can be accounted for by the fact that he has never owned a dangerous idea, never dreamed a dream. With good luck he will one day be Governor.

He introduces the famous General, and the old soldier speaks:

"San Juan and El Caney . . . Manila Bay . . . I said to Admiral Dewey I said . . . and we gave them if the ladies will pardon me hell . . . and you could see the dead on the beach in the morning . . . washed up on the shore . . . and I agree with Sherman that war is hell but . . ."

Home is the place where, after one wanders, after one has seen the bigtowns and the small towns and the open road between, he comes to because it is the place that Mama and Papa, when they came West, chose to settle in. They might have chosen Missouri or Kansas. But they chose Illinois. And, having chosen Illinois, they might have settled in Peoria, Mattoon, East St. Louis. But they chose Springfield. An accident of circumstance.

Home is a house with one's own special window looking out upon the Governor's lawn.

Home is the city that might have been a city in Kansas or Missouri, or that might have been Quincy, Moline or Vandalia. But it is Springfield, and he feels a responsibility for that city altogether unlike the responsibility he feels for other cities. Because Springfield is home.

It is the place where, if he were spun around fifteen times like when he was a kid and played at spinning himself around to see how dizzy he could get, he would, no matter how dizzy, retain that sense of direction which one has nowhere but in the city he calls home. Usually it is the city where one is born and lives those first fifteen years and roams the streets with no purpose, no destination, just roaming to be roaming.

Home is where he can pick up the telephone book and find on every page the name of someone he knows.

Home is where American English is spoken just a little bit differently from the way it is spoken anywhere else, and the ear is attuned to that difference: home is where, no matter how fast people talk, he can understand them.

Home is where he knows the cop at Capitol and Fifth, the ladies of the Abraham Lincoln Public Library, the *Journal* reporters, the City Commissioners, the manager of the ball club, the custodian at Lincoln's tomb.

Home is where, at the busiest intersection, somebody is likely to shout his name.

And if one has a vision of a perfect world composed of perfect nations composed of perfect cities home is the city one sees in the image of that vision. The home-city is the model. Athens was Socrates' world. Florence was Dante's.

Home is where the riot was. He had been on the road at the time, but he has heard endless accounts from numerous people, and what it boils down to is two dead Negroes (one shot to death, one hanged from a tree in the Edwards School yard) and four dead whites (two killed by Negroes, two by well-intentioned white rioters with bad aim) and a fire set by persons unknown in the Lincoln home which was quickly extinguished and the arrest of a number of schoolboys belonging to a gang called the Black Cats, each of whom had a black cat tattooed on a forearm. Three days of terror and bloodshed; the easy official explanation of the whole embarrassing thing is that it was all the work of the boys with the tattooed arms. Three days and three nights of murder and arson that everybody would like to forget and nobody can.

It could break loose again today. Jim Jeffries, after five years of retirement, is tangling with Jack Johnson this afternoon in Reno, and everyone—that is, most people—sitting at the square and listening to the speeches keep a part of the mind on that momentous event.

The State Senator, seated on the platform from which the General speaks, is handed a bulletin: at the end of two rounds both Johnson and Jeffries are on their feet. He hands the bulletin to the General who relays the information to the crowd which cheers because the feeling is that the longer it goes the better are Jeffries' chances and because, if the sour truth be known, the General is rather a bore. The people are restless. The day is cruelly hot.

A Black Cat: *Hoooo-ray! At least when there's something to cheer about it's like having something to do. I wish something would bust loose. Not a riot or anything like that, naturally, but just something. It is hot. Maybe a small fire where nobody got hurt. Just a fire in a field because it seems like there's never anything exciting happens just go to work and come home and Sundays go so fast and sometimes I think I might go*

down to St. Loo or up to Peoria where my brother lives and his wife and
things always happen up there. I hope Jeffries licks that black. He won't.
It oughtn't to be allowed for an old white man to be made a fool of by
a nigger. Something could bust loose. You could tell he was a General
even if you never knew the way he stands with his shoulders so square.
I wish there was a war.

Home is where there is a square that there is one of in almost
every city he has seen yet which is somehow different from every
other square.

He sits high in the buggy beside Papa on the square. The sun is
on Papa's beard, and the beard is gray. When Vachel came home it
was gray, and it is grayer now, almost as gray as it can get. Papa
sits with his left hand on his right thigh, his right elbow resting on
the back of his left hand. With the fingers of his right hand he plays
with the hair of his very gray beard, and Vachel studies Papa's
hands and knows the feel of those hands, remembering when he
came home and his blistered foot was swollen half again as big as itself, and he sat at the table in the kitchen with Papa opposite, with
his leg stretched out and the foot in Papa's lap, and Papa pressed
one place and then another until he found the center of infection.
When he found it Vachel howled, and Papa said he would cut it and
drain it. He sterilized the silver scalpel. Vachel said maybe the foot
would go down by itself to its own size, but Papa came with the scalpel, and he took the foot in one hand and braced it between his
knees, and held it there, and with the other hand he carved a half-
inch square dead center where the pain was, and blood ran, and pus,
and it did not hurt as much as Vachel thought it would hurt because
the learned hands were swift and deft and strangely gentle, and in a
week the foot was back to size.

Except that there will always be the half-inch scar that will fade
over time but never wholly disappear, and the scar will be there
always like the scar on the chin that is fading but will never wholly
disappear, and the scars will be reminders of various adventures
undertaken when Vachel was young and went adventuring in search
of himself, roaming to be roaming.

Maybe Papa still hopes, even now, even this late, that Vachel
will yet forsake adventuring for medicine. It is hard to know what
Papa hopes or thinks. He is a silent man, brooding and self-con-
tained, and he sits silent now, looking out upon the citizenry that

has come in the name of Independence to listen to the speeches, and
he knows that before the day is out he will be called upon to apply
the learned hands to firecracker burns and a sunstroke case or two,
even as, two summers ago, there were rioters with broken scalps and
burns and fractured bones who gathered in the name of something
else and were wounded in the name of something quite different
from Independence. He will mend the wounds today as he did two
summers ago. He does not ask questions. He only mends wounds.

"There was a song we sang, and we will sing it all together. You
know how the song goes Tramp tramp tramp the boys are marching,
only we sang it to different words, and if I sing it you will get the
spirit of what we went through." The voice of the old soldier raised
in song is an old voice, but a voice that likes to sing, and when he
sings the veins of his neck rise and fall, blue from up close, black
from the distance, and the voice in song quite captures the crowd,
and the crowd joins him in the chorus, singing because people like
to sing together and because there is no music as exciting as the
music of many voices in song, and the old soldier bellows "Chorus!"
and once, twice, three times the people accompany him in the chorus, louder each time as the new words (a few of them meaningless
but somehow right) become as familiar as the old tune. "All together!"

Damn damn damn the Filipinos, cross-eyed kackiack ladrones.
Underneath our starry flag, civilize 'em with a Krag,
And return us to our own beloved homes.

Home is where he comes limping to on the foot that is half again
as big as it ought to be. And the place called home is different, old
buildings replaced by new buildings, dirt roads hard-top now, a
new church where an old church was or where there was no church
at all.

But that is not the difference. The difference is in him. He has a
theory. He has seen cities and open roads, and he has met many
people, all kinds of people, and somewhere along the road he developed a theory, and he has come to believe a thing that men have
believed before and will believe after until the theory is either
proved or, by some unforeseeable, cataclysmic occurrence of history,

disproved, and the thing he believes is this: that man is fundamentally good, that he may yet be better, that he may in time live a life so good that he will weep for the millions and the millions who lived their lives in pain and darkness and fear in the two thousand years before Christ and the two thousand years that came after.

He thinks he has proved that theory. Papa would say he has not proved it because Papa is a man of science, and proof is proof only when the thing happens every time, unfailingly, like fire destroying paper and water destroying fire, happening every time. That is proof.

But Vachel is not a man of science. He is a man of faith, a Romantic. And when he was a stranger and alone and he knocked in the night there were people who would admit him to their homes and share with him their little, and he talked with them, sometimes talking until dawn, and he learned to know them, and they him, and he and they learned to trust one another, and natural fears dissolved, and he found that between them and him there was a bond: they shared poetry together, and they sang the old songs, and they knelt and prayed together, and they slept with no door between. He had proved a Romantic theory.

At least he thought he had proved it. The man of science would say that it was not proved because it did not happen every time, and as a matter of fact it did not. But if it had happened only once, just once, it would have been proof enough for Vachel.

Thus, when he came to the place where home was he saw the city different, and every man he met he looked at and believed in, knowing that that man embodied the love and the trust of which the world was made and which had somehow become submerged. He reasoned that a city is only people one by one, and since there is love in each man and since the city is only the one man multiplied there must be a lovelier side to that city. He set out to seek the loving face of that city.

The final chorus of the fierce song is ended. The General sits and the Senator rises, calling "One moment please one moment please," and the disassembling crowd, hot and weary and anxious to get a good place along the route of the parade, pauses reluctantly an instant to hear the Senator, and the Senator announces that at the end of the fifth round Jeffries and Johnson are both on their feet. There is applause for Jeffries, and—for the Senator—a kind of muffled acclamation, as if by the act of bringing good news he is reaffirming his loyalty to Jeffries and his enmity for Johnson. The Senator rejoices that the bulletin came in time: of such sturdy stuff are Senators made and unmade in Illinois.

The crowd disperses, seeking strategic positions, those who are luckiest finding seats on the curbstone, those who are less lucky forced to stand behind, those least lucky of all obliged to hoist children to their shoulders so that the children may see and never forget this last sight of the fading old soldier who did what he did wherever it was to the Cubans or the Spaniards or whoever they were and in so doing kept Springfield safe from whatever it was that would have happened if it had not been for the old soldier.

On the high seats behind the horses Papa and Vachel ride slowly, feeling the first breeze of the day, eying the lengthening shadows, hearing from afar the brass band and the cheering people. They lag farther and farther behind the people who, as the last of the parade passes, disengage themselves from the crowd and become transformed, no longer a crowd but, rather, small family groups or people from the same neighborhood, beginning the homeward trek after the long day and the long speeches and the exciting parade, having paid their last respects to the flag and Independence and the old soldier.

Nothing had broken loose. Papa had been busy, but not as busy as he had expected to be. Two firecracker casualties. One boy will lose an eye.

Beside the carriage, on the curbstone, a little girl who had not been able to see the General and who wanted very much to see him now waves at Papa. She is told that he is the General. He waves in return, and she is delighted. She will remember, almost forever, the day she saw the General with the gray beard, and the blond soldier beside the General who waved at her too.

And then there is the silence which seems to be a deeper silence than is usual at this hour on this street but which is actually no deeper than usual, only seemingly deeper because the noise of the day was great. The fireworks have been expended; now and then someone, finding on the street or in a pocket an unexploded fuse, dutifully, without enthusiasm, discharges it.

Nothing broke loose. It seemed as if something would break loose, but nothing did. Vachel is glad that the speeches and the parade

are over and that the final report on the fight did not come when
the people were a crowd and the day was at its hottest. He wonders
who will win. He supposes Johnson. He is not much interested in the
fight despite the fact that he has bet five cents with Mama on the
outcome. He wishes he could remember which way he bet, who
took who. He will claim Johnson.

It is strange how a brass band and an old soldier captures them.
One by one, if he met them that way one by one in their own houses
they would read poetry together and sing the old songs and talk
politics. That was how it was when he made the journeys afoot.
They always talked politics. And half of them would agree that an
old soldier is essentially a bad boy grown up and given a uniform to
hide the black cat tattooed on his arm, and the war song is an evil
song and Cubans and Spaniards and colored folk and white folk are
nothing but people with different names and different colors. They
would agree to the words. What happens to people when they become a city?

Home is the place where he knows who is who in the house next
door. He sits at his table where he does his writing, leaning back
and looking idly out the window at the house next door, relaxing
for a moment from the writing of the poem he has always been
meaning to write about the man who lived in that house and walked
that lawn back when Vachel was sixteen and Bryan came.

Nobody has lived there since. Only Governors. There has not
been a *man* in that house since John Peter Altgeld lived there and
served the land and the people and helped to create the unrest that
swept the valley from Chicago to Cairo.

How came there such a man to the house next door? And if there
was one such man there can yet be another. He will write of the
one and thereby suggest the possibility of another, and he makes
notes on the poem he thinks he is now ready to write sitting by the
window and looking out upon the mansion of the Governor. He
makes of the notes two lines.

*The mocked and the scorned and the wounded, the lame and the
poor that should have remembered forever, . . . remember no
more,* and he sets the lines aside and returns to his notes, and the
notes become the fragments that then become whole lines *To live
in mankind is far more than to live in a name, to live in mankind,
far, far more . . . than to live in a name,* and whole lines become

the whole poem, and he copies the poem, and he changes words, and then he changes words again, and again, and again, and he knows that although he has been a month on the one poem he has not quite said what he wanted to say. But he has come as close to saying it as he can come, at least for now. The things he did not say he will say in other poems.

For the present it is done, and it sits on the table before him, and he wonders how he ever had the nerve, the courage, the audacity to write a poem. It is only words, and he must be a fool or a madman or both if he thinks that a quiet poem can make a greater noise than a brass band.

Who will read the poem?

Mama and Papa will read it. They will like it, too.

He could strike off a copy and send it to Olive in China. She will like it. She shares his sentiments in most matters, which is why she is a missionary, he supposes. They are both missionaries.

The widow bereft of her crust, and the boy without youth,
The mocked and the scorned and the wounded, the lame and the
    poor . . .

He wishes he had a magic lamp that when he rubbed it everything would become absolutely silent and his voice would have suddenly the power of thunder and he could then read his poem to the widow and the youthless boy and the mocked and the scorned and the lame and the poor down at the square. Maybe they would remember the poem next time they cast their ballot.

They turn off Capitol and onto Fifth, and they do not speak, and there is a deep silence broken only by the drumming of the horses' hooves. In the twilight the gray beard is dark again, like years ago when it was dark. Papa says that he is hungry.

Vachel is hungry. He hadn't thought about it until Papa mentioned. Mostly he is lonesome, lonesome and alone. He supposes that they are not synonyms. He is always thinking about words. He supposes that lonesome is how one feels even though there are people around and alone is how one is, physically, as when one is alone in a room or somewhere out on the road. Sometimes he thinks he would like to take to the road again because he was never lonesome even though frequently alone. He is alone and lonesome.

Maybe that is not exactly what the words mean. But that is how he is.

Except that he is never absolutely and positively alone or lonesome because home is also the place where there are other people who are in many ways like himself. They would be alone if he did not exist, and he would be alone if they did not exist. They find one another.

How do they find one another? They do not have a sign on their door like a doctor or a veterinarian or a blacksmith or a dentist, although, one night, half seriously, they talked about it, saying would it not be nice if a man or a woman could hang out a shingle saying Socialist or Liberal Democrat or Peddler of Dreams or I Believe In The Single Tax, and they laughed about it, and then what it bogged down in was a discussion of what could be put on a shingle that would apply to all of them.

Duncan McDonald said why not put up a sign saying Debs For President.

Vachel said that if everybody else would do the same and if Papa permitted he would hang out a sign saying I Protest.

Susan Wilcox prefaced her idea with a story. She said that once there was a boy in one of her classes, whosit's boy down at the bank, and she gave him Browning's whatsit to read beginning *Oh to be in England now that April's there* and he could not read it because how, he said, could it be April when it is December and two weeks to Christmas. She would hang out a sign saying It Is April and keep it out all year except of course in April if everybody else would.

They thought they might form themselves into a club, Susan and Duncan and Maydie Lee and Vachel (it is Maydie Lee's house where they usually meet) and call themselves the It Is April Club or the I Protest Club or something like that like back when Hawthorne and Emerson and Thoreau and Parker and the rest had a sort of a club that was never in any way official which some of them called The Club of the Like-Minded although they never really agreed on anything any more than Vachel and the rest agree on anything.

Willis Spaulding does not even agree to the idea of a club. Willis is a City Commissioner. He believes that a political man might

leave the city better than he found it by becoming a part of a going political concern like the Democratic Party (Willis is a Democrat) and working within that party and standing at least a chance
of shaping policy and winning office. If, he contends, you hang your
shingle out and the shingle says I Protest or April In December or
Debs For President that is all very nice and you are probably a
very decent person with your heart in the right place and you will
probably go to Heaven which does not have a fixed two-party
system. But you will not win any elections in Springfield Illinois.

He wins elections. He will win them time after time, as long as he
cares to make races. He has a rare genius—the ability to fight unpopular fights and come back and win the next election as neatly as
the one before. The Country Club finds him offensive, and year in
and year out he fights the Country Club which during business
hours runs the Brewery and the banks and the big shops and the
mines, and year after year he defeats the big interests. They try to
buy him and find him unbuyable, and they try to smear him and
find him unsmearable because nobody can pin anything on him
except the Democratic Party label and a few luncheon-club badges.

The secrets of his heart and mind they cannot know. His heart
holds a secret which his mind ponders. He has a plan: he will build
a lake in Springfield where there is now no lake, ending drought
where there is drought, giving to many people the waters of the
skies which now belong by special arrangement with certain City
Hall politicians to a certain few people laying claim to the sky and
the waters thereof. It is all very legal. If Vachel does not think it is
legal it is because Vachel is a poet and not a lawyer or a judge. Willis says that things which are poetically illegal are frequently legal
enough according to law.

So Willis is a Democrat and in his heart and mind a member of
that club which has no name and no dues and no bylaws and which
could never vote decisively on anything because its members agree
on nothing except those basic principles which anybody who believes in democracy and poetry with a few socialistic ideas mixed
in would naturally believe in anyway.

And he finds Willis. Willis does not hang a shingle before his
house saying Down With The Country Club or The Water Belongs
To The People, and yet he finds Willis, and he is glad, and Willis is
glad. Willis, too, is lonesome and alone.

It was on account of the poem. They would have found each

other sooner or later anyway, but this way it happened a little sooner. It was all very roundabout and vexatious at the time. Afterward it seemed amusing. But certainly it would have happened sooner or later because anybody who could conceivably belong to the club that is not a club but just people winds up some night at Maydie Lee's. Everybody in Springfield who is slightly socialistic gets to know everybody else of like mind. It is almost occupational: Papa knows all the other doctors, every plumber knows all other plumbers, lawyers know lawyers, druggists know druggists and preachers know preachers. Probably all burglars know all burglars.

He wrote the poem and then there was nobody to read it to, and he telephoned Susan who is always happy to criticize his poetry, and a stern critic, too, and she invited him over to her house, and he folded the Altgeld poem as yet untitled and put it in the breast pocket of his coat and hoisted his collar up high on his neck (it was raining that night) and he walked as far as the Statehouse, and then the rain came down hard and he stopped for an hour under the eaves, waiting for the rain to stop. He wished he had a title for the poem. The birds sang in the rain.

When he finally got to Susan's there was a note in the box saying she had gone to Maydie Lee's, and he knocked on a neighbor's door and told the lady there about his appointment with Susan and the rain and how probably she waited until she could wait no longer and did the lady have a telephone and could he use it. The neighbor lady said why didn't he say what he wanted in the first place, and he called Mama and asked her if she knew Maydie Lee's address, and Mama said no, not offhand, but she knew Maydie Lee's brother's address, meaning Willis, and the neighbor lady stood with her hands on her hips, looking at him at the telephone and at the trail of water that traced his course through the front room, and he decided not to telephone Willis but to go there instead. He went through the rain to the house where Mama said Willis lived, and it was dark, and he went up on the porch, and in the dark there was a man there, waiting for the rain to stop, and Vachel asked him if he was Willis, and he said he was not. There was the slightest burr in his speech that Vachel figured was maybe Scotch or Irish. He said he was Duncan McDonald, and they shook hands and waited for the rain to stop, or at least to ease, and in the course of time the man asked Vachel if he believed in socialism.

Vachel said maybe he did and maybe he didn't. He was, he supposed, a democratic socialist or a socialistic democrat. He was not sure which way the words ought to be arranged.

Duncan McDonald said he had come to argue with Willis. They had not had a good argument together since the night before last. Duncan had books in his arms with which, he said, he could prove certain things about the goodness of socialism which Willis had not agreed to the night before last. He said he would lend Vachel the books if Vachel would promise to read them and discuss them afterward. He assumed that Vachel was a friend of Willis, and he assured Vachel that he loved Willis and believed in him and would vote for him any time, but he differed with Willis on strategy. Duncan believed that both parties were the instruments of capital, and he thought that the only way to improve the system was to change it.

Then they moved out into the rain together and headed toward Maydie Lee's (Duncan had been there before) and Vachel, much to his annoyance, scarcely got a word in edgewise all the way over.

Duncan was a miner. He had seen darkness, he said, and working in darkness he had come to believe in light, and Vachel thought that was a rather poetic way to put it. Duncan said the whole system was darkness, that men went to work in the dark and came home in the dark, and as a result their minds were dark, and their lives were dark. Unless, he said, there was a good union, and he asked Vachel if he believed in unions, and before Vachel had time to answer Duncan told him about the miners' union and how it worked, how it fought and was fought, and how he believed in unions, not only his own but all brother unions, and he warned Vachel against the sin of buying things that did not bear the union label—cigars, neckties, whatever. Vachel said he did not smoke cigars. Because, said Duncan, the union label means that the man who made that article to which the label is attached went home that day by daylight. People, said Duncan, are a damn sight more important than things. Vachel agreed.

The rain came heavy then, and he and Duncan ran the last two blocks to Maydie Lee's, and when he got there she took his dripping coat and he dried his face on a handkerchief. There were, he recalls, some Women's Trade Union League people there that night, down from Chicago to lobby, the legislature being then in session, but after a while things emptied out a little and all that were left were Susan and Maydie Lee and Duncan McDonald and

Willis Spaulding and himself, and for some reason he felt more at home there than anyplace in Springfield since he came limping back to town.

He edged the talk around to the poem that he just happened to have with him and which he would not be too shy to read aloud if they absolutely insisted, and they coaxed him sufficiently, and he went to his coat in the other room and came back with the poem that was wet and smudged from the rain, and he read it aloud, and he was surprised, as he read it, how much of what Duncan had said was in it, and how much of Susan and how much of his lonesome self.

And that was how he found Willis.

Only Duncan and Willis and Maydie Lee are at Maydie Lee's tonight. They seem to have been expecting him. On the round mahogany table there stands a glass containing one generous chunk of ice. "Yours," says Maydie Lee. "There's a pitcher in the kitchen. Give it a little shake first," and he goes to the kitchen for the pitcher of lemonade. There is always a pitcher of lemonade. In the winter there is always the bottomless coffeepot.

"Let's build a fire," he says, returning with the pitcher. "Who won the fight?"

Nobody knows, and nobody seems to care. Duncan removes his necktie, opens the two top buttons of his shirt and blows downward at himself. He twists his necktie in his hands, absently picking at threads. He is always picking at threads in ties. It is a union-made tie, not the best for the price. But the man who stitched it went home that day by daylight.

"Nobody'll come down tonight," says Willis.

"Can't blame them," Duncan says.

Nobody seems to care. Tonight they will sit as quietly as possible, nursing the lemonade, and the only significant sound shall be the sound of ice in the glass, and there shall be only the silent presence of one another because it is too hot to care whether anyone comes or not or to care about anything at all except maybe to hope that a breeze will come up out of somewhere and freshen the night.

It seems that the globe has stopped spinning and that all the business of the world is held in abeyance, waiting for the breeze, a cool tomorrow, that good works and evil works alike are suspended for the night because of the heat that makes one want to sit silent and still and creates the impression that all men and all women everywhere are sitting silent and still like this, waiting for the heat to pass and the breeze to come.

"There was a thing in the *Journal* window," Duncan says. "They were still fighting."

"Now," says Maydie Lee, "one of them is a colored man. Which is that?"

"That's Jack Johnson," says Willis.

And nobody really cares.

Except that each hopes in his heart, and each knows that the others hope in their hearts that Jack Johnson whaled hell out of Jim Jeffries this afternoon at Reno.

Which, in fact, he did.

There will be other nights like this at Maydie Lee's.

But mostly the nights are not like this at all. Usually, at Maydie Lee's, there are many people and much talk, people seen perhaps once and no more, people seen again and again over the years. Except for Susan the few Springfield friends who are friends now and will be friends forever (to the last, to the very last, Duncan and Willis each at a corner of Vachel's coffin at the very last) Vachel first met here, at Maydie Lee's, summer, winter, ice in the glass, the bottomless pot of coffee, and he will gain from them, as he gives to them, the hope and the courage and the strength and the will that come from knowing that in being lonesome and alone one is never wholly alone, never positively and absolutely lonesome.

On the round mahogany table, beside the cream pitcher, beside the bowl of ice, Henry George's great book lies finger-marked. Here and there in the book scraps of paper mark the points of particularly memorable passages. The yellow-tinted cover of the book hangs loose, and someday the last binding threads will break, and the cover will be lost. Still the book will occupy its central place, reminding whoever comes to Maydie Lee's of the central theme. The fading letters on the cover of the book state that theme: *Progress and Poverty*.

Vachel will write a Single Tax poem to celebrate Henry George, and he will bring the poem as he brought the Altgeld, and he will read, *Come, let us see that all men have land to catch the rain, have grass to snare the spheres of dew, and fields spread for the grain,* and they will not agree on the merits of the poem. They agree only to listen to it when he brings it newborn, to study it from first to last, to commend and advise, suggest and deliberate. All agree that poems must be written and testaments and documents composed, dreams dreamed. They agree together that progress has been, and is, possible, that the central question is progress and poverty, the stark paradox of want in the midst of plenty. They are Romantics.

They will leave a singular mark upon Springfield. They will not be cheered at courthouse square or wined and dined at the Country Club. There will be no brass bands for them, no fireworks, no parades.

But in the far time it will be possible to say that because Maydie Lee was here suffrage was extended, and because Susan was here each generation sees and feels in ways its mother and its father could not see and feel, because Duncan was here the workingman goes home by daylight, and, because Willis was here, there is water where for generations there was drought.

Their heroes, over time, are the men and women of distant cities, distant villages, Tom Johnson the Single Tax mayor of Cleveland, Golden Rule Jones the mayor of Toledo, Jane Addams, William Jennings Bryan, Henry George, John Peter Altgeld, men and women who, like themselves, once upon a time sat plotting change and reform somewhere in somebody's house on the outskirts of some town or other.

It is the kind of group one finds in any village or any city, and, like all such groups, they often feel alone, lonesome. They feel, sometimes, that protest is futile, that December is December and can never be April.

Yet, even at the point of despair, they maintain hope.

And in the far time Duncan and Willis, each at a coffin corner, will remember the rainy night when Vachel came with the Altgeld poem and read it aloud to them because there was nobody else to read it to in all of Springfield, and how, because of them, he was able to keep faith with himself, and how, because of all of them, because of Maydie Lee and Susan and Duncan and Willis and Vachel and the sometimes people like Charlie and the rabbi they left their singular mark upon the city, giving to that place which they all called home a conscience, a soul. And the conscience and the soul will live after the old soldier is forgotten and the parade has passed and the crowds have gone home and the brass band has played the final note.

Late, very late, he leaves Maydie Lee's with Willis and Duncan, and at a corner they part, bidding one another good night and going their three ways through the dark silent night. When there are no longer the sounds of their footsteps behind him Vachel becomes aware of the whisper of a breeze on his cheek. The faint breeze is cool on his wet forehead. He feels altogether better than he has felt all day, less lonesome, less alone.

He lets himself into the house, locks the door behind him and goes swiftly upstairs with his shoes in his hands. Home is the place where one goes swiftly through the dark house without lighting a light.

2

Papa is good. After the first of the month the bills must be paid and he is not always certain how he will pay them, and for a time he is silent and irritable behind his gray beard, and then they are paid as they are always paid. Papa is proud that he owes not a penny in this world.

He works hard. He does not push himself as he once did, but he makes his rounds faithfully, doing his duty as he sees it, winding about Springfield in his ancient, familiar buggy (the young doctors have automobiles) and paying his bills and keeping his pantry stocked and the house warm in winter and the ice chest full in summer, and he tries to dismiss from his mind the sight of Vachel round-shouldered at his table; particularly on and about the first of the month when the bills fall due the sight of Vachel troubles him. It is somehow wrong that a man already thirty shall rise late in the morning and spend his day in a disordered room drawing pictures and writing verse round-shouldered at a table as if there were no bills to meet, no obligations, no responsibilities. It is probably too late to expect a reformation in Vachel. Papa thinks Vachel is a man who has never quite grown beyond boyhood. (Mama fixes it, and Vachel goes into southern Illinois—Little Egypt—to spread the dry word for the Anti-Saloon League, and he goes dressed in a black-tailed coat like a preacher. He talks in the coal towns at the union halls. He does not deceive himself that whisky can be outlawed: there must be a substitute for liquor. There must be a gathering place as attractive as the saloon, and the vacant place in the Illinois life must be filled with something equally satisfying, stimulating, and he talks to the miners of art and literature Christ

Ruskin Henry George women's suffrage and public ownership, of everything but abstinence, and he comes home empty-handed, having forgotten to pass the hat, for which lapse he is dropped from the Anti-Saloon League.)

It is too late, Papa thinks. There is something in Vachel demanding of him that he draw pictures and write verse, and perhaps the young doctors with their new knowledge will discover a cure for the inkwell disease that makes an otherwise sensible young man allergic to living as other young men live, that lashes him with invisible chains to the chair before his table, that gives him no desire in life but to put words upon paper, striking from his nature the love of flesh, of rich food, of property, of position. It is unnatural.

The walls of Papa's waiting room are decorated with Vachel's drawings. There is a Map of the Universe and a Village Improvement Parade, and in such idle moments as there are Papa pauses in his work to study them, and the more he studies them the more he likes them despite an inner suspicion that they are nonsense. Each time they gain in meaning as each rereading of the Book itself leaves Papa with the glow of new discovery, and Papa will not take Vachel's drawings down no matter how many times a day folks squint with mixed amusement and amazement at the walls and look at Papa as if to say so that is why he spent how many years Chicago New York and the Lord's good time traipsin the country a bum. Papa gives them look for look. It is his business and none of theirs what Vachel does with his time, when he rises in the morning and when he goes to bed and if he burns his light at night long after good people are asleep. It is Papa's business and nobody else's. It is Papa's money that supports Vachel in his adult infancy Papa's money in Vachel's belly and nobody's business what Papa does with his money it is his and he earned it by the sweat of his face like it says in the Bible. Besides, when you look close and try to study it out and not sit like asses reading old magazines you will see there is much good sense in the drawings there is Mammon fearfully large in the Map of the Universe and is it not true are you not compelled first to consult with The God Of The Purse no matter if you are half dead or half eaten away until at last in the shadow of death you come to me, physician. Fools! He is my son and I keep him for better or worse you shelter your own I shelter mine and where were your sons when the riot was on did they weep do they weep yet as mine wept and weeps still or were they out smashing heads do they know who Dante was do they know their Bible heroes have they been going about since they were old enough to think trying to do what Christ would do in a place where if Christ came you would not have him in your clubs!

Papa likes the Queen of Bubbles as well as any. Vachel sells it to The Outlook for ten dollars, but that is not why Papa likes it. Papa likes the inscription beneath the drawing, written in Vachel's extraordinary hand. One thing about Vachel his penmanship is magnificent. Penned across the bubbles is a poem, the allusions of which are not entirely clear to Papa, but beneath the drawing Vachel has written *All my true friends are petitioned to pin this poster on the parlor wall for fifty years, never to be ashamed of it and to explain it in all its details to the world,* and Papa knows a good deal more about Vachel each time he reads the words, a good deal about a wish for love, about the need to be understood, to communicate, the need to have his labor seen.

Vachel goes with the ten dollars and a copy of the Queen of Bubbles to Norval Taylor's print shop, and Norval prints twenty copies. "Might make it smaller and save," says Norval.

"No," says Vachel, "it must be big. Like a poster. It's for hanging on the wall and you should be able to see it across the room."

"Like a picket carries," says Norval. He does the printing for the streetcar union.

"Sort of," says Vachel.

"Gonna sell them?" says Norval, holding the drawing at arm's length.

"Give them away," says Vachel.

"I do mailing," says Norval. "No extra charge except postage."

"No, I'll take them myself." He has twenty friends in Springfield who will be willing to hang his drawing on the wall for fifty years. With the remainder of the ten dollars he takes Susan to see *Battle Hymn of the Republic* at the Sangamon Theater, and afterward they have ice cream and coffee at Loper's.

3

On the walls of Willis Spaulding's office in City Hall are pictures of Willis dressed in his public clothes and smiling his best political smile, and Vachel smiles when he sees the pictures because the people do not know how, behind the smile, Willis dreams his dream,

and how, behind closed doors at Maydie Lee's, he explains in a tone
of confidence how he will take the water from the few and give it
at cost to the many. "If I get that one thing done before I die,"
says he (he is Vachel's age), "I'll die feeling I was useful in life."

"Now Vachel," says Willis, leaning across his desk, "there's nothing here you'd like. You'd be bored." He knows, as Papa knows,
that Vachel's strongest need in life is to write poems and draw pictures.

"I can't help it. I owe it to Papa."

"I bumped into him the other day. We chatted."

"A good man," says Vachel. "Sometimes stormy, but on the whole
a noble citizen. You don't hire City Hall poets," he says, and he
laughs.

"Not this year. Someday," and Willis does not laugh. In the picture behind his desk he is smiling and cutting a ribbon across a new
roadway and dressed in his best public clothes and reaching with
one hand for the hand of the Governor.

"Governor either," says Vachel.

"The worm."

"Just thought I'd ask."

"Seriously, Vachel, not a damn thing I can think of." On the wall,
to the left, in the picture, Willis at a ground-breaking smiles
broadly and shovels the earth, and beside him the dignitaries stand
looking toward the photographer. But now he does not smile. "For
the most part there's typing and filing. Ever drive a truck?"

"I could learn."

"Filing's not so bad."

"I can file all right."

"Worst damn monotony on the face of the earth."

"How much does it pay?"

"Depends."

"On what?"

"On your party."

"Oh?"

"Never knew that?"

"No." Vachel smiles.

"Ever wheel cement?" Willis bites his lower lip thoughtfully.

"No."

"Pays better than filing. Also gives you a hernia by the time
you're forty."

"I might do it awhile. Six months, say. Tell you, Willis, I got an idea for some printing I want to do. If I had a little money."

"See there's a long line of people voted regular and I have certain —certain . . ."

"Obligations."

"Sure." In the picture on the wall to the right Willis dressed in his best public clothes pins a medal on Mordecai Turner who has worked twenty-five years for the City and never missed a day of work and was late only twice. Now Willis does not smile. "Damn tricky situation," he says. "And you wouldn't like it, Vachel. You're not cut out for it. Not that anybody is cut out for boredom and hernia."

"Hernia wouldn't worry me," says Vachel.

"It's the boredom. I don't know how folks do it. Really, I don't. Damn funny thing the way folks'll just stick to a job. Year after year. Hating it all the time and never throwing it over. And trying to tell themselves they don't hate it. Damn funny." Willis swings sideways in his chair and sits looking at the wall. He rubs his nose thoughtfully. Vachel watches the tip of the nose in profile. Up and down. Up and down. God he loves Willis! Sometimes he wishes he could be like Willis and keep his mouth closed and have a nice neat office and fit in with all the regular people and at the same time work in his own quiet style and make life better in some important way for people. Up and down goes Willis' nose. He looks at his watch. "I got a luncheon date. Let me call you."

"How are the chances?"

"Maybe good. I might get you something."

"It'd be the thing I need right about now."

"Silly damn luncheon clubs," says Willis, adjusting his tie. "Vachel . . ."

"When do you think you'll call me?"

"Vachel . . ." says Willis again. He is a little stern. "Vachel, if and when you're on a job if anyone asks you're a Democrat. Not a Lincoln Democrat. Not with a small *d* or any other kind. Just a Democrat. You and your father. You're Democrats." Willis pulls a comb from his pocket and combs his hair with great care. Then, quietly: "Somebody took a shot at Duncan last night."

"I know. I heard."

Willis poises his comb in mid-air. "And you're never to go about boasting what a great friend you are to Duncan."

"Never," says Vachel, rising from his chair. "If anybody asks I'll say I hardly know him. Just to speak to. Which way you headed?"

"Good. The Lincoln. Let's go."

Vachel thinks he might mine coal. He waits on Duncan Mc-Donald's doorstep in the late afternoon, thinking that he will mine coal with Duncan.

The sun blazes huge and red, low in the sky. He wonders who shot at Duncan last night. The thought of being shot at is terrifying, and he imagines that Duncan is terrified and will come home through the alleys. Who would shoot at Duncan? He shivers slightly. He would rather be shot at, though, than shoot.

Then he sees him, and he comes ambling long-legged up the street with the sun behind him, a perfect target, Vachel thinks, silhouetted black against the low, red sun, a tall, thin man, wiry, mostly arms and legs, and Vachel stands and walks toward Duncan, and for a fraction of a second Duncan slows his pace and stiffens, and then he sees that he who might have been a foe is only Vachel, and he quickens the pace again, and they meet and turn together up Duncan's walk. Duncan sets his lunchpail on the stoop, takes his mail from the box, and he unlocks the door, and they enter. "You go to work before the mail comes," Vachel observes. "I'd have to change my habits."

"Much before," says Duncan. He studies the envelopes before opening them, and Vachel offers an opinion to the effect that he sleeps best in the later morning hours because he usually writes until midnight or after, and Duncan, in turn, offers the opinion that a man must choose between the pen and the pick. "They don't mix," he says. "I've told you before. Forget it."

And Vachel thinks, seeing Duncan, seeing how Duncan is honorably black from the dust of the mine, and how he is tired but somehow tired in a healthy way, that if a man—Vachel, say—went into the mines and dug the coal he could then claim a rightful place in his city because he would then be like other men; and if he Vachel were like other men and labored as they do at dirty but honorable labor he would then belong to the city in a way he does not now belong. He phrases the thought aloud.

"Absolute nonsense," says Duncan. "Sometimes you talk nonsense." His teeth are very white and his tongue very red against the deep black of his dust-black face. He wears a big green union button on his cap, and when he removes his cap his forehead is half-white and half-black and his hair is pressed flat where the cap was. He stands reading his mail, fingering the switch of the light attached to the cap. He has always thought it a mockery that the light makes the cap heavy; he says sometimes that if he were a poet he would write a poem on that theme, how the light makes the cap heavy.

"I hear that somebody shot at you," says Vachel. "With a gun."

"It wasn't a bow and arrow."

"Doesn't it worry you? Who did it?"

"Sure it worries me. I don't know." He tosses his mail aside. "Company people I suppose. That'd be the safest guess. About nine-thirty it was. There was a bunch of us on the way home walking in a bunch down Sixth just this side of—I think—Jefferson. I forget just where because I took off, not exactly pausing as I went. There's too many men losing fingers in the couplers and we had a meeting and some men I never saw before came by in a black car. Never saw the car before. They pulled up to the curb beside. They said 'Which is Duncan McDonald?' and we all sort of guessed what was up. I guess it's an instinct maybe, and we all scattered every which way, and somebody spotted me from the car. So I guess there was somebody in on it that knew me. I don't know who. I sure wish I knew who. But he must of known me because I was the one that was fired at. I kept moving right along." He removes his jacket and his shirt, and he invites Vachel to join him in the bathroom. He plugs the sink and runs the water and mixes a gritty powder with the water and washes the black from his arms and his neck and his face.

"If I applied at the mines would they take me? Would I belong to the union first or afterward?"

Duncan talks into the water, bubbling and talking at once. "You got two legs, two arms? They'll take you. Sometimes they'll take you with less. Get you cheaper that way. You'd sign on first and join the union after. But don't be a fool. What do you want to go around all your life creeping and crawling on your belly? Man was born to walk vertical. Besides. I didn't tell you. I'm thinking I might quit it."

That would change things. Part of the glory of mining, of course, is the idea of Duncan. Vachel has had the picture of Duncan and himself side by side down in the mine. He would simply ask to be put to work beside Duncan, and there would be plenty of time for good talk together.

"If I could get some capital I been thinking I might open a book-shop." He rubs his face vigorously with a rough towel, and his skin glows pink. He is clean again. He dips a toothbrush into a second gritty soap. "It gets into your teeth something awful. I think it gets beyond them down to where you can't brush it out. It's the places that you can't brush out that worry me."

"You'd be a capitalist," says Vachel. He stands beside Duncan with his arms folded, fairly certain that he has now put an end to Duncan's bookshop plans.

"You can be a capitalist and not believe in capitalism," says Duncan, his mouth full of toothbrush. "You suppose slaves believed in slavery?"

Vachel likes the idea of a bookshop better than the idea of the mines. In an instant the bookshop becomes a reality. He sees him-self selling books across the counter. "You'd need a good clerk."

"I'd need somebody I could trust."

"I am available."

"Given up mining, have you? Given up writing?"

"You don't make a living writing."

"You don't make a living doing anything else. You live. You eat. Is that living? Stick to your pen, boy. Write books for me to sell. There's light in books." Vachel follows Duncan to the bedroom, and Duncan changes into gray trousers and brown shoes and a white shirt and a bright tie, and the tie is ragged where he has plucked at loose threads. "Let's go get some supper," he says. "I'd sort of like to get back before dark tonight."

Vachel tells Mama she need not rise early with him, but she does. Every morning as he comes downstairs he smells the good break-fast odors rising from the fresh fires of the stove, and Mama stands sleepy-eyed waiting for him, and she kisses him and takes the warm food from the stove and places it on the table before him beside the halved grapefruit or the quartered orange or the blue-black prunes or whatever and she neatly cuts the toast into triangles and spreads the butter, and the coffee tumbles black into his cup.

He is grumpy these mornings. Mama brings him his necktie and he slips it over his head and pulls the knot against his neck without looking up from his cup. "Twenty of," says Mama, and at length he brings the cup to his mouth just one more time, and then he rises and Mama stands behind him with his coat, and she walks with him to the door and opens it standing out of the draft, and then she closes it behind him and goes to the window and pushes aside the curtain and watches him move with a swaying, sleep-walking motion down Fifth and out of sight. He does not turn to wave.

Afterward, on Capitol, he moves east with the crowd in the freshness and cleanness of the early morning, and why do they come from warm beds to breathe the morning between home and shop and home and office and then hide themselves away? It is not worth it. If he is going to leave his bed why tantalize himself with a quarter hour in the clear, clean morning? What for? It is not as if, at the end of the day, he will have the strength to write and draw.

In the musty room at the end of the corridor in City Hall the gray cabinets are choked, and every year one third of the cabinets are emptied into a bin in the basement, and every three years one bin is carted away in a truck and the papers burned, and everything is alphabetical, all the paid bills going alphabetical through the cycle from cabinet to basement to flame. On a table in a box marked FILE the new day's work lies before him, and Willis was right as Willis is often right, it is boring boring as hell and the pink slips must never be mixed with the white. Mordecai Turner explains it all to Vachel wearing in his coat a medal that Willis put there after Mordecai's twenty-fifth year. Mordecai thinks Willis is as great as if not greater than Woodrow Wilson. He has a wife and five grown children and twenty-one relatives, and Mordecai leads them by the hand to the polls whenever Willis is up for election. Willis said it would bore Vachel and it does. Vachel lunches each day with Mordecai Turner, and he feels now a feeling of belonging, and he walks with the people in the morning, and he lunches with them at noon and leaves with them in a group at night, and he is like everyone else in his coming and going. He is not outcast, and A is for Johnny Appleseed striding westward alone planting seeds as he goes and leaving new trees in straight rows behind and B is for Daniel Boone blazing his peaceful way west and B is for General Booth of the Salvation Army the only general who never fired a gun and C is for Christ and Crane and Clemens and old Columbus found the wrong place but at least he went somewhere beyond the curve of the earth looking for the place with Marco Polo opened at his table before him and Marco Polo went places Columbus did not stay home filing pink slips in gray cabinets for Queen Isabella and D is for Debs and Duncan McDonald and E for Ezekiel went blowing his trumpet and warning the people F for Saint Francis Lord God bless those who peaceably endure.

"Not that it matters," says Mordecai to Vachel. "It all gets burned up anyway. But I like a man who takes a job and does the best he can."

"I'm doing the best I can. You can't expect a man to understand all this complicated procedure right off the bat."

"True," says Mordecai.

"They've been working on this confounded alphabet ever since the Greeks and you can't expect a man to pick it up all in a week."

"No you can't," says Mordecai, and at night, undressing, forgotten pink slips slide from Vachel's pocket fall to the floor he leaves them there tumbles into bed thinking G for Henry George and H for Hiram College and the good old days and I for Ingersoll and Ishmael exiled to the desert for marrying wrong, and up and down the alphabet derived from the Greek and letters swim before his eyes and the last thing he sees before sleep is Mordecai's medal bouncing B for boredom on Mordecai's B for breast.

At the end of the week he sees Willis, and on Monday he begins work at the pumping plant, and Mama feeds him two eggs instead of one in the morning, and there is no need for a necktie.

At least it is outdoors. There are blisters across his palms, and after two days the blisters harden and become flesh. He wheels cement with two men who do not speak English. They wheel their barrows along the boards placed end to end from the mixer to the pump. They show Vachel how to tip the barrow handles upward roll the light load easy you do not carry much cement that way but you do not care and the men at the mixers do not care and the masons do not care. The job pays a man enough to feed him and house him more or less and give him the strength to come again tomorrow.

After a week he is accustomed to the pain in his back. It is as if he has always had the pain and he would miss it if it were not there as a nagging spouse is missed after he or she is gone, and it cannot go on for long as it could not go on for long in Mr. Marshall Field's basement, as he has never been able to remain anywhere for long. He wants to write, and he does not want to do anything else. He

wants to be saying things because there seems to be so much in
need of saying, and suddenly he is aware that something invisible
like the invisible thing that crushed Bryan is crushing him, too, and
forcing him into silence, even as Susan sad-eyed forbade him to
make his speech long ago.

And after the second week Vachel quits his job at the pumping
plant and the pain in his back eases and disappears and his head-
aches stop and the hard calluses soften, and perhaps he will never
write good poetry at all but he will never know until he writes a
long time and writes all the bad poems out of his system. He does
not feel that a man can write good poetry at night after wheeling
cement all day. In his room he sits round-shouldered at his table
writing poems and making notes for more, and A is for Abraham
Lincoln and B is for Bryan and C is for the colored races and D is
for Daniel in the lions' den and Z is for Zion and Y for Yankee Doodle and W for Booker T. Washington. He wishes he were a centi-
pede and could write with his feet.

4

Newsboys on bicycles three abreast proud and important fall
away down the side streets and send the papers skimming above
the lawns and sliding along the porches to a final stop against the
front doors, and the ambitious boys, the ones who will get somewhere in life, double back to the *Journal* for another loud stand
shouting *paper paper* at the busy corners. They do not shout *Journal*. Everyone knows it is the *Journal*. There is no other.

And it is read, and it is believed. "I saw it in the *Journal* and it
must be true." Except that it is not what is said that is truth alone,
but what is never said and what will never be said so long as one
million dollars are required to launch a newspaper.

In Norval Taylor's union printing establishment Norval with
infinite patience goes over the figures with Vachel. "You see," says
Norval, "it don't come cheap."

"Then I'll go broke," says Vachel.

"All very well. But I can't do business that way."

"I don't expect you to. I'll go broke alone. You see," says Vachel,
"going broke is a way to show them. You can get crucified for an
idea or sent to jail or burned at the stake. But the thing that really
convinces people is when you go broke."

"Anything you say."

Together they go over the job again. Vachel edits very carefully, and editing is not an easy thing for him because Vachel is fond, perhaps overly fond, of every word he has written. It seems a shame to strike thoughts he struggled hard to capture. "I find," says Norval, "that after you edit it out you never miss it. Sometimes I'll edit on my own a little here and there and the customer never notices."

"I'd notice."

"There's a knack," says Norval. "Look. Here." He reads: "Many of the Statehouse Politicians and all of the Country Club people utterly abhor this ideal. Their bitterest sneer and deepest hate are for those who take the ideal seriously. Okay. Many of the Statehouse Politicians. Out. Many politicians. All of the Country Club people. Country Club means people automatically. So: All the Country Club. Utterly abhor. Now when you abhor you might just as well leave it at that and not do it utterly. Let's take the whole thing. Many politicians and the Country Club abhor this ideal. Their sneers and hatred are for those who take it seriously. Ideal is understood so there's no sense repeating it. That saves half an inch. So the Springfield craftsman will hammer out other things than horseshoes on these anvils for the next hundred years." Norval touches his pencil to his tongue. "Okay. Springfield will hammer other things than horseshoes for the next century. I knocked you out eight words."

"But that's not how I wanted it."

"Well you ain't a millionaire. When you're a millionaire you can write like Shakespeare."

"No, I want it the way I had it. And I think I'll raise the price to five cents."

Norval whistles between his teeth. "Why not make it five dollars while you're at it?" They will not sell, and Norval knows it. (A decade hence they will sell for five dollars apiece.)

"You're a Gloomy Gus," says Vachel.

"I'm a realist."

"So am I. Five cents."

In the big manila envelopes two for five at Coe's Book Store Vachel fires his poetry east, and it almost always comes back, and each time the postman comes along Fifth Street with Vachel's ma-

nila envelopes jutting from his leather pouch it is an instant of tor-
ture, a moment of doubt, and the postman strolls smiling up the
walk, and Vachel smiles back. "Nice day." "Fine day, fine day,"
and Vachel takes the mail from the postman's hand and shuffles through it and turns and climbs the steps to the house.

It comes back. It almost always comes back. The returning
envelope is addressed in Vachel's own hand and creased down
the middle where he folded it when he sent it, hoping as he did so
that it would never be in his hands again, that the poem would be
bought and printed. But it comes back self-addressed, and the
poem within did not set the world on fire the editors regret they
are reluctantly compelled to return the enclosed it becomes necessary to give precedence to other contributions the editor begs to
be excused from the ungracious task of criticism comes back with
a printed form and sometimes a few words in ink too radical sir both
stylistically and from the standpoint of idea sir are you acquainted
with our magazine it is often helpful to study our magazine before
contributing in order better to conform with our style.

But Vachel will not conform because he wants to write poetry
the way he wants to write it, and perhaps someday somebody will
publish it. He will live to be one hundred and five.

And the envelopes rebuke him, saying perhaps you are not a poet
perhaps you are merely convinced you are a poet the way all madmen wander about convinced they are Christ or build themselves
an ark convinced the world will end on such and such a day, the
way they are convinced all the world is crazy but them.

He tells himself he is a poet, and when there is delay, two weeks,
three weeks, and no envelopes, his hopes rise and he tells himself
this is it! and a day later the envelopes come in a flurry and he is
madman again and it is hard to say fine day fine day to the postman. (Current Literature accepts one poem. And out of New York
the city of stone an editor-poet named Witter Bynner writes to say
he admires Vachel's work, and Vachel promptly sends Witter Bynner one hundred poems with instructions to throw out the bad ones
and show the rest around to all the editors he knows, and Witter
culls thirty and almost sells the rest to Small, Maynard & Company, book publishers. Almost, but not quite, and for two months,
while Small Maynard is reading his poems he is buoyed by the vision of his poems in a book. He awaits the postman each morning,
and each morning he peers hopefully for the publisher's envelope

and the letter which will say Dear Vachel pardon our delay in writing you concerning the seventy poems but without further delay
permit us to say we will publish them with pleasure and distribute
them with energy and support them with all the resources at our
command. Folks will sit up and take notice in Springfield. Folks
do not read widely in Springfield, and assuredly they do not read
books of poetry, but they must respect anyone who has written a
book and furthermore had it published. He will be vindicated, and
people will not laugh behind his back as now they laugh, sneer.
They do not laugh and sneer to his face, but he knows they laugh
and sneer, and it is painful, and the letter comes at last *Dear
Mr. Lindsay We are returning to you the poems Mr. Witter Bynner
so kindly recommended to our attention we do not feel we are in a
position to publish them at this time,* and the blow rocks him and
fills him with new doubt about himself: how long can a poet go on
writing for himself and his Mama and his Papa and a few friends?
A poet must be heard. He does not write for his own amusement.)

Meanwhile, while waiting, he writes long letters to Witter Bynner telling Bynner how he started the War Bulletins and told all
Springfield to go to hell in so many words on the first page and how
he supposes he (Vachel) has worms in his skull please tell Small
Maynard if they take the seventy poems he will allow them to publish a further volume. Long long letters with no objective point,
concerned only with the pleasant Sabbath morning and the noises
of little birds outside his window and the sun in the Governor's yard
and by the way he is sending along a new poem The Rose and the
Lotus because he (Bynner) is good enough to like Vachel's poems
and because there must be someone to talk to sometimes he thinks
he will pick up and go calling on poets in England. How does that
strike you would you care to come along?

And Witter is perplexed because he has written to other poets
and they do not come pouring out their hearts through the mail. He
reads the long letters with fascination, and by the time he has answered one there are two more on his desk. This is a strange fellow
that empties himself to someone he has never met. Witter rereads
the letters at a single sitting. He replies briefly, but he destroys the
reply. People cannot return cry for cry. What does one write to a
stranger sitting somewhere in a place called Springfield Illinois
why does he not leave and go somewhere else?

Long long letters from somewhere in the sticks because no one will listen to him or publish him or believe in him Dear Witter Bynner you must write to me sir here in Springfield lonely as hell and brimstone.

War Bulletin Number One settles slowly into the receiving tray of Norval Taylor's press. Norval brings the crank of the press to the position of rest, wipes his hands with a long downward motion on the skirt of his apron and reaches into the tray. He holds the ink-wet pamphlet aloft between the tips of his fingers, scans it and hands it to Vachel.

At the table in his room he sits looking at the mountain of printed matter and wonders just what he will do with seven hundred declarations of war. There are no boys on bicycles to carry them up and down the side streets and to hawk them at Sixth and Capitol because the boys do not work for the love of labor. It is money that makes the mare go. Duncan is right. And there are no advertisers and no easy Billy Sunday answers, no contests, no comics, no sports, no classified advertisements, no social page, only Mammon the soul of the spider leering from the pages, and a man carrying a banner and marching in something called a Village Improvement Parade, and across the banner it is written FAIR STREETS ARE BETTER THAN SILVER GREEN PARKS ARE BETTER THAN GOLD.

There is an attack upon the Country Club. Vachel does not plan to sell many copies at the Country Club.

It occurs to him that he will not sell many copies anywhere. He thinks he will go into the street and sell them the way he sold his poems in New York. The thought chills him. It begins to look to him like a dead loss and he should have figured out before he printed it just how he was going to sell it, and now it is too late and the Bulletins in piles of fifty sit on his table declaring war in a voice so low that nobody hears and nobody runs with fear or sets to work rebuilding the city according to the instruction of the Bulletin.

He thinks he will give it away. He will send it to all the friends he ever had, to the union halls where he spoke for the Anti-Saloon League, to all the little magazines, and he will look up all the addresses of all the poets he ever heard of. He will put a pile on the table of the YMCA reading room. Somehow he no longer has the nerve to go peddling door to door as he did in New York. He supposes he should not have declared war unless he was prepared to carry it through to the end; he is not the soldier he was, no longer so young, no longer so strong, and money makes the mare go makes the wheels go round or so it is said, and he has no money and a war cannot be fought without money.

Yet there must be further War Bulletins because he states in the first that there will be, and for once in his life he must go through with something and do it complete and not run away as he has run away every time he sensed disaster. God help us to be brave!

He has saved a little money from the City Hall job and from the pumping-plant job. It is somewhere in this room and he will find it, and he will mail the Bulletins as far as the money will take them, and he will give them away in Springfield to anyone who will take them. This (he vows) is the last plunge, the last tract. Dear Witter Bynner hereafter I surrender to the age.

It is a bad dream. At Coe's Book Store, on the magazine rack beside The Saturday Evening Post, War Bulletin Number Two (its price reduced from five cents to nothing, henceforth as free as bread and butter in a hospitable house please pass the fire from mind to mind and the labor is amply rewarded) catches the August breeze through the open door. And free as it is it is not bought. It is maddening. In and out of Coe's all day the people come, and one day, for a full hour, Vachel stands and watches the people, and they inspect the magazine rack, and sometimes, curious, read the announcement concerning the new price, and they smile but do not trouble themselves to carry a Bulletin away, and sometimes they read down the column of his lead editorial, *Why I Fight,* but they are not interested. "A *Post* and a *Journal,*" they say. Is that all they can say? Can they not be roused or angered? They cannot, and it is a bad dream. The people come and go along the same route every day a *Post* and a *Journal* and it does not interest them that Vachel makes war upon them.

They are not afraid of him. If only they were afraid of him and would shoot at him at night as they shoot at Duncan! He is as dangerous as Duncan, and he cannot make them see it: he would change their lives and make them march in a Village Improvement Parade and take away their gold and make them worship God instead and take away their charity games and make them worship universal plenty and take away their miracles and make them worship possibilities.

He declares his conviction that beggary is the noblest occupation of man!

It is there in print and they will not read it and become incensed.

He asserts his intention to beg tomorrow and forever rather than write a line he does not want to write!

And they do not care if he begs he may remain and beg or leave no one cares what he does with his life there are no sentries along the roads leading from Springfield. They would not miss him if he left. They scarcely know that he is here. They ignore him. They do not care what he writes about or what he will not write about.

War Bulletin Number Two, plentifully remaindered on his closet shelf.

War Bulletin Number Three. Christ is a Socialist. Saint Francis the king of the beggars is the noblest of all the saints. Heaven? He is skeptical about Heaven.

I want you to join my gang! I do not want to join yours!

And they do not care whom he joins or whether he joins at all a *Post* and a *Journal* the key is in the river and the door is never locked he may go when he pleases.

At least they hated Lincoln and hanged John Brown and chased Ingersoll out of Illinois and lynched Lovejoy. At least they shoot at Duncan and despise Jack Johnson, and why does the printed word not stir them to wrath. At least they made Dante leave town.

But if the people think about Vachel at all it is to say that he is put up to it by Duncan and the Socialists or by Rabbi Tedesche and the Jews (there is an article concerning Jews in War Bulletin Number Five) or by the minority wing of the Democrats (the fine hand of Willis Spaulding behind the scenes), something they put him up to down at Maydie Lee's. But they do not think about Vachel much. There are always odd sticks with special messages, and they come and go and have always come and gone, and it never matters. They are swallowed whole and laughed down and ignored and their banners fall to the dust and their books go out of print and their pamphlets yellow and wither, and business proceeds as usual. The river is never diverted in its bed.

"The thing to do," says Vachel to Norval, "is to make it a decade magazine. I'll put it out in twenty and then again in thirty and forty and so forth."

"Anything you say," says Norval. "If I'm here you come see me." They shake hands.

On the twenty-ninth of May wearing high-topped brogans yellow corduroy pants a bright green flannel shirt a black sombrero, and carrying War Bulletins and a pamphlet entitled Rhymes To Be Traded For Bread printed by Norval Taylor on a pay-when-able basis, Vachel walks west against the crowds on Capitol Avenue. He thinks he will stroll to California.

CHAPTER TWO

Land of the free. 1912. 1913.

Gainesville Florida. On the railroad platform a white man pokes his hand up through the open window of the coach. "Mr. Washington, let me shake your hand." Booker T. Washington reaches down, and the white hand clasps the brown. "Mr. Washington, you're the greatest man in this country."

"Oh now," says Washington, "what about Teddy Roosevelt?"

"Used to be I thought Roosevelt was the greatest. But then he ate dinner with you and that queered him with me."

Las Vegas Nevada. In a return match Jack Johnson toys with Jim Flynn for nine rounds and cuts him up and pounds him where it hurts, and finally, when he feels like it, when he is good and ready, he sends Jim Flynn to sleep. Folks don't like it.

Washington D. C. The Anti-Saloon League calls for a Constitutional Amendment to institute prohibition.

Illinois. Women win the vote seven years before women win it nationally.

Senator William Lorimer, a black-mustached Chicago lumberman, is recalled by the people of the State, and unseated. The people cannot be fooled all of the time.

Springfield Illinois. The public schools are thrown open for political meetings, thus bringing politics out of the back rooms, or so it is hoped; with women casting ballots for the first time the people outvote the private companies by six hundred and sixty-eight votes to win a public light-and-power plant.

The New Nationalism is supplanted by The New Freedom. The Square Deal. Ninety million self-governing people. Arizona and New Mexico join the Union and the flag has forty-eight stars and the people rejoice in the new bigness. They see progress in bigness. Parcel post and the income tax, a Secretary of Labor, the direct election of Senators.

The people. The common man. The celebrated man in the street. The farmer and the factory worker, shopkeeper, schoolteacher. He rejoices in

160

his bigness and his strength and the way America grows from the sea to the sea. (When he says America he means the United States.)

Panama. The French could not build the canal but America can build it, can resist disease and sliding earth and make the oceans do what America wants them to do.

Two hundred and forty million cubic yards of earth!

Four hundred million dollars!

A lock canal, and nobody ever thought of *that* before!

It is magnificent, and the people are proud of themselves and the way they build eternities on shifting sands and the way they govern themselves, and they have a right to be proud.

They are good people. There are no better people on the face of the earth or between the covers of the history books.

They will labor for days to pull a kitten from a well, and they will go sleepless a week to nurse an ailing neighbor, and they will go five hundred miles to a funeral believing they are honoring the dead and comforting the bereaved, and they will give nickels and dimes to build a church to God or a monument to a hero or for any cause described to them as good, and they will send green bills through the mails to total strangers, and they will plow a neighbor's fields and adopt orphaned children and build red-brick schoolhouses and go hungry to educate their children, and they will believe anything that is printed or spoken from a pulpit or a platform or shown to them in a picture or on a label or in a catalogue or told to them by a salesman because most people are honest and do not quite believe there is dishonesty in others, lechery, avarice, gluttony and sloth in salesmen, preachers, pleaders and professors.

They are for the right and against the wrong, and they believe that bigness is progress and a soldier's death is honor, and they believe they govern themselves because no one has shown them different. They do not easily recognize illusions.

Yet it is not wholly an illusion: the people unburdened themselves of a King, and in time they overthrew slavery, and along the way they taught themselves to read and write, and they reduced the length of the working day, and they took children from the factories and sent them into red-brick schoolhouses, and they do not lynch or riot as much as they once did, and they do not pass the death sentence so often or imprison the insane any longer. Little by little they have won for themselves prerogatives no people ever possessed, and by sheer weight of numbers, despite literacy that is not wholly education, bigness that is not progress and a freedom that is not wholly freedom, despite illusion dressed as reality the people move forward, seeing sooner or later through the mist of words and deception, sifting true from false and right from wrong.

And in the welter of the names and events of their short history the heroes that were never really heroes fall by the way, and the men who made revolution remain. The heroes are Washington, Jefferson, Jackson and Lincoln, Emerson, Thoreau, Roosevelt, Wilson.

"The people have a right to make their own mistakes." The mistakes: a quick happy war with Spain; the time we ran out on Bryan. And maybe it is not us, the people, because we are good. Maybe it is the system, like Mr. Wilson says. Maybe it is our unregulated self, like Teddy Roosevelt says.

Baltimore. Bryan behind and pushing, and the words sound familiar, and the Convention dumps Clark for Wilson. (A young fellow answers the roll from New York: F. Roosevelt. Related? Hell no, sixth cousin, something like that.) And Wilson says *So what we have to discuss is not wrongs which individuals intentionally do—I do not believe there are a great many of those. There are some men of that sort. I don't know how they sleep o' nights—but the wrongs of a system* sounding like Debs the Socialist but still and all a Democrat. (And we always go and hear Debs, the whole family of us goes, but we never vote for him the Democrat man brung a turkey Thanksgiving and a candy stocking Christmas.)

Chicago in August. Bull Moose. Theodore Roosevelt. *Property shall be the servant of the people and not the master* and they sing Onward Christian Soldiers and Battle Hymn of the Republic, and, to the tune of The Wearing of the Green:

> We stand at Armageddon and we battle for the Lord,
> And all we ask to stead us is a blessing on each sword;
> And tribes and factions mingle in one great fighting clan,
> Who issue to the battle behind a fighting man.
> Then let the traitor buckle and the falterer go fawn,
> We only ask to follow where the battle line is drawn.
>
> We stand at Armageddon, where fighting men have stood,
> And creeds and races mingle in one common brotherhood,
> And here from day to darkness, we battle for the Lord;
> Thy blessing, great Jehovah, grant on each impatient sword.
> And in the righteous conflict we pledge one sacred word;
> We stand at Armageddon and we battle for the Lord!

And it sounds like songs they sing in a Socialist meeting or a union hall, but it is not socialism it is Roosevelt. And those are the words and they were always the words here in America, and they will always be the words and a man can vote for them and still get his turkey and his candy stocking. But it is not Wilson or Roosevelt who brings it about.

It is the people pushing upward pushing someone pushing John Peter Altgeld pushing Bryan pushing Wilson, the people in their own slow way.

Chicago in June. "We are the party of Abraham Lincoln." Honest and unresisting, Mr. Taft clings to what he thinks and says what he means: The word dollardiplomacy is born. He opposes Initiative and Referendum. He looks about him and he finds that the corporations are not in politics the way some people say they are, and that is the way he sees it. *Why should we be afraid to tell the people that they are not fitted to select high judicial officers? They are not.* "We are the party of Abraham Lincoln."

And the people given a chance will vote for what they want because the people are not as dumb as some people think.

A myth? The people a myth?

Add it up! Split it three ways among Roosevelt, Wilson and Debs, and still there are only two states left for Mr. Taft and something that once was the party of Abraham Lincoln.

General William Booth dies.

The people mourn. And they mourn because they believe the Salvation Army saved lives and fed the hungry and was truly devoted to God, and it did, and it was, and people are forever reaching out to help other people, and forever reaching for God.

Perhaps it is true, as some of his critics say, that General Booth helped people but did not help mankind, but all he knew was people, and mankind never came to his door, only people, and he organized the City Colony and the Farm Colony and the Household Salvage Brigade and Rescue Homes For Fallen Women and the Deliverance For The Drunkard and the Prison-Gate Parade. He was the Poor Man's Bank and the Poor Man's Lawyer, and he was so busy feeding the poor and sobering the drunk and rescuing fallen women all his life that he never had time to change the system or find out why drunkards drank why women whored and why the poor were poor, and he was so busy running from troops in England and police in America he never had time to do anything but lead his Army.

A book: *In Darkest England and the Way Out.*

He dies blind, and people mourn, and he never saved the world, but he saved a few people. It is a thing people can understand and weep in their beds about because most people, even in this new time of Wilson and Roosevelt, cannot see clear to the roots of things. Not yet. They mourn him because, like them, he labored to pull the kitten from the well.

Chicago. A tiny lady named Harriet Monroe, a pince-nez jiggling across the bridge of her nose, rents an office on Cass Street and furnishes it with a desk and a chair and two empty file cabinets and a wicker rocker for visitors, if any. Downstairs and around the corner is an Italian restaurant called Luca's. It will be an intimate place to take guests, if any. At Luca's wine is served before, with, and after meals, and all poets love wine. Across the door of her office it says: Poetry: A Magazine of Verse, except that as yet there has not been an issue of the magazine and no stampede of poets to Cass Street, and not much chance of a magazine of verse surviving in Chicago or anywhere else.

There has been little poetry in the land since Whitman. There have been Robinson, Stephen Crane, Moody, and Markham and one or two others, and Markham is known for one poem alone and Crane and Moody are dead, and only two magazines in the land willing to print good poetry: in St. Louis William Marion Reedy publishes his Mirror; in New York John Sloan and Art Young and Robert Minor spark the radical Masses, and these magazines are not on reading tables in almost every home the way The Saturday Evening Post is. The chances are that Miss Monroe will flounder and at length lock her door and go away disappointed and re-educated.

But this is the time of Wilson, and Bryan at his right hand, and a great hope in the land after the long silence, and everything and anything is possible. Harriet Monroe writes letters to all the poets she knows of, at home and abroad. She writes to anyone she thinks might possibly invest a little money in a magazine of verse. And there come in reply a great flood of good poetry, and warm letters, and money from people who are not poets but who hate to see poetry dying its slow death in the dark, and time and again the magazine will linger on the point of death, and it will not die. "We hope to offer our subscribers a place of refuge, a green isle in the sea, where Beauty may plant her gardens, and Truth, austere revealer of joy and sorrow, of hidden delights and despairs, may follow her brave quest unafraid." Each issue of the magazine is to carry Whitman's words: "To have great poets there must be great audiences, too."

There is never a great audience. In its very best days there are three thousand readers. But for the poets Poetry is escape from darkness and silence to a place where they may be seen and heard and write the new poetry their own way. A green isle in the sea. New poetry. New poets and a new diction *Chicago, Hog-Butcher for the world, Tool-maker, Stacker of Wheat, Stormy, husky, brawling, City of the Big Shoulders: They tell me you are wicked*, and out of Chicago come new voices. Harriet Monroe's pince-nez will jiggle triumphantly on the bridge of her nose.

Until now nobody has ever heard of the Illinois poets—Carl Sandburg up from Galesburg, Edgar Lee Masters of the Spoon River Valley, Vachel Lindsay up from Springfield; a Missouri bank clerk named Eliot, Sara Teasdale from St. Louis, a farmer named Frost, a hundred more.

Nobody has yet heard of a midwestern paint manufacturer named Sherwood Anderson of Winesburg Ohio; of Sinclair Lewis from Zenith; of the young men and the young women of the long valley of the Mississippi, the valley of Huckleberry Finn, of revolt in the villages against Mammon driving poetry beyond incorporated limits to the point of death in darkness.

Something called The Literary Revival, packaged in the books between the zero years and the Twenties.

1

NOTES ON a further journey.

In the early evening on an abandoned railroad siding just west of Jacksonville Illinois an old man sits on an upturned crate stemming gooseberries. "Evening," says Vachel, removing his hat and rubbing a hand along the sweatband.

"Evenin," says the man, looking up. "What you got?"

"Poems and pictures."

"Ain't got no money. Eating berries and livin in this here boxcar and not buying so much as a loaf a bread on the market."

"I'm not selling anything. I'm trading poems for bread. Or if not bread, then something to eat. And a place to sleep."

"Preacher?"

"Preaching a gospel of beauty."

"Damn good idea. Take a load off your feet."

Vachel squats on the ground beside the man and they stem berries together until it is too dark to see, and then they get up stiffly and wipe the pale juice from their hands and climb into the abandoned boxcar. The old man lights a lantern. "Go ahead and read me," he says, "and then show me your pictures. Pull up a box." Vachel slides his drawings and poems from the waterproof oilcloth in which he carries them. "Got any good pension poems?" says the man, leaning back on the crate that serves as a chair. "Have some berries. There oughta be some good pension poems wrote, and some prohibition poems and some poems on the sins a preachers."

"I'll read the titles and you take your pick. The King of Yellow Butterflies."

"Oh hell."

"The Grave of the Righteous Kitten."

"Nope."

"Why I Fled from Duty."

"That's more like it. Keep a-goin."

"The Soul of a Butterfly. Indirectly it's a pension poem. According to my scheme the butterfly is beauty pitted against Mammon. Mammon is the soul of the spider."

"Keep a-goin."

"Machinery."

"Let's try 'er."

Vachel reads Machinery and the old man listens attentively, tilting his head to one side, but not fully understanding. "What else?"

"The Perfect Marriage."

"Hell, that's all dead and forgot with me. I had two wives and they didn't turn out."

"The Leaden-Eyed."

"Give it a whirl."

And Vachel reads: "Let not young souls be smothered out before they do quaint deeds and fully flaunt their pride. It is the world's one crime its babes grow dull, its poor are ox-like, limp and leaden-eyed. Not that they starve, but starve so dreamlessly, not that they sow, but that they seldom reap, not that they serve, but have no gods to serve, not that they die but that they die like sheep," and the old man says read it again, and Vachel reads it again.

"Now there's a damn fine poem. Who wrote it?"

"I did. I wrote all these."

"No."

"Really."

"Well gimme more a them kind."

And Vachel reads Dreams in the Slum and his poem on Lorimer the unseated Senator, and his Altgeld poem, and the old man sits straight and still, listening, *sleep on O brave-hearted O wise man that kindled the flame—to live in mankind is far more than to live in a name.*

"Them's damn fine poems. That's what she oughta be. Pension poems, not tulips and lilacs and all like that. That Lorimer! Hep yourself to berries. Eat your berries and I'll sing," and the old man goes to a dark corner of the boxcar and brings forth a guitar and dusts it with his sleeve and seats himself again. "I know some you'll like," and he plays John Brown's Body and Hell's Broke

Loose in Georgia, singing high and excited, and now and then his voice cracks, and he refuses to notice or pause. "I got to play fast or die. Sing right along."

But Vachel cannot sing. The lantern light dies and the old man sings, and when he is weary he asks for the Altgeld poem again, and Vachel recites it and the old man sings until he is breathless. "I ain't used to it. Used to be I could sing all night and never get tired. Old guitar got a couple a flabberdy strings besides."

"It sounds fine," says Vachel.

"Well thanks," the old man says, and he returns the guitar to its place in the corner, and he pulls the sliding door closed. "You'll stay the night," he says. "Sleep flat out the long ways," and they lie the long way to avoid the raised crossboards, and the old man snores open-mouthed.

It is like the early journeys. Except that it is different, and the difference is in Vachel.

The countryside is the same, and the people are the same, and the difference can only be within himself, in the new understandings and the new outlooks, in new knowledge absorbed over time, the nights at Maydie Lee's and the things that Duncan McDonald said and the things Willis Spaulding said and the way they work in unalike ways toward much-alike goals.

And Vachel is older, and the sound of thirty is a young sound because it was a long time ago and now he is past thirty. And he has done a lot of thinking about the world and what it is and what it ought to be, isness and oughtness, and more specifically about poetry and what it should be and do and how it must talk about people in the language people speak and understand, and how it might even be necessary to discard all the old methods of poetry the way Dante threw Latin out the window and wrote in the language of the street, and Wordsworth did something of the same. The radical becomes traditional and there must then be a new radicalism, and the idea grows within him, and if he walks alone it will grow and form and come clear in his head and shape itself in his hands. It is not like the first journey when he walked alone.

Now he is not alone. With him, beside him, is the idea. He is pregnant. An idea, and on the road across Illinois the idea can be pondered. At home it is not possible to ponder. In Springfield a man is not properly observing his duties and obligations unless he is

visibly at work. He is not supposed to be sitting and thinking. He
is supposed to be digging with his hands or building or studying
business documents at a desk in an office or writing for the newspaper or preaching in a church or arguing the law.

Across the big river and into Missouri, and the countryside is as
it was on the earlier journeys, but it is seen differently. The big
river. The great Mississippi. Once there were steamboats lighted
at night, and music on the river, and he read in all the books of the
romance of the river, and it is still the same river but he does not
see steamboats or hear music: he sees frame houses on sagging stilts
beside the water, and the lean faces of the children, and young men
and young women walking old and stiff with dampness in their
joints, and at night there are steamboats and music and he must
try to put out of his mind the fact that in the darkness by the river
people live in rotting houses. And he cannot.

And he cannot go singlehanded and uproot the stilted houses
and carry the children to better land or carry the men and women
to dry places, but he can do the one thing he can do: he can write
his poetry and try with words to make people see and feel, cure
them of the disease indifference, fill them with a love of living and
the hope of change, and post his drawings on their walls and read
to them the three poems he describes as his theory and solution of
American civilization. "I am preaching a gospel of beauty."

Damn good idea.

At least on the earlier journeys there was a place to go, and now
there is nowhere. The place was home, and he loves Springfield and
wishes it may be another Athens another Florence another Oxford
and he went home and lived with that in mind, and he could not
remain home because they ignored him, and when they were not
ignoring him they were laughing at him. Now there is nowhere to
go. He cannot go home. He can only go on and on toward unfamiliar cities peopled with unfamiliar faces, and he wants to go
home. And he cannot. He tries not to think too much about himself.

He tries to think only of the poems yet to be written, and of how
he can write poems about people that people can read and understand,
poems in the American language full of American noises, and
maybe it will never be poetry for the ages, but at least it will be
poetry for now and help people here and now to improve their
world, and in every generation there will be better poetry, and eter-

nity will take care of itself in the hay in the stable near Warrensburg Missouri falls asleep thinking.

At breakfast (breakfast is not always part of the bargain, but it is usually offered) the farmer reads up and down the ponderous columns of the Kansas City *Star*. "Hmpf," he says.

"What?" says his wife.

"Old General Booth. He died."

West of Warrensburg Vachel strikes the Kansas City highway. He does not like the main highways speeding automobiles he does not like are noisy go too fast the idea of life is to slow down not speed up. The people in the cars rush by stare blank-faced at him, and sometimes children wave and he waves back, symbol of gasoline steel age at night two onrushing lights in a straight line through the darkness whatever they hit they hit do not care the road splashed with squashed animals died blinking into the lights. It does not seem to Vachel that the automobile is put to good use.

In the thorny hedges beside the road a red bird sings a song Vachel never heard before. He asks an old Negro man, "What is that bird? I never heard it before. No doubt a Missouri bird." "That's a Rachel-Jane," the old man says.

"Nothing else?"

"No. Juss Rachel-Jane." It sings *plee-whah plee-whah* and now and then its song is drowned by the noise of passing cars, but it does not stop singing, and Vachel's mind being what it is and operating the way it does he thinks the bird sings a protest, and he loves the Rachel-Janes because they protest as he himself protests goes wandering writes in his notes that beggary is an act of defiance and revolt.

In a way, it is lonely revolt. The road is lonesomeness and the people are nameless in the houses where he is sheltered and at the tables at which he eats, and suppose the revolt proves endless, what will happen to him then when he is too feeble to walk the roads, and where will he ever find a home, and the old Negro man asks, "Where is home at for you?" and Vachel is almost ashamed to say because of what happened there between Negroes and whites.

"Springfield," he says.

"Which one? There's a number a Springfields."

"Illinois."

"Wasn't Lincoln from there?"

"Yes he was."

"Well," and in the cabin with the Negro man and his wife Vachel recites and gives away some drawings of the Village Improvement Parade. He bathes in a tub behind the cabin, and they eat and pray together, and Vachel tells them stories he has heard of Lincoln.

"You ought to write a poem," the old man says.

"I've got one going."

"A real rosy poem," the old man says. "Somp'n I could read without my specs, and no Latin. I get to readin ever so often and then of a sudden—whosh—come to the rhyme and there's a mighty chunk a Latin spread out."

"No Latin," says Vachel, laughing.

"Nor no French."

"No. No French."

"Nothin but plain ole American."

Out of Belton Missouri on a line slanting south into Kansas, and the Rachel-Jane still singing in the hedges, and the sun hotter than it was earlier in the month. On the road, in the distance, a speck becomes a man, and a puff of dust rises beside him, and as Vachel walks the man grows larger and his arms are seen apart from his body, and his legs show themselves separate and distinct, one from the other, and the face assumes the pinkness of life, and the man grows and becomes alive in motion, and they meet. The man half-stops, hesitant, tentative. Vachel stops. "Loneliest damn state in the union," the man says.

"Well, I'm going clear through," says Vachel. "California."

"Harvestin?"

"No."

"Me neither. What you got when you're through? Smoke?"

"No. Thanks."

"Who's gonna win the fight?"

"Which fight is that?"

"Flynn and Johnson."

"Oh, I don't know," says Vachel. "What difference?"

"Heap a difference. Well. Think I'll push on. They'll be harvestin early on account a the hoppers if you're thinkin a harvestin. Smoke?"

"No thanks."

And the man moves on in a circle of dust and smoke, and in Kansas the grasshoppers raise midgins of dust in the road. They chew tiny round holes in green leaves. They climb up Vachel's trouser legs, and he shakes them to the ground. They get under his shirt, and they work their way inside his hat, and once, in the afternoon, awakening from a nap, he finds two large holes in his hat and a network of holes in his shirt. He scatters the grasshoppers with a sweep of his arm and they hop away, and always they return, and he cannot kill them. He thinks he might kill them, and the dead would be a warning to the living, and no one would ever know that he broke the rules of Saint Francis. Yet it does not matter whether anyone would know or not. *He* would know.

In the fields beside the road the farmers spray the trees and the earth with a white liquid and kill the hoppers in defense of the land and the crop.

It is a gesture, and a part of his protest, and Vachel cannot kill them though they eat holes in his clothing. They live, and he cannot kill something which lives, not even in the lonesomeness of the road where no one would know or see, and they spoil his sleep at night and eat away the sombrero which was new when he started, and his shirt. He thinks he might harvest a few days and earn enough money for a new shirt and a new hat and then get out of Kansas. The man was right: Kansas is the lonesomest state in the union.

The map shows big circles, and beside the circles are the names of towns, and when he arrives the town is a livery stable drugstore square wooden hotel all rolled in one. There are no saloons in Kansas, and he thinks at first he will like Kansas because the saloon is outlawed, but it is much like Missouri, and empty and silent at night and hot by day, and sometimes he is tempted to wire Papa for railroad fare and turn around and go home and fight it out in Springfield the best way he can. Sometimes he thinks the best thing to do is to surrender to the age and go home and be a proper boy as Papa advised him long long ago standing over him in the barn with a length of old harness in his hand.

And then, all the way through Kansas, in the instants of deepest loneliness, the Rachel-Jane sings against the noises of steel and gasoline, and at Osawatomie someone has erected a John Brown statue John Brown was never a proper boy, and at Emporia William Allen White edits the local paper, and the symbols give him strength and he pushes west with his clothes full of holes Osawatomie Emporia Cottonwood Falls Florence Newton Punkin Center north and west along the Arkansas River. And always when he is lowest in spirit, out of nowhere, at a turn in the road, at the crest of a hill, in a shelter from the rain, someone or something revives him and sends him hopeful westward again.

The Mennonite wheat is early and abundant, and ordinarily they do not hire people from the outside world. If they do, they do so with special care.

Among the Mennonites every man is a preacher. He wears a neck-tie whether in church or in the fields, and the women wear black because they think it mortifies the flesh, and they go barefoot, and the white of feet and hands and face against the black of their garb is not, to Vachel's eye, effective mortification. They are beautiful.

In the Mennonite lodge at night, before a low fire, he reads to them the poetry of his gospel, and they sit silent and do not show by word or face that they hear him. "Are you done?" an elder asks at length, and Vachel says yes, he supposes so, and the Mennonites rise and go through the fields to their cottages.

If it were not for the wheat they would not have him. He is pagan. In their church they will have no organ, and they have no leader because every man is a preacher, and everyone has read the one book many times; after they have gone Vachel sits in the lodge alone reading Menno Simonis' *The Wandering Soul* by the light of the dying fire.

The Mennonites sing from white hymnbooks. Singing, they are alive. They are a strict people. (In the fields the necktied men do not talk among themselves because talking is profane, and on the second day the silence begins to oppress Vachel. Beside him a young man bends at his work. "Did you ever hear about the swearing hen that laid deviled eggs?" says Vachel, and the young man straightens quickly and his lips tremble. "We do not tell jokes about swearing," says he. The young man begins to sing and thereby to cleanse himself, and up and down the line the others join him, not breaking the rhythm of their labor, singing *When I behold the wondrous cross on which the prince of glory died My richest gain I count but loss and pour contempt on all my pride. . . .*)

Yet they are a prideful people. They live in themselves and sing their own songs. They are hostile to strangers, and they will not undersell their wheat. They keep themselves fanatically clean.

And now and again a Mennonite boy or girl slips away in the night and disappears in the wide outside world, and his name is not spoken, and almost always he or she returns and the matter is never mentioned, and all the world's people but them will go to blazing fire in the end, and they recognize no way of the world but their own.

Every man is a preacher, but they do not seek converts. "In the end the world will come to us," an elder tells Vachel, and Vachel wishes he could feel that in the end the world will come to God, but he is not so confident as the Mennonite elder; he feels that each preacher must go to the world with the gospel hymns or the poems or whatever. But he does not argue with the elder. It would do no good.

They have settled all questions. They have found God within their fenced fields, and they worry a little but not too much about the price of wheat. They do not have a jail and they do not commit suicide and their doors have no locks and there are no madmen among them, and they own no automobiles because there is nowhere worth going, and they read only one book because all else is profane. They do not care what is decided beneath the dome at Topeka or in Washington or anywhere else, and they do not read the newspapers except to investigate the price of wheat, and Vachel wishes it all could be decided in his own life as it is in theirs.

But there is a world beyond the fences.

At Ellinwood with the money the Mennonites gave him Vachel buys a new suit of clothes. He reorganizes himself, slipping his belt from the old trousers through the loops of his new ones and almost leaving his wallet in the old pants but then remembering and going back. The wallet has in it the cardboard onto which he pasted the Browning lines Mama sent him at Hiram, and it would be a shame to lose it.

"Harvestin?" the haberdasher asks.

"Yes."

"Plenty a harvestin near Great Bend. You'll know when you're in Great Bend they'll be a gang a farmers standin around cryin into their handkerchiefs lookin for hands. Go up to them and they'll stop their cryin and write down your name. Ten eleven miles."

"Thanks."

"Foller the fight? Damn! Someday somebody gonna give that

black sonofabitch his due. Don't let on to them farmers you want work bad. Let on like you don't give a damn one way or the other."

Near Great Bend Kansas in the fields in the lanes between the rows the men sing *Oh Paddy dear and did you hear of Mary Jane McGee how all along with Timothy she thought it was his knee,* and Vachel does not sing because he cannot sing and because if he could sing he would sing a better song than they sing *Oh the sun shines bright on little Red Wing as she lays sleeping there comes a-creeping a cowboy,* and at night in the big barn the men lie on their bedrolls in the cool darkness pass the bottle from hand to hand and drink jealously sing *This lovely Indian maid she always was afraid that some buckaroo* and Vachel on a mat of hay not drinking not singing looks upward through the roofless loft at the stars the harvest moon, and at length the men sleep, snore, and now and then talk aloud in their sleep.

In the morning, in the fields again, the harvesters sweat the liquor from their bodies and by afternoon are ready for song again *Oh does she?* (tenor) *Yes she does.* (bass) *Oh will she? Yes she will. For me? For you. Tonight? Tonight.* And all together *She will bake a pumpkin pie for you tonight* laughter the wheat man on a bronco coming down the rows saying "Faster. Faster" and the men muttering and momentarily working faster but then resuming the slower pace, and a tenor in the middle of the twenty-some-odd stanza of the Two-Timing Gal from the One-Horse Town collapsing from the heat and dying soon thereafter and buried after dinner in an acre of manure, and at night in the barn the drinking and the singing as if it had not happened.

And suddenly Vachel wants to write poetry again. He wants to write of harvesting how the seed is planted nourished how it grows fragrant and ripe is taken from the earth given to the world. He wants to go somewhere where it is cool. He wants to sit holding a tablet of clean paper in his hands, and a sharp pencil, and he asks the wheat man for his pay, and the wheat man laughs because nobody gets paid until the end of the week. Lines of poetry form in the mind build themselves into stanzas, and he wants to write now, today, while the harvest idea is still fire in his brain, now before the picture becomes confused with drunken men and the clumsily manipulated lines of dirty songs, and death and discomfort. All of a sudden, having walked across three big states, he is ready to write again. He is restored by the thing he sees in Kansas, by the smell of the harvest by the whisper of possibility he hears above the muttering and the sleeptalking and the songs in the barn at night in the fields by day *Oh, I have walked in Kansas through many a harvest field, and piled the sheaves of glory there and down the wild rows reeled* lost in a speculation upon possibility as the men are lost in bootleg drink.

Because there is nothing harvested here but pain and death and a few dollars to take a man back where he came from what the man had said on the road *what you got when you're through?* lies thinking how he might borrow the melodies of the songs sung to a thousand sets of words all over the land

We stand at Armageddon and we battle for the Lord
Oh Paddy dear and did you hear of Mary Jane McGee

borrow the melodies as a base for the new poetry write words of his own make people sing *his* words *his* heroes. Then after the people have come to poetry that way they will be ready for a further step, for better poetry, the way they have always come one step and one step and one step forward. Poetry ought to be brought out of the libraries and out of the universities. It ought to belong to the people.

He cannot sleep. He slips into his shoes and steps over the sleeping men and out of the barn and into the fields, and the more he thinks about it the more certain he is that at last he has struck upon something big. People like poetry! They have always responded to poetry. Sing to them Carry me back to Old Virginny sing to them The sun shines bright in my old Kentucky home and they will weep though they have never seen Virginia nor ever been within five hundred miles of Kentucky fastening their minds upon words and the picture the words create and Bryan is words Roosevelt Wilson are words the Bible and the Declaration and the Proclamation they are words, only words.

And in the beginning God created the heaven and the earth, and the earth was without form, and void, and darkness was upon the face of the deep
And when in the course of human events it becomes

necessary for one people to dissolve the political bonds which have connected them with another and to assume among the powers of the earth the separate and equal station

And all persons held as slaves within any State shall be then, thenceforward and forever free.

And Lincoln at Gettysburg was poetry and Bryan was always poetry and the war slogans were always poetry, and the gospel hymns, and people are forever supporting good and bad causes so long as the rallying cries are poetic enough Tippecanoe and Tyler Too Fifty-Four Forty or Fight Remember the Maine Are You Washed in the Blood of the Lamb? Sixteen to one no cross of gold. Billy Sunday and General Booth, and Washington and Jefferson, and Lee and Lincoln and McKinley and Bryan, and everyone who ever bore a banner wrote poetry across it and knew how to swing the words around and make people follow as the children followed the piper.

He wonders how the idea will sound in the morning. He has always had a lot of good nighttime ideas, and then in the morning they are not really so good. He has written a good deal of nighttime poetry and then in the morning torn it up and thrown it away. Yet this seems like a good idea, even in the morning, after the sleepless night.

On the afternoon of the fourth day in the wheat in the fields near Great Bend Kansas the men stop singing suddenly. It is too hot. Heat rises from the ground, and their bodies no longer perspire. They are drained.

The hoppers, are more abundant than ever, and the more the men kill the more there seem to be, and the men grumble because their liquor is gone and the wheat man will not advance any money.

The wheat man is in a nasty mood. He is not pleased with the way the wheat is coming. He thinks there ought to have been more wheat.

He is not pleased with the men. He thinks they ought to have more interest in their work.

And he is not pleased with a bronco called Dick, a colt loaned to him by his widowed sister in Hutchinson, and he boasted to her that he would break Dick to the bit, as a man named Jeff Hatten in Springfield Illinois some twenty-odd years before boasted to his townsmen that he would break a gelding named Tough or know the reason why, and the two men, the man in Illinois and the man in Kansas, never knowing, never seeing, never dreaming one of the other, first in the presence of an unformed boy and later in the presence of the drifting man which the boy had become, perform in far separate times an act of vengeance: for in the hand of the Kansas wheat man, now in the summer of nineteen-and-twelve, a snake whip becomes instrument of vengeance, and a bronco named Dick belonging to a widow woman in Hutchinson, becomes, of vengeance, object, and the sounds of vengeance are echoes close to the ground of the curling, cracking whip and the bleating and crying and anguished squealing of the baby bronco, and the colors of vengeance are red and white, and the red is blood on the flanks of the bronco and the animal's foaming mouth is white and a red-white rib is exposed between lips of broken flesh.

There is a necessity for vengeance, and the man with the whip is not aware of the reasons for the necessity, nor are the men who straighten to watch. Nor is Vachel aware. Vachel is only aware that the end of the process is death, and that in instants of silence a Rachel-Jane calls shrilly *plee-whah plee-whah* from the hedge near the road, and he stands stark and stricken and watches the living thing die upon its side on the dry, hot ground, whimpering, bleating, pleading in its final moments, then straightening its legs and arching its back and looking a last time at its killer and expiring in its own running blood, silent now, as if to say I have at least regained my dignity, and lying still and dignified in the blood which soon ceases to run, soon stops and becomes brown like the brown earth.

And the drifting man who stood once long ago in the field of Jeff Hatten in Springfield Illinois somehow hoping that the gelding would vanquish the man, stands now and watches as the carcass of the bronco Dick is hoisted to a wagon and rolled away, and then he turns quietly again to his work, for it is only an animal and he is no longer a child, and nothing has happened here that will, in a week, be remembered.

And yet he will remember it, and he will make of that which is not worth remembering a memorable poem, and the bronco that would not be broken will be alive and dancing in the poem that will be read after the wheat man and the hired hands and the poet himself have found, as the animal has found, a dignity in death.

Because, in fact, the unformed boy who became the drifting man became in the process something more than a drifting man: he became one who learned to look upon the goal of life as the emergence of the will and the soul and the spirit over the reins and bits that make of the human being a creature of toil, oxlike, limp and leaden-eyed, the man with the hoe, the man beneath the yoke.

And for the boy to become such a man there was somehow the necessity to journey, and there was a first journey and a later journey and a third journey, and it was now, upon this journey, that the colors and sounds and sights became full-meaningful, and the gelding that he saw long ago in Jeff Hatten's field he sees again, now, except that now it is Dick the bronco, and it is dead, but this morning it was blood and bone and flesh and brain as man himself is blood, bone, flesh, brain, spirit and soul, and it was a defiant bronco as man is defiant, and it was, for reasons unknown, a bronco that would not be broken, and the drifting man who saw it die is a man who for reasons known and unknown drifts and journeys and will not be broken.

And he sees now, clearly for the first time, that his defiance is his virtue and his drifting is in fact not a drifting but a straight path leading a true course toward fulfillment of a duty to his fellows, that the submissive man is the unremembered man because he is the curse of civilization, and the defiant man, the man who will not be broken, is the man who, like Dick, will be the hero of song and story in the far time when unbroken man looks back upon the gloomy history of his sad and vengeful ages.

Vachel thinks that perhaps the idea he had in the night was not such a good idea after all. And maybe he is crazy maybe not a poet and will never be maybe people are right they say *If you are a poet why don't I see your name in the newspapers and magazines?* maybe he does not see the world aright the way madmen never see the world as it really is. Maybe he is crazy.

In the night he collects his poems and his drawings and sets off without his pay down the dark road toward the west.

How can he write and hope people will feel about things as he feels about them when the things he sees are never the things most people see sees everything cockeyed and upside down. He wants to write a poem about the road stretching west, automobiles, grasshoppers and the Rachel-Jane and to everyone else the automobile is progress and to him it is something less thinks grasshoppers dream grasshopper dreams and have grasshopper lovers and he cannot kill them hears rebellion in the cry of the Rachel-Jane on a road of plentiful symbols that only he seems to see and only he seems to hear, and a love that is big beyond itself loves big ideas democracy brotherhood plenitude, and most of all he loves people, and people drive him from his city and kill his symbol with a snake whip and send him despairing to the road again.

Yet by daylight he is thinking, plotting, planning a way to compose a great new song of celebration. Maybe it ought to be based on a gospel hymn to begin with, or maybe the names of the towns all strung together to be recited aloud as a train caller would recite them.

South from Great Bend Kansas beside the dry bed of the Arkansas River Pawnee Rock Garfield Larned and Spearville, Dodge City Cimarron Charleston and Pierceville, Garden City Lakin Mayline and Syracuse, Medway and Coolidge and across the line to Colorado, and the mountains in the distance suggest a thousand symbols and start the wheels of his mind churning again with imaginings, not of the bigness or the highness of the mountains but of the way they are close to the sun and the stars and the moon and the way they defy him to draw them or write about them.

The topmost peaks are white with snow, and nobody really looks at the mountains Holly Granada Lamar Las Animas La Junta and nobody really looking at the mountains because the only thing about the mountains is that automobiles boil over in them they cut off the wind and send down water and people come from all over to look at Pike's Peak. And maybe if a poet really wants to get something across to people he must keep himself in check and not deal in special, vague and mystical things; he must try to see as other people see, and he must at the same time be just one short step ahead of the people, not two or three or half a dozen because the people move ahead just one short step at a time.

It begins to come clear. He walks, and he trades his rhymes for a meal and a bed, and he talks to people, and here and there he works a day in the fields or paints a barn or hoes a garden or chops wood, and all the time he listens and it begins to come clear: the thing to do is to employ the symbol people can recognize, to give meaning to that which is known but which is not understood, to hold hands with people and go with them the one forward step, and

after that to take the next and the next. That must be the duty of
the poets in this generation and in the next, and in the generations
that follow, and the ultimate poem will come in the ultimate time,
after the names of the earlier poets will have been forgotten, and it
will not matter because the goal is not great poetry but a great hu-
mankind. To live in mankind is far more than to live in a name.

He thinks back to the past, to the times when in the midst of
people there were rejoicings within him, and everybody felt rejoicings, and then it fled and the mood of the instant was gone: he
might write of the time when Bryan came and the world seemed
about to take one forward step and then it never took it because
Bryan went away on the railroad and the mood was not sustained.
If one could write a great Bryan poem full of all the shouting and
the hopeful singing and the cheering! Then every time a person
needed to he could pick up the poem and get in a Bryan mood
again. In a poem forgotten moods can be re-created he could put
his heroes into poems thinks he ought to go back and polish up all
the heroes in the old poem he wrote in New York might work in a
few new stanzas on Wilson Roosevelt maybe a Booker T. Washington poem or a General William Booth poem or both then when the
heroes of the present are firmly established move on to newer people, to less respectable people, the one step and the one step, and
ultimately to the mountains and the mystical mysteries.

And when were the times of rejoicing? They were the times when
people were singing around him, carols at Christmas, hymns at
church, the Mennonites coming alive when they sang together in
the fields, harvesters at their best when they were singing might
write a great clean harvest poem to be sung to the tune of scythes,
sickles and pitchforks, the old man in the boxcar coming alive
when he sang. Even the Republicans sang when they broke with
Taft and hoisted Roosevelt to their shoulders, the Socialists always
sing at their meetings, and there are union songs now, and in the
cotton the black slaves sang and kept alive their hope, and the people sang in Springfield when Bryan came. And there were the times
he stood singing in the street at night with the Salvation Army, and
he had felt wondrously good.

2

Mama and Papa have for some years camped during the summer
at Empire Colorado. It is not camping in the woodsman sense;

they are too old for that. They sleep at night on cots on a platform tent two hundred feet off Route 40, and Mama does the cooking on a fireplace grate, bringing the food down from Glen Arbor Lodge just across the highway.

Mostly it is a place where Papa can sit by day and let the mountain sun bathe him. He sits with his eyes closed, feeling the warmth of the sun on his lids. One eye is dead. He claims he can still see with it, but he cannot see, not really see.

Mama still has the old bounce. Time and age have not so swiftly overtaken her. She is still embattled. She has given up some of her club work (and the clubs have died behind her) but she is still the president of Via Christi in Springfield and she is still intensely concerned about the state of the world. She is still Mama.

They sit on a big warm rock on the hillside near their tent. Below, a mountain stream makes water noises on the smooth rocks, and on the highway above the automobiles pass westward and their tires hum on the new hard road, and life is still a thing ahead of Mama and Papa, not a thing to be looked back upon as old people in storybooks always look back upon life and never ahead.

Except that now and then they look back, and when they do it is not without satisfaction and a sense of having lived a good and proper life and lived outside themselves for other people, yet taken care of themselves, too, and sent two daughters into the world to marry and do good and people the race, and Vachel they forgive as the mothers and fathers of artists always forgive and somehow with slim means support and assist because it is their child as a child born deaf or blind or malformed or weak-minded is always still the child of love and the flesh of the flesh and the blood of the blood.

On the curbstone in Pueblo Colorado in the early morning Vachel sits wondering what to do. He told everyone he was going to California and he must go. He thinks he will cut down into New Mexico and shoot across the desert prove to everyone in Springfield that when he says he is going to California he means he is going to California. He will go to Los Angeles and settle down and write the new kind of poetry.

But Mama and Papa are up in Empire he could make it in a couple of days feed up and maybe borrow a few dollars, and then too not feel so lonesome and down in the mouth the way he has been feeling. It is a terrible lonesome feeling he has been having all along the way growing more and more lonesome. On the road there is no one. On the road it is a day here a day there he never knows anybody's name. He is never really at home anywhere nobody to love him kiss him as Mama will do if he should go on up to Empire. And there is nobody he can really explain his new idea to. Everybody listens very politely, but they do not understand the way Mama would understand.

Going up and seeing Mama and Papa would be almost like going home, and what he wants to do really is to go home and be somewhere and feel that he belongs to something because suppose the new idea fails the way all his ideas have failed! He is expecting rather a good deal—expecting some new kind of poetry to catch on when people have been accepting the same old poetry for such a long time. Then where will he be when the new idea fails? He will be somewhere far away in a strange city where he has never been before, and then in the end he will go home a failure as he went home from Hiram, as he went limping home from the East. At least he was young then, and now he is not so young.

Yet he must try the new idea. If he does not try it he will always wonder if it might not have worked after all, and he will never really be satisfied unless he tries it.

He decides he will compromise and go up to Empire, but just for a visit, and then he will come back down and go clear to California the way he planned it.

He travels the road north beside the mountains to Denver, and then he goes west, into the mountains, to Empire, and he finds Mama and Papa on their warm rock beside their tent, and when Mama sees Vachel coming down the hill she gives a little cry of surprise and gets up from the rock as fast as she can and kisses him the way he knew she would, and Papa squints at Vachel with his one good eye and shakes Vachel's hand and rubs his beard against Vachel's chin, affectionately, playfully, and it is good to be somewhere at last where he does not feel lost and alone. "It's just a visit," he says. "I'm going to California all the same," and Mama hardly hears him because all she can do is stand looking up at him. "My but you're tan," she says.

"I've been in the sun," he says, and he laughs.

"Oh, Vachel," says Mama, and she hugs him and kisses him again and straightens his hair, and whatever they say about

Vachel, whatever anyone may say, he is good: he always comes back; he is never lost to her. "Go wash your hands," she says, and Vachel goes side-step down the hill to the stream and lets the water run over his hands and lets the sun dry them, and Mama spreads butter in a hot pan and fries three eggs and browns bread and warms coffee, and she watches Vachel eat the eggs, and he tells about all the places he has been since his last letter, and Mama says not to talk with his mouth full.

"It's wonderful here," he says.

"The nights are cold," Mama says. "Papa wants to go home."

"We both want to," says Papa.

"You'll come," Mama says.

"No. I've got something yet to work out. I've got an idea."

"You can work it out at home."

Papa turns from them, setting his face toward the sun again.

"It will be winter," Mama says.

"I've got to try it first and then maybe I'll come home. It's a new idea. Maybe I need a new place to try it in."

"Always new ideas," says Papa. "There haven't been any new ideas. In Springfield the young pups think they have all kinds of new ideas. In the end they come back to the hot-water bottle and the mustard plaster."

"This time it's something real. At least that's the way I feel about it and if I don't try it now I never will."

"What is it?" says Mama.

"You were going to be the biggest man in Chicago," Papa says.

"Papa," says Mama, sharply.

"And then when it's not New York it's the road, and then it's home again and away again . . ."

"Take something like a good old gospel tune," says Vachel.

"That's what I said when you were beginning," says Mama. "I said the religious themes . . ."

"With a twist," says Vachel.

"It can't be twisted," says Papa.

Vachel thinks he might as well not talk about it because the only way to do it is to go ahead and do it. "When are you leaving? I'll go as far as Denver with you and put you on the train."

In Denver Papa puts Vachel up at a hotel and gives him two dollars for a pair of new trousers, but Vachel goes to the moving picture instead, and he spends the rest at Elitch Gardens, and on the following day he sets out again for California.

3

Wagon Mound New Mexico on the straight road between Raton and Las Vegas. Vachel wonders how it got its name, but nobody knows, and when he inquires folks look at him and scowl. "Just asking," he says.

The railway agent is young and very smart, and he knows how many people live in Wagon Mound and what they do, and he knows what he would do with the Spanish if he could and he knows all about the Indians and how they won't work for a living but sit around letting the Government take care of them, and he tells Vachel that Wagon Mound is called Wagon Mound because that's what it was called when the white men came and drove the Indians off the land and built the place up and made it pay.

"There's a formation in the mountains. Looks something like a wagon," says Vachel, pointing east through the window of the railroad shed.

"Well I'll be damned," the young man says. "Maybe that's how they come to call it Wagon Mound. Beats me. Where you bound?"

"California I hope. Los Angeles."

"You got a hell of a ways to go."

"I know. I have a sort of an uncle in Los Angeles."

"California's not a bad place. Where you from?"

"Illinois."

"I saw in a book one time how you could take Illinois and dump her twice over in New Mexico and still have lots left over."

"That may be. I think I might take the train to Los Angeles."

"Oh you think so?" The young agent's tone is abruptly different. "It'll cost you forty dollars not a penny less."

"I was thinking I might fix up a corner of an empty."

"Well you got another think comin. The railroad ain't on a charity basis. It'll cost you forty dollars."

"I've walked a long way."

"You should a thought a that before."

"I didn't know it was so big."

"Well it is, and you should a thought before. This here is the third biggest state in the union. It's bigger than Arizona. Don't you ever read books? If you'd read books you'd know."

"Well then, may I send a telegram?"

"You got the money you can send a telegram anywhere in the whole damn world right from here." He slides a telegraph blank across the counter to Vachel, and Vachel picks up a pencil, and the pencil is moored with a string. He composes a wire to Papa, and the agent reads it and smiles. "Lost your nerve did you?"

"This isn't my brand of nerve."

"That's what they all say," the young man says, counting the words in Vachel's wire.

"Then, too, there's nothing ahead but desert. It's so far between places."

"You should a studied up on that beforehand. Eighty-eight cents. It's one a the biggest damn deserts in the world, maybe the biggest except for Egypt. Doctor Vachel Lindsay, six hundred and three south fifth street Springfield Illinois Papa my feet and my spirit have given out forty dollars will get me to Uncle Olan love Vachel care Western Union Wagon Mound New Mexico."

"That's right."

"Eighty-eight cents."

"We'll take it out of the money when it comes."

"That's impossible."

"Just go ahead and send it," says Vachel.

"I tell you it's impossible. Besides, then you'll be short on the fare."

"Well, ask for forty-one."

"It's impossible. It's against the rules. Suppose he don't send it?"

"Just go ahead and send it," says Vachel. "He'll send it. If worst comes to worst the Western Union Company will be out eighty-eight cents. Send it!" Vachel's voice is very stern, and the young man turns and goes to his machine and pulls his green eyeshade down over his eyes the way he has seen old-timers do, and he sends the telegram.

(On the road somewhere north of Wagon Mound it had all fallen into place, all the pieces of the puzzle, all the elements of the new idea, and Vachel never knew and will never know just how it happened. It happened the way it happens to a stonecutter splitting a section of marble, tapping lightly lightly maybe ten thousand times and all of a sudden the block splitting neatly, and that is how it happened with Vachel, with one light stroke, one more stroke, one light tap after the ten thousand tappings of the thirty-plus years.

(He had been thinking of the people he might write a great swinging song about, of Bryan, of Roosevelt, of Altgeld and Booker Washington, of Lincoln and Boone and Henry George and Eugene Debs and General William Booth of the Salvation Army, and when he thought of Booth he knew it must be he and no other. And when he thought of Booth he remembered the gospel tunes remembered how he felt and maybe how everyone feels when the great hopeful hymns are sung and how the hymns are lovesongs and God-songs and songs of peace and songs of a better future day and how when he sang them he felt close to the singing people about him.

(He thought about Booth and how the thing that bothered Booth was the agony of people in slums jails brothels, sickness and drunkenness and blindness and lameness and all the things that are a part of poverty, and these are the things that always made Vachel unhappy and restless. They are the things that make him write poetry in the first place.

(And to Booth the ugly were beautiful and the meek and the poor were blessed indeed because to Booth it was always more than just words it was in the doing and Booth went out and did it.

(And now he was dead and Vachel saw Booth at Heaven's gate, and the gate of Heaven became in Vachel's mind the wide door of the old fossil limestone courthouse on the square in Springfield, and Booth with flying beard marched around and around the courthouse square, and he was blind and yet he could see, and Jesus came out of the courthouse to greet the General and to welcome him, and Booth went into Heaven, and behind him went the drug addicts and the crippled and the flophouse bums and drunks and whores and convicts, all the leprous dispossessed of the world.

(And they were singing The Blood of the Lamb and pounding tambourines beating bass drum strumming banjos piping upon flutes, and Booth entered first *Booth led boldly with his big bass drum.* Already a line. *Booth led boldly with his big bass drum, Are you washed in the blood of the lamb?* Already two lines, and a great deal more ready to fall into place, and Vachel knew he had to go somewhere to write it out, and there was nowhere to go because he was afraid to go home again like a whipped pup with its tail between its legs. And he had no money, and then he thought about Uncle Olan who was a sort of uncle and he lived in Los Angeles and taught at a college, and he was always inviting Mama and Papa and Vachel to Los Angeles, and they never went, and Uncle Olan would give him a room and feed him and let him write for a week or so or however long he needed to get the Booth down on paper, and after that he would go home and settle down. And Vachel knew that he must write this poem and try out the new idea and stand or fall on the outcome.

(To be sung to the tune of The Blood of the Lamb *Booth led boldly with his big bass drum, Are you washed in the blood of the lamb?* to be sung with bass drum and tambourines and banjos and flutes and the new idea came clear the big marble block split soundlessly down the middle, and then he was in Wagon Mound New Mexico sending a telegram the young man was counting forty dollars and twelve cents into his hand, and he was buying a ticket and boarding a train and changing trains at Albuquerque and outside the window was New Mexico desert and Arizona desert and the trainwheels leading boldly washed in the blood of the desert and Uncle Olan was shaking his hand and showing him the guest room asking about Papa and Mama and saying how good it was to see him washed in the blood of the lamb.)

Uncle Olan's hired girl Doris spreads a fresh sheet across the bed in the spare room. She pulls the corners tight, and Vachel helps, standing faced toward Doris on account of the hole in the seat of his pants.

Uncle Olan brings Vachel a pair of trousers and a towel and soap and some writing paper and some pencils and a small table, and he draws the shades against the August sun, and the room is cool and dark. Uncle Olan and Doris withdraw, closing the door behind them, and for Vachel there is an instant of terror: for an instant he cannot remember why he came or what it is he wants to write. Then the instant is gone, and he remembers.

And he is afraid because it is now or never, and the great idea of the road must be transferred from mind to paper, and he cannot go on forever planning and running and finally failing, and the lines that sang in his head on the road must sing on paper now.

And then the first two lines, set to paper for the first time, and then he pushes the paper to one side of the table and takes another and writes another line and sets that aside, and most of the lines that he composed on the road are still with him, and he writes them down, and on another sheet of paper he makes notes of ideas that are not quite lines and he jots down words that are not quite ideas but that now must be developed, and the words must become ideas and the ideas must become lines, and all of it must pound along as the first line pounds, suggesting the bass drum, and as he writes his confidence returns. Six sheets of paper become a stanza, and the stanza suggests the exact nature of a second stanza, and he must not forget as he works that there are to be banjo stanzas and tambourine stanzas and flute stanzas. He does not forget.

He rereads, and when he is done he is aware that he has been tapping his feet and pounding the frail table, and he does not at first hear the knock on the bedroom door. "Is anything wrong?" says Uncle Olan through the door.

"No," shouts Vachel, "everything is right," and he goes to the door and opens it and puts an arm around his uncle's shoulders. "Let's have some coffee," he says, and they drink coffee in the kitchen.

"Doris," says Vachel, as she prepares the supper. "Do you know what raiment is?" and she pauses at her work and stops to think. "I've heard it," she says, and she runs her tongue thoughtfully between her lips. "Give me a hint."

"Suppose certain people were clad in raiment," says Vachel.

"Then it would be clothing," she says.

"Good," says Vachel. He must use songs that people know and words that people understand.

The first day and the first night the momentum carries him. He works all of the first night, and at dawn he goes quietly from the house with his papers in his hand, and he walks. On Sixth Street, in the park, he sits beneath a palm tree, organizing the pieces of paper. One by one he crumples them and throws them away when they no longer serve him, and when he is done a solid core remains, and today about that core he will build again, and each day he will build until the core is a whole. He has written many poems, and he knows how the process goes for him.

It is work. It is hard work, and by the third day the core is the rough whole, and by the fifth day the rough whole is considerably smoother, and in seven days the seven stanzas look like a poem and sound like a poem, and maybe there will be changes here and there as there are always changes to be made, but at week's end it is a poem, fixed, and ready to be read aloud to someone.

It is a poem. It is not the usual sort of poem. It is not an orthodox poem. It is a new kind of poem, heavily musical, and its heroes are people who have never before, in quite the same way, been the heroes of poems, and Jesus comes walking out of the courthouse like anybody walking out of a courthouse anywhere.

And now that it is finished Vachel is sad to think that there is little chance of anyone's publishing such a poem.

He bids good-by to Uncle Olan and to Doris, thanking them for everything, and with the new money from Papa he buys a train ticket to Springfield. He enjoys the ride. He sits looking from the window at the fine smooth Arizona desert, at the mountains, at cities and towns and rivers, and the West is behind him, and Missouri and Illinois are the bright colors of autumn, and it is as if a great weight has been lifted from his shoulders, as if the thing he came west to do he has done, and no matter what happens now, at home, he has done what he has been trying a long time to do. Now and then he rereads his new poem, and at length he is home and the journey is ended, and he thinks that maybe next year he will go walking somewhere again, but he will not.

He does not know it now, but his walking days are over.

Book III—PATRIOT

CHAPTER ONE

1

MISS GLORIA FISK, chief librarian of the Abraham Lincoln Public Library in Springfield Illinois, has learned to smile a little. She has not learned to smile a wide smile as if she really enjoys smiling at people, but she has learned to smile a little, and that is a gain. She has, for the most part, overcome her fear of children, her fear of city officials, and her fear of the general public. She is fretfully aware that children sometimes gigglingly refer to her as Miss Glorious Fits, but over the years the pain of this knowledge has subsided within her until it is really no pain at all.

Over the years she has grown. She has matured. The six-dollar weekly wage she once received is now thirty, and the pompous dignity she once affected is now the natural dignity of middle age. She no longer assumes the power of censorship: whereas once she outlawed *Huckleberry Finn* on the grounds that it was ungrammatical and irreverent, now she cautiously encourages its reading; whereas once she refused to authorize the purchase of books containing either nude pictures or doubtful words, now within limits she houses them in the name of Art and Truth; she has softened in her attitude toward Walt Whitman; she has altogether relented in the matter of admitting periodical literature into her library; she has made adult books available to children.

The change within her has come not because she has lowered her morals but because she has raised her sights.

She is still deeply, hopelessly and endlessly in love with books. Her hallmark is a soft rag which she carries with her throughout the day and with which she dusts the exposed surfaces of shelved volumes as tenderly as she would have caressed a lover had she ever had one, and when she dies it will be reported upon her gravestone *Gloria Fisk 1860-1935 She Devoted Her Life to Books.* (When the poet Vachel Lindsay was a child she did not smile at him because he was a child, and then for a long time he was gone, and now he is a man and she smiles, and she does not smile at all men. But he is a writer—a creator of books—and to her a writer is a creature apart, and so she smiles.)

Gloria Fisk is the library. The building has been remodeled, expanded, refurnished and renamed. Wooden steps leading from the street have been replaced by concrete. All manner of alteration has been effected within the building. Like her, the library has changed and grown slowly in subtle ways over the years.

And the library is Springfield Illinois because all that will remain after the men and the women pass on are the documents they leave behind, not buildings, not streets, not homes, not speech. Only documents. This much she knows and has always known. If she has never learned to smile broadly or to love human beings well or to retreat for a public instant from a studied dignity, she has nevertheless known this—this respect, this worship of the documents.

In the beginning, in her beginnings, there was Lincoln, and five books about Lincoln when she came, and she set them aside on a shelf in a corner, and then she moved them to a table just inside the entrance to the building, and on the table she placed a card PLEASE DO NOT TOUCH. And later there were ten Lincoln books, and then suddenly there were twenty, and in time there were a hundred, and she set aside an entire section and placed a sign above it BOOKS ABOUT ABRAHAM LINCOLN, and now she did not forbid the touching of the books. They were for loan. They were borrowed and returned and then they were borrowed again and returned again, time after time and year after year, and the hundred books were three hundred, and added to the books were newspaper clippings and photographs and letters signed by Lincoln and the deed to his home at Eighth and Jackson. And it was never and it is not now within Gloria Fisk an adoration of Lincoln; it is only that he was a figure of earth and a person among persons, and in the documents she keeps him and preserves him as she keeps and preserves all things that seem to her worth saving, the record of all things, of riot, fire and drought, manners and customs, all that may in some future time be matters of interest to somebody, anybody, who may care to concern himself or herself with events in the life of Springfield Illinois.

From the library files Miss Gloria Fisk removes the recent application of Vachel Lindsay for a borrower's card. Upon it he has signed his name in agreement to the proposition that he will observe the rules and regulations of the library, and he has designated two persons resident in Springfield who in the borrower's opinion will attest to his responsibility. The persons are Willis Spaulding and Duncan McDonald. Upon a separate sheet of paper Gloria Fisk types the words *Card showing signature of Vachel Lindsay, a poet of Springfield, Autumn, 1912,* and she staples the sheet of paper to the card and places the joined documents under the letter *L* in a cabinet in the basement marked *Pending,* and beside it, the following January, she places several pages clipped neatly from Poetry: A Magazine of Verse. The pages contain Vachel's poem, General William Booth Enters into Heaven, and at a later date, in the margin beside the title of the poem she makes the notation: *Susan Wilcox informs me that Vachel says he received twenty-two dollars for this poem,* and she signs her name, and the date, and she climbs the stairs from the dark cellar and resumes her duties above.

She reads all of Vachel's published poetry. She has no opinion about it. He lives on Fifth Street and is therefore a part of Springfield, and she is the library and the library is Springfield, and all that is written about or by or within Springfield is to be dated in ink and properly filed, and she has no opinions: it must all be saved. Everything. And the cleansing of time will determine the relative value of the hundreds upon hundreds of scraps of paper and newspaper articles and magazine writings she saves. It is not for her to make decisions.

She is not aware that the magazine, Poetry, marks the birth of a new spirit in American verse. She is aware only that her periodicals budget must now include Poetry and Reedy's Mirror and The Seven Arts and the Little Review and The Masses and others, and even The National Rip-Saw because Eugene Victor Debs edits it and people are always coming in and looking up things about Debs. She is for a time blithely unaware that there are scores of new names, the new poets, Williams and Stevens and Pound and Fletcher and Frost and Eliot and Bynner and Lowell and Untermeyer and Tietjens and Corbin and Kilmer and Seeger and Tagore and Teasdale and Aiken to name but a few. She is somewhat more sharply aware of Masters and Sandburg. They are from Illinois. There is a new playwright: *Thirst, and other one-act plays,* O'Neill, Eugene G.; Anderson, Sherwood; Lewis, Sinclair. It is not for her to note movements and directions. Soon she will feel the great new strength that is in the literature, the protest, the revolt. For the time being it is primarily Vachel's name she looks for: The Santa Fé Trail, in Yale Review; Kansas, in Forum; The Broncho That Would Not Be Broken, in Seven Arts; the Illinois Village and On Reading Omar Khayyam (During an antisaloon campaign, in central Illinois), in Current Literature, and she removes Vachel's poems from the file under *L* and prepares a separate folder marked with his name, and the folder grows fat and bulky with pages clipped from magazines, a poem on the Panama Canal in the Boston *Evening Transcript*, Yankee Doodle for Metropolitan, and three poems on Mark Twain and a poem urging peace with Japan and a poem calling for a curse upon kings and a poem striking out against war in general, and sometimes two poems in a single week, and the folder marked Vachel Lindsay now splitting at the seam. Gloria Fisk transfers the growing file to a large envelope which she removes from the cabinet marked *Pending* to a locked case on the main floor. And she always smiles at Vachel when he comes to the library.

Over time, Springfield, like Gloria Fisk, has softened its attitudes and broadened its tolerance and deepened its awareness. The streetcar strike is bloodless, and the drought in the valley is accompanied not by despair but by thoughtful study and intelligent action (the vote in 1916 favors public ownership of utilities). The city is prepared to regulate itself, to organize its better self against its more selfish self (in 1914 the Russell Sage Foundation is engaged to make a survey of Springfield's needs), and if there is someone among them fooling with poetry then let him be, let him go his own way, let him write, let him speak.

Springfield is growing up, and if one has never read a single line of Vachel's poetry one nevertheless reads in the *Journal:*

Chicago—at Mandel Hall a dancing group is performing to the rhythms of the poetry of Springfield's own poet, Vachel Lindsay, of 603 South Fifth Street. . . .

New York—Collier's, the national weekly, announced today that in its issue of September 6 it will devote two and one half pages to a personality sketch of Springfield's own poet, Vachel Lindsay, of 603 South Fifth Street. The article will be accompanied by a large photograph of the poet. . . .

Chicago—The magazine Poetry announced today that its $100 Levinson award for the outstanding poem of 1915 will go to Vachel

Lindsay, Springfield's own poet, for his Chinese poem, The Chinese Nightingale. Mr. Lindsay lives at 603 South Fifth Street.

And something in the *Journal* to the effect that John Masefield and William Lyon Phelps and William Dean Howells and William Butler Yeats have at one time or another had laudatory things to say about Vachel's poetry, and Bob Mann of the *Journal* is not at all sure who these men are, but he has heard their names and so it must be reported, and the newspaper clippings go into Gloria Fisk's big envelope. The New York *Times* suggests that 1914-1915—with the publication of Aiken, Lowell, Frost, Masters' *Spoon River Anthology* and Vachel's book *The Congo and Other Poems*—is probably the brightest period in American poetry, and Bob Mann knows that if the *Times* dares to say so he may say so in the *Journal*, and so it is said. And something about a poet named Witter Bynner touring the country and reciting Vachel's poetry, and something about Vachel's reciting in a poets' series in Chicago, and everything clipped and dated and placed by Gloria Fisk in her Vachel Lindsay envelope: Abraham Lincoln Walks at Midnight; The Booker Washington Trilogy (including a Simon Legree poem and a John Brown poem); A Rhyme for All Zionists; The Leaden-Eyed; The Fireman's Ball; The Kallyope Yell; When the Mississippi Flowed in Indiana.

And then, rapid-fire, the books, and a space on a shelf to be cleared, and a special section all his own. *General William Booth Enters Into Heaven and Other Poems. The Congo and Other Poems. The Chinese Nightingale and Other Poems.* And it all happens swiftly, beginning with the time of Booth and the end of the walking days, and ending afterward as swiftly as it began, but now, in the quiet time in Springfield, going forward swiftly. Gloria Fisk stands Vachel's two tramping books, *A Handy Guide For Beggars* and *Adventures While Preaching the Gospel of Beauty*, beside the books of poetry, and he signs his name for her in the front of each book, and she smiles, and the books to her are the end-all because they are the documents, and documents do not die.

In all, there are six books in the four good years, beginning with the time of Booth and ending with the time of war when all the forward upward motion stops, when the building and the softening and the deepening cease and the documents no longer matter.

But now, in the good quiet years, war is but soft thunder far away. It does not touch Springfield Illinois. War cannot come; it can fall only where all rains fall when there is faraway thunder—somewhere on the plain beyond the city.

Springfield Illinois. March, April, May, 1914.

An adult act. An act of self-study, self-contemplation, a searching of itself, an asking: *What is wrong with me? Tell me what is wrong with me for I want to know!*

Into Springfield, at the City's own request, come eleven young men and women, and you do not like them: six of the eleven wear thick-lensed glasses and the flat-bosomed women walk a little like men, and the men talk a little like women, and you can look at them and tell they are Jews and atheists and no doubt Socialists.

In point of fact only two are Jews and one an atheist and one a Socialist behind on her dues, and they come with a suitcase filled with square white cards, and at night in their rooms in the Abraham Lincoln Hotel they write about what they see during the day, and the men go into the women's rooms and the women into the men's as if it were wholly proper. They read their reports to one another. They tabulate and check, retabulate and cross-check, and they go back tomorrow and ask the same questions all over again, and you let them come and go as they please because in an adult mood in an adult time you ask questions about yourself.

They begin with the children. They go with tape measures and footrules, and they tell you: floor space in your schools is inadequate, the lighting is wrongly located, ventilation is poor, fire escapes are inaccessible; drinking fountains bubbling too close to toilets, urinals too high for the boys, seats too high for the girls, salaries too low for the teachers. And you have spent your money to put a high polish on your schools; but you do not spend money for books. Mental deficiency, chorea and tuberculosis among your children, and nowhere to play, and nowhere to dance except in the saloons, and you can stand at Fifth and Monroe and count in thirty minutes four hundred and sixty-two girls and eight hundred and thirteen boys with nothing to do and nowhere to go.

One hundred and ninety-eight saloons and fifty-five houses of prostitution.

(All they can give you are facts and figures, and you live by facts and figures, so you understand. They talk your language.)

Your downtown buildings stand back to back and side to side and most of them are firetraps, and seven thousand four hundred and thirty-one privies flow merrily into seven thousand five hundred and thirty fresh-water wells, and railroads cut through home lots, and factories and dwellings stand wall to wall, and you did not know until now that two thousand of your people are diseased and penniless, and you should know because you contract their diseases and pay in a dozen other ways for their poverty. You are on the one hand greedy and on the other hand foolish.

At The Home for the Friendless the children are undernourished. Illegitimate children and the children of divorces are not permitted in the Home: they must starve elsewhere on their own. And you would not permit it if you knew, because you love children. But you did not know.

And now the facts are out, and you are ashamed, and you study the picture of yourself unmasked, naked, and you wince but you do not turn away because you are growing mature, older, wiser.

According to your view the insane, the drunk and the venereal are criminal. But you do not think it is criminal that the hungry die on their knees in your missions because you make them pray before you will feed them. It happens. It really happens! (Names, dates and places on request.) And you demand three hundred dollars and a property deed before you will shelter your aged in the Home, and you send your blind and consumptive and epileptic to the County Poor Farm, and your girl-children serve industry in your factories, and small boys serve as trappers in your mines, and your Factory Inspection Department is a fraud and a farce and you know it.

Death in your factories and high talk in your churches, seven-day weeks and three-dollar days. Bright's disease and typhoid fever, marasmus and inanition, and you drink Decatur's sewer water, and milk polluted by dairymen who on the Fourth of July orate to you on the duties and responsibilities of citizenship, and some of your judges are for sale across the board, and your newspapers don't tell the whole truth and you give your policemen medals instead of money and you wonder why the police are corrupt, and your commission form of government is commendable but some of your commissioners are dishonest. (Of all the City departments, it is found, only that under the direction of Commissioner Willis Spaulding issues literate reports and meets its obligations to the people.)

The City neglects to care for its trees; the trees are rotting at the roots.

(And you know all this and a good deal more. The stories you could tell! And the jottings on the white cards become a big green book entitled *The Springfield Survey: A Study of Social Conditions in an American City,* and up and down the Valley, in other cities, they laugh at you, and you are ashamed.

(Yet you are glad, and in a way you are proud: you had the courage to look at yourself, and in this time, in bold resolution, in earnest editorial, in inspired sermon, you promise yourself that you will do better henceforth. And you mean it, and here and there you even make your beginnings.

(But there is yet to be the interruption of war, and for some reason you will never again be where you are now in the good, quiet, forward, upward time.)

2

Mama is halfway planning a trip to Toronto to the national convention of the Christian Church, and she is halfway not planning it at all because she thinks Vachel might get married any minute. Her suitcases, half-packed, stand open on bedroom chairs.

She greets the mailman on the porch, and he tips his hat to her. He is of the older generation. She takes the mail from his hand. There is a letter for Papa, two for her, and six or seven for Vachel.

He, like her, has been watching for the mailman. He takes the six or seven envelopes from Mama and thumbs through until he finds the one for which he has been waiting, and Mama stands watching, neglecting to open her own mail, and Vachel, with the open letter in his hands, shuffles toward the staircase, feeling his way as he goes. Mama observes at length: "I noticed there was something from Sara."

"One letter," says he, continuing his reading.

"Anything—anything new with her?"

"One letter," he replies.

"I'm talking, Vachel." When she was young she answered when she was spoken to. "What does she say? Is there anything new? Vachel, I'm talking."

"I'm sorry, Mama. I wasn't listening. No, nothing new. She has new stationery with something on top. It looks like a flower. She says it's a teasel."

"Anything—else? More personal?"

"She says she had a grandpa who owned a steamboat."

"Most interesting."

"Maybe I'll have some stationery made. I want on my coat of arms a bronco, rampant."

And Mama completes the packing of her bags and goes off to Toronto against her better judgment: she thinks it would be wiser to stay at home and keep an eye on Vachel and not let him say the wrong things to Sara. She has promised him the house if he marries. In the old days when somebody promised you a house you got married. But she goes on to Toronto hoping something will break one way or the other and end the suspense before she returns.

Harriet Monroe, too, thinks, at least in the beginning, that something might be made of it, and she brings them together for the first time in the office of Poetry in Chicago. She—Harriet—is just old-fashioned enough to believe in the necessity of the proper introduction, and she introduces them properly and formally, Miss Sara Teasdale of St. Louis and Mr. Vachel Lindsay, Springfield, and they clasp hands, and her hand is cold, and he says, "You have a cold hand," and she says it is on account of her blood which does not circulate as other people's blood circulates. "I lack a layer of skin," she says.

"Pooh!" says Harriet. "You have the same skin as anybody else," and Vachel laughs because he thinks it is some private joke. It is no joke. Sara is quite certain of her facts: she does not know how many layers of skin a person has, but she is positive that she has one layer less than everybody else.

Actually, in a very real way, they have met before. Sara has read with interest, if not complete approval, much of Vachel's poetry. Once, some years before, she received copies of the War Bulletins in the mail. It was at a time when Vachel was sending War Bulletins to anyone he thought might be interested, and Witter Bynner had given Vachel her name and address, and he had sent the Bulletins down to St. Louis with a note expressing the hope that she would immediately declare war on St. Louis, as he had declared war on Springfield. She had smiled. She thought it was a joke.

(She, too, had once been the spirit behind a magazine. It was called The Potter's Wheel. It was issued monthly. There was but one copy of each issue, and the single copy was passed from hand to hand among friends until, at some point in its travels, it fell apart from handling or was lost or was, in someone's curtained study, placed flat upon a bookshelf and forgotten. The idea of distributing it widely, or of urging that it be read by people who did not ordinarily read poetry, never occurred to her. When she first saw Vachel's War Bulletins, and saw that they were addressed to an entire city, she thought it was a joke, and she smiled.)

Vachel has read Sara's poetry. "You have little birds in it, and it softens it down," he says. "I can see why," and he takes her hand in his again. "You are a lily, and I'm a bass drum in a street parade."

"You," says she, "are an unquenchable noisy boy," and she laughs.

"There's a table at Luca's," says Harriet. "Let's not be too late."

She feels that she has performed a service. She has introduced them properly, the frail girl and the noisy boy.

Later there is the first ride together on the Alton, the first of many rides together between Chicago and Springfield and between Springfield and St. Louis on the train which is always so slow when Vachel is alone and which, when they are together, is never slow enough. She sits close to him, away from the drafty window, and sometimes the sun is behind her, and it illuminates her golden hair, and he lifts his hand and touches her hair, and the first time together, after the lunch with Harriet at Luca's, he insists that she come to Springfield for a night or two nights or as long as she wishes and occupy the extra room because there are empty rooms in the old house now that the girls are away and he will show her Springfield where Booth marched and Lincoln walked because it is a holy place and with all its faults the place of as many possibilities as any other place on earth. Surely she would want to see it having read the War Bulletins and all.

And she explains, this first time and several times thereafter, that she really must get home, for mother is failing, and has been failing for years and years, and she herself is coming down with a nasty cold which she caught, she thinks, standing in the snow.

"Standing in the snow?"

"I like to stand in the snow."

Too soon the train slows for Springfield, and he rises and does not look back but goes unsteadily down the aisle, and before the train stops he is off and running beside it and looking up at her through the window and waving his hat. She hopes he will not fall. Then the train stops, and he stands smiling up at her, and he indicates with a gesture that this is Springfield, as if it were a holy place, and after a time the train starts, and he is gone from sight. Sara looks through the window with new interest at Springfield Illinois. She has never really looked at it before. For her, the distance between St. Louis and Chicago is always a long barren mile which must be covered, that and nothing more, and she peers, and sees, and thinks: so this is what he loves!

She finds it ugly. This! she thinks. Steam and steel and smoke-red coal-black buildings, littered streets, a newspaper afloat in the wind, artless architecture and railroad shacks and workingmen in patched overalls eating from lunchpails on a plank laid across a grease pit, stockingless women with shopping bags entering and leaving dim shops along the railroad right-of-way. This! This rudeness, this brutal and hopeless city that looks like all the brutal and hopeless cities of America.

This he loves. Or perhaps he only pretends to love it. She cannot believe that he loves it, although she understands that there are men and women who love the land and believe in the land and contend that the land holds a promise. In her own way she wishes it well; she never quite despises it, yet she never quite loves it or trusts it.

Out of nowhere beside the railroad track a signboard glides swiftly into her vision.

GOOD-BY

COME AGAIN

SPRINGFIELD

There are the railroad trips together, usually between Springfield and Chicago. Sara prefers New York, possibly because it is more European than Chicago. She has been to Europe, where she had a splendid time until her portable electric stove broke down, and she much prefers New York to Chicago. But mother is failing, and she cannot roam too far, and Vachel is glad for that—not that her mother is failing but that there is a thing that keeps her close.

Usually he meets the train at Springfield. He climbs aboard as close to the front as he can, and he wanders back through the coaches, seeking the girl with the golden hair. She has saved a seat, and he asks permission to sit beside her, assuring her that he is a respectable young man of a good Springfield family, that he is a poet, but not violent, and that he has credentials to prove it. He produces, then, the work he has done since last they were together, taking from his breast pocket a growing poem which, says he, is to be dedicated to a girl from St. Louis.

It is a delicate poem. He calls it The Chinese Nightingale—a song in Chinese tapestries—and it grows beneath his hand, little by little, until it becomes a very long poem speaking of his vision of peace, of eternal spring, and of love in a way that he has never known love before.

She admires the poem. He wishes she would admire it more vehemently, but vehemence in Sara is subordinate to cool analysis. She is craftsman, analyst; it is he who is heat, passion.

One would think they are in love. One sitting near to them might hear the respectable young man from Springfield address the tall, slender, golden-haired girl by names which are rather unusual, but tender, and if the eavesdropper does not understand the allusions he understands perfectly the tone. The young man calls her Cordelia, calls her Gloriana, tells her that he has at last found an angel-friend, that he lives in the palm of her hand, that their coat of arms will be a teasel and a bronco, rampant, and they will live to be one hundred and five.

They are thought to be in love, and it is rumored that they will marry—in a church in Springfield, it is rumored, in the office of Poetry, in the ancestral Teasdale home on Kingsbury Place, St. Louis.

It seems to Vachel that it is she for whom he has waited, that their lives crossed belatedly, over time, in a patient way, and that was how it should have been, first the knowledge of each other, and then the presence of each other, and now there is, or so it seems, the marriage of minds, her hand upon his, softening and deepening both himself and his poetry. Though there be miles and miles between them he feels her presence, sees her face, her hair, knows her smile, her voice. In this presence he composes the best song of his days.

And everything he ever wished for is now. Multitude and solitude and plenitude is now, and when he writes a poem it will be read, and when he speaks he will be heard, and this a poet needs as he needs bread. On this he grows, and his substance multiplies, and it seems to Vachel now that after the long lonesomeness he is at peace with his city.

Once in January, and twice in February, and many times in the spring, he climbs high-spirited aboard the Alton and rides the hundred miles to St. Louis. "Mama," says he, "you can get me in an emergency at the Christian Publishing Company." "Very well," she says, and she gives him five dollars from her purse, and she knows, and he knows she knows, that he will be nowhere near the Christian Publishing Company or any other publishing company in St. Louis, and she warns him, "Vachel, you be nice and say the right thing and remember how frail she is. She looked frail to me." (When Sara comes to Springfield Mama is always concerned about how pale and frail she is.) "And don't insist upon walking," says Mama. (In Springfield Vachel took Sara walking all over town, seeing the sights.)

"No, Mama," says he. "She said we'd go look at the boats."

"It will be cold by the river."

"We'll dress up warm."

And betweentimes he is home and at work, and his room looking out upon the Governor's yard is as it always was, a bed and a chair and a table and crooked bookcases standing at a list because he was never good with tools, and a cabinet in which nothing is filed quite right, and it does not seem to be the same room at all because he remembers it mainly as a place of defeat where everything defied him and his drawings emerged as clear upside down as right side up, and nobody understood his poems, and once he wrote a speech and Susan made him throw it away and write it over because it was not proper. And now so much comes so easy to his hand, and after it is written he will send it away and it will be published, and he will be paid for it and not feel the need to look away from Papa all the time, and people do not look at him cross-eyed on the street any more because he is known to be a success in his field.

The atmosphere of his room is different because the times are different, because as if on a single morning the poets have arrived, and they are being listened to, Carl Sandburg on Chicago and Edgar Lee Masters on the Spoon River Valley and Vachel on Springfield. All Illinois is under fire from the poets.

Carl comes down now and then, and he walks with Vachel, and Vachel shows him all the Lincoln sites because Carl is doing a big Lincoln book, and Lee comes now and then to visit his mother. And in Springfield folks do not wholly approve of Carl's view of Chicago, and they do not like the realism of Edgar Lee Masters. But the poets may come and walk in Springfield and be read and heard as any dissenter may practice his dissension, and this is the atmosphere that invades Vachel's room and cleanses it and makes the work easier.

Out of the past, long dormant, the ideas come alive. They become poems, and they may be read and understood, and Vachel is young again because he feels young and the atmosphere is young, and after these poems will come better poems. He will live to be one hundred and five, and when he is eighty he will write the best poems of all.

Everything is now. Now is Sara and love. Now is youth and the best songs of his days. Now is solitude when he wishes. Now is multitude and plenitude. All are the clean atmosphere of his room.

3

But there is this about love: love is not only the meeting of minds, but also the meeting of bodies. And solitude and multitude and plenitude are not enough if the man is to be complete.

Of this part of life, of this incompleteness in himself, Vachel is aware, and sometimes it troubles him, disturbs him, sends him searching within himself for the answers to unanswerable questions: why is there no completion? why has there never been?

Why will there never be until, in a great show of strength and courage, he will at last conquer the dark fear and become complete?

What are the roots of the fear? He does not know. And, lest the questions plague him to distraction, lest they sap the energies of his mind, he pours his strength and his love into his work, assuring himself that he loves cities and open roads and peace and eternal spring and the brotherhood of men and the vision of a perfect city, and that if a man love these with all his strength he is powerless, drained of love, and he cannot then give himself to the love of flesh.

And thus it is that between the frail girl from St. Louis and the robust young man from Springfield, between the search for security and the quest of Utopia, between the cool hands and the warm hands, between the teasel and the bronco, the lily and the big bass drum, the potter's wheel and the bulletins of war, between the portable electric stove and the open road, between the daughter of the ever-failing mother and the son of the vibrant and powerful messenger of Christ there is the brief, tender meeting of minds, but never the union of bodies.

4

Multitude.

The fifty members of the Noonday Luncheon Club stomp like small boys into the big dining room of the Abraham Lincoln Hotel. They are free for an hour. They tuck their white napkins under their chins and fall joyfully into chairs about the big horseshoe table, and Rolf Nielsen thumps with his gavel—"Gentlemen!"— and they rise and bend their heads, and the prayer is offered, and then joyfully again they seat themselves and reach with hungry eager hands for their food, and someone overturns a water glass, and they laugh. They bend their heads over their food. They eat hungrily. Roastbeef mashedpotatoes browngravy peasandcarrots icecreamandcoffee.

Vachel eats sparingly. His stomach throbs. He is nervous. Midway down the table Willis looks up at him and winks, and Vachel winks back. Willis wears an orange badge. It says, NOON-DAY MEMBER, "WILLIS." Vachel wears a blue badge. It says, NOONDAY SPONGER, "VACH." Beside Vachel Rolf Nielsen pushes back his coffee cup and stands and raps once with his gavel, and the clatter of dishware ceases. Rolf's round belly hovers over his water glass, and Vachel reaches and slides the glass away from the edge of the table. "Gentlemen," says Rolf. "I am reminded today of the story about the old darkey." Laughter, and Rolf's upheld hand demanding silence. "The old darkey was in charge of engaging a speaker to speechify at the church supper, and he wrote away to Chicago and New York and Cleveland and a number of other great cities and he could not get anyone and he finally decided that the best he could do would be to have the local preacher say a few words, and he addressed his congregation thus: Brethren and sistern ub de congreegation, Ah has run among de greatess ramifications" (Rolf Nielsen's dialect stories have long been considered priceless, and there is appreciative laughter) "and obfuscations and difficulminations and have decided that for this evening we kin all listen to our own Preacher Rufus. He may not be Ralph Waldo Jones nor Henry Ward Washington, but he is our own, our very own." Laughter and applause. "And so today we have among us our very own. He needs no introduction. Many of us have read his famous poem General Booth Entering Heaven in Poetry magazine and his other famous poems in—elsewhere—and many of us are familiar with his mother and father, long-time Springfield residents and tax-paying citizens."

There is polite applause. Vachel's finger tips are cold, and he warms them, wrapping his fingers about his coffee cup. His heart pumps hard and his stomach makes strange sounds, and Willis catches his eye again, and winks again. Rolf Nielsen consults his watch. "According to custom all speakers must conclude their remarks by five minutes of. It is now twelve twenty-seven. I present, with great pride, our own local poet, Vach Lindsay," and Vachel stands and bows to the applause and waits for silence. Cigarsmoke floats blue across his vision. The faces about the horseshoe are turned upward toward him.

"Gentlemen," he says, "I have waited a long time for this opportunity. I have always wanted the—opportunity—to address you, and I am proud to be permitted at last into your company. I can't get it out of my head that I have a thing to say to you. It is good of you to give me thirty minutes of your time, as I am giving thirty minutes of mine. It is sometimes thought that a poet does little but wander in the woods waiting for divine inspiration, as if God were only to be found somewhere out there, but this is not so. That is, misconceptions about how a poet spends his time. I work quite as hard at my trade as you gentlemen do at yours, and maybe harder. So my time is valuable, too.

"Awhile back I distributed a series of bulletins in which I declared war on this town. I now declare a truce because I feel at peace at last, and I want to outline my truce terms briefly. As simply as I can state them it is this: I do not intend to join your gang; I want you to join mine." There is laughter, and everything within Vachel relaxes; his stomach and his heart cease their noise and their heavy pumping. "I plan to fight your gavels and your clocks to the end of the chapter. I am determined to make this place —this city—a more beautiful and a holier place than the Chamber of Commerce ever dreamed of. I aim to make you get the titles of my poems straight, and not only mine but a lot of other people's poems. The *Journal* writes a bit about me now and then and it always gets the facts backward. Certainly it gets the spirit of the things—the poems—somewhat twisted," and the men laugh bass laughter and look down the line at Bob Mann of the *Journal,* and Bob Mann leans back and laughs and discharges a great cloud of smoke. "In time Springfield will be poetry-conscious and art-conscious. In time we will have had enough of silly ledgers and business methods, and we'll turn to the arts, the fine arts and the art of living sensibly. For myself, I do not plan to give an inch in my fight for a better Springfield."

Applause.

"I told Rolf Nielsen I'd recite General William Booth Enters into Heaven" (applause) "but I don't think I will. I've recited it four hundred and forty-four times here and there in town, and my jaws ache. You may read it for yourself in my book, *General William Booth Enters Into Heaven and Other Poems,* which you can get at

Coe's or Barker's. If you are a little rusty on how to buy a book someone there will show you how. It is not much more difficult than buying a ticket to a vaudeville show. Or you can get it at the library. I am fast learning, to my surprise, that the best way to hide a poem is to put it into a book.

"Now, there's another thing. Books. Before I'm through—before they lay me away in Oak Ridge—I plan to get across the idea that we ought to read books here in Springfield, and when I say books I do not mean newspapers or pamphlets or magazines. I do not mean folders issued by life-insurance companies. I mean books. I was brought up on books. I often carry a book with me, and it amuses me when people look down at it and then up at me and say What've you got a book for? as if reading is something you do only in school. It's time we took books seriously and made them a part of our civics. There's a lot of good books and a lot of good ideas in them sitting over at the library while we waste our time reading financial reports and crop quotations and things that won't mean a thing next week.

"We ought to get out and support our library."

Applause.

"I have a new poem coming out in the Metropolitan magazine pretty soon. I recited it awhile back in Chicago at a dinner given by Poetry magazine, and then I got a letter from Metropolitan asking me not to recite it any more until after it's published. Otherwise I'd read it today. It's a rather long poem called The Congo, and I want to tell you something about it and how it was born.

"Metropolitan asked me for a theme poem. I wasn't sure—I'm still not sure—what a theme poem is, but I worked myself into a theme mood. I got to thinking how one of the big problems we have here in Springfield is the problem of colored people."

A nodding of heads.

"There aren't any colored people at this table today. If there were we might talk it out with them."

Silence.

"So I set about writing a big theme poem, and it was big all right, and maybe it will be misunderstood. But nobody here ought to misunderstand it because you have the villain of the piece right here before you to tell you what's in it and what it all means. Occasionally I read something about myself and my work in a scholarly journal, and I learn that I am full of all manner of subtlety and theory and that I am indebted for this or that literary mannerism to gentlemen I never read and barely ever heard of. This amuses me. The thing about my poetry is this: the sermon and the proclamation are the important thing; my poems are weapons on a strenuous battle-field. I am fighting for a better Springfield."

Applause.

Rolf Nielsen touches Vachel's elbow, and Vachel looks down at Rolf's finger pointing at the face of Rolf's watch. Vachel's time is half gone, and among the men on the rim of the horseshoe three rise and move heavily tiptoe out the door, but for the most part the men remain in their places. A waitress circles the table with coffee.

"The Congo is a porridge of many things. Mostly it is protest. I protest the quaint custom of burning people alive as we some-times do in the Southern states, and I protest that ugly week end we had here in town a few years back. Partly the poem is a hymn of praise to some good books I've read—*Uncle Tom's Cabin* and W. E. B. DuBois' *The Souls of Black Folk*. As much as anything it's an attempt to remind us of a document issued by a chap who kept store hereabouts and practiced law and generally got looked at cross-eyed by the Country Club set because he didn't own a dinner jacket. He used to sleep late on Sundays and forget to go to church, and they named this hotel after him, and I'm not so sure that if he were alive he'd be invited to join this club because he never kept his boots clean and most of the time he owed somebody money. He was what you'd call a poor risk. Well, we forget about the document. We name the hotel after him, and barber shops and schools and poolrooms and saloons and streets. But we forget about the docu-ment.

"So before I let you gentlemen get back to work I'd like to read a Lincoln poem hot out of the oven," and Vachel reaches into an inside pocket and brings forth a sheaf of yellow paper, and Roscoe Root of the Brewery starts to rise from his chair, and Willis beside him touches Roscoe's knee, firmly, and Roscoe lowers himself into his chair again.

"No title as yet," says Vachel. "Tentatively, Abraham Lincoln Walks at Midnight in Springfield Illinois."

"I got to go," whispers Roscoe to Willis.

"Shhh," says Willis.

"It is portentous, and a thing of state that here at midnight, in our little town a mourning figure walks," and the men about the table are trapped. It is a familiar sensation. They remember it from school where they were trapped and sat squirming in hard seats, and now at night, at home, with empty hands, often they sit feeling lost and unfulfilled because in idle hours there is, for them, nothing to fill the empty minutes, nothing for the mind.

"A bronzed, lank man! His suit of ancient black, a famous high top-hat and plain worn shawl . . ."

And the lines have a motion and a rhythm, and tell a story, and some of the men listen now, and their cigars go dead in their hands, and some listen but do not comprehend, and some are at the edge of slumber, and someone with a copy of Berryman's Fiscal Procedures fans himself slowly, and Vachel looks up for an instant at the fluttering white paper, and the man lowers his fan and sighs. Vachel reads:

"He cannot sleep upon his hillside now. He is among us:—as in times before! And we who toss and lie awake for long breathe deep, and start, to see him pass the door." And reading, he thinks: let it fall where it may, and it falls upon the unwilling and is instantaneously forgotten, and it falls upon those who feel the sway of the lines and may in a moment rise from their seats and leave and in the minutest, least visible way, be changed, and it falls upon one man or two or maybe, at the outside, three, who feel and long have felt the ironies, men aware of injustice and inequity who would set the world right if they could, but who, to keep flesh on their bones, work at the business of business and banking and buying and selling and know in themselves that the great gift of life is wasted upon nonsense, and of the three perhaps one in a future time, in a moment of crisis, will desert his past and by some quiet deed reject an old way and awaken a new idea and divert his fellows and in the long run win his point, as in the long run the persistent minority has always imposed its view on the doubtful majority.

"Yea, when the sick world cries, how can he sleep? Too many peasants fight, they know not why, too many homesteads in black terror weep. . . ."

And Vachel thinks of his reading as a single stroke against the high thick wall of conscience, and it will not be this stroke, this reading, but this, added to all the other readings and all the other attacks, multiplied, accumulated, the further straw and the further straw. This much must be done, and the men shift in their seats and look at their watches, and Vachel pauses once and fixes upon his listeners eyes they cannot resist, pleading, demanding.

"He cannot rest until a spirit-dawn shall come;—the shining hope of Europe free: the league of sober folk, the Workers' Earth, bringing long peace to Cornland, Alp and Sea. . . ."

The men remain to hear him out, and when he is finished they applaud and push back their chairs. Rolf Nielsen pounds twice with his gavel to officialize the adjournment, and the men wrestle into overcoats and wrap scarves about their necks and glance quickly at themselves in the glass door and adjust the angle of their hats, and then they are gone, and only Willis and Vachel remain. "I was as politic as possible."

"You did fine," says Willis. "I like that poem."

"It needs work." Vachel folds the yellow papers and returns them to his pocket.

"Sit awhile and cool off. You're sweating."

"So I am."

"You're allowed to keep the badge."

Vachel unpins the blue badge from his coat. "I wonder if anything took."

"Everything takes."

"You're an optimist."

"Hell I am. I'm a politician. Everything takes."

Plenitude.

After breakfast a walk by way of the post office to clear the mind and drain the nose and heat the blood. By noon Vachel is at his table, resuming where last night he laid down his pen and screwed the cap tight on the bottle of ink. It is a long sitting. By suppertime he is weary. He lies flat on his bed for fifteen minutes. His spine relaxes.

He goes downstairs, and he reads the *Journal,* and he sets the table for Mama, and afterward he wipes the dishes and stacks them away, and in his room again he clicks on his light and takes from a corner of his table a parcel of unanswered mail.

The letters come two or three a day. He answers them in order. They are the letters from the people, the voters, and they come handwritten from everywhere, from people he has never met in cities he has never seen, and this is the plenitude, the reward. His replies sound one like the other. He tries at first to make each answer different from the one before, personal and intimate, but it is difficult. He tries to sound warm and friendly because these are the people, this is the great audience that must make the great poets; his answers are brief, and they sound much alike, and to dull the formal edge he draws on each a daisy or a smoking inkpot or a dove, and as long as they last he sends out the War Bulletins he could not give away in Springfield. In distant places the letters are read and saved because the poets do not usually write, except to one another, and when they write it is an occasion. In far-separated places the voter does not know that the letter sounds much like many others.

And after the letters to the strangers the letter to Sara. He writes five for every one she writes him, and Mama says it is bad policy. Mama says he ought to match Sara letter for letter, no more and no less, and Mama is right, and he makes up his mind he will not write so often or at such length, but then, because there are so many urgent things to say, he abandons Mama's policy and goes back to his own, and in his letter tonight to Sara he announces the urgent things the first buds on the trees in Washington Park today he saw two robins a lady robin and a gentleman robin and the lady kept flying up into the trees and hiding among the leaves and he wanted to stay and see how it turned out but he had to get home and work on the Chinese nightingale poem he is dedicating it to her it was to be a big surprise but he will tell her anyway, and today in a book he had not looked in since the New York days he saw Reni's painting *Aurora* and one of the nymphs in the painting looks like her and this is an urgent thing and cannot wait, and he thinks that on Saturday he might drop down and visit the Christian Pulishing Company of St. Louis, but then again he thinks not because the Russell Sage people are coming for the Survey and he wants to be on hand to greet them, and somehow Sara has never been as overjoyed as she might be over a thing like a Survey coming to dig down to the roots, and why, and why has she not written since almost a week ago, and did anyone ever write like this, the page after page, because if he is being silly, or foolish, stop him, and the urgent thing is that on the streets in the distance every golden-haired girl is Sara, and today he was reading The Lyric Year again for the twentieth time, not reading it really, just looking at Sara's name on the page, and his own name a few pages over, and is this not the lyric year, the best year that ever was *Your hand is on my head and on my heart.*

And he is terribly sorry about Saturday, but expect him next Saturday and every Saturday in all the years, and all the days between. At the bottom of the tenth page he makes his mark, a heart. *I send you as much of my heart as you choose, view it as a poundcake. With love, Vachel,* and writing her name on the envelope is the last small pleasure; he affixes the stamp upside down; and as he seals the envelope he remembers suddenly the dozen urgent things he meant to say but did not say. They are the things he can say to her only in the privacy of love.

He puts aside the sealed, stamped envelopes and the packages of printed matter and the unanswered mail, and he turns again to his work. He does not write. He goes over the work he has done by day, tapping out the meters once more, checking his spelling, going back to his source books, perhaps rewriting a line, polishing polishing polishing, sometimes discarding an entire poem. Until now it always hurt to throw away a day's work, but now it is easily done. Now there is time. Now, among his books at night, searching for a word, he may lose himself in byways and side roads, coming back at last to the work at hand.

He is suddenly aware of the quiet of the city. Outside his window is darkness. Mama has long ago passed his door and said good night.

Solitude.

And afterward, when his eyes blur and the pages of the books fall into the habit of jumping before his eyes, he knows the day is done. He tightens the cap on his bottle of ink, and he goes tiptoe through the dark house, downstairs and into the street, and the hot blood cools and his eyes are bathed in restful black. He walks twice around the Governor's square, and then he re-enters the house and locks the door behind him Mama is always warning him to lock the door last thing at night, and in bed ten minutes later he is asleep.

The day is done. It was a good day as all days are good days now, now in the lyric year.

5

Spring becomes summer.

Willis Spaulding and a party of men in a Brewery touring car roll southeast out of town. They hold their hats in their hands. The breeze is cool on their foreheads. "Tell us where," says Lester Heck, and Willis nods yes.

Of course they know where. Every year in the first heat of summer they ride out four miles with Willis to inspect the site of Willis' lake, and the breeze is good on their moist brows, and on the way back they will stop for a beer at Kendall's just outside town. Every year they stop for a beer.

But first they must look at Willis' lake. One always goes out with Willis to look at his lake as one always stops and smiles at a child *look at my dolly she is real.* Lester parks the car on the muddy shoulder of the highway. It is always muddy here, and the seven men climb down from the car and walk stealthily across the road and through the wet fields behind Willis. At the crest of a rise Willis pauses, and the men draw up beside him, and they stare east, and Willis tells them again as he tells them every year, pointing: "All this is wet land. It stays wet. In drought weather it's wet. You can believe me or not. Come out in the middle of summer and see for yourself. Don't take my word for it." The men descend the rise and stoop to feel the ground, and the ground is wet, as Willis says. Every year the ground is wet. "She drains off down Sugar Creek and Lick Creek. Maybe she even comes down from Horse Creek for all I know. Ask an engineer. Ask Scowles. Don't take my word for it."

"We believe you."

Willis holds two fingers aloft. "One, water," he says. "Two, beside water, recreation. Swimming. Maybe even sailing. Every year we have a water problem."

"It's vexatious," Lester says.

"It sure as hell is. Here you got water cheap and a place to play. Scowles says there's enough water here for a hundred thousand people. Believe Scowles if you don't believe me. He's not what you'd call a dreamer."

"No," says Lester, "he's not," and the men turn and go back up the rise and down the other side and across the fields to the road. On the concrete highway they stamp the mud from their shoes, and they climb back into the automobile, and Lester swings it around and heads toward town. "Some beer?"

"Don't mind if I do." Curt Stapp of Sangamon County Trust always looks forward to the morning. He likes to get out of the bank once in a while.

"Count us all in I guess," says Roscoe Root. "Willis?"

"Sure," says Willis.

"You ain't mad," says Lester. He is always afraid that Willis will be angry.

"I'm never mad."

"Because even if you was mad there's nothing anybody could do. There's the water people, and if I do say so myself there's the Brewery people. I'm nobody. People think that when I say something the Brewery has got to back it. No sir. There's stockholders."

"I know all about it," says Willis.

"So don't be mad at me."

They stop for beer at Kendall's. The long tables hold six, and Willis on a folding chair sits at the end of the table, on the aisle, and down the table on his right and on his left the men sit talking, and it seems to Willis that this was how they sat last year, in exactly the same order, Curt and Lester and Burr Davis, Buster Lennon and Roscoe Root and Phil Smith, and who was it whose table was prepared in the presence of his enemies every year they come and look at his lake. It is decent of them to come. He likes them. And they will fight his lake, and he will fight back, and when he has created a lake where now there is swamp they will come to his lake and swim in it and sail their boats and drink the water.

"Three, six, seven," says Kendall. "Thirty-five cents."

"Here, let me," says Willis. He takes change from his pocket and spreads it on the table before him and counts out the money and puts the remainder back into his pocket. Every year he buys the beer.

And beer will go to a dime, and then be forbidden altogether, and before it is back there will be a lake, and cheap public water, and children splashing in Lake Springfield, and full sails on the water, and the water flooding white over Spaulding Dam near the Vachel Lindsay Nature Trail. Burr Davis and Phil Smith will be dead, and Willis will be older, much older, and he will never pass Kendall's on the lake road without remembering how every summer, ten and twelve times a summer, he came out to show people his lake, and how on the way back they often stopped for a beer.

6

Dry summer is wet fall.

The Alton from St. Louis pulls dripping into Springfield. On a

handcart under the open shed Vachel sits swinging his legs, and
when the train comes he lets himself down from the cart and walks
out into the rain, looking up at the coaches as they pass, his gaze
moving jerkily from car to car. He has been waiting half an hour.
Mama says he should never be right on time; she says he should
come running up at the last minute, but he cannot: it is not in him
to play coy games. The train slows, and he runs forward on the
wet platform, and he sees her at last. Her hat is a big green affair
with a white Paradise feather, and she smiles when she sees him,
and he runs to her and takes her hands in his, and her hands are
cold. Her teeth chatter. "Such a day," she says. The rain runs down
her face. A large drop wavers on the tip of her nose, and falls, and
Vachel catches it or pretends to catch it, and then, when they are
inside the station, he goes with fist closed over the raindrop and
buys an envelope and a stamp from Mrs. Holly at the newsstand,
and clumsily, with his free hand, he addresses the envelope to himself and affixes the stamp and puts the raindrop inside and mails
the envelope, and Sara laughs. "I forgot an umbrella," she says.

"Mrs. Holly," says he, "two St. Louis *Globes*. As I rule I don't
support the *Globe-Democrat*. But when it rains it rains. I woke
up and it was raining and I was afraid you wouldn't come."

"I almost didn't. I almost missed the train."

"Well, you didn't. This is the last day. It'd be a shame to miss it.
It's not far."

"I should have brought a cape."

They go down the street with the newspapers over their heads,
across Washington, across Adams, and down to Monroe. Sara
keeps close to the buildings, but even so her clothing is wet, and
her teeth chatter, and the newspaper on Vachel's head grows wet
and soggy, and he throws it away, and his hair falls down over his
eyes, and the good gray suit is wet and dark. "This is wonderful,"
he says. "I come almost every day. This is the last day. Tonight's
the big dinner. I'm going to recite. I missed two days."

Sara is cold, and her nose begins to run, and she knows she will
be sick because she is always sick after being in the rain like this,
and her hat, she fears, is the worse for the experience.

"I missed two days on account of the pen-and-ink book. They
kept writing and asking me when. So I did two days' work on it.
When I was down and out they never even answered my letters.

Now they write me all the time. I think they have special people
doing nothing all day but writing letters to me. So that was the
two days I missed."

They turn up Monroe and cross the tracks. "Vachel," she
says, "let's wait." She stops and stands close to the building.

"It's only a block," he says. "I tell you. Let's run," and she does
not move. She stands, breathing heavily, and he takes her arm, and
she runs beside him, and he skips, and he sings, "Just one more
block for to tote the weary load, it's summer and the old folks are
gay. I changed the words. I got a big long letter from the National
Association for the Advancement of Colored People, writ by Mr.
Spingarn personal. They didn't like certain things in The Congo.
Well! I didn't know. Live and learn. So I don't sing darkey and
words like that. Just one more block for to tote the weary load, it's
summer and the old folks are gay," and at the end of the block Sara
stops in her tracks. She struggles for breath.

"This is it?" she says.

"Yes." He laughs. "It'll be warm inside."

She stands in the rain on the corner, looking up at the Armory.
"It's hideous. It's—it's fabulous."

"In Springfield," says Vachel, "we never do things halfway. When
we build an ugly building we make it *ugly*. This structure, young
lady, contains all the worst features of Gothic and Renaissance with
random samplings of baroquerococo, a special new central Illinois
variety of taste at its baddest."

"But Vachel. How can you make fun? How can you live with it?
I can't go in," and she draws away, and he grasps her wrists, and
he laughs.

"We'll do better. Give us time. We're young."

"It's like doom," she says. "The middle ages did so much better.
I've seen them. Jee-*zuz* Christ." She looks up in awe at the Armory.

"Come," says he. "Out of the rain. Inside is the new Springfield."

Inside, to the left, two busy ladies preside over the information
booth. It is early in the day, and the crowd has not yet begun to
come. Before the day is over the people will come and trudge
slowly from booth to booth in the big Armory. Despite the rain
the people will come, and to Vachel the sound of the shuffling feet
is a magic and a wonder. Here, ten days ago, five cannon stood in
the middle of the floor, and today the cannon are gone, and Vachel
helped to roll the cannon out. Today, in the middle of the floor

is a mobile stage, and upon the stage, throughout the days of the Exposition, amateur players have been acting out the findings of the Springfield Survey. They are poor actors, and it does not matter, and along the walls, silently, motionlessly, puppet figures act out further findings, and the drama is big, the drama of Schools, the drama of Charities, the drama of Industrial Conditions (Vachel has been the barker in Industrial Conditions), the drama of City and County Government, of Public Health, Recreation, Infant Mortality, Prostitution, Alcoholism, Parks, Crime, Delinquency, Newspapers, Water Conditions.

Above the midway a large sign hangs from the high, steel-raftered ceiling: WHY?

It is a village improvement parade, and Vachel long ago drew wishfully big posters of a Village Improvement Parade, and Norval printed them, and Vachel could not give them away, and the figures in Vachel's parade carried banners, and the banners read FAIR STREETS ARE BETTER THAN SILVER GREEN PARKS ARE BETTER THAN GOLD and A CRUDE ADMINISTRATION IS DAMNED ALREADY and GOOD PUBLIC TASTE IS DEMOCRACY and he could not give his drawings away free in Springfield.

And now the people have come to the village improvement parade, and they see themselves mirrored, and they are ashamed, and the Armory is no longer ugly, for in time, Vachel feels, after the shame has become action, after the poverty, after the darkness, after the crude administration, there will be good public taste, and the Armory will come down brick by brick, and the cannon will stand before the courthouse, a relic of the past: *This instrument, known as a cannon, was used as a weapon of warfare by the First Regiment of Illinois in the olden days when men made wars among themselves.* It is a dream, and today the dream takes form, and the people come, and they bring with them a damp smell (it is unpleasant), and in an hour the hardwood floor is slippery with black water. The people move soggily from exhibit to exhibit, pressing, crowding, staring, pushing, and the children cannot see, for their eyes are at the level of adult hips, and they cannot see and they cry, and hard wet hands are pressed against their mouths. "Shut up!"

Around and around the people go. The coffee concession is a bottleneck. The coffee drawn black from silver-plated urns comes steaming from the spouts into paper cups and the cups are handed hot from finger tip to finger tip, and the chilled people bring it hot to their lips, and sometimes cups drop to the floor and coffee spills upon the children, and the children squeal. The smell of hot coffee commingles with the smell of people, with the sour smell of soiled children, with the musty smell of damp and sweating people.

Vachel holds aloft a cup of hot coffee. He works his way with the shuffling crowd, back past the exit to the information table, and Sara takes the cup and drinks. "At eleven there's a movie," says Vachel, "and at twelve there's a drama. Why don't you go see the movie? Straight down at the other end. Don't be bored."

"No," she says, "and what's the movie?"

"Mrs. Tubbs," says Vachel, "what's the eleven-o'clock movie?"

Behind the information desk Mrs. Tubbs consults a schedule. "Dear me," she says.

"What is it?" says Vachel.

"Here," says Mrs. Tubbs, and blushing she hands a schedule to Vachel, and he reads it and hands it to Sara, and she reads it, and she does not blush. She looks at Vachel and she smiles a little. She finishes her coffee.

"Vachel," she says.

But he is gone.

At eleven o'clock at the north end of the Armory the curtains are drawn about chairs set in a semicircle before the screen. The program announces the eleven-o'clock showing for adults only, and thus the presence of a great many children is assured, as well as adults, and the film snaps twice, and each time it breaks there is laughter, and Sara sits cross-kneed on a folding chair. Beside her a stout man lights a cigar.

Social diseases CAN be cured. If YOU have a social disease, or if you know anyone who has, or if you suspect (imagine) the presence of such a disease anywhere, here is what to do: The words move slowly across the screen. The stout man removes his cigar from his mouth, and his lips move slowly, and his eyes widen as he pursues the words. "Say miss," says he, "did you catch the last of it?"

She does not reply. How slowly they read!

First, consult a physician (doctor). Speak freely to your doctor. He is your friend. He will help you. For a long time the words are bold and still on the screen, and then they melt away. "Say listen," shouts the stout man, rising, "can't you slow that machine down none?" The operator stops the machine. "Folks," says he, "shall I slow it down?" There are cries, yes yes, and the stout man sits again and looks at Sara. "We done it," he says.

She leaves. Outside the Armory she stands a moment in the rain, breathing deep. Coming and going the people brush against her. "'Scuse," they say, " 'Scuse, miss." Women look sideways at Sara as they pass—sideways, and up at the green hat with the white Paradise feather.

Vachel forgets. It is impossible, and yet it is so. In the great crush of people there is no world, no person, only this, not Vachel, not Sara. He has no food in his stomach, and he does not feel the emptiness. His feet are wet and cold and he does not feel them. He goes around and around with the people. "Twelve o'clock," he is shouting. "See the great drama. See Murphy the cop foil the hoodlums." His hair, still damp, clings to his forehead and falls forward over his eyes.

"Mr. Lindsay where's the great drama?"

"Center stage, madam. Twelve o'clock."

The curtain rises. The backdrop is a city street. From the wings two unmistakably desperate characters run with pistols to the center of the stage, and they turn and shoot behind them, and Murphy the cop, seemingly in the direct line of their fire, comes swiftly onstage. "Missed," he says.

First desperado: Gads.

Second desperado: We missed. Worse luck.

Murphy: Stick them up.

Desperadoes (together): You will never take us alive.

Murphy: Indeed I will. Men, I see that you are very young. I should guess your ages at sixteen. You are not yet hardened criminals. . . .

But Vachel does not remain to hear the story. He drifts away, and somewhere between an old day and a new day he is lost and forgetful. He has never been drunk, but he supposes it is like drunkenness, the numbness of the body, the circling of faceless people, and then, recovering, sobering, he sees nameless, familiar faces, all the faces of the past, shopkeepers and schoolteachers, policemen and politicians, the faces of schoolmates, all the people who ever came to plot with Mama the Christian crusades, all the people he ever saw in Papa's waiting room. And they have all come to see

Vachel's Mother Springfield and his Wise Old Owl, and to march around and around in a village improvement parade. It is a powerful liquor, and he is drunk. It is love at last, after the years of wooing, and this was the first love, this city and this people. This was ever and always the only love.

(There is Sara, and he loves her as well and as wisely as he can, and now and always he will love her and dedicate poems and books to her, and he will carry with him on later journeys, different kinds of journeys, a miniature of Reni's *Aurora* because one of the nymphs reminds him of Sara, and seeing her name on the page of a book, or in a newspaper, will give him always a moment of anguished regret. He loves her because she is beautiful and because she is frail, because her poetry is tender. Now, in the lyric year, she is near to him, and he to her. Her hand is on his head and on his heart.

(But in the lyric year it is not Sara who fulfills him. It is the old love, the first love, the mother Springfield. She is the womb from which he sprang, the breast at which he fed, the lover who sent him away, once, twice, three times, and it is she to whom he returned three times a virgin lover. It is she whose love he sought, and now, it seems, has won, and in the ecstasy of triumph, in the moment of climax, all else is forgotten.)

And suddenly he remembers. "Mrs. Tubbs," he cries, "where has Sara gone? Have you seen her? She was here. Right on this chair."

"That was this morning. I don't know where she went. Have you tried—you know?"

"Well go look," says Vachel, and Mrs. Tubbs goes obediently and looks, and Sara is not there, and she is not at the moving picture and she is not at the great drama, and she is not among the latecomers circling the floor of the Armory, and Vachel goes round and round, looking. He telephones home.

"No," says Mama, "she's with you."

"No no. She's not."

"She must be."

"No, Mama. No!" and he hangs up the telephone.

On the floor of the Armory the Survey Volunteers push the exhibits back against the walls. The portable stage is lifted and moved to one side. Vachel lends a hand. Brooms and mops are produced, and someone thrusts a broom into Vachel's hand, and he sweeps, and Mrs. Tubbs takes the broom from him, and he protests. "You rest," she says. "You have a big night ahead."

Tonight he is to make a speech and recite a poem, and Sara was to be beside him. He telephones the railroad station. "A young lady very beautiful a green hat and a white feather."

"No, not here."

"She must be. Where else can she be?"

"Look . . . mister . . ."

Long wooden tables are pushed end to end on the Armory floor, and white cloths are spread, and food comes in covered trays, and the people arrive and stand talking in little groups, and Vachel knows he ought to leave and get the six-o'clock train for St. Louis.

He leaves the Armory. It is still raining. He buys a ticket and he waits, and the train comes, and at the Armory the people will wonder and look at one another and shrug their shoulders, and it will be as if he has deserted them, as if he does not care.

He returns to the Armory. The people are seating themselves at the long tables. There are fifteen hundred people. At the speakers' table Vachel sits between Mrs. Burr Davis and Mrs. Phil Smith, and they keep saying things into his ears people place food before him he eats behind him Tod Pennington places his hands on Vachel's shoulders leans down whispers confidentially, "Little strengthener Lindsay old boy," and Vachel smiles and shakes his head no. "Up to you old man," says Tod. "A drop or two in your coffee cup? Sure you couldn't go for it?"

"I'm sure," says Vachel, and Tod moves away, and the speeches begin, and they are the same speeches—the presidents of the knife-and-fork clubs, the commissioners—and because of the presence of ladies there are no jokes of the sort one does not tell in mixed company, and because of the presence of Negroes and Jews there are no jokes that might be offensive to them. Otherwise the speeches are the same, and this is the night Sara was to be beside him. He had pictured it they were to have smiled sidewise held hands below the table she and he together were to have known that the speeches were words without logic, and it was not to have mattered because each knew that a city must live long and develop slowly; tonight was but a single step, and in the single step he and Sara were to have rejoiced (tonight there were Negroes and Jews and women, and Sara always asks, "And what about women?"), to have celebrated a stride, not victory but a stride. This he and Sara were to know and feel together. (Or did she know it? Or did she feel it? Or did she even care?)

He does not hear. His feet are wet and cold, and then somehow he is standing, and there is applause, and he is speaking. "I rejoice," he says. "This is the largest gathering I have ever addressed under a single roof. I have been addressing intimate audiences, but I feel that I am at last catching bigger fish. There are a lot of big fish here tonight. The biggest fish in Springfield, one might say. And I may add—it's a good night for fish," and as the laughter dies Vachel preserves the silence. He does not speak again immediately, and in the few seconds of silence the crash of rain against the building is clearly felt, and the laughter rises again, and applause follows. It is a good trick, and Vachel is pleased with the gods, and in the next breath he is himself again. The laughter and applause restore him. The generous noise of the people dispels the misery of the moment before: the people is the city, and the city is the loved one, and Vachel is the lover, and now the loved one is lover, too.

His voice is clear and strong. It carries to the farthest tables. "This has been the most wonderful day of my life. There are assembled here the most contradictory factions in town—people destined to take opposite sides in many a future argument. Or political campaign. I see in the southwest corner of this arena Duncan McDonald, Nell McDonald, and their contingent of fellow Socialists. I see elsewhere a number of ladies and gentlemen who come— so to speak—direct to us from our Brewery. I see the Republican delegation. I see the scattered Democracy, a greater and a lesser wing—a better and a worser element if you like. If there were as much faculty for co-operation among hostiles in the nation of Mexico as there is under this arsenal roof tonight there would have been a government down there some time back.

"I should like to recite a poem. The *Journal* mistakenly reported yesterday that I wrote this poem especially for tonight. It is not so. As it happens, I wrote the poem a long time ago because I took my own Springfield Survey a long time ago. The *Journal* could not have known this, of course. It is entitled: On the Building of Springfield."

He recites slowly, prayerfully, in a meditative way, his voice floating out across the Armory above the heads of his listeners. He recites in a conversational tone, and only the diners seated within twenty feet of him can see that the veins of his neck rise and fall with his efforts. His left hand is upon his hip; his right hand is raised above his head, the fingers outspread. His head is tilted backward, his eyes half closed. His face is grim. It is hard work. It is not an easy task to recite in a conversational tone to fifteen-hundred people. Slowly, prayerfully:

> Let not our town be large, remembering
> That little Athens was the Muses' home,
> That Oxford rules the heart of London still,
> That Florence gave the Renaissance to Rome.
>
> Record it for the grandson of your son—
> A city is not builded in a day:
> Our little town cannot complete her soul
> Till countless generations pass away.
>
> Now let each child be joined as to a church
> To her perpetual hopes, each man ordained:
> Let every street be made a reverent aisle
> Where Music grows and Beauty is unchained.
>
> Let Science and Machinery and Trade
> Be slaves of her, and make her all in all,
> Building against our blatant, restless time
> An unseen, skilful, medieval wall.
>
> Let every citizen be rich toward God.
> Let Christ the beggar, teach divinity.
> Let no man rule who holds his money dear.
> Let this, our city, be our luxury.
>
> We should build parks that students from afar
> Would choose to starve in, rather than go home,
> Fair little squares, with Phidian ornament,
> Food for the spirit, milk and honeycomb.
>
> Songs shall be sung by us in that good day,
> Songs we have written, blood within the rhyme
> Beating, as when Old England still was glad,—
> The purple, rich Elizabethan time.

He pauses and shifts his feet slightly. Now conversation becomes exhortation, recitation becomes plea, and prayer becomes demand. Those of his hearers whose interest has flagged are forced by him to become alert again. In the pause, as the pace changes, a rustling, a shifting of bodies, a clearing of throats, and whispers, disturb the silence. And then there is silence again, and the first demanding words are fired forth. They are angry and vehement:

> Say, is my prophecy too fair and far?
> I only know, unless her faith be high,
> The soul of this, our Nineveh, is doomed,
> Our little Babylon will surely die.
>
> Some city on the breast of Illinois
> No wiser and no better at the start
> By faith shall rise redeemed, by faith shall rise
> Bearing the western glory in her heart.
>
> The genius of the Maple, Elm and Oak,
> The secret hidden in each grain of corn,
> The glory that the prairie angels sing
> At night when sons of Life and Love are born,
>
> Born but to struggle, squalid and alone,
> Broken and wandering in their early years.
> When will they make our dusty streets their goal,
> Within our attics hide their sacred tears?
>
> When will they start our vulgar blood athrill
> With living language, words that set us free?
> When will they make a path of beauty clear
> Between our riches and our liberty?
>
> We must have many Lincoln-hearted men.
> A city is not builded in a day.
> And they must do their work, and come and go,
> While countless generations pass away.

The echo dies. Somewhere a pair of hands claps, once, palm against palm, and then stops. All else is silence. Vachel sits, and the silence seems long. It lasts perhaps five seconds, and then applause begins, and the people stand, and the clapping of hands is the music of Heaven, and after a time it slackens and dies, and the people move toward the exits. There was never such music as this. There was never such a day or such a night.

The rain stops by midnight. The pale moon rides the sky. The train floats south, and all the night is beautiful, and the music of clapping hands still sings in Vachel's ears.

South of Alton the train rumbles across the steel bridge, and the moon image floats on the calm water of the Mississippi.

In St. Louis, at Sara's, an elderly servant sits waiting in the dark for Vachel. She is told that he will come, and he comes, and he raps heavily, and the old woman lights her way through the dark to the door. She opens it. "Do you know what time of night it is?" she says. "What do you want?" She is fond of Vachel. He has always been kind to her.

"I came to see you," he says.

"I'm proud," she says. "Sara's not home." On the hall table, behind the old woman, the green hat with the white Paradise feather is soiled and spotted with rain. "She ain't home."

"Please. I must see her."

"Would I fib? To you would I fib?"

"No," says he, "you wouldn't," and he plunges back into the dark and down the silent street.

Daylight comes. The train moves up the Missouri side, and back across the river into Illinois, and up again to Springfield, and he is home. He is weary. He feels nothing.

Mama fries eggs, and he eats them, and the postman comes with an envelope addressed in Vachel's hand. It contains a raindrop.

CHAPTER TWO

1

THROUGH THE WINDOWS of the Springfield post office the summer-morning sun slants across the faces of boys and men grouped in readiness beneath the flag. On either side of the group the fathers and the mothers and the sisters and the envious too young brothers stand peering over one another's shoulders, looking at the young faces, and the lovers, too, stand watching, and all sound is subdued as sound is always subdued at times of sad, uncertain parting.

Outside the windows, on the avenue, the firemen's band plays thumping holiday music, and small boys march with ten-cent flags sewed to wooden sticks, but inside the post office those who wait and those who watch seem not to hear the music. A yellow cross-eyed dog sits openmouthed with flapping tongue on the sunny floor. He looks upward at his master, and now and again the gentle master-hand reaches down and caresses the yellow head, and once, turn-ing sharply to the window, the yellow dog barks angrily at the music.

Vachel threads his way through the people and drops three letters down the chute and turns and goes back through the sun-swept area to a point of vantage near the door. He hoists himself onto a ledge, and he looks out upon the heads of the people, and now and again during the waiting minutes he thinks that the heads that turn toward him, and the eyes that meet his, do so in a mood of resentment, and he is not sure.

In the sunlight they are young faces. On most the first sprinklings of beard show silver in the sharp brightness, and the faces are smooth childhood faces, and some are splotched with the last traces of adolescent acne, and most of the young men whose faces these are have never been anywhere or seen anything or done anything or even sought answers because they have not yet had time to pose questions, and of the twenty-one men in the sunshine twenty are white and one is black, and within the twelvemonth one will be dead and one will be legless and one will be legless sightless and speech-less in a basket labeled *Sans Identité, Soldat Inconnu.*

Vachel sits on the ledge and braces his heels against the post-office wall, and he listens as the names are called and the answers given. The sergeant in command is a slim man who carries himself with a military air, and to the young men he appears extremely soldierly, and the truth is that the first sound of gunfire on the range at Camp Dix turned his stomach, and he was sent to Spring-field Illinois to work in the recruiting office, and he is just as glad. He pronounces the oath, and the young men with upraised hands repeat it after him, and he arranges the men in ranks of four with the Negro lad pulling up at the rear, and the men right-face clum-sily sheepishly and drift behind the sergeant to the post-office door, and the music stops, and behind the sergeant the men meander out of line. Good-naturedly he halts them and raises his hand. "Break ranks and form behind the band," he says.

The men file from the post office. One man lingers and bends and caresses the yellow dog a last time. "Now you stay," he says. "Don't you follow," and the young man starts to leave, and the dog follows, and the man turns with a desperate look to Vachel. "Mister," he says, "please hold this dog awhile," and Vachel smiles and takes the dog in his arms, and the dog struggles, but Vachel holds him. The band resumes its thumping, joyful music. Five minutes later it turns the corner at Capitol and Fourth and pro-ceeds to the railroad station, and the yellow dog runs frantic in the street before the post office. "Come come," says Vachel. "Calm down." And the dog becomes calm and trots warily but conscien-tiously behind Vachel up Capitol, through the Statehouse, out to Lincoln, and across to Washington Park.

In the park the young mothers push carriages. The babies sleep. Old men sit drinking the sun. A bare-chested boy mows the green grass noisily, and the smell of the fresh-cut grass is sweet and good, and the nostrils of the yellow dog quiver. Vachel goes to the Park Department supply chest in the corner of the pavilion. The Washington Park caretaker, protesting at first that such an ar-rangement was unheard of, after a week-long struggle with his sense of duty gave Vachel permission to store his typewriter and writing materials in the box. He agreed to leave the box unlocked during the day if Vachel would "guard it and be responsible," and

Vachel, in turn, agreed, and now he bends and with some effort lifts his new typewriter and carries it to a shaded table. He returns to the box and kneels and gathers up a bundle of papers.

For a time he sits staring at his machine, and finally he inserts a clean sheet of paper and rolls it into place. Thinking: the first step in writing is the insertion of paper into typewriter. The paper sits naked and inviting. He punches the keys and writes six words, and immediately he returns the carriage to the margin and covers the words with x's and m's. Often it is noon before he writes the first words of the day, and then he writes until suppertime.

Under the table the yellow dog lies at Vachel's feet. Vachel has named him Woodrow. "Silly Woodrow," says Vachel, "you got the whole park to run in." But the dog likes the smell of Vachel. (And the sun-sprayed faces crowd the poet's vision, and here he sits writing, and tonight he will eat warm food at a clean white table tonight he will sleep in his own room. The weight of the inequity oppresses him. Where will they sleep tonight and whom will they kill in the morning? It is the killing Vachel fears. The boys must kill! And should he not be among them, and Mama says think to yourself what would Jesus do, and Jesus says in the presence of Judas *put up again thy sword into his place: for all they that take the sword shall perish with the sword,* and Jesus says *Ye have heard that it hath been said, an eye for an eye, and a tooth for a tooth, but I say unto you, that ye resist not evil, but whosoever shall smite thee on thy right cheek, turn to him the other also.* It is the killing, not the dying; there is time to die, and there are noble ways to die. He thinks he might die someday on a pyre with a Negro, burned alive, or he might die with workers on a strike. There are ways to die, and there are yet other ways, and to die for France is easy enough, and meaningless, because the massed men die for too wide a principle and therefore no principle at all, and when Vachel dies he will want it known exactly why. He has one life, and it must have meaning or it is no life in the first place, and what would Jesus do why does he come back again and again to Vachel? Why does he make things hard for Vachel? Why does he whisper words in Vachel's ear?

(With his own hand Vachel writes: *This is the sin against the Holy Ghost: to speak of bloody power as right divine, to go forth*

killing in White Mercy's name, making the trenches stink with spat-
tered brains, tearing the nerves and arteries apart, sowing with
flesh the unreaped golden plains, and now comes all the world asking Vachel to do in the name of Jesus the thing that Vachel thinks
Jesus would not do himself, and what does a man do does he do
Jesus' work or the world's work? To Vachel it has always been clear,
and he has written, *This is the sin against the Holy Ghost: this is the*
sin no purging can atone: to send forth rapine in the name of
Christ: to set the face, and make the heart a stone. Four years ago
he wrote the lines, and they are still his lines to the last syllable.
Vachel stands upon all the lines he ever wrote, and the view does
not change simply because the times urge change in the name of
one nation or another. Jesus Christ is still Jesus Christ yesterday
and now and next year and forever.)

Below, on the green, the young mothers talk among themselves,
and Vachel hears them and he cannot look. He cannot face them.
He can only think, where are their men?, as they are thinking,
and he imagines that they look up at him, and he thinks he hears
them speak his name. Their eyes are upon him. Round-shouldered
above his typewriter he feels their eyes, and he is wifeless and child-
less and where are their men, where are they now, this instant, are
they dead dying crawling somewhere toward death with the un-
conceived children of the mothers in their loins? Are they dead
somewhere on the deep wet sands of the ocean? Are they somewhere abed in the city of Paris, and who is abed with them?

The old caretaker, with a knotted cane, climbs the steps of the
pavilion. "Morning," says he.

"Morning," says Vachel. The yellow dog crawls from beneath
the table. With his wet nose he investigates the old man's trouser
cuffs.

"Moving right ahead," the old man says. He reports to Vachel
every morning on the progress of the war. "Still think we ought to
surrender?"

"Yes I do," says Vachel, and the old man scowls and stands looking down sadly at Vachel.

"Must be good to sit around all day and not have no work to do."

"Oh, I keep busy."

"Putterin," the old man says. "Putter putter. If I was young I'd find plenty to do—these days." He raises his cane, vertical at eye level, and he squints along the length of the stick. "Pah-*koo*," he says. "Ever fired a piece? Pah-*koo, koo koo koo.*"

"My dear fellow . . ."

The old caretaker turns and goes down the steps. He winks at the young mothers, and they titter. It is everyone's privilege to titter at Vachel nowadays, to bar him from the luncheon clubs, to cut him on the street, to wound him as only a lover can be wounded.

By noon the day's writing is begun. It is to be a prose book, but prose, for Vachel, is a more difficult medium than poetry, and it is not a very good book, and he knows as he writes that in many ways the work lacks power and coherence. It is a dream book, a dream of Springfield Illinois in the year 2018, and like the sequences of a dream the sequences of the book rush blurred across the white pages, and he thinks it would be a better book but for the pressures and distractions, the eyes of the young mothers upon his back, the echo of war, and scornful laughter in Springfield Illinois, and sometimes he wonders why does he write at all why each day punish himself to celebrate his dream why give of himself and his faith why work to save the people with one hand while with the other he must defend himself from them.

The Golden Book of Springfield, by a citizen of that town, being the review of a book that will appear in the autumn of the year 2018, and an extended description of Springfield, Illinois, in that year.

And he gains, in the deep dream, a kind of peace, an escape to a future time, and it does not matter to him that no one now alive will see that time or live in the dream. It matters only that men someday will live such a life in such a place, and Vachel is content to describe the time, though he will never live it.

(Duncan McDonald long-legged straddles the pavilion rail and reads Vachel's manuscript and sets it down page by page, and when he has read all the pages he squints his eyes and rubs his chin. "No stalling," says Vachel. "Out with it," and Duncan laughs a nervous laugh because he knows how many months Vachel has worked on the book. "Well I tell you," he says, "it's all very well to dream of paradise . . ." "But?" "But paradise don't come leaping over the wall. I don't say you got to write a Socialist book. But you got to have some idea *how.* I don't know. It's confused. You and I been over this ground before."

("I take the romantic view of history."

("Sure. So do I. In lots a ways being a Socialist is being romantic. But it just doesn't come like that. Not even in a hundred years. The factor isn't time; it's what people do in the time. You give us a hundred years. God knows I'd like to be alive in a hundred years and live in your golden Springfield. But what goes on in the meantime? What brings it? How?"

("You think I skipped too fast over the meantime."

("I think you did." Duncan disengages his legs from the rail. "Let's let it cook awhile. We'll talk some more. I've got an appointment."

("Thanks for reading it." "Any time," says Duncan, and he goes down the steps and ambles across the green into the distance, and Vachel watches him go until he is out of sight, and then he turns to the book again.)

But he cannot write of today and tomorrow, of the necessary meantime that must precede the ultimate peaceful day. He must leave the present and the immediate future, for the present is painful: the present is war and death and the shelling of Paris, and the great good he always sensed in the people of his city is somewhere buried for the time. He does not know what has happened to it, or where to find it. Heavy confusion sits upon his head and upon his heart and upon his hands, and here in the quiet park, pausing an instant in his work, he sees himself apart from himself, grotesque, ridiculous, a spectral figure making thin noises upon a writing machine, spelling out Utopia while the globe trembles explodes and the men die and the women weep and the children grow fatherless. He cannot write of today and tomorrow; today is lost and gone, and tomorrow will be spent picking up the pieces. He has lost today, and he has lost his mother Springfield, and there is nothing left to love but the far future.

(Springfield Illinois. 2018. The far future. Here he belongs. He claws at the soft earth, at the splintered coffin, at the outspreading roots, and he rises from the grave through the dead weeds. He finds the new race of man, a sturdy crossbreed, living in a city that has painted away its drabness, an orchard city of clean streets, a perennial fair, the New Earth, the New Springfield, and he smells the incense of civic genius.

(The radicalism of the Twentieth Century is the conservatism of today. Here a finishing school stands, the last vestige of American plutocracy. Here is the University of Springfield. Here is Truth Tower, sometimes called Edgar Lee Masters Tower. Here is a building designed by a Negro architect. Close by, on Mason Street, is Rabbi Ezekiel's Heretical Synagogue, and here, as elsewhere, radical bishops preach, and everyone calls everyone *cousin*, and the children have painted on the walls *No man is too awkward to dance*. Three ballet companies happen to be in town at the moment.

(Men and women work at the same jobs. Everybody belongs to a union. The city has a woman mayor. The majority of the people attends the University. All labor is noble. Above the union halls and above the Cathedral the world flag flies. New citizens swear the oath: "I will support the Constitution of the World Government, the Constitution of the United States, the laws of Illinois and the ordinances of Springfield. I will observe my duty to my neighbor, become an expert workman and a member of a guild." The heroes are Harriet Beecher Stowe, Jane Addams, Lincoln, Johnny Appleseed, Debs and Haywood, John Brown and Elijah Lovejoy, and there are no tenements, and the Ku Klux Klan is a forgotten sickness of the dead past, and the guildsmen march in anticoal parades, and artists are scorned who lick the boots of the rich.)

It is a daydream set down upon paper, revolt against the present, projection into the far future, a wish, a plea, a suggestion of possibility, a lover's cry, an inept book written in a bleak time by a saddened lover at a table in a park in a drab smoky city with a cross-eyed yellow dog at his feet.

The United States of America. 1917. 1918.
The lyric year is ended.
William Jennings Bryan, a pacifist, is gone from Woodrow Wilson's cabinet; the big voice is not heard in the land. Of Wilson it is said: he is the unhappiest man in the history of the world. It is close to truth. About him crowd admirals and generals. With them he shares the reins of government. The men he loves by instinct he moves swiftly against, swiftly, efficiently: he sends Debs to jail in Atlanta. It is the system, says Wilson, quoting a last time from a half-forgotten text, and the men who always loved him now fight him: La Follette breaks his hand pounding the table for peace; Jane Addams makes the circuit: "A man's primary allegiance," says she, "is to his vision of the truth. He is under obligation to affirm it." Ailing, she takes to her bed. The doctors call it pleuropneumonia, a medical term meaning heartbreak.

The big voices are still: this is not a time for primary allegiances.

William Allen White draws the picture:

"The whole liberal movement which had risen so proudly under Bryan, Theodore Roosevelt, and La Follette, was tired. The spirit of the liberals was bewildered. The fainthearted turned cynics. The faithful were sad and weary."

Reedy's Mirror dies. The post office bans The Masses and the staff is tried for sedition. The threat is effective: the hostile press closes its doors and sells its stock for scrap. (Twenty years later the righteous Judge Manton who heard the case is jailed for peddling justice.) But now, in the funk time, while the admirals and the generals play at war with an unwilling Wilson, it is Manton and ten thousand of his kind who interpret the law and decide what the words mean.

The free press goes under. The English language itself is retooled to power the war machine: honor now means victory, progress means a battlefield taken or a bridge destroyed or a village occupied, principle is treason, pacifism is villainy, might is right, sauerkraut is liberty cabbage, murder means heroism. The map of Europe is the new primer, for the Book is set aside and the soldier's manual becomes the Book, dissension is a criminal offense, death is glory, blood is wine, and a world can be made safe for democracy by men who never dreamed a democratic dream, never spoke a democratic word, never struggled upward through the soft earth, the outspreading roots, the dead weeds, toward the democratic air.

It is not a time for poets. Alan Seeger dies. Joyce Kilmer is killed at Picardy, and afterward, in the books, they will print one poem of Kilmer's and two or three of Seeger's and append a scholarly note to the effect that they were never very good poets, not really. Who knows? They were young and unformed and half-grown, and who knows what greatness died in their brains when their bodies died? The dead are dead, and with them the lyric year dies.

Illinois. One hundred years of statehood. A century of democracy. Race riots in East St. Louis.

Twenty miles northwest of Springfield the remains of the settlement of Salem are unearthed. A bonanza! It is rebuilt as Lincoln knew it. Here he chopped wood and clerked in a store, here he wooed Ann Rutledge and lost her. From here, on behalf of the residents of the thirteen cabins, a telegram was sent in 1860: "Tell Abe Lincoln that we remember him and that we and our houses will stand behind him." Here, under glass, for posterity, a soap dish Lincoln once used, a pair of gloves he once wore, a faded scarf, an ash tray that once sat upon his desk. Picnic tables. Free parking.

Springfield Illinois. A letter in Lincoln's hand, long lost, now found, takes a dim view of the war with Mexico, a dim view of war in general, but the letter is somehow misplaced. At the tomb in Oak Ridge four soldiers and their ladies listen attentively to the authoritative statistics of the guide: "The body of Lincoln lies thirty inches north of this cenotaph, facing east and six feet below the ground."

It is not the Springfield it was before the war. It no longer asks itself questions about itself. The citizens who three short years ago surveyed their city, if they think at all of the matter, think sheepishly of the gesture. It was an assertion of their strength of purpose, a proof of their power to rule themselves wisely, to shape their own lives. And the war killed it, and now even their sons are not their own, and they must sing the war songs and buy the Liberty Bonds, and the city will never again go shamelessly about the business of reforming itself. It does not now invite dissenters to address its luncheon clubs. On the floor of the Armory gray-green cannon occupy an old familiar position.

Of Springfield's best-known poet the New York *Times* writes: "If he is a little mad it is because his head has bumped so many times against the stars." It is an improper suggestion: he is not mad. He is in a state of shock and sadness, for the lyric year ends suddenly, and he was unwarned. It ends upon a single day. It is as if in midsummer the pages fall from the calendar and dark February is suddenly revealed. It is as if a loved one in one's arms melts into air and the lover is left with his arms encircling nothingness. (Sara Teasdale, quite unexpectedly, marries a vice-president of the Royal Baking Powder Company; he will shelter her, not make her run in the rain in her new hat, not force her into the midst of a multitude.)

Sara is gone, and the mother Springfield too is gone, and his arms are wrapped about air, and he cannot write well or think straight in this awkward, unhappy posture. But he is not mad. He will absorb the shock. He will find somewhere a calendar marking a new lyric year. He will try to force the words back into the frame of the earlier meanings.

But he is not mad. The mad are the men who silenced Bryan and shattered the hand of La Follette and broke Jane Addams' heart and killed Kilmer and Seeger and burned the magazines and mislaid Abe Lincoln's long-lost letter. Who are the mad ones? Is Vachel mad? Is the world made safe for democracy? What is written in history on the pages of the New York *Times?*

2

At Empire Colorado, by the running stream, Papa bends and dips his hands into the water, and the rush of the water pulls upon his wrists and arms and shoulders, and he fights the water. He strains against the current and with a great effort draws back from the stream and turns and walks away from the water, the way he came, feeling his way with his wet hands because his eyes see only shadow, and he falls.

From the platform of the tent Mama sees him and drops the greased pan she holds and runs to him on aged legs and tries to lift him. "Don't try," says Papa, and Mama leaves his side and goes up the hill and across the road to the lodge, and men come and lift Papa and carry him up the hill.

On the train out of Denver he seems better. In the compartment he lies very still, but his eyes are open and he is conscious of alternating shadow and light. Mama sits beside him. Gently she feels his forehead, and then her hands move down across his face and through the white fleece of his beard, and Papa reaches upward through the dark and touches her cheek, and with a last show of strength he draws her face toward his. "Mama," he says, "I am dying."

"Don't say that," says Mama.

"Why not? It's true." Papa never reaches for dreams.

On the shelves in Papa's study the black notebooks stand side by side. At the base of each a strip of surgical tape bears a date in ink. There are thirty-five notebooks. In late years the entries have been few, for the old folks pass away and the young have no faith in the old, and Papa was not so busy at the last. In the notebooks the names are ranged page upon page, the names and the ailments and the fees, and a blue circle is drawn about the name when the fee is paid, and once or twice or sometimes more often on every page there are names not yet encircled in blue. It is Papa's old-fashioned way. Nowadays one pays the young doctor or the young doctor does not come again.

Vachel takes the notebooks from Papa's shelves and shakes them upside down thinking maybe Papa put into them something he meant to be found after his death. Vachel ties them with cord and carries them to the cellar and stands them in a corner with all the precious instruments that were Papa's because all that was Papa's must be saved.

He was the balance. His going unsettles the scale. He was husband and father to two who in their separate ways made the saving of the world their workaday task, and only now, side by side at the descended end of the scale, do the two survivors feel with something close to sinking fear the awful absence of Papa who was ballast. (At table, just the two of them, they share a roasted fowl, and Vachel stands and carves, but the knife is not sharp, and he goes and sharpens the knife, and still it is not sharp, and he laughs, and Mama holds the meat steady with a fork aimed like a sword at the breast of the fowl, and at length shredded sections of meat are disengaged, and Vachel goes to rinse his sticky hands. "Papa always did the carving," Mama says.)

Papa was the carver of meat and the mender of fences. He fed the horses and patched the roof when it leaked, and he shoveled the snow and sprinkled rock salt on the walk, and he earned the money and he knew how to spend it, and he knew how to putty window glass and when to water the lawn and trim the hedge, and he put screens in the windows in spring and took them down in fall, and he knew when a tree was sick and what must be done to save it, and he loved one God and voted one party and went to his grave in peace. He had hoped to live the war out because he had a curious turn of mind: he liked to know who won wars and elections. But of late years he was inactive; he was too old to ride in Democratic parades as once he rode in the Grover Cleveland victory parade. He was the leavener, the less spectacular but indispensable alloy, and without him the mixture boils fast in the pot. (Once the bank calls. It is something about taxes, and Mama is on her way out the door. It is Via Christi day and Mama has never been much interested in taxes anyway. "Here, Vachel," she says, and she hands him the phone and goes, and he listens awhile, and Mama comes back for a book she forgot, and he puts his hand over the mouthpiece and asks her, "Who is this?" and she tells him, "The bank." "Oh," says he, "what do they want?" "Well listen dear they'll tell you," and he listens. "You don't say so," says Vachel. "That's not good I suppose. But I'm in the middle of an Andrew Jackson poem and one on Kilmer. You know Kilmer. He was killed in the war. Nice boy. Big round face. Terrible thing. Well, one on Jackson and one on Kilmer and after that shoot right out and round up some money." A pause. "My dear fellow . . ." says Vachel. "What's wrong?" says Mama. "Nothing," says Vachel, but the blood has drained from his face. "My dear fellow there can't be that much of a hurry about anything and you can just call back another time when your liver is sweeter," and he hangs up the phone. "Why, Vachel! That wasn't nice," and Mama goes out the door again, this time with her book.)

Papa liked people to knock before entering his study, but Papa is gone, and it is almost with a feeling of guilt that Vachel goes bursting into the study in the early November morning. He takes the big dictionary from Papa's shelf and opens it to the pages at the back where all the flags are printed in color, and Papa never liked people to tear pages from books, but Vachel tears the pages from the book. He takes the scissors from Mama's sewing basket and the paste pot from the kitchen cabinet. He walks very quickly to the park.

In the park Woodrow runs to greet him. Vachel made a bed for Woodrow in a corner of the pavilion. Today he forgets to bring Woodrow's meat wrapped in a napkin.

Today is different. The church bells ring, and in the empty park Vachel can hear, downtown, in the distance, the sound of collective rejoicing. Through the park the old caretaker comes swiftly toward Vachel. He forgets to lean upon his cane. His eyes shine and his cheeks are wet, and he hugs Vachel. "This time it's real," he says. "This time it ain't false. They're ringin the bells and tootin the fire horns and throwin stuff out a the windows. Ain't ya glad? Let's go down. Ain't ya glad? Why ain't ya laughin?"

"I'm laughing."

"You don't look like it."

"Inside I'm laughing." With Mama's scissors Vachel cuts the flags from the pages of the dictionary. He trims them carefully, and one by one he sets them on the table before him.

"She's over," the old man says. "At eleven they stop the firin and they all come home. My boys is comin home."

"You're lucky," says Vachel, not looking up.

"Damn right. I tell ya now—I was scared. I didn't tell nobody, not the old woman nor nobody. But I was scared. They went and they fit and they done well by theirselves. Two hours and she'll be over. Hear the noise! By God there ain't been a noise like this in a long time."

"Hold these down," says Vachel, and the old man places his hand on the pile of paper flags to protect them from the breeze, and Vachel unscrews the paste pot. Woodrow, on his hind legs, sniffs. He sets his paws on the table and sniffs expectant at the good smell. "Down," the old man says, rapping Woodrow's paws with his cane.

Vachel takes the flags one by one from the pile and spreads paste on the back of each, and he pastes the flags of all the nations to a sheet of white paper, and the old man watches. He thinks Vachel is crazy, but he likes him because nobody loves an old man and nobody listens to him, but Vachel usually listens, and they have had good talks in the park together, and Vachel is mad but the old man likes him. "How'd it go on that business with the bank?" the old man asks.

"Fine."

"You got the money?"

"No."

"Seems like if ya'd rustle around a bit ya might get it. If I had it I'd loan it."

"Thanks. Now don't let this blow away." Vachel goes down the pavilion steps and breaks a twig from a tree, and with the old man's knife he slits the twig halfway down the middle and inserts the paper, and then he binds the top of the split twig with a length of shoelace, and then he waves the flag.

"She's right pretty."

"Yes. Isn't she. What time is it?"

"Halfway ta nine-fifteen."

"Wouldn't you think they'd stop it right when the decision was made. Why do they wait?"

"They *got* to wait."

"Don't be silly."

"Why—they got rules. Ya got to have rules."

"Suppose you were one of the people that was shot between now and eleven o'clock?"

"I wouldn't like it. But I don't suppose I'd complain. How ya gonna regulate things if ya don't have rules? How come ya ta talk? Ya ain't been interested in the damn war since she begun, so how come ya ta get interested in it all of a sudden when it's over? I'll tell ya. I never told ya, but I'll tell ya now. There's people done talkin. About you."

"What they say?"

"Nothin. They say it's mighty queer. You."

"What else?"

"Ain't that enough? Let's go downtown. They're blowin the horns and ringin the bells and makin a mighty fuss."

"Yes. Let's go. I got to get some meat for Woodrow. Come along, you silly dog. What time is it? I think if they know it's over they ought to stop the shooting."

Downtown the shops are closed and Vachel cannot buy meat. From the windows and roofs jubilant hands send a rain of paper into the streets. The bells ring and the horns blow, and strangers kiss, and the compact weight of the people moves solid and unresisting down Capitol toward the Statehouse. "No use," the old man says, "ya can't get through."

"I got to get some meat for the pup," says Vachel. "There'll be some place open," and the old man turns and moves with the crowd, and Vachel holds his flag above his head and seeks the bare spaces in the body of the people, and he darts through them, and behind him the yellow dog keeps his nose at Vachel's heels, sensing Vachel's mission, and strangers kiss and embrace, and salt tears flow, and hearts are full, and all the tensions snap and all the fears are ended, and the frozen waters at the mouths of all the rivers of the world are melted by the warmth of peace. And peace will be forever.

Book IV—JOHNNY APPLESEED

CHAPTER ONE

1

HIS STUDENTS at Baylor University find Dr. A. Joseph Armstrong a decent sort of a fellow and not like professors of English are supposed to be, all wrapped up in their books and all, and knowing very well those wormy old dates and all but never knowing to save their souls how to make change for a dollar and never getting any fun out of life and half the time creeping around in the dreary old library and all. He is not like that. They do not know anyone who *is* like that. Yet he does hit Browning awfully heavy and practically anything that comes up it reminds him of something Browning once did or said and all. He is the sort of a fellow that if his house caught fire he would rescue his books and never mind the *valuables*.

It is a fair and reasonable judgment. Armstrong has a great love for Browning, a large love of literature in general, poetry in particular, and an almost fanatic conviction that, if every citizen of the world were to swallow a generous dose of good poetry upon rising in the morning, tomorrow's students would find today's history a good deal more digestible.

Armstrong, like most learned men, knows a little bit about many things and a great deal about one or two special things—in this case Browning; like all learned men he stands in hourly awe of the happy happy majority which so happily knows how to make change for a dollar and so happily considers that if this is all one knows it is also all one needs to know.

The most alarming thing about it is that there is almost nothing that anyone can *do* about it. As he grows older (he is still a young man) he sadly learns to accept the fact that between himself, his kind, and the happy happy many there is a point of no meeting. Now, if Browning were a purebred horse or a revolutionary type of automobile . . .

Waco Texas is much like Springfield Illinois, and Armstrong, like Vachel, sometimes feels very much alone.

245

The two men have never met. Armstrong has read Vachel's poetry and has found it exciting and has read it to his students (he conducts a course in Modern Poetry, one of the first such courses offered in a reputable university) in the hope that they, too, will discover excitement, and a few of them do. But most find it exciting only to whatever extent it can be said that poetry is exciting because poetry can never really be exciting in the same way that things are really *exciting* exciting like a horse or an automobile and all.

But they are interested in Vachel Lindsay—the person—if not in the poetry, Armstrong having wisely mentioned that Lindsay, unlike Robert Browning, lives and breathes, and that furthermore he is not an Englishman in the nineteenth century but an American in the twentieth. This makes things a little more exciting, if not for good literary reasons at least for good human reasons. The class seems willing at least to sip the tonic if not to throw back the head and drain the cup, and the slight brightening of the faces before him quickens within the professor an idea that has long been idea, never action: if Waco will not come to poetry he will bring a poet to Waco and maybe if Waco sees a poet it will believe that poetry after all is the labor of a live hand, and having seen a poet Waco might then read a poem, and having read a poem Waco might then read another, swallowing its tonic in small doses at first, more generously as time goes by. The ultimate history of Waco Texas might then be more digestible.

He has heard that Alfred Noyes plans a summer tour of America, and, with all the confident enthusiasm of a young man whose fresh idea has yet to clash with practical consideration, he writes to Noyes's agent, extending on behalf of Baylor University an invitation to the British poet to visit Waco.

To which the agent in question replies with a courteous but categorical no, on several grounds: Waco is a long way off the beaten path, Southern tours have proved unprofitable in the past; the reply hints that Dr. Armstrong is in all probability the only human being south of the Mason-Dixon line who cares to be visited by Noyes. However (the agent states) if ten public lectures can be arranged in addition to the one which Dr. Armstrong claims to be able to arrange at Baylor, and if they can be paid for at professional rates, the agent on behalf of Mr. Noyes will take the matter under consideration.

Eleven professional lectures. It seems a large order. Armstrong, sitting at his desk with the agent's letter before him, spreads beside it a large map of Texas, and he views with mixed feelings that out-sized forty-eighth part of the Union which, much like the other forty-seven, is a source of combined wonder and chagrin to all who thoughtfully behold it, and he knows, or thinks he knows, the futil-ity of asking the state of Texas to pause for an instant to listen to someone as little informed as Mr. Noyes.

But then, setting aside cool logic and subduing for the moment certain grave suspicions concerning Texas, he proceeds to write letters to every institution of higher learning in the state. Would they like to have Mr. Noyes? Will they hire him a hall? Can they provide an audience?

They would, and they will, and they can, or so they say, and he finds himself suddenly in business though he never meant to get into business, and he assures Noyes's agent that professional rates will be paid, he—Armstrong—to guarantee the sum, though (se-cretly) he is distressed by the sight of himself adventuring in high finance like this.

Noyes comes, and after Noyes Masefield, and, after Masefield, having run out of Englishmen for the moment, Armstrong writes to Vachel in Springfield, and Vachel replies transport me and feed me and send me home safe with a hundred-dollar bill pinned in my pocket and I will go up and down Texas letting them see me and hear me. I can recite (writes Vachel) five times a day on a good night's sleep and a fifty-cent breakfast.

And Vachel comes, and he recites twelve times in four days, and after Vachel, totting up accounts, Armstrong finds himself five hundred dollars ahead of the game. He buys five hundred dollars' worth of books for the Baylor library.

Vachel has tried, on several occasions, to interest professional lecture agencies in what he describes as his platformidability. But for a variety of reasons no lasting connections are made.

Platforming is a business, and Vachel seems to them less inter-ested in business than in carrying a message, and while it is cer-tainly noble to wish to bear a message it is not always sure-fire at the ticket window. The agencies always advise their lecturers to have a message, but they are always careful to add that the mes-sage must never offend. And he wants to be Johnny Appleseed,

advancing upon bare land and leaving in his wake a forest lush
with growth, but this is scarcely business because the bare lands—
the towns and the middle-sized cities—have never paid off though
of course it is admirable to wish to be Johnny Appleseed, for he was
a noble fellow and while it is regrettable that we do not have more
Johnny Appleseeds these days business is after all business. We
speak from experience.

Vachel argues: there are one hundred fine poets in the land, and
they are singing on an island to themselves, and I will go and make
the way easy, and after me the poets will follow; and he is fore-
warned by the hardheaded agencies that it has never been done and
cannot now be done and probably can never be done what island.

But there is then the Texas conquest, or that which seems to him
a conquest, twelve recitals in four days, and John Brown and
Abraham Lincoln publicly celebrated deep in Dixie, and it seems
to him a conquest.

Now, home again, he writes to Armstrong: if we have done what
we have done down there to Mason and Dixon why can't we do the
same in the other forty-seven? And Armstrong who is young like
Vachel, and who believes like Vachel in improbable people like
Johnny Appleseed and who, like Vachel, has no practical business
experience behind him to remind him that THINK not DREAM is
the byword and the password and indeed The Word itself, proceeds
to arrange a tour that will carry Vachel, according to his request,
from Springfield to Connecticut, from Connecticut through the
Atlantic South, thence westward to California, then home.

They call it their Transcontinental. It may flop on its face halfway through Indiana, but for the present it is their Transcontinental. They will do one and one only (in the space of three years
they will do three), Armstrong directing it from Waco, sticking
colored pins in the map and writing the necessary letters and arranging for the collection of the fees which, they strictly agree, shall
never exceed one hundred dollars per engagement, Vachel supply-
ing the lungs, the noise, the racket, the clamor, the poetry and the
song which, together, are the message, the peppermint-flavored
tonic.

The first Transcontinental goes according to plan, Springfield to
Springfield via New England, Dixie and the Far West, a bold in-
vasion conceived and conducted by two teachers in strange dis-

guise, one posing as a lecture bureau, the other as a platform attraction.

2

Near Empire Colorado, on the rocky hillside, Mama shows Vachel the place where Papa fell. "I was standing here," she says. "The tent was here. I had something in my hands, and I looked down towards the water, and I could see that something was wrong," and below them the rushing stream beats itself upon the rocks. "That was the sound. The same sound." Mama looks up at Vachel. "Then I ran down to him, and I couldn't lift him, and I went over to the lodge for help."

"Show me," says Vachel, and he leads her away from the spot where, for so many summers, their tent was pitched. He puts an arm around her and helps her up the hillside, steadying her, guiding her. "There's no sense going back over the ground, Mama." At the road they wait for an approaching car to come and speed past, and they cross the road.

"I couldn't find anyone at first, and then I found a man and he went and got some other men, and we went back for Papa," and they mount the porch of the lodge and sit in the rocking chairs.

This year they are renting rooms. Mama saw that Vachel was tired when he came home from the tour, and she said if he stayed home he would work at his things in his room and answer his mail and not rest, and so they came to Empire, and every day they sit on the porch chairs and rock themselves and look across the valley at the twin peaks of Mount Lincoln and Mount Douglas.

It is restful. The lines of fatigue have disappeared from the corners of Vachel's eyes. He sleeps long nights, and by day he sits studying the curves of the mountain horizon, and in the afternoon he walks into Empire and buys the Denver papers, and he returns and reads them until suppertime, and soon afterward he goes to bed. After a week he is rested.

The Denver papers are full of news of Woodrow Wilson. He is home from Europe, and the feeling is, at least in the United States Senate, that his pockets were picked at Paris, and anyhow the Senate is weary of generous sentiment and fine talk, and they will not go along with Wilson, and the President says he will take to the road, go to the people. He will speak to them from train platforms and in public halls. He will go up and down the land, and his doctors say he will die if he does, and the Senate says let him go let him go it will win him nothing, and Wilson says to hell with the doctors and to hell with the United States Senate, for thousands have died and thousands more lie armless and legless and speechless and sightless and mindless in hospital baskets, and what if one more dies and the one more is he—Wilson. He will go.

It is good to read. Vachel reads it in the Denver papers in the half-light of evening on the porch of the lodge. It is couched in newspaper language, but Vachel has learned to read between the lines. He has read much about himself in the newspapers, and always it is not quite himself, and one must learn to read between the lines. Wilson will go to the people because the people's servants in Washington are no longer a part of the people, because something happens to a man when he becomes a Senator, and he forgets his October promise, and now and then in November the people cleanse the Senate and seat other men, new promises, as the people did in the Novembers of Jefferson Jackson Lincoln and Wilson, and again the new Senate forgets and betrays, and the people go again in a new November, and mark their ballots, and hope, and again the Senate puts the people up for sale. Now Wilson will remind the Senate. He will go to the people. Vachel reads it in the Denver papers in the half-light of evening, and something expands and contracts in his throat, and his hands tighten on the newspaper.

And he lays aside the paper and he thinks as he has thought before suppose there were a hundred Wilsons and a hundred poets and a hundred new Bryans and they all set forth at once on a hundred different trains and made a powerful noise in the land among the people!

The half-light is now no light at all. The moon has not yet risen. The mountains meld with the dark of night. A breeze sweeps the porch of the lodge and flips the pages of the newspaper. Vachel hears Mama's step at the far end of the porch. "Vachel?"

"Yes, Mama."

"Don't sit up too late."

"No, Mama."

"Good night."

"Dream of me, Mama." Five minutes afterward he leaves his chair. He walks a bit stiffly because the cool of the night has caught him unaware, but by the time he reaches his room the stiffness is gone. He opens his door, and then, without entering, he closes the door with a bang that Mama down the hall can hear, and he tiptoes down the hallway and out into the night.

He could not sleep if he wanted to. Why try? He has slept for a week, and he is rested, and he does not want to sleep. He thinks he wants to write. He has done almost no writing since before the tour began in the spring; he thought he would write on the trains, but the trains were too unsteady, and he thought he would write in the hotels, but people always came to see him the instant he arrived. He tried to write once in the library at Yale but a young man kept circling about him to make sure he was not writing in library books, and the young man made him nervous and would not go away.

He walks on the highway. And Wilson will ride the unsteady trains and sleep in the crowded hotels, and Wilson knows, as Vachel knows, that victors have always gone to the people, that that is how Jefferson smashed Hamilton how Jackson dethroned the Adamses Lincoln bested Douglas and Wilson and Roosevelt and Debs split Taft three ways. Wilson knows.

Bryan knew.

And Vachel thinks now of Bryan who lost yet never really lost, lost only the office McKinley won the office and McKinley is forgotten and Bryan but beginning to be remembered, and McKinley lived in the office and Bryan lived and still lives in the heart and brain of the people in mankind not in a name his own line from the Altgeld poem Bryan came to Springfield and Altgeld gave him greeting the people cheered sweating in the sun sang John Brown's Body and Marching Through Georgia went into the tree to weep almost twenty-five years ago a quarter of a century he was sixteen and all the world was sixteen and Bryan went to the people rode the rocking trains and slept in the wooden hotels because Bryan knew. . . .

And now is the time, and he turns in his tracks and walks more swiftly than he came, and he tiptoes down the hall of the lodge to his room and searches among his belongings for papers—the clean side of letters, envelopes, the bare white spaces of magazines, newspapers, an old laundry list. He shakes the ink down in his fountain pen. There is no time to go look for ink. The time is now, and he must write. He hopes there is enough ink in his pen. He is fresh and rested and his debts are paid, and a fountain pen will write on indefinitely when one wets the point with spit, and a stubby pencil lasts forever, and the time is now because Wilson will go to the people in the manner of Bryan.

In the margin of the *Rocky Mountain News: In a nation of one hundred fine, mob-hearted, lynching, relenting, repenting millions . . .*

On the back of an envelope: *I brag and chant of Bryan, Bryan, Bryan. . . .*

On the back of an envelope: *When Bryan came to Springfield, and Altgeld gave him greeting, Rochester was deserted, Divernon was deserted, Mechanicsburg, Riverton, Chickenbristle, Cotton Hill, empty. . . .*

On the back of a letter: *And Bryan took the platform and he lifted his hand and cast a new spell. Progressive silence fell in Springfield, in Illinois, around the world. . . .*

In the margin of the Denver *Post: July, August, suspense. Then Hanna to the rescue, Hanna of Ohio, rallying the roller-tops, rallying the bucket-shops, threatening drouth and death, promising manna, rallying the trusts. . . .*

Lines, and notes on further lines, an excursion into the past, twenty-five years into the past, into boyhood, a portrait in words of a crusade that was dead and then came alive, today, in the Denver papers, and the moon is low, and rising, and the sky is black behind blacker mountains. Mount Lincoln and Mount Douglas can be seen from Vachel's window, and now and again he looks up and sees them, and the sky lightens, but the sun has not yet risen.

On a sheet of plain, white paper, suddenly discovered in the breast pocket of the linen coat he wore from Springfield to Empire: *Where is McKinley, Mark Hanna's McKinley, his slave, his echo, his suit of clothes? Gone to join the shadows, with the pomps of that time, and the flame of that summer's prairie rose. Where is Hanna, bulldog Hanna. Low-browed Hanna who said: "Stand pat?" Gone to his place with old Pierpont Morgan. Gone somewhere . . . with lean rat Platt. Where is Altgeld, brave as the truth, whose name the few still say with tears? Gone to join the ironies with Old John Brown, whose fame rings loud for a thousand years.*

The sun is up, and Mama knocks upon his door. "A minute," he says, and afterward she returns.

"Did you fall asleep again? You forgot to turn out your light." He gets up from the table and reaches for the light and snaps it off. He gathers together the letters and the envelopes and the torn strips of newspaper, and he piles them in a corner of the table, and he meets Mama at breakfast, and she kisses him. "You didn't sleep. You were reading. I can tell."

"I was writing."

They sit, and breakfast is brought, and Vachel begins to eat, and between the grapefruit and the eggs something that eluded him by night is in a twinkling captured, and he leaves the table and strides down the hallway like a man taken suddenly ill, and the eyes of the diners follow him, and they look at one another and shrug.

With a spit-wet pen in the margin of the comic page of the Denver *Post: It was eighteen ninety-six, and I was just sixteen and Altgeld ruled in Springfield, Illinois,* a simple straightforward line that is not so easy as it looks, and the pieces fall into place. Now they are dim and faint on scraps of tattered paper, but he has the framework of a poem, and after he has slept a bit he will arrange the papers on his bed and build upon the dim faint lines and join them together and make a song that will sound like Bryan and look like smell like rising dust on Springfield streets, and perhaps it will make all people feel as Vachel felt when he was sixteen, in Springfield Illinois, and Bryan came.

He returns to his breakfast. He recovers his paper napkin and tucks it beneath his chin, and he looks about him sheepishly, but Mama has explained to everyone how it is when poets are in the throes of composition, and everyone is very sympathetic, and between the first and second helping of eggs it happens again that the elusive idea of the night becomes words by day at an inconvenient moment, and Vachel excuses himself and departs in haste from the table.

Later he returns and finishes his cool coffee, and Mama can tell that the poem must be over.

On a crumpled napkin with the flattened surface of an inch-long pencil: *Where is that boy, that Heaven-born Bryan, that Homer Bryan, who sang from the West? Gone to join the shadows with Altgeld the Eagle, where the kings and the slaves and the troubadours rest.*

3

Somewhere, possibly in the mountains near Empire, Vachel lost the house key. The loss is not discovered until, standing with Mama on the porch in the early September evening, Vachel sets their bags down and plunges his hand into the pocket where the key should be, and does not find it. He goes through all his pockets, and Mama goes through her purse, but the key is nowhere. "Strange," says Mama.

But it does not matter because, before leaving for Empire, although Mama reminded him twice to do so, he had neglected to lock the windows from the inside. He tries a porch window, and it slides open, and he climbs through and steps gingerly over the mail that the postman has kindly slipped under the door, and he admits Mama to the house and then goes out for the bags. And they are home.

Stooping, Vachel gathers up the mail. There are a few letters for Mama, but most are for him, and he takes them to his room and drops them on his table. He throws open his window.

There are two letters from a firm in Los Angeles. He compares the postmarks, opening the earlier letter first. A moving-picture company has seen advance copies of *The Golden Book of Springfield* and thinks it might be interested in filming the book. Lord! Lord! Vachel could go touring for nothing if he sold a book to the movies. But the deal is off in the second letter. *After lengthy consideration it has been decided* and so forth and so forth because there is no love angle. Vachel smiles a crooked smile with half his mouth. No love angle? What is the book if not a book of love? Who loves man or woman with greater passion than Vachel loves Springfield? *We are always on the alert for screenplay material in which young people find solutions to their problems* and so forth and so forth, and Vachel tears the letters in two and drops them into the basket.

Through the open window comes the Springfield smell, an odor Vachel has known nowhere but here, an unnamable and unidentifiable smell, the odor of no single thing, the compound of a hundred or a thousand objects. Sometimes, faintly, he has smelled it elsewhere, faintly and fleetingly, but here by his window it is constant and pervasive, and he associates the odor with Springfield, with childhood and youth, young manhood, a riot, a war, a rainy day in the First Regiment Armory, and with the present. It is an admixture which in a laboratory might be analyzed and found to be so much coal and so much corn and so much Brewery and so much railroad and thus and thus many people, proportionately, and nowhere but in the Springfield air are the proportions identical. He is but dimly aware of its presence, yet it affects him and creates in him a mood, as soft music, dimly heard, suggests a mood. It assures him he is home again, and here he would like to remain and never move a foot beyond the city limits. Here he longs to sit at his table and compose a finer, more mature poetry than he has ever written, and walk among the people he knows and has always known, and stroll on Fifth Street and on Capitol Avenue, and stand by Willis and fight for a lake and public water, and stand by Duncan and fight for Duncan's right to be heard. In all cities there are Fifth Streets, and long avenues comparable to Capitol, and one or two or as many as six Duncans and Willises fighting unpopular fights, in all cities people, in all cities a prevailing sour-sweet odor, yet this is the city Vachel knows best and has longest loved, and this is the house though it be like a million or ten million others across the land.

No matter! Someday he will return and write the great songs within him. Now, upon his table, are invitations from everywhere. He slips them into a large manila envelope addressed to Professor Armstrong, Baylor University, Waco, Texas. Mail which has been forwarded to him from the publisher, or from magazines, he hurls into the basket: if people do not know by now that Vachel lives in Springfield Illinois it means they have not read him at all, and he will have none of them until they have read his books; Springfield is in all his poetry and all his prose, in the lines and between the lines, in the titles and in the margins. An envelope addressed *Vachel Lindsay, Springfield,* will reach him, because even the Government knows who he is and where he lives.

He will go, as Johnny Appleseed went, as Wilson is going. Transcontinental a second time. Soon he will return, and remain.

It is really something quite new in poetry. Noyes and Masefield have come and gone. Now and then a United States poet, to pay his way across the country, lectures or recites and goes on to his destination and never returns to lecture or recite again in the midland cities between the coast and the coast. The poets are quite sure there is nothing but desert between New York and Los Angeles, or if there are cities they are empty, and if there are people in the cities they are a peasant people because all that is worth hearing or reading is spoken or written in New York, Paris or London, or perhaps in Chicago, and Chicago is the far far West, and roughly speaking the Mississippi River is a body of water flowing north and south between Canada and Mexico, bordered by states indistinguishable one from another, Ohio Iowa, Illinois Indiana, Kansas Arkansas, and Kansas City is the capital of Kansas and Minnesota is the capital of Minneapolis, and Memphis is a city of Egypt, and Birmingham is in England, and Santa Fe New Mexico is a place where artists go when New York bores them, and how much postage do you put on a letter to New Mexico, and if poets stir from New York and travel to Los Angeles it is to go with the blinds drawn and an order to the porter to arouse them in Albuquerque that they may look out of the window at the Indians.

And maybe they are right. Maybe there is nothing between the oceans but an unpoetic peasantry, Indians, cactus, and wild horses. But Vachel thinks they are wrong. He will show them that between the oceans there is more than a wasteland. He will sow the seeds as Johnny Appleseed sowed them, and they will take root in the fertile earth, and other poets will follow and nourish the trees.

"Give away all you own," Johnny Appleseed said, "and in an aftertime you will have two beautiful wives."

"Be kind and men will follow you," Saint Francis said.

And Vachel goes wandering in the fashion of his heroes, the wanderers, who went to see if the wasteland was really a wasteland, and in an aftertime the poets will follow, or so he thinks.

He has wandered before. He has gone on blistered feet into hostile towns at strange hours, and suspicious night watchers have shone flashlights in his eyes, and, half-joking, bearded men have threatened to hang him, and dogs have barked the alarm at his approach, and the food has been bad and the beds have been hard. But there is more than a wasteland between the oceans. He knows.

And now it is different. Now he wanders on speeding trains, and he is met at the railroad stations by committees which have planned for weeks to welcome him, and they have fought for the honor of carrying him in their automobiles from depot to hotel, and they have wrangled for the privilege of feeding him his meals, and if once he came nameless to strange towns, now he comes known, and the committee has double-checked the spelling of his name and triple-checked his time of arrival and four times checked if he will have with him wife or friend. But he comes alone, and in the downtown shops there are posters in the windows, and his name and the date of his coming are painted upon them, and now it is the mayor who greets him and awards him the key to the city, and now it is the president of the college, the superintendent of the board of education, photographers with flashing bulbs and newspaper reporters with pointless well-meant questions, and high-school students with memory books to be signed and the local poet laureate with an armful of his own writings. Only on the trains is Vachel alone. In the towns and cities he is besieged. It is wonderful.

CHAPTER TWO

1

SOUTHERN INDIANA is cold. Three appearances a day to keep warm in Evansville, two a day to keep warm in New Harmony, a cold church, a warm church, a cold library, an overheated library, a chilly schoolhouse, Benton where the train broke down, Mayfield where he stifled a sneeze in the middle of The Congo. Blytheville Arkansas. Memphis. Little Rock.

Texas. Austin to Georgetown, Georgetown to Cameron, Cameron to Giddings, Giddings to La Grange, La Grange to San Antonio, a few restful days with Armstrong in Waco.

The people will listen. They may not always agree. They may not always understand what Vachel is driving at, but they will listen. They file into the public halls, uncertain and skeptical, and once captive they remain two hours, three hours, because there has been no one quite like Vachel before. Once seated they do not leave.

He stands before them with a hand upon a hip, the other hand upraised, his head thrown back, his eyes partially closed. He waits, and soon there is no sound among his hearers but those distractions which Vachel has learned are inevitable, the whimper of a baby unused to the night hours, the hissing of a steam radiator, the clamor of traffic outside an open window; before the evening is over the noises will abate, the baby will sleep or come fully awake. Before the evening is over the uncertain people on the hard seats in the public hall will be chanting with him, singing with him of heroes they have never praised before, and they will never forget Vachel in the afteryears: they will disagree as to the color of his hair and his height and his weight, and they will never be quite certain what year it was he came. They will tend to the belief that his hair was blond, as it almost was, and they will remember him as taller and heavier than he was, and they will be inclined to place the year of his coming sometime back before the war, because it seems so long ago, because it seems somehow that he came in a good time. They

cannot quite recall the songs they sang that night, but then, thinking, they remember there was one about Solomon because Vachel
made Old Man Grantly get up there on the stage and be King Solomon, and Grantly died before twenty-four but not long before, and
there was one about General Booth and he made Jughead—he's at
the college now—he made Jughead go home and get his bass drum,
so that was ten years ago, Jughead being then only ten years old I
know because his ma was carrying Priscilla and Priscilla's ten now,
and I guess he must a stood till near midnight cause I remember he
said he'd stay just so he didn't miss the train to Portland.

They remember.

They remember, and they call him Vachel. Because somehow he
was the sort of person you called by his first name, because somehow you knew him.

God you could never forget because it was like we was as much
a part a the show as him, and I remember when he come down
through the aisle to go for the train he was sweatin like he'd been
diggin or plowin, and we all stood up and we give him a yell, and
when he got to the door he turned and waved and we all waved
back and stamped our feet, and I never saw him no more after
that.

The colleges are different. They are bright little worlds unto
themselves. They are usually somewhere at the edge of town, and
there is always between the people of the town and the people of
the college a slight suspicion, each of the other.

On the college campuses, nine times in ten, there is an air of mis-
trust of existing institutions. At nine colleges in ten Vachel can relax
a little, for if he says Dante he need not explain all about Dante.
The professors and the students, on the whole, are at least faintly
aware that a poem cannot be read or heard as a specific report on a
specific occurrence, like a police blotter or a report to the board of
trustees. They can be made to understand that Springfield Illinois
is every city, and John Brown is a symbol of man in the fine state
of rebellion, and John Peter Altgeld is a symbol of public man cher-
ishing an ideal without conceding that public life necessarily cor-
rupts, and Bryan is a symbol of a man with faith in the people, and
the poems to which the college girls dance on the chapel stage sym-
bolize a graceful life and look toward a graceful time when no man
shall be too awkward to dance. These things he need not explain

at length in the colleges as he must explain them in great detail to the townspeople. These are large, meaningful symbols that a great many people, even if not all people, may understand. Vachel's idea about poetry is that it ought to be widely understood. Even those who cannot now understand it may sometime comprehend its meanings.

The children of the colleges crowd the chapels. Few have read his poetry, but most have heard his name, and they come, and they listen, and they hear, as any hundred or any thousand brains hear a single sound, some with pleasure, some with delight, some barely hearing at all, and of the hundred or the thousand many soon forget and some will always remember, and a few will not only remember, but remember, too, that the day Vachel came was a singular day, that the thing that happened in the chapel that day was the singular thing that happens in every inquisitive mind, the momentous thing, the reading of a certain book, the class under a certain professor, the one memorable experience that seems, in retrospect, to have worked the great change and to have made of the child a different adult.

In the afteryears they remember:

It was twenty-one because in twenty-two I graduated, and I remember because I was up front on the north side of the chapel that's where the juniors always sat they still sit there. I was a business major, and I went because I had missed assembly three times already and couldn't afford to miss again, and I heard him and I went to Professor Pringle now dead, and I wanted to switch over to English and write poetry, but it was too late because I was an upper junior by then. But everything was changed after that. Everything in my mind was changed. It was in my mind all the time, and this day it changed, like that, like you snap your fingers, and I went on and I got my degree in business—now they call it Business Administration—and I got out in twenty-two and I went into business, and I went down in thirty-one, and the day I knew I was a goner I didn't go to see the bank or my wife or my lawyer. I wrote him a letter. I don't know why. You tell me why. I guess maybe I was never in business, not after that day he came, not before thirty-one and not since, and I never vote like a businessman nor really ever think like one nor act like one. But how else you going to live? He did something to me that I guess was going on inside me before he came, and I guess it would of gone on, but I remember that day the best. Like I wrote him, he disrupted me. He made me wonder about myself and the way I lived. Whether that was the best way. He disrupted me.

And this is chiefly why Vachel comes—that he may disrupt the young. He comes for a small fee or for no fee at all (none at Tuskegee, in Alabama, where the chapel faces are brown) and he must have lunch with the Board and tea with the faculty wives, and it is wonderful, as such a life must always be wonderful to one who has spent childhood and young manhood writing poems that no one would print, developing theories that no one was interested in, shouting without ever being heard.

In the morning, in the cool chapel, Vachel sits half-hidden on the stage. He is directly behind the speaker, a gray-haired man whom the student-body president has described as distinguished.

The distinguished man is not a very good speaker. He has read somewhere that an effective orator must now and then strike his fist upon the lectern, and this he does at intervals. Each time he pounds he produces a spectacular noise, and the students, eyes upturned, are unmistakably fascinated by the energy with which the gentleman punishes the wood. Their eyes are upon his fist, even as Vachel's eyes are on the speaker's fist, and their minds, like Vachel's, are upon other things.

It is a morning in spring. It is amazing, Vachel thinks, how morning revives him. Last night he was tired, and he had half a mind as he often has when he is tired to cancel his dates and go home. In his pocket at this moment is a letter to Armstrong. Vachel did not mail it last night because he suspected that he would feel different this morning.

(The speaker is ready to strike again. All far-off thinking must be suspended until after the blow falls. It falls.)

And this morning, after the good night's sleep, Vachel feels different, indeed, refreshed and vigorous, as a young fighter, between rounds, his wounds repaired, the salts administered, his breath recovered, feels refreshed and vigorous and ready to fight again. Vachel reaches into his pocket for the Armstrong letter. Quietly he withdraws it, his eye upon the speaker's fist, and when the hand again comes down Vachel tears the letter in two, and no one can hear the sound of the tearing paper. He puts the torn letter into his pocket. It is amazing what the good night's sleep will do.

The distinguished gentleman has a deep pleasant voice. He gave a new dormitory to the university last year and now he is telling how much it cost and how he got the money to pay for it. But a dormitory, he is saying, is more than just a dormitory, derived from the French, meaning *to sleep,* more than just a place to sleep, but a place of fellowship, and fellowship is more important than just living, for fellowship is the essence of good business and learning to be a leader of men. As John D. Rockefeller has said, quote, I will pay more for the ability to direct men than for any other ability, end quote.

Vachel is wondering, as perhaps others are wondering, whether it is painful to the hand to be brought repeatedly into violent contact with the hardwood lectern; perhaps there is some secret method of smiting the wood, a certain angle at which the fist is held at the instant of contact.

At length the speaker reaches, or seems to be reaching, concluding remarks. "The real business of the day," he says modestly, "is really not my own few words but the awarding of a scroll to a very distinguished gentleman sitting here now behind me and ready, I know, to bring you a message from the world of poetry." Among the audience there is a general shifting, a stirring, a sense of anticipation: the morning chapel sessions are never very interesting, but there is always the hope that the next speaker will have something lively to say or do. Once, last year, there was a strong man on the program, and the time passed quickly that way lifted heavy things with his teeth tore the Chicago telephone book in two with his bare hands. And now there is Vachel, and please God let him be either brief or good and get through quickly because Dr. Bush has yet to speak, and it is spring outdoors.

At the lectern Vachel unrolls the scroll and pretends to be reading. The letters, spelling compliments, are drawn with a broad-point pen by the student generally thought to have the finest hand on campus, curled in accordance with that student's belief that a scroll, to be impressive, must contain curled letters. But Vachel is not really reading. He scarcely sees the scroll. He is stalling, thankful for the opportunity to stall, for the gift of time, the matter of seconds during which he can rally himself, regulate his breath, noiselessly clear his throat. In his belly a full-grown cat crouches and snarls, stretches, sharpens its claws and then, at length, relaxes and is still. A fearful silence settles upon the chapel.

It is the silence of the sweltering crowd that waited near the

Statehouse for the first word from the silver tongue of Bryan; it is the silence of the classroom on the first autumn morning waiting for the voice of Susan Wilcox. It is a unique silence, the traditional courtesy the American people have been willing to give to most American spokesmen, the right to speak, after which there will be the right to hoot—or, worse, to ignore—and the right never again to give to that spokesman the courtesy and the silence he begs.

He must now shatter that silence. He must bombard the empty silence, pour into the courteous ear the speech of his brain and the cry of his soul. He must prove, in the space of an hour or less, that he brings a message from the real world, not, as the gray-haired dignitary insists, a message from a peripheral world of poetry. He must be more exciting than the strong man, more compelling than the beckoning outdoors, and he must be all this in an hour or less.

He rerolls the scroll and places it on the shelf beneath the lectern where the Bible rests. In his belly now the snarling cat is ready to spring. Vachel says nothing, neither thank you nor greeting. He tilts his head backward and raises an arm, and the cat seems to become rigid and tense, and then to spring, and Vachel shudders with the effort of first delivery, and his first words knife the silence, sounding in the empty silence like the crashing sounds they represent, felt, by him, and by his listeners, in the stomach's center.

BOOTH LED BOLDLY WITH HIS BIG BASS DRUM, and silence is ended. A few students turn with pleased surprised looks, one to the other, stiffening, and then relaxing. This just might be better than the strong man after all, or if not as good at least different, and chapel hour has been such a horrible bore since God knows when that if only this man will be different . . .

The first words give him confidence, draining away the tensions, annihilating the fear that his voice will fail or his legs buckle or his mind go suddenly a white and paralyzing blank, and the later lines come now without the effort of conscious memory, like water following water over the hump of a fall, and he knows, before two stanzas are completed, that he has earned a certain attention, dissolved a certain skepticism, removed the fear that he, like nine chapel hours in ten since God knows when will be such a horrible bore.

After the Booth there is applause. He listens intently. Applause must be more than the polite clapping of hands. It must be more. It is essential that it be more, just as surely as it is essential that a lover's kiss be more than the polite contact of lip and lip. Applause must carry with it the demand for a further poem.

He is satisfied, on this day, that it does, and that the delivery of the further poem will be more than a gentleman's fulfillment of an agreement to recite some poetry for the better part of an hour. "I want you to hear the Altgeld poem," he says. It is the first time he has addressed the chapel directly, prosaically. It is a deliberate procedure, a small, strategic deception which he justifies on the grounds that most audiences seem to be more interested in him as a man after having heard him recite at least one poem. There is the expected reaction—a tittering, the realization of the half-obscured fact that he is not poet-machine but poet-man. "It's a poem about a man who was a neighbor of mine back home in Springfield Illinois, which is my home city. He lived in the Governor's mansion, which is just across the street from my own—somewhat smaller—family mansion. He was the best neighbor who ever lived in that house. He never loaned us a cup of sugar or swept our walk when we were away. In fact, I don't think I ever spoke to him, and I don't think my mother or my father ever did either. But he was our best neighbor."

The small deception succeeds. Vachel can tell by the depth of the silence, by the angle of the upturned heads. He has learned to know the meanings of sounds, of applause, and he knows now, on this spring morning, that he has won for himself the attention of this restless chapel, that he has forced the attention from Booth to himself, and now, in turn, from himself to Altgeld.

His hand is again upraised. He sees briefly in his mind's eye the memo he once made on the reading of this poem, *with the interruptive quality of a mortuary chant, breathed softly and slowly*, and there is no sound, once he begins, but the sound of Vachel's voice, and they listen because, now knowing the poet-man, they are interested in his neighbor of long ago, and as he recites he recalls, as the poem always forces him to recall, Papa with his *Journal* across his knees and Mama in her apron when he read the poem to them, and how, on the same night (was it the same night?) he went into the wet dark and down to Maydie Lee's and read the poem there to Maydie Lee and Susan and Duncan and Willis and Henry George on the table, and now, breathing softly and slowly the lines of the tender poem he sees through half-closed eyes the many before him who were once so pitifully few, the round mahogany table which is now the crowded chapel.

Applause delights his ear: they would hear more about his neighbors, more about Springfield which is, it would seem, a place not too different from their own home towns. The volume of applause tells him what he hopes to hear, sends echoes from the chapel walls, delighting him, his ears, his whole being, and the echoes cry more, *more*, and he smiles a wide smile, the first smile of the morning, and he mops his damp forehead lightly with the tips of the fingers of his left hand.

"Once I took a walk along the Santa Fe Trail. I walked from Springfield Illinois to Wagon Mound New Mexico."

"Walked?" pipes a voice from the front row.

"Yes, walked. Once in a while I rode a little way in an automobile. Walking is good for the spirit, and it was against my rules to ride. But sometimes my feet got a little tired of being spiritual." (The warm laugh, the exact response, the gentle wave of laughter telling him that a bond tightens between himself, the lone man at the lectern, and the collective face below.) "Suppose we take a walk together."

They would like to take the walk with the gentleman from Springfield wherever-it-was, the friend of Booth, the neighbor of Altgeld.

The Santa Fe Trail: *now delicately, to an improvised tune, now with great speed, now a rolling bass, with some deliberation, now in an even, narrative manner, now like a train caller in a Union Depot, now very harshly with a snapping explosiveness, well-nigh in a hush now, then louder and louder, faster and faster, now sonorously, ending in a languorous whisper,* and they walk with him, hearing the sounds of horns, of automobiles passing westward, hearing above all the shrill, brave call of the Rachel-Jane, and sensing now that the man behind the lectern is leading them somewhere, that the long walk is meaningful, more meaningful than the strong man lifting heavy things with his teeth, that Booth and Altgeld and the Rachel-Jane all march together in the one parade.

There is the bronco, Dick, who died dancing.

There is John Brown.

"But I must request," says Vachel after the John Brown, "that if you beat your feet you do it softly, and with proper respect for the

advanced age of this chapel," because a few have begun to beat
their feet, and when they begin to beat their feet on the chapel floor
and their fists on the arms of chapel benches he knows that he has
won them. He knows that when they have forgotten themselves and
have begun to do naughty things in hallowed places, shouting as he
directs them in stained-glass-windowed chapels, that he has begun
to win them for himself and for the things he is trying to say to them
of Altgeld and Booth and the Rachel-Jane and John Brown—the
broncos that would not be broken of dancing.

He will try the Bryan, he thinks. Usually they want The Congo,
but he prefers the Bryan. He is, he says, in a Bryan mood this morning, and he tells of the time that Bryan came, when he was a lad
younger than anyone in the present audience—"I think it was the
summer before I went and spent three years in college and learned
a lot of things that weren't even in the catalogue and came away
none the worse and maybe somewhat better"—the summer when
the world was to be set free, or so it seemed at the time. And the
world is still waiting to be freed, waiting for the young Bryans.

He recites, and reciting he knows that there, below, somewhere on
the benches a young Bryan sits. There is one on every campus, one
young man who is one generation wiser than Bryan, and it is for him
he sings, for the one young man or the one young lady, most of all
for him, and for the rest as well, even as Susan sang to all her children and yet sang to him alone and sent him unbroken, unharnessed,
into the world beyond the classroom.

Yet after the Bryan there is one more song to sing, and just time
enough. The pace changes, the voice is lowered, and he sings the
song that is sweeter and deeper than most of the others, not the protesting cry of the bird in the hedge but the mystic song of the
Chinese nightingale. It is the song he wrote for Sara, the quiet song
celebrating the quiet time after the street parade has passed the
window. It is his song of love, his declaration of faith, of belief in
the eternal spring that must come after the battles of Bryan and
Booth are won. It is the sort of poem Vachel hopes to write and write
again after he is home for good and settles down to greet his old
age.

They have come with him to the end of the street parade, to the
place of quiet. They are silent now, listening, silent in a way they
were not silent before. The large hand of the chapel clock completes

the turn, comes full cycle. Vachel, too, has almost completed the cycle, and he knows by the sound of the soundless silence below that he has done, in this hour, as much as one man can do. He has scattered seed; no man can do more.

The nightingale song is almost over. Vachel's voice is rough and dry, and he breathes deep before delivering the last lines, and then they come forth, lower and lower, almost a whisper, *They spoke, I think, of peace at last. One thing I remember: Spring came on forever, Spring came on forever. . . .*

The seed is scattered. His work in this place is done. He bows, first at the benches below, then at Dr. Bush and the gray-haired gentleman onstage, and he walks swiftly toward the open door. The cool air of the spring morning is good against his flushed face. From within the chapel there is prolonged applause, the scraping sound of many feet, the opening of doors, and he is pleasantly aware, walking swiftly toward the railroad station, that Dr. Bush will speak but briefly, if at all, to an emptying chapel, and that the words of the gray-haired hard-fisted corporation soul will be forgotten altogether.

A young man runs after him with the rolled paper he left behind, and Vachel takes it and thanks the young man. He claims his luggage in the tiny college station, and the young man insists upon carrying it to the train.

And the train will sweep him from this college town to the next place, and tomorrow, in the next place, revived again after the night's sleep, he will scatter the disrupting seed as he has scattered it here, disrupting the children of the next place as he has disrupted them here.

It went well this morning. Some days go better than others, and today went well. He knows. He has learned to judge by response, by the quality of applause, by the degree of attentiveness, by manifold signs which are neither visible nor audible, but which exist to guide him and to help him perfect his method.

Once aboard the train he opens the window of the coach and flings away the halves of the letter he wrote last night to Armstrong. He writes another. *Dear A.J. . . .* He writes that all goes well, all goes well in the bigtowns and in the small towns, and on the campuses, and soon the people will be ready to be won, and after the forty-eight states are captured he wants to disrupt England. And after that somewhere else in the English-speaking world, and there is no telling how far the thing will go once the poets get moving to the places where the people are.

Dear A.J., Hurrah! . . . and he folds the letter into the shape of a cocked hat and addresses the hat and stamps it and gives it to the porter to mail, and the porter laughs, and Vachel laughs, and the train gains speed, and the wheels sing on the silver tracks, and all the world is the new green of the new spring.

A frail man could not awaken refreshed every morning. But Vachel is a strong man. He lives clean, not for the sake of cleanliness but because he knows he must live a long life, because he must have strength in the later part of life for the greater poems, and because he must have strength, now, to sing to the people and stir them and set their imagination afire and show them worlds they might never know and dreams they never dream. He has always lived clean, and now he is glad because when he calls upon strength it is there within him, ready, and he need not fear spending it. It will be supplied again in the night.

He gives the appearance of doing his work easily, but his secret is that behind the appearance of effortlessness lies a history of hard labor. Before each presentation, with hand upraised, he refers himself to the reading directions he has appended to many of the poems, for his own use and for the benefit of readers of poetry, such as they may be. When he was young and his mind was a storehouse of theory and fact and fancy words—before he put away theory and fact and fancy language and became a man of action—he knew that such aids were called rubric, and now he has forgotten the fancy word, and the aids are simply the means of making hard work look easy.

The rubric:

Altgeld: with the interruptive quality of a mortuary chant, breathed softly and slowly.

Congo: a deep rolling bass, solemn, a rapid climax of speed and racket, a philosophic pause, shrilly like wind in the chimney, now a whisper with emphasis on the delicate ideas, light-footed, pompous, now with great deliberation and ghostliness, now with overwhelming assurance, good cheer and pomp, now to the tune of Hark, Ten Thousand Harps and Voices, now dying down into a penetrating, terrified whisper.

It is hard work, and it is worth the work, and he goes, now shouting, now whispering, louder and louder, faster and faster, and behind him the poet-politicians will pick their way over the ground that he has broken, and they will keep the course because he has blazed the trail, and the thing that died when Bryan went under, and the thing that died a second time in the great pointless war, is coming alive again. Vachel feels it: he is pumping dead air from the smothered lungs and breathing fresh breath through the bloodless lips as Dr. Page of Hiram College Ohio exercised the limbs of the cold corpse to make the blood flow red again.

2

He is the first American poet to recite at Oxford. This fact is uncovered by the correspondent of the St. Louis *Star*, although it is ignored by the British press, the British being somewhat less interested in statistical matters than Americans.

But they are more startled than Americans by Vachel's rather noisy approach to poetry. There is not, between Vachel and Oxford, an easy and intimate exchange, as there is between Vachel and Louisville or Vachel and Minneapolis, or even Vachel and Boston. Vachel is out of the West, and he comes openhanded and free-tongued, and kings and class and protocol and the sacred mumbo of Oxford have never been sacred in the Mississippi Valley. They are not sacred to Vachel.

And poetry is not sacred. It may be shouted in Westminster Abbey or bawled from the highest roost of the Nelson Monument. It does not matter where anywhere will do just so long as it is not allowed to die in the books, and the King may hear if he cares to come and listen, but Vachel has not planned on going to the King because it would be a strictly limited group at the Palace, and a stupid one at that, and Vachel wants the crowds, as at Oxford and Cambridge, at the Athenaeum, in the Ruskin Museum and in the public halls of London.

They are quiet crowds. At Oxford, between two dons in the front row, Mama sits proud, a little disturbed by the unnatural stillness, but proud. John Masefield welcomes Vachel, and Sir Walter Raleigh, the critic, says a few noncommittal words, and the poet Stephen Graham, less reserved than Raleigh, introduces Vachel with positive enthusiasm, and Vachel thanks Mr. Graham and Mr. Masefield and *Mister* Raleigh, and Sir Walter's eyebrows come together in a scowl and Mama thinks maybe things will liven up some, and they do, but not much, because Vachel is out of the far, far West, and if it is English he speaks it is a rather queer sort and really not English any more than it is English that is spoken on the docks of Southampton or in the mills of Liverpool, and it may be poetry he recites but it is not what Dr. Johnson would have called poetry.

Vachel is reminded of a story he has always liked, of the time Mark Twain went to Boston and found to his embarrassed sorrow that what was roaring funny in Missouri provoked only anger in Boston, and he tells the story, and Mama laughs, and he laughs, and Stephen Graham laughs, and here and there among the audience there is laughter, but that which is funny in the United States of America is not at all funny in learned London circles.

After the first recital Vachel is somewhat at a loss to choose his poems. John Brown is no hero in Britain, and General William Booth fled England at the invitation of the King's regiments, and the British upper classes much preferred Lee to Lincoln at the time, and who is Johnny Appleseed and where is the Santa Fe Trail and if it is so noisy why are there not codes to regulate the noise? And the poem they like least and the one that stirs them the most is the John L. Sullivan poem, and Mama says Vachel ought not recite it any more, but he laughs and says he likes to stir folks up.

"May I ask," says a Cambridge gentleman, rising, and clearing his throat, "if this John L. Sullivan was the Irish prize fighter?"

"Oh yes," says Vachel.

"And you write poems in America about Irish prize fighters?"

"Indeed we do," says Vachel, and the gentleman sits. "Frost and Untermeyer have also agreed to write Sullivan poems. Was there some point you wished to make?" and the gentleman from Cambridge rises again and clears his throat once more and waits for perfect silence. "I have made my point," he says.

Yet it is a good summer. The weather is good and the hotels are comfortable and not too expensive, and if the learned of London do not agree with Vachel in matters of poetry they are nevertheless courteously interested, and he drinks tea with lemon and nibbles dainty cookies and talks good talk in the rooms of the tutors and dons and fellows. In the fall he recites in the public schools which are not quite so public as he thinks they ought to be, and he rides about London with Mama and Stephen Graham, and twice they go into the quiet countryside, and Vachel almost feels that he would like to buy a cottage here and live the simple life write half the day walk the other half think in the meadows. But the feeling does not last long. Besides, his money is gone, and he could not buy a cottage if he wanted to. He has just enough money to get back to Springfield. In October they sail.

And home is the place. The United States is the place. England is fine, but the United States is the place. Here, here in the new young country the public schools are public and there are no kings, and Vachel is glad to be home again. He will stay; for this, the young land, is the world's hope, still the new world openhanded and free-tongued, and one may try whatever he thinks is worth trying, and the heroes are the General Booths who fled old countries and found homes here, and the people are the British who never went to Oxford and the Germans and the Irish who would not serve kings, dissenters from a hundred lands, here.

And on the statue in the harbor the tablet says to old Europe: "Give me your tired, your poor, your huddled masses yearning to breathe free, the wretched refuse of your teeming shores, send these, the homeless, tempest-tossed to me: I lift my lamp beside the golden door." And he could not see the tablet from the rail of the ship, but he knew it was there, and he knew the words that were written upon it, and this has always been his idea of the union of states, the reason for its being, the reason it is worth saving, and if this is not its reason for being then there is no reason. It has always been Vachel's reason for being: the young country must be kept forever young. It must always be the golden door. And new ideas must be forever tried, and new songs sung.

In Springfield on the first Tuesday after the first Monday in November Vachel casts one vote for James M. Cox and F. D. Roosevelt on the Democratic ticket, and then he packs his bags, and he leaves on the southbound evening train for an extended tour of the country, a third Transcontinental.

Transcontinental.

The United States of America. The Twenties. A young man with a stuffed wallet, a young lady with false flattened breasts.

We don't know where we're going but we're on our way.

We're here because we're here because we're here because we're here.

Yes, we have no bananas.

I'll say she does.

United States Steel is at 90 and a quarter. Bet a dollar on United States Steel and watch it run. Watch the dollar grow. It never grew so fast before. Bet a dollar on Florida land and watch the dollar grow. Bet a dollar on the New York Central. And the young man with the fat wallet bets a dollar on steel and never puddles steel, bets a dollar on land and never works the land, bets a dollar on the railroad and never goes near the railroad, and the dollar soon is enough and more than enough for a quart of genuine Canadian whisky distilled in a barn just west of Kansas City and stamped with a Canadian label printed in New York and sold by a cousin of a captain of police to the young man with the dollar in Little Rock Arkansas. Quick, dearie, run, put another dollar on steel and another on railroads and buy me two lagoons in suburban Miami (under the turquoise sky) and another quart of Scotch whisky made in Boise Idaho while I finish up this crossword puzzle, and tonight we'll play at contract bridge with Mr. and Mrs. George F. Babbitt. And the young man humming shaves his face with his new revolutionary safety razor.

I'll say she does. We don't know where we're going but we're on our way. We're here because we're here because we're here because we're here.

The man of the hour is George Folansbee Babbitt, and he lives and works on Main Street in Winesburg Ohio and in Zenith and in Springfield Illinois, and he has many aliases.

He is a good hand at poker but his wife insists that he learn contract bridge. Poker is still his favorite game, and next to poker he likes golf, and his heroes are Red Grange and Jack Dempsey and George Herman Ruth and Charles A. Lindbergh, and now and then he reads a well-recommended book. He reads *Main Street* and *Babbitt* and *An American Tragedy*, and he goes with Mrs. Babbitt to hear Vachel Lindsay when he comes to town, but there is not time, really, to think about books or to read poetry. The books are concerned with people Babbitt does not recognize. They are somebody else. They are not he. They are not the Main Street he knows. Dammit, they are *not*.

"Ted and Verona went to a dance after dinner. Even the maid was out. Rarely had Babbitt been alone in the house for an entire evening. He was restless. He vaguely wanted something more diverting than the newspaper comic strips to read. He ambled up to Verona's room, sat on her maidenly blue and white bed, humming and grunting in a solid-citizen manner as he examined her books: Conrad's *Rescue,* a volume strangely named *Figures of Earth*, poetry (quite irregular poetry, Babbitt thought) by Vachel Lindsay. . . . He liked none of the books. In them he felt a spirit of rebellion against niceness and solid-citizenship. These authors—and he supposed they were famous ones, too—did not seem to care about telling a good story which would enable a fellow to forget his troubles. He sighed. He noted a book, *The Three Black Pennies,* by Joseph Herge-sheimer. Ah, that was something like it! It would be an adventure story, maybe about counterfeiting—detectives sneaking up on the old house at night. He tucked the book under his arm, he clumped downstairs and solemnly began to read. . . ."

He reads a paragraph, and he throws the book down, and in the morning Myra, straightening up the living room, will carry the book upstairs and put it back on Verona's shelf where it belongs.

Babbitt does not know, and Myra does not know, and Ted and Verona but faintly sense, that all the great books and all the great poems of the hour are an attack upon him, the man of the hour, and Babbitt fights back and does not know that he fights, but he comes perilously close to winning his fight against the writers and the poets. By ignoring them, he fights, and he scatters them and panics their ranks. The weak turn tail and flee.

Eliot's poem, The Wasteland, is the last great thrust of a poet threatening to be great, but he has fled and abandoned the fight, as Ezra Pound and Amy Lowell have fled, and from the safe distance they turn their guns upon their ranks. Says Amy: Edgar Lee Masters is too dirty, and Sandburg is too democratic, and Vachel Lindsay she thinks is fine when he writes of Chinks and Niggers. In the disorder of the retreat she fires upon friends. Of Pound and Eliot she says: "Each has more brain than heart." The rout is complete, and the hundreds who never threatened to be great follow the leaders and wave the same banners from the rails of sailing ships: Down with the Heart, Let the Brain Rule. To Hell with Babbitt, He is not Worth Saving. Down with the History Book, Up with the Greek. Away with the Simple Word, Give us a Good Old-fashioned fourteenletter word in Greek or Chinese if Possible that Nobody Can Understand and Nobody Will Want to Understand. Babbitt is not Worth Saving.

The New Yorker Magazine: "Not for the old lady from Dubuque."

In the defaulted land the smart set kneels facing Baltimore, and Mencken is God in a land where wisdom is knowing where and what to buy and when to sell, and United States Steel is 109 and a quarter and the dollar bill stretches as far as anyone wants it to stretch. God says: up-lifters and world savers were and are all mountebanks; even in a depression no one will starve in this Republic; I do not believe in democracy, but it is amusing; the liberal movement is half a dozen gabby Jewish youths meeting in a back room; democracy is a 'disease; all problems are insoluble; what this country needs is a genuine aristocracy; Thoreau,

Lincoln and Bryan were frauds; the League of Nations idea is clinical evidence of democratic psychopathology ("the old Peruna bottle" is Mencken's term for the League).

Oh, that Mencken! In a Whoopee time, when the financial page is Scripture and the prophet is Charles A. Lindbergh Mencken shall sound like The Word in the land.

The gods are dead and dying. Bryan dies. Debs dies. Woodrow Wilson removes to a house on S Street, in Washington, but he is seldom home. He is abroad in the land with a few faithful beside him to support him when he stands to speak, to nurse him through feverish nights, to spray his raw throat and spoon broth through his lips and brush the gray hair with a soft brush to hide his baldness, for the people must see that Woodrow Wilson is still Woodrow Wilson ("the self-bamboozled Presbyterian," according to Mencken) even if he is not, which he is not, for he is a dead man walking and talking as though he were alive, and his heart beats and his eyelids open and close as any man's, and his fever rises and falls and rises and falls, and he mumbles of a league of nations and a time of peace, and one day, as expected, the heartbeats stop and the eyelids close and do not open and the fever falls and the mumbling ceases, and he is dead. Mumbling, they die. Bryan, Debs, Wilson. They thought Babbitt was worth saving. They did not know that democracy was out of fashion. But it is. It is gone with the ankle-length skirt.

Sacco and Vanzetti. They confuse illusion with reality. They hear the rumor that this is the free land, and they read on the tablet in the harbor, this is the free place, the golden door, and they make the mistake of believing what they hear and what they read, and they speak too free in the new land, and they are heard, and they must die.

In another time it might not be so, but now it is nothing to the young man with the folding money or to the young lady with the false bosom or to the poets who cannot be bothered with unpoetic things like people, or to the smart set kneeling facing Baltimore. And the good shoemaker and the poor fish peddler sit to die. "I wish to forgive some people for what they are now doing to me," says Vanzetti. "Good evening, gentlemen," says Sacco.

Mencken: "In no other country known to me is life as safe and agreeable, taking one day with another, as it is in These States."

Oh, that Mencken!

And the folding money is real, and in such a time one need not seek leaders to follow, and Debs may lounge in jail, and die, and Bryan was never really sophisticated nor profound nor learned in Greek, and Wilson was a good wartime President but the war is over and who are we we should worry our heads about a couple a Wops in Boston? Let 'em fry! Fry all the Reds! United States Steel is 129 and a quarter.

We're here because we're here because we're here because we're here. A good cigar is a smoke. I'll say she does.

Harding and Coolidge whip Cox and F. D. Roosevelt. Mr. Harding is a good hand at poker, but Mrs. Harding wishes he would learn to play contract bridge.

Mencken: "No other such complete and dreadful nitwit is to be found in the pages of American history." But Mencken votes for Harding. A time of confusion.

Warren Gamaliel Harding is the friendliest handsomest man ever to live at the White House. He looks like a statesman. He is loyal to his friends and they come from Ohio at Warren Harding's call, and the light burns late above the poker table in the Blue Room, and they keep track of their debts in the margins of the books Woodrow Wilson used to read. *Progress and Poverty.* Thorstein Veblen. *The Speeches of William Jennings Bryan.*

"John, I can't make a damn thing out of this tax problem. I listen to one side and they seem right, and then—God!—I talk to the other side and they seem just as right, and here I am where I started. I know somewhere there is a good book that will give me the truth, but, hell, I couldn't read the book. I know somewhere there is an economist who knows the truth, but I don't know where to find him and haven't the sense to know him and trust him when I find him. God! What a job!"

Back to normalcy, says Warren. He is pleased with the new word he is told he has coined. Warren is just folks, and the old friends gather round and talk of Ohio days and slide the cards across the table and United States Steel is 149 and a quarter and Warren deals good hands to old friends.

Teapot Dome. It takes a dollar to make a dollar, and old friends study the cards, and the land and the oil thereunder and the profits therefrom go to the good old friends that came to the aid of the party and never work the land or pump the oil. Warren is just folks. A million dollars or thereabouts for old friend of a friend Harry Sinclair and a million apiece for further friends of friends. Blackmer. O'Neil. Stewart. John what is this business about armaments? Why don't they leave me alone John? Back to normalcy I say.

He looks like a statesman. He walks and talks like a President ought to walk and talk. He is the friendliest man who ever lived in the White House, and he dies of poisoned crabmeat. Or so they say. Or was it suicide? Or murder? Mrs. Harding always hoped he would take up contract bridge, and she never liked his friends, and they will build a statue in Marion Ohio of the handsome gentleman who left his poker debts behind in the margins of the books Woodrow Wilson used to read.

CHAPTER THREE

1

THE DIFFERENCE between the first big tours and this, the last big tour, is not unlike the difference between the earlier tramps afoot in the South and in the Midwest, and the later tramp into the West: in the beginning it was a search, and he went hopeful, preaching a gospel of beauty and thinking he would find a great something worth finding, and he found the rhythms for a new kind of poetry; and now, on this big tour, he must find something new for the new, later time. He does not go from town to town and city to city for the joy of riding the trains; he does not go for the money. The tour must be something more than the repetition of earlier tours.

And it is. There are soft carpets now on the floor of the lobby of the Evansville hotel, and last time the floor was bare wood, and Rotary in Nashville has doubled its membership, and you needn't go down the hall to take your tub bath you can shower private in a tile shower with a glass door without ever leaving your room, and you can pick up your telephone and ask for what you want, and Mr. So-and-so who used to run the hotel he doesn't run it any more; he manages it. One of our new services is a public stenographer would you like a public stenographer?

In Atlanta a dentist pulls an aching tooth, and Vachel takes a pill to ease the pain, but the pain continues, and in Macon he tries to engage a dentist, but the dentists do not work on Sunday, and he goes to a dentist in Columbus on Tuesday, and the dentist observes that somebody pulled the wrong tooth. "Well then, pull the right one," and he pulls it, and he gives Vachel two kinds of pills, one for easing the pain and the other because the first pill will make him sick.

See how the town has changed! Why there wasn't a house beyond the old well, and now they've built it up all the way to the ball park, and the man who ran the newspaper he doesn't run it any more; he edits it, and the lad, you remember the lad he was studying journalism at the State University and he's a big help to me. Mr. Lindsay, how old are you?

Forty-one.

Are you married?

No.

Are you planning to get married?

I guess not. Not at present.

What kind of a poet would you say you are mainly?

A love poet.

What is your favorite poem?

Offhand I'd say . . .

One question we always ask. You notice that we have two-way traffic on Broad and very slow progress in both directions. The paper's position is that if we made Broad one way going north and Jackson one way going south we'd speed things up considerably. Would you care to comment on this?

No. I'd say that if the paper's bent on speeding things up that'd be the way to do it.

And the halls are filled with people, and whatever may have been the irritations of the day they are forgotten because here are the people stamping their feet and beating their hands as always. If there is a fine shade of difference between his first visit and his second the people are not aware of it. They cry for Booth and The Congo, and Vachel is for a moment reluctant. He protests. "I've recited them until my jaws ache. You can read them for yourself, you know," and the people mistake the slight weariness in his voice for due modesty, and they chant, *Booth led boldly with his big bass drum Are you washed in the blood of the Lamb?* and Vachel smiles now and he raises his hands. "All right. All right. But I did rather hope you would discover some of the better ones," and he closes his eyes and inclines his head and remembers the rubric, *Booth, to the tune of the blood of the Lamb with bass drums and banjos sweet flutes and tambourines,* and if there are no drums or flutes or banjos or tambourines in the house then he must be all of them, no matter if his tooth aches or he is tired or a little dizzy on the platform as he sometimes is these days, not knowing why. And they do not notice that Vachel yanks out a middle stanza of Booth, and they do not notice here or there a new word for an old one because the old one slips away somehow, nor do they notice now and then two lines inverted or two words transposed or forgotten altogether. People do not notice syllables dubbed in to keep the meter when the memory fails; they do not know Vachel's work that well.

They are still not buying the books. In a sense they are failing him, making this big tour just like the last, as his fellow poets in turn are failing the people, fleeing to Europe or clinging to one another in tight little groups in lower Manhattan, Santa Fe New Mexico, or in a few square blocks near the University of Chicago.

He has the feeling that it was not a very good recital, certainly not as good as the last time he was here. Nevertheless, afterward, the few come forward as they always do, to see him close-up and to ask and tell the important little things that for some reason or other are no longer quite as interesting to hear or to answer as they were the last time around.

(A middle-age lady with silk-gray hair and a middle-age man with a fatherly smile: "Will you sign a book for us?" "Certainly," says Vachel, and he holds forth his hand for the book, and they have no book. "I guess we'll go get one," the lady says, and she and the gentleman turn and go in great haste through the crowd, and Vachel turns to other people and forgets the middle-age couple. But they return and hand him a book. It is a Bible, and he opens it to the blank endpage. "You can say, for George and Henrietta," the fatherly man says. Vachel pens: "I did not write this book," and he signs his name and the date and the place, and hands it back, and George and Henrietta smile at him and he smiles back at them and it is not quite the smile they remember from last time when he smiled and his teeth showed through so white and wide and his whole face creased from chin to brows and it seemed at the time that smiling was the big thing in his life. They said to each other then: it must be the big thing he likes to do best on account of the way it was such a wide and white smile and how it was not only his lips but his whole blooming face.)

And then the full halls are empty again and he goes into the night, and outside the hall the man with the paste pot spreads milky liquid on the backs of the squared sections of the new announcements, and he pastes the sections square by square over Vachel's name and picture, and above the announcements is the single fixed word, *Coming,* and Vachel stands a moment and watches. "Always something new," he says.

"Always something new," echoes the man with the paste pot. "If it's not one thing it's another," and he runs his short-handled squeegee up and down and across the new face and the new name and the new date, and the excess liquid paste runs down the wall to the walk. The workman stands back to admire his work. He looks at Vachel. "Like it was built in," the workman says. "Well. G'night," and he goes down the street with his pail and his brush and his squeegee. He turns the corner. He is gone.

And Vachel is alone, and the aches of early evening return. He forgot them in the press of the recital, as he always can forget them, but now they return, and maybe the good night's sleep will scatter them as the good night's sleep used to do.

(Taxi? Where to sir? Nice night ain't it? Yes, nice night. Where are we? Oh yes. The Statler, please. The Raleigh. The Century Club. The Davenport. The Copley-Plaza. The Brown Palace. The New Washington. Hotel Fontenelle. The Troy Club. The Jefferson. The Rice. The Ben Franklin, please. The Oxford. The Huckins. The Chisca, please. The Brevoort.)

In the smaller towns Vachel usually walks to his hotel, and except in bad weather he makes it a slow, calm walk, and always it is a lonesome walk, and in the new-carpeted lobby old sleepless men and ladies sit talking softly in the leather chairs, and the clerk asks what number please, and Vachel does not remember there are so many numbers clerks taxicabs. "Lindsay is the name." "Oh yes sir yes sir," and the clerk takes the key from Vachel's box and the notes good people always leave asking Vachel to luncheon tomorrow to supper tomorrow.

And the bare room that is Just Like Home except that at home there are no rates and regulations pasted on the walls and the water faucets at home do not spring shut when one removes his hand to lather his face and at home there are never old whisky bottles in the dresser drawers and the smell of bad whisky in the smell of stale room not Just Like Home at all.

They are not the sort of rooms where Vachel can set up shop and get some writing done. He knows writers who can do their work on trains or in waiting rooms or on an upended suitcase wherever they are Masters wrote most of Spoon River on the backs of napkins and Sandburg can whip out a pencil any old time and go to work, and Vachel wishes he could do the same, but he cannot. Everybody works in his own way, and Vachel cannot work on stingy little hotel tables by bad light they put the small-watt bulb in so you don't use too much electricity, and now and then he tries, but he knows that if he starts to work the blood will run hot again he will never get to sleep, or if he gets to sleep he won't be up in time to catch his train, or if he manages to catch the train he will be exhausted by tomorrow night before the lecture even begins. And that would be letting people down, and the reason he is here, the first and only reason is that he must reach the people Woodrow Wilson Appleseed alone in the bare room and he has never liked being alone.

In the hotel corridors lights shine beneath the doors, and behind the doors people are talking laughing, and he envies them. After his lectures he sees the people leave the halls, and they go arm in arm, men and women and men and men and women and women, and hardly anyone is alone. Everybody has somebody, and he has nobody, and maybe he should have gone wherever it was he was invited tonight, and he could have worried about tomorrow tomorrow. Besides, it will be hours before he sleeps.

He undresses. In his pajamas he sits by the window in the dark. This is the worst time of all, when he is tired and sleep will not come, and he sits and listens to the sound of snoring in the rooms on either side of his, and he gets into bed and tries all the tricks he ever heard of counting sheep thinking of the sea whipped cream poured from a bottle lithe lines of a cat in motion, or turning on the light again and reading bad poetry in the hotel copy *The Golden Treasury* or the duller sections of the hotel Bible or Saturday Evening Post fiction or the local telephone directory. But sleep will not come. "Three eighths of an inch of pre-Prohibition whisky," said the salesman on the train. "An eighth of an inch at a time. Then get under the sheet, no covers, and think about it and drink it in your mind over and over again. It's all in the mind, I always say," and Vachel thinks maybe it is all in the mind because he cut down on coffee and cut the recitals a little bit short, but sleep will not come. "Sit by the sea," said the doctor in Memphis, and he would go sit by the sea if he could, but the people live on land, and land is where the troubles lie, not upon the sea.

And the sea is a lonely place, and he is lonely enough, and the people come two by two to his lectures, never alone, and two by two they leave, and the twosomes, detached from the crowd at the end of the evening, are still in each other's company and he is alone, and he has always been alone, and it is not enough to love the great mass of good people because the great mass is nameless as the farmers in the houses by the highways were always nameless and Vachel always came and went alone. He has always been

among people, and he has always been alone, at Hiram College
Chicago New York on the open road he was always among people
and always alone. And in Springfield he was never quite a part of
the people because if people were praising the city he was declaring
war upon it, and if it was fighting a war he was refusing to fight, and
if it was fighting white against black he was writing poems in praise
of John Brown and Booker Washington, and if they were saying
the secret of life is labor he was saying that beggary is the noblest
occupation of man, and they hated Socialists and he wrote and
printed and gave away free an essay on Christ the Socialist. And
now, in the very midst of adoring people he is still alone, and they
sleep and he cannot sleep, and they remain within the limits of their
towns and cities and he is forever in motion from place to place, and
he was not quite right for England but he is not quite right for these
states, either.

(Exclusive interview: World-renowned love poet Vachel Lindsay,
41, took a firm stand here today in favor of the abolition of two-way
traffic along Broad Street.)

Only now, in the sleepless night, is he aware of loneliness and
weariness. Tomorrow is another day. Maybe tomorrow night he will
sleep as he used to sleep, and then, the day after tomorrow, he will
roar like new again.

(Madison Wisconsin. Witter Bynner, after the show: "It's fine,
Vachel, fine. Beats me how you do it. Me, my throat gives out all
the time." Vachel laughs and pumps Witter's hand, and they embrace
each other because it is good, when one is on the road, to cross paths
with another poet. "It's what comes of having hog-calling ances-
tors," says Vachel.)

"Rum," says Witter Bynner, pouring from a bottle into two hotel
glasses.

"No thanks," says Vachel. "Maybe you have a little ginger ale
around."

Witter looks over his shoulder at Vachel shoeless on the bed, his
head propped with pillows. "Where would I get ginger ale? Where
you headed? Which way?"

"Milwaukee tomorrow night."

"I'll go that far with you. I'm pooped. I'm going home. Too bad
we can't go farther together. Drink your drink."

Vachel balances his glass beside him on the bed, but he does not drink. "I go clear to the coast before I go home. I think I'm going to be tired by the time I get back. I'm tired now."

"Oh you're probably better off than you imagine. When a fast-moving character like you slows down a little it's more noticeable than in somebody like me. I go for the money. Then I hole up until the money runs out."

"Well, I like to get into the small towns, too. . . ."

"I know." Witter holds the bottle to the light and squints and pours himself a short ration. "You can burn yourself up that way."

"A couple weeks' rest and I'm set again."

"Sure."

"I am!"

"Sure. I said sure."

"I feel fine. A little tired."

"You're always a little tired before you're a lot tired. Frost got sick on the road and gave it up. . . ."

"Frost is Frost. People are built different."

"You're just a human being. Remember?"

"I'm not going to do it forever. Don't worry about me, Prince Hal."

"I'm not worried. I'd just rather see you write verse and let the ladies' clubs imagine your face."

"You've got to go to them, too."

"Why? Suppose we all went to them. Nobody wrote anything. All the people who write were knocking themselves out at the Rotary clubs. What have you written the past couple of years? Anything? Don't answer. I know the answer. Drink your drink."

"I really don't like the stuff, Hal. Couldn't we get some soda water somewhere?"

"You can't spend half your time on the road and be a poet the other half. You can't divide yourself into departments like a university." Witter sets his drink down and sits beside Vachel on the bed. "I'm not scolding, boy. Don't think I'm scolding. But this isn't the last generation that's ever going to be on earth." He grasps Vachel firmly by the shoulders. "Who in hell appointed you to save the world?"

"Nobody. Myself, I guess." Vachel laughs. "Maybe I get it from Mama."

And Witter laughs and retrieves his drink. "Forget it. Finish up your tour and come down to Santa Fe. Better still, drop the tour right now. . . ."

"Oh, I couldn't. . . ."

"The hell you couldn't. You've got poetry to write and you're not writing it. You didn't save Madison tonight. You were good. But you didn't save it. And you won't save Milwaukee tomorrow night."

"Suppose there was me tonight, here, and somebody else tomorrow night, and somebody else Friday."

"But there won't be."

"Well, there could."

"But there won't. There won't be me, for instance. And I don't feel as if I'm fleeing the ship. Take care of yourself, boy. A live Vachel is better than a dead one."

"It's not as bad as all that. I feel that I'm winning. Everywhere I go I feel that I'm winning a little bit. I can see it in people, and in the letters I get. In the things they say. They don't read books, but they'll come out and listen to people."

"Have it your way. You're probably right." Witter studies the level of the rum again, starts to pour, changes his mind and corks the bottle. "Which way do you go from here?"

"Down through St. Loo. Tulsa. Then Albuquerque I think."

"Maybe you'll spend a couple days in Santa Fe."

"Maybe I will."

("Porter, if I sleep will you wake me in Springfield like a good fellow?" "Be glad to, sir. You want to send a wire, mail a letter?" "No, I just want to be awake." "Maybe you want to make a telephone call, see a party?" "No, I just want to be awake. I just want to look out the window.")

Quite unofficially it is Vachel Lindsay Week in Santa Fe, and he is delighted and flattered, and he protests that all the fuss is a good deal more than he deserves, but he enjoys it, and when he is asked to recite two or three poems at Sarah McComb's lawn party he recites three or four. There are few audiences like this anywhere, and he is at his best, and he does not yank out stanzas, and in fact he does not want to. There are no audiences like this in Muncie or Evansville or Boston or Minneapolis. This is an audience of fellow poets.

Vachel has always been popular among the poets of America.

He has not taken sides in their private arguments. He has always felt that the issues of poetry are side issues in a wider fight. He is fond of saying, "Any friend of mine is a good poet." He has not troubled himself to write devastating replies to Amy Lowell and he will not declare himself as to whether Ezra Pound is madman or genius. He will recite his poems and listen to the good talk and laugh at the stories about the good old Sanitarium days and the hoax that Witter and Ficke pulled when they called themselves Knish and Morgan and advanced the Spectric theory of poetry, and he will laugh until the tears run about the time the gang drank a quart of Taos Lightning and everybody wrote two lines and they put the lines together and God what a poem came out, and Witter does his imitation of the preacher and John Sloan goes through the business of finding the hair in his soup, and what happened, Vachel, between you and Amy in Texas?

"Nothing really," says Vachel. "It was a big dinner for the Baylor anniversary. A jubilee I think they called it. And Markham introduced Amy and she talked about herself for an hour and forty minutes and about subtlety in poetry. I forget all what she said, but she never mentioned Markham, and there was the great old man right beside her. Well, then I spoke for ten minutes or so about Markham and what a great old man he is, and Amy never got the point. So she's not mad at me. But Markham got it. So nothing happened between me and Amy."

And they talk about the issues of poetry and drink up the pre-Prohibition liquor (Vachel has sarsaparilla) and open up the cases of old wine and remark upon displacements in So-and-so's poetry and promise they will never breathe a word of it beyond this room, and they read aloud the latest letter from Paris and play a continuing game called Bory-may (nobody knows why) where you take fourteen words any old words just so long as most of them rhyme with one another and everybody writes a line using the rhyming word at the end of the line, and you write a sonnet that way and Jesus what comes out it is the funniest goddam thing you ever heard. So who has won the fight, Vachel, between Jessie and Harriet? And they all look at Vachel. Harriet Monroe and Jessie Rittenhouse have been scrapping in the public prints over which one of them discovered Vachel.

"I don't know," he says. "I stopped following it a long time ago.

I have the feeling I discovered myself, and Harriet helped and Jessie helped. God bless them both."

They are good, sweet people. They are the Santa Fe Volunteer Fire Department, and they put out many fires in their town, and they raise money for the New Mexico Association on Indian Affairs, and they sign petitions and discomfit the Mayor of Santa Fe and the Governor of the state of New Mexico.

The seven days of Vachel's week go swiftly in Santa Fe, and he would like to stay and make the week a year and maybe make the year a lifetime and maybe soon forget that there is a troubled world beyond Lamy.

They tempt him. They plead with him. *Who in hell appointed you to save the world?* And they are like the Mennonites in Kansas, and Vachel is comfortable among them because they are devoted to a cause of their own and a book of their own and gods of their own, and he will come to them again and again, miles out of his way. But he will never learn his way around town and never be quite sure of the route between the Plaza and Camino del Monte Sol.

On the morning of departure, in the house behind the house behind Alice Henderson's he awakens from the dream that is the continuation of the events of the night before. There had been firelit faces turned toward him, voices asking again and again *why? why? who in hell appointed you to save the world?* over and over, the same question framed in as many ways as there were faces. And he could not phrase an adequate answer, and the shadows of the firelight danced on their faces, and as he sat before the hearth the heat of the fire made him dull and sleepy, and at last he begged to be excused on the grounds that he had an early-morning train to catch, and he left for bed troubled and confused, and he dreamed dreams of trouble and confusion.

Now, in the cool morning, splashing his face with clear water, breathing deep the air of the new day, his mind seems alive, and he wishes it had been so alive last night before the hearth. He wishes he might have one last word with the circle of friends who told him in the kindest way they knew that what he is doing is futile, that people in the mass are mindless and unfeeling, that poetry is for poets, that he pursues a ghost, a specter, a spook. Democracy, some said, is an illusion—a pleasant illusion, but an illusion all the same.

He knows now, too late, the perfect reply: What ghost, what

specter, what spook, ·what illusion would you rather I pursue? I will wake them up, he thinks. I will go from house to house and ask them the question that is the answer to theirs. But no, it would not do to wake them up. They would only be grumpy. Besides, he has a train to catch.

He forces his suitcase shut, and he leaves the little house. He is greeted by his Spanish neighbor who carries in his hand a loaf of fresh-baked bread, and Vachel insists that he cannot take it, and the man insists that he must. "Also the horse," says the man.

"I'll eat the bread," says Vachel. "But I draw the line at the horse."

The man does not laugh. He leads Vachel to the two-seater wagon, and they climb up, and the man speaks in Spanish to the horse, and they go bumping down the Camino to the place where the autobus waits.

He should have told them: Sure, laugh at Harding. I laugh at him myself. Laugh at Babbitt, too. I often laugh at Babbitt. But Harding is Babbitt's man, and if you would demolish Harding you must first win Babbitt. You who have quick minds and you who read the wise books, you are turning your backs on Babbitt. We must go to Babbitt, he thinks, meeting him every day at some turn of the corner, in church, on the job, in the union hall, at the luncheon club. We might even have Babbitt to dinner some night, painful as the prospect may be, or ride in Babbitt's car on a Sunday afternoon or play poker with him on a Thursday night or go with him to the ball game when the locals are in town. At the very least (he should have said) you can talk with him across the back fence or on a park bench or at the general store or in the Turkish bath.

Babbitt is a man with a tremendous potential. He will listen. He has always been a good listener. He'll lend you money if he has it and feed your dog when you're away and help you mend your fences and visit you in the hospital and pray for you on Sunday. He will suddenly appear with a gift in his hands in that instant of distress when the wise men you thought you could count on are much too busy writing critical essays in fourteenletter words. Or they'll be in bed asleep.

"Why do I always think of smart remarks too late? They're all in bed. They're good people. So is Babbitt. He's a good fellow."

"He's a good fellow," says the Spaniard, gravely. "Very good fellow."

"They'll be asleep because they were up late last night talking high talk."

"Very good fellow."

"This is where the bus comes."

"Si."

"What do you charge for the lift?" The driver shakes his head from side to side, no. "I insist."

"Adios, señor. Hasta la vista." He addresses his horse. He is gone.

There are, besides Vachel and the driver, three men in the autobus. They are salesmen, and they came to Santa Fe to sell to the shops on the square, and now, their work done, they stare sleepily at the open country between Santa Fe and Lamy.

On the day coach between Lamy and Albuquerque the three are twenty. They sit in groups, laughing together at stories they have heard before. Their name is George F. Babbitt.

Look at him! God look at him!

He is weary of the train ride.

Then why does he go?

He is driven.

What drives him?

He is driven, Vachel supposes, by a sense of duty, and he rides the train out of that same sense that makes him do most of the things he does. Convince him of a duty and he will perform that duty. Show him a god and he will pray to that god because he feels the need to pray. Show him a luncheon club and he will join that club because he likes to laugh with his townsmen. Give him a badge and he will wear it, a newspaper and he will read it. Give him a car and he will drive it, and he will love his cigarette lighter and his good cigar and his safety razor and contract bridge and crossword puzzles because he has been convinced that those are the right and proper objects of love, and that which he is told it is right and proper to love he will love because he wants to do the right and proper thing.

Vachel knows Babbitt. He has shared a meal with him in Florida, in Georgia, Ohio, Kansas. He has recited poetry for Babbitt in the schoolhouses of Zenith, in the theaters of Zenith, in the churches and the temples and the colleges of Zenith. Babbitt comes to listen because Myra Babbitt tells him it will be cultural. He believes in Culture.

Vachel will write a letter to Santa Fe, he thinks: I have read about Babbitt in all the books. You have read the same books. He is the hero of all the books. He is the hero of The History of the Great Revolution and the hero of The History of the War to End Slavery and the hero of The History of the War to Make the World Safe for Democracy. Babbitt freed you at Quebec unless you were black, in which case he freed you at Richmond, and he was certain he was saving the world for democracy in the Argonne, and he bled and died because he thought he was in the right, because he thought bleeding and dying was the way in which he might establish the rightness of things. He went to the polls for Jackson and Lincoln and Bryan and Wilson in his time, and if he goes now for Harding he goes convinced that he is doing right by himself and Myra and Ted and Verona and his country and his God.

He is a man to be reckoned with. Tell him that Warren Harding is just folks and he will vote for Warren. Convince him that the Scripture reads back to normalcy and he will vote for the Scripture. He will be deceived once. And he will be fooled a second time. And if the times are right he will lose his way a third time because George is not a fast thinker or a deep reader. He is a plodder. He is a foot soldier. He will march behind evil men in a first war and in a second war. But he will not go marching and dying forever. It may take disaster to awaken him, but somewhere along the way he will indeed awaken. And you—you must bring him awake. You must help him to see disaster before it overtakes him. He understands more than you think. He understands himself better than you think.

If only you could see him as I see him now! If only we could know him as I try to know him! If only we could trust him, and him us!

Might write a stern letter between trains in Albuquerque, he thinks, suspecting that he will never write the letter, but imagining that he has written it and they are reading it aloud by firelight before the warm hearth:

On these trains, in the towns, everywhere I go I keep running across a fellow named George. Don't sell him short (that's George's phrase) and take care you don't mock too loud the old lady from Dubuque. She is wife and mother and sister to George, and they kneel to false gods and put their faith in folding money that after being too far stretched will tear at the middle.

They make mistakes. They do incredibly foolish things, savage, wicked, brutal things. I remember a race riot we had once at home. But I remember Bryan, too. I know that you all laugh at Bryan now. He said, "The people have a right to make their own mistakes." If he said nothing else, that much should make him famous. An illusion? Maybe. But what illusion would you rather I pursue?

The people—they will sift and resift the sands that record their hours, their days, their generations, and they will separate pure from impure. Do not mock them or desert them. Show them better gods and they will get up off their knees and stand facing a new way. Ultimately they will read the poems and sing the songs of the men and women who remain among them in the counterfeit time when the folding money masquerades as the real thing and the natural breast is flattened and hidden and the cynical god receives his mail in Baltimore.

They are I and I am they, and the wasteland is I as well as they, and if George F. Babbitt will not come to me wherever I am I must go to him in Zenith if it kills me, and it might, and someday George will do something for me.

CHAPTER FOUR

1

HE PICKS UP the tour again on the fifteenth in El Centro California, and he is in San Diego only a few minutes late for an eight-o'clock program. It is a long, steady pull up the coast, two days in Los Angeles and four in San Francisco with side trips to Oakland and Sacramento and two to the University at Berkeley, one for a group called the Neo-Literati because the Neos are boycotting everything sponsored by the English Department and would not recognize Vachel's appearance the night before.

The train is ahead of schedule, and in Salem he catches five hours of sleep and has a very satisfying evening and goes on in the morning to Olympia, and some students are kind enough to drive him to Tacoma after the show, thus saving him not only fare but a long wait in the bus station, and everything goes smoothly in Tacoma, and on Wednesday morning, the first, he hits Seattle, a little pooped, to use Witter's word, but full of zing and high spirits and still rested from the week in Santa Fe. He checks in at the New Washington.

There is a telegram from sister Joy, from Springfield: Mama is ill with pneumonia and he must come home, and more by habit than because he is aware of what he does, he goes about the business of making himself at home in the hotel room—setting out his toothbrush and hairbrush and comb and razor, and he washes out some socks and underclothes and tries to collect himself and figure out just what to do.

The chief thing, he thinks, is not to get flustered. He decides to send wires canceling dates for a week ahead, and after he gets home and sees just how things are he can plan ahead a little better. He sends the wires and telephones the Seattle Woman's Club to cancel tonight's date, and then he checks train times. There is no train until tomorrow morning. He calls the Woman's Club again and says on second thought he can fill the bill tonight. He showers and shaves and then some newspaper people come—two men and a woman—and he ends up having supper with them. Then he taxis to the hall.

It is not a good show. It starts well but it bogs about the middle when it occurs to him that if Joy has left three children in Cleveland to go all the way to Springfield Mama must be a good deal sicker than the telegram indicates. It is hard to keep his mind on what he is doing Mama a hard one to keep down. If she is ill she will remain so only as long as time will allow will be up and at it come the next meeting of Via Christi the next visit of missionaries back from China en route cross-country to the home office in New York. But why did Joy come down from Cleveland?

He does his best for the Woman's Club, and he cuts the program short at half past ten with the feeling that he has let the Seattle folk down. It is eleven-fifteen before he is out of the hall. It is two-thirty before he is asleep.

On the nine-fifteen out of Seattle he tries to read, and for a while he makes a go of it, but Mama keeps coming back crowding his mind with herself in a thousand postures at the telephone a pencil in her hair presiding at table clubroom First Christian Church leading the Springfield auxiliary of the Anti-Saloon League holy war against the demon rum chin to chin with Lester Heck of the Brewers' Protective League battling him to the ground and defeating him at last for better or for worse. He smiles to think of Mama how she follows Christ, how she has won and lost crusades and earned undying friends and ferocious enemies, and her friends adore her and her enemies call her unspeakable things, and taken all in all Springfield is richer for her presence and Vachel is wiser for her guidance. He is Mama's son. He was never quite Papa's. The world-saving drive comes from Mama, and if there were one hundred thousand like her in the land, breeding another two hundred thousand of her kind, one Olive and one Vachel, it would be a different land, for the most part a better land, certainly a more Christian land, a shade too doctrinaire perhaps, but the doctrine is a good one if followed down the line. *Ask yourself what Christ would do, and then go do it* what Mama always says and always does. Jesus Christ directs Mama's household and woe to the bigot will be good to sit beside Mama and hold her hand and maybe read to her from Dante or Browning although Mama of late has become a little suspicious of Browning on the grounds that he never belonged to a missionary society. Well never mind he will read to her from whatever she wants to hear they will talk about the old days and the days ahead. Vachel has not yet had a real good discussion with her on Prohibition whether it is working out or not.

All night he thinks of her. He lies stretched on his berth, his hands clasped behind his head, smiling up into the dark: Mama intervening when Papa with dark brow was angry with Vachel; Mama at the cleared dining-room table striking off with unhesitating pen a powerful address to be delivered in powerful voice to the women of Springfield; Mama the spokesman for the women, striding with set face up the Statehouse walk to remind the Governor of a forgotten promise; Mama of the tender hands; Mama pure in a city that is, to her, shabby and ill-kept and unmindful of its duties to its citizens; Mama tender in a city where man is often cruel to man, where some men labor that others might play and some feed high and others barely at all and children sometimes starve and the ailing sometimes die when the dollar that buys golf balls or a book of crossword puzzles or the latest *Who's Who in Contract Bridge* might have gone for a basket of food; Mama a bright light in a city of much evil dark. And Springfield is fortunate that Mama lives on Fifth Street, and they may laugh at her and insult her and ridicule her crusades and thwart her efforts and call her Old Lady Do-Good, but she has marched seventy-four years toward the Holy Land and never lost her way (Seventy-four! Who would think!) and better far better a do-good than a do-nothing.

And when he was at Hiram College, and afraid, and wondering whatever would come of him, she sent the Browning lines *Grow old along with me, the best is yet to be,* and he held the paper in his hand and thought how, yesterday, it was in Mama's hand, and he was not afraid. He still carries the paper in his wallet. It has outlived many wallets. And he pasted the paper with the inked lines on a piece of cardboard, and now the lines have faded to invisibility, but he can still read them because he knows what they say, and Mama wrote them at the dining-room table with her powerful tender hands.

And she has marched seventy-four years in the Army of the Lord loving God and Democracy, and Vachel remembers the church plays (Mama called them colloquies to deceive the Puritans) and Mama writing all the speeches for all the gods and all the nations, and Vachel was Cupid (he had long curls down his back) and the first time, when he was afraid to go out in front of all the people,

Mama put her hand on his bare shoulder and pushed him just the slightest bit, and the hand was warm, and love and courage were there in the tender hand, and it warmed him and made him forget that he was afraid, and he went out in front of all the people with his painted cheeks and his paper arrow, and he was not afraid.

And he remembers, too, long, long, long ago, one Christmastime when Grandpa Lindsay came from Kentucky and the old blind patriarch, seeing with his hands that Vachel wore curls, took Vachel's hand in his and demanded to be led to Mama. "Daughter," the old man roared, "boys don't wear curls," and the curls were sheared from Vachel's head.

Yet they were never really sheared at all, for they remained, and they are there yet, invisible golden strands draping his shoulders, and he knows they are there as surely as he can read the Browning lines that are not there, and he can almost feel them because he was Mama's, always Mama's, never Grandpa Lindsay's, never Papa's, always Mama's, maybe (could it be?) too much Mama's, too little himself. He wonders could it be, as often, in moments of stress such as now, he has had cause to wonder whether Mama's unnatural strength gave him not only strength, but, in its way, made him also weak, incomplete. When she wrote the speeches for all the gods and all the nations did she also write his?

On Monday, in Chicago, between trains at the terminal, he telephones home, smiling and thinking of Mama, thinking how now she hears the ring and says she will get it it is probably for her, and the ringing stops. "Hello," says Joy. "This is Vachel. Joy? How are you? How are the babes? How is Mama?" And Mama is dead.

The funeral is Tuesday morning. The ground is hard and the men use picks as well as shovels for the slow work, and there would have been more people but some didn't come up from the church because the weather is so cold. It is a fine service, and a sad one, and Mama is eased gently into the open earth beside Papa and the three babies, and Joy cries quietly, holding Vachel's arm, and Vachel stands with his lips tight and big tears frozen on his cheeks, and wisps of steam rise from the warm, open earth, and it is good to think of Mama and Papa warm below. The shovels make a cold noise scooping the frozen clods from beside the grave. The grave is filled in.

The mound is higher than it would ordinarily be because the earth is frozen. The mortuary man claps Vachel on the shoulder and explains that the mound will disappear when spring comes and softens the earth, and the mortuary drivers start the motors in the shining black cars as the people drift from the graveside. The rubber-tired wheels crunch on the gravel as the procession rolls down and out of Oak Ridge leaving Mama to lie once again beside Papa.

On Wednesday morning Vachel sees Joy off on the train, and in the afternoon the house becomes alive again. The telephone starts to ring and people start to come, and Vachel begins to pull himself upward from sad depths, knowing that the world's business goes forward even when the world has lost someone as strong and as central as Mama. He tells himself he must get interested in living again, and he goes to the telephone table and studies the memo pad on which, in Mama's hand, are three names and numbers to be called no later than the first, and Vachel smiles and tears the sheet of paper from the pad and crumples it and throws it into the wastebasket beneath the telephone table. He makes his own notes on the pad: wire Armstrong and thank him for the flowers and tell him the tour will pick up again on the twenty-first in Omaha, and call the man and okay the headstone, and while he is making the notes the doorbell rings and he admits three Via Christi ladies, and the lady who seems somehow to be the spokesman says "You remember us," and he remembers the faces but not the names, and he says, "Of course. Sit down. I was just brewing tea. Tea?" They say yes.

"How do you feel about hard maple?" says the lady who is spokesman.

"Hard maple?"

"For your mama's tree."

"Oh yes. Yes, hard maple is fine. I think Mama would have liked it."

"We thought right by the library would be an appropriate place."

"The most appropriate, I should say."

"We thought we would plant it in the spring and then after it grows we might put her name on a plaque. You know how they plant trees for soldiers. She was a soldier."

"That would be nice," says Vachel.

"And you think she would have liked hard maple?"

"I know she would."

"Something's boiling," says one of the other women.

"The tea water," he says, and he hastens into the kitchen and takes the pot from the flame, but before he has time to pour the telephone rings. The *Journal* wants to check on a few things for the funeral notice, and Vachel fills them in and commends them on the accuracy of yesterday's obituary.

A gentleman comes from Sangamon County Trust Company. He is a past vice-president of the Brewers' Protective League, and the three Via Christi ladies eye him as they might eye Judas. But he smiles at them, and they all have tea and talk about Mama and decide this is as good a time as any to go through some of her papers. "We feel," says the man from the Company, "that since your work keeps you on the road so much we might just take the business of the house off your hands," and it occurs to Vachel for the first time that when he leaves Springfield again there will be no more Lindsays in the city and nothing but silence and darkness in the house.

He rounds up Mama's papers and sets them on the floor beside the tea table, and the man from the bank and the ladies from Via Christi pull up chairs about him. Together they begin the work of dividing the papers into two piles, a Via Christi business pile and a miscellaneous pile. The Via Christi pile is the more interesting. The miscellaneous pile consists largely of correspondence with the Sangamon County Trust Company, mainly concerned with tax arrears, evaluations and assessments, all of it exceedingly dull, much of it sent to Mama to be returned immediately with her signature affixed, but Mama never got around to signing things as she should have, or, Vachel surmises, ever really generating much interest in affairs between herself and Trust. The man from Trust shakes his head sadly and begins to arrange the neglected papers in chronological order. "I tried to interest your mother in a number of things," he says, "but she was always lukewarm."

"Here's one we never saw," says a lady from Via Christi, and the three women put their heads together and read a sermon in Mama's hand, and the man from Trust winks at Vachel, and Vachel goes around behind the ladies and reads along with them. It is a lecture beginning with the thought that the good Christian citizen flavors two salads, one his city and the other his church, and Mama struggled in the paper for half a page, trying to keep her metaphors straight. She had written: "Let us flavor the salad of Springfield civic affairs with the garlic of the church," and then she had drawn a line through *garlic* and presumably gone on with the intention of inserting a better word later, but she never did.

"You see," says the man from Trust, showing Vachel a letter. "I tried to interest her in stock. She could have covered taxes with the increment."

"She had a way of putting things," says the lady from Via Christi.

"When Mama gave her fixed, consecutive attention to something Lord help the villain she was after."

"She was a soldier."

"How about you?" says the man from Trust. "Are you interested? Men understand these things better." He laughs.

The three Via Christi women glare icily at him.

"I might be," says Vachel, coming around from behind the ladies and seating himself by the tea table again. "Not right now, though. I think I'll just close it and lock it."

"It's not yours to close and lock. There's taxes and . . ."

"I don't understand these things," says Vachel, and he rises and goes around behind the women again. "You know, Mama was right. Garlic was wrong but the idea was right. It's all in the choice of your figure. Here. Flavor civic affairs with the spice of the church. Maybe spice isn't right either. But it's nearer the idea Mama was after. Something sweet yet strong from the kitchen. That's what she wanted. Maybe a specific spice, like thyme or curry or nutmeg. But not garlic."

"You could rent the house."

"Yes. I could rent it."

"Or we could rent it for you. Why not let us handle it while you're away?"

"Listen, everybody. Here's a letter from China. It's from Olive."

"That's my sister," Vachel explains to the man from Sangamon County Trust Company.

"In this land the Confucian order of society is not unlike the ideal Christian order, with the scholar and sage ranking highest and the soldier the lowest, because the soldier only destroys. . . ."

"Say," says Vachel. "Sage is a spice. Now!" He circles around behind the women again. "Get back to that business about putting the garlic of the church into civic affairs. Right here. Flavor the salad of civic affairs with the *sage* of the Christian church. You see!

You have a double edge there, sage meaning wisdom and yet being a straight kitchen term, too."

"My my."

"Then am I to understand that we may manage the rentals?"

"Yes," says Vachel, "if you think that would be best."

"And you're not interested in stock at this time."

"No."

"Do you mind if I take these papers with me to overlook?"

"No. Go right ahead. Just one thing. If you rent don't rent out my room. From time to time I'll come home."

"Here's something," says one of the ladies. "A letter from President Wilson. Signed in his own hand. I am pleased to know that the women of your organization in Springfield Illinois have joined me in my continuing efforts to impress upon the people of our nation the necessity to establish a permanent and supersovereign League of the nations of mankind."

"Let me see," says Vachel.

"Good day," says the man from Trust.

"Good day," say the ladies, not raising their heads from the Via Christi papers.

"Good-by," says Vachel, "and thanks for everything," and he pulls his chair around beside the ladies, and they drink tea together and go through Mama's papers until suppertime.

And then he is alone, completely and terribly alone in a way that he has never been alone before, not ever, not in the darkest days, and tonight will be the first night she will spend beneath the earth they bury folks so fast you would think they would allow a longer time in the house. The man said the mound would go down by spring.

He sits at the kitchen table waiting for the tea to steep where Papa said he sat waiting for the tea to steep when Vachel was born upstairs. Papa told the story over and over again the older he got the more he told stories over and over again. He could remember what happened forty years before but he was hazy on what happened yesterday or this morning. He always had it good in life when he sat here waiting for the tea to steep it was at least a time of being born, not a time of death like now, it was a time of the coming of people into the house not a time of the departure of people until there is nobody, like now, nobody but me.

There was Olive. He thinks he might send a cable to Olive and ask her to come home from China and live with him and comfort his soul which needs comforting as much as the average Chinese needs his soul comforted. Then he would not be alone like this with Mama the first night in the cold ground hearing the story again from Papa how he sat at the kitchen table steeping tea the day Vachel was born.

The tea grows black.

You would think he would have been upstairs seeing what could be done for her not sitting idle in the kitchen for she bore him in pain it was the hardest birth and there were six and she ought to know having gone through six three died and in their way were lucky to go quietly in babyhood not knowing the pain and the agony and the anguish of growing with her and then suddenly to get called home like that and finding her gone when always in the back of the mind there was the idea that someday after the long journeys he would be home for good and they would live to one hundred and five together and die on the same day and never be alone, either of them, never be alone like this like a man who is lighter than air drifting off into space with no beacon below.

She was all he ever had there were women and they came into his life and as soon were gone. There was Sara she came and was gone married to a gentleman of means Untermeyer says a little like a diplomat on a secret mission and a little like the head usher in a funeral parlor. And there were other Juliets and they came and were gone and she was rooted like a beacon light and always kisses me and loves me after every journey and defends me and asks nothing of me in return but that I be her boy and remain in the paths of righteousness and dwell in her house forever.

The tea is black and cold, and he pours it down the sink, and the mood of the morning returns, and he knows, as he knew this morning, that life goes on, that death is but death, and it will come when it will come.

Susan would know what to do, and he goes to the telephone and makes the connection, and she answers, and he does not speak, and she says twice, puzzled, "This is Miss Wilcox. This is Miss Wilcox," and then, "I thought that when we reached high school we no longer played pranks," and he presses noiselessly upon the cradle, breaking the connection, restoring solitude and silence.

Old ties must be loosed, old memories banished.

She lies tonight with Papa, the first night after the brief separation. He lies alone tonight, wakeful and thoughtful and terribly alone in a way he has never been alone before, and he knows within himself (no disrespect to Mama) that if she was beacon she was also, quite without meaning to be, that great force that stood between himself and his own completeness. He will become complete.

CHAPTER FIVE

1

IT IS HARD, writes Vachel in a letter from Denver, to get interested in the game of living again. He rereads what he has written and strikes the word *game* and writes above it, *business*, because it is not a game. It was never a game.

Yet it was never a business, either, and he strikes the word and writes above it, *problems*, and immediately scratches it out and draws an arrow to the margin and writes the word *game* again.

It is not a game. It is not even a fight, or if it is a fight it is not the sort of fight it once was. At least it used to be a fight for a cause and now it is only a way to live, and when a day's work is only a means to the end of working again tomorrow the day's work is so much waste.

He thinks he will go tramping again get out from under the trouble is he is only a man not some kind of lecture box you roll out onto the stage wire up and switch to the On position it runs until somebody shuts it off like a sausage machine or a phonograph, and Vachel is not something to be packaged and shipped around the country like Uneeda Biscuits. He thinks maybe he will write some magazine stories the way the magazines want them written and stock up a whole lot of money and then do the writing he wants to do, and he goes downstairs to the lobby of the Brown Palace in Denver and buys a Saturday Evening Post and comes back upstairs and loosens his tie and takes off his shoes and stretches out on the bed studying the way the Post likes its stories written. It certainly looks easy. He supposes that all he would really need is a stomach for it and maybe a few days of not reading the world news so's to get in the right frame of happy mind, and in the middle of a story called Uncle Jonathan's Calendar by Avery Van Avery he falls asleep.

At least it all used to be a sort of a game and a sort of a fight, as to any young fighter fighting begins as a game of honor and skill, and the initial bruises are a part of the game, wounds to be proud of, and the second in the corner is someone to be loved because he makes the fighting possible and laughs when he mends the wound, but the next time the wound is not so funny, and the wound re-opened a third time is downright painful, and the game of fighting is not a game any more and has nothing to do with honor or skill, and the throaty roar of the people is not the exciting music it was in the beginning, and the lights begin to hurt the eyes, and the flat-tery of newspaper people and hotel bellboys and Pullman porters becomes transparent and sickening, and the young fighter remem-bers all the generous things he was going to do with his money, but he does not do them because he knows that the strength to fight is the gift of youth, and he is no longer young. At forty-three he is infinitely older than he was at thirty-eight. His lungs trouble him now. There is an infection inside his cheek which ought to be oper-ated on. Larger simpler longer plans, he thinks, less evangelistic and more realistic. The economy of energy. He is mightily impressed by the fact that Caruso used to get five thousand dollars a night.

He has been here before, or so it seems to him. There is a term in psychology meaning that I seem to have been here before, that all this happened once in the past. The students on the chapel benches would know the term. They are full of terms which they come upon in books of psychology. Everybody in college studies psychology these days as if it were a new thing. It is an old thing with a new name. Freud will someday be as popular as Babe Ruth. It explains everything, or at least it explains everything sufficiently because after all nothing is really puzzling any more. Everything is good. Everything is hunky-dory.

He knows that he has been here before because he remembers this chapel, and whereas it is true that all chapels look pretty much alike each chapel has, nevertheless, certain distinguishing fea-tures. Strolling up from the college station last evening the feeling first came over him—that he had been here before—because chapels are not usually located so close to the railroads. That much he remembers from the time before. The trains kept him awake last night, and as he lay awake he remembered how it was the time before, how it was morning and the smell of spring came in through the door as it comes now, and there was a lectern like the one before which he now stands, and a shelf beneath, and a Bible on the shelf. His hands search for the Bible, and it is there, and he remembers now that they gave him a scroll upon which, in curled letters, something was stated to the effect that he had made notable contributions to American life and literature. He wonders if Freud will ever really replace the Bible.

BOOTH LED BOLDLY WITH HIS BIG BASS DRUM, *to the tune of The Blood of the Lamb, with a bass drum beaten loudly, with banjos and sweet flute music, tambourines to the foreground, and, at the last, reverently sung, no instruments,* and afterward applause which seems to be loud enough to be described as enthusiastic and which seems to invite a second poem. He is not quite sure what it means.

"I used to live in Springfield Illinois. I don't know where I live any more. I seem to live mostly in a Pullman berth. But at home, a long time ago, most of you hadn't even been thought about yet, I had a neighbor named John Peter Altgeld. Do any of you remember Governor Altgeld of Illinois?"

No hands are raised. No voice is raised.

Wearily, *with the interruptive quality of a mortuary chant,* ". . . sleep softly, eagle forgotten . . ." and he remembers, as always he remembers, the Altgeld poem on his tongue, Susan and Duncan and Maydie Lee and Willis and Mama and Papa and the night the poem was born and how, over time, the few who heard it on the first night have become a multitude. But now he is also sharply aware that the men and the women of the age of Altgeld have gone day by day the way of the beautiful neighbor. And the new generation is a new age, and they listen now, attentive, polite, dutiful, and he chants the chant exactly as he chanted it here before, and he listens to the sound of the listening silence, and it is not the same silence that once it was. Booth. Altgeld. A bass drum. A walk he once took from Springfield Illinois to Wagon Mound New Mexico, the bronco that would not be broken, the Rachel-Jane, John Brown, and the songs evoke no chapel echoes. There is no warm laugh today at that point at which there is always responsive laughter. The feet do not begin to beat. Something is gone both from him and from them.

Before the Bryan poem he pours water from the pitcher into the glass, and, half-turning, he glimpses behind him, on the chapel stage, the young man who introduced him. The young man smiles. He is the president of the student body, except that he is not called president but chairman, and he is not president of the student body but chairman of the student committee which is an altogether different thing. It sounds more like a corporation that way, and everyone is corporation-minded because the corporation is here to stay, and things are, as the young man said in his introductory remarks, hunky-dory. And the young man's smile says proceed, you are doing nicely and it is all very entertaining, proceed. And he does not feel at all like proceeding.

He sets his glass down beside the pitcher, and he proceeds, and he sings of Bryan as if it were the first time, *I brag and chant of Bryan, Bryan, Bryan,* coming down hard on the magic name, square-jawed, his chin thrust forth belligerently as if the intensity of delivery can force his hearers to feel the thing he feels about the name that was once so much more than a name.

And he knows as he sings that the sad truth is that Bryan is dead, *Defeat of the young by the old and silly, defeat of my boyhood, defeat of my dream,* that the young have grown old and silly at twenty, and the dream indeed is dead because the young are old before their time, and it is hard to sing and be brave, to exhort those who are not brave and do not want to be exhorted. Yet he sings angrily, as if anger were contagious, as if he can spread anger and infect the chapel and make the boys and the girls on the benches below know anger as he knows it, and when he is finished they applaud as before, and he bows and smiles, and the bow is not deep and the smile is not real.

He thinks that he has done enough for one morning even though the chapel clock has not yet recorded the full hour. He hears applause. It is loud, and it is good to hear, and he waits for the demand that he recite again, just one more song, but he does not hear that demand in the applause. He hears only the clapping of hands, a much different thing from applause. At the rear of the chapel a door is flung open, and sunlight floods the passage, and then the light is blocked by the dark press of bodies moving from the chapel to the sunshine beyond.

The young man shakes Vachel's hand, insisting but not too hard that it was a most delightful program and Vachel must come again sometime. Then the young man is gone, and Vachel is alone in the spring sunshine, walking between the chapel and the college station, knowing now, with certainty, that he has been here before. The last time he was here a young man ran after him with the scroll he had forgotten.

It is a morning of doubt. It is not the first such morning. On many mornings and on many evenings the song sounds wrong, off-key, and it seems sometimes that he is a man singing to himself on an open plain, far from any other human ear, like a shepherd on a hillside singing only to his beasts.

Students pass him on the walk. They nod to him, and they smile, and the smiles, he thinks, are complacent smiles, and he knows that this new generation looks upon him as a rather older man with a lot of interesting but rather old-fashioned enthusiasms. He had sung to them his anticorporation song, the song of Bryan, and they clapped their hands and filed from the chapel. They think it is an old song, sung by a congenial rather older man who fought a fight, and lost. The corporation has won, and everything is hunky-dory now. He wonders, boarding the train at the college station, whether hunky-dory complacency will ever really replace old-fashioned things like courage and the will to resist.

He goes in a figure eight, down from Denver through the south-west, westward to the coast and up the coast, rounding out the loop of the figure at Spokane and descending south by east toward Denver again, and he is not Johnny Appleseed planting as he goes, leaving green orchards behind, and he is not Daniel Boone clearing the wilderness road and blazing the overland trail, and he is not St. Francis conversing with the birds. He is a man with a territory, a salesman with a sample bag, and the thing he is hawk-ing is poetry, and the poetry is something the salesman devised and perfected long ago when he was young and newly indignant.

He carries with him a thick package of crisp two-by-two cards, held together by a rubber band. On the cards are written the first lines of stanzas. He shuffles and reshuffles the cards on the lectern before him as a guide to help him remember poems he once knew but is somehow forgetting.

He is a travelingman, looking older than his years, by trade a poet, of necessity a weary citizen of the railroad and patron of the hotel that is Just Like Home.

He is at that time of life at which an artist may expect to feel within himself a new flourishing, a new creative strength, when the heat of youth is cool but far from cold and wisdom new-discovered makes the poet at forty-plus look back upon the work of his

younger days, and smile. And the books he wrote in the younger
time he hides in a dark corner of a lower shelf. It is a time when
an artist is neither young nor old, and yet both old enough and
young enough.

And he is lonesome for comforting sounds and comforting hands,
and there are no sounds in his life but the sound of applause, the
sound of crowds, and the complimentary gurgling of nameless
people who come to hear him because listening is easier than reading his books. He thinks that if they loved him they would buy
his books and free him from the flat-wheeled railroads and Rotary
clubs in endless rotation, and there are no tender hands now that
Mama is dead.

(In Salt Lake City, browsing in a secondhand bookshop, he
finds in an old volume a reproduction of Reni's *Aurora* in which
one of the nymphs looks like Sara, and he buys the book and tears
out the page and carries it with him, and in the hotel rooms the
first thing he does upon arrival is to stand the page on the dresser,
and it is there to study.)

He is a sick man. He is sicker than he knows. The trip-trip-trip
beneath his shirt is explained in Gray's *Anatomy four dollars*
which he never read and in Johnson & Johnson *The Circulatory
System six dollars* which he never read either, and the dripping
sinuses are something he should have read about in Goldstein but
never did, and the night fever is something Woodrow Wilson could
tell him about if he were not dead. A human body is not a machine.
It can resist much. But it cannot be bounced on railroads indefinitely. After a time the parts rebel: the stomach rejects bad food;
the lungs are not kitchen sieves that may be upturned and scraped
clean in a spare moment; the heart can pull so hard and no harder.
And the bodymachine has a thinking apparatus, and it thinks and
feels and has a spirit, and the spirit can be injured. The body must
sometime rest and be restored. Vachel at forty-three is infinitely
older than Vachel at thirty-eight: a single night's sleep does not
rest his body.

And the tired body saps the mind. (It is the railroads, he thinks.
It is the way they run the railroads and the kind of people that
ride them and the way they are damp and smoky and ill-smelling
and never on time.) He thinks what he ought to do is stop everything and go somewhere away from the railroads away from people,

and just write. He has new things to say, and old things that he has said once and is now prepared to say better. More than anything, he wants to write about the big things, and there are big things to say in a time like the present. And the only trouble is that the only way Vachel can write is by going somewhere quiet and sitting perfectly still, not touching pencil or paper for maybe a week, just sitting idle and letting things take shape in his mind, and then picking up a pencil with no serious intentions at all and letting the pencil go how it will on the paper, and then, after a dozen or a hundred false starts, after another week, settling down to the task of writing.

He thinks he will stop awhile and go somewhere and write and then when his money runs out he can go touring again except in practice it is hard to give time to writing running a race against a dwindling purse that is not very fat to begin with a big big problem, *big problems,* and he smiles because it is rather in the nature of understatement, because the problem of getting older and wasting away in the ripe time of life and feeling sicker day by day and wanting to write and having no place to go and write and being forever bounced about by the railroads and forever asked by pawing crowds to recite old poems he is tired of reciting and writing books that are widely reviewed and seldom bought and being lonesome with no companion but a nymph that looks like an old love these are bigger than big.

And nobody knows because there is no one day in and day out to see. There are only letters to dear friends, to be collected in a later time from Witter Bynner in Santa Fe and Harriet Moody in Chicago, Armstrong in Waco Texas, Untermeyer in New York, a doctor's report, a bank statement, diaries written in a degenerating hand, the reminiscences of people who gave him the spare room when he came through town, and they remember that he sang well and laughed and was uncomplaining, and now that the subject comes up, yes, why yes, he was tired, damn tired. But he thought he was Johnny Appleseed. "Give away all you own," said Johnny Appleseed, "and in an aftertime you will have two beautiful wives." And he thought he would give away all he owned, his voice, his heart, his lungs, his purse, because he believed in people and thought they were worth the trouble, and he thought he owned more than he owned.

2

In Springfield, shortly after midnight, sitting erect in his berth with his nose pressed to the window, looking out into the lighted station, Vachel decides quite impulsively that he has had enough. He dresses quickly, frantically, and takes a last look about him for things he may have forgotten, and finding nothing he rushes awkwardly with his suitcases in his hands, up the narrow passage of the sleeper. He alights, and a young man with a black-peaked cap takes his bags and leads him to a taxi, and Vachel gives the young man the address and they ride through the quiet streets. "Will you do me a big favor and carry the bags up?" Vachel asks, and the young man says sure, sure, and Vachel digs into his pocket for his keys and he slides the key into the lock, and the lock does not turn, and he withdraws the key to look at it, but in the dark he cannot see. "Do you have a light?" he asks the driver, and the driver says sure, sure, and he sets the bags down and reaches into his jacket pocket and brings forth a handful of matches, and he strikes one on his shoe and together they inspect the keys in Vachel's hand. "That's the one," says Vachel. "These others are suitcase keys," and he feels with a thumb for the hole of the lock, and he brings the key to the lock and inserts it and twists to the right and twists to the left, but the lock does not turn. "Let's look at the lock," he says, and the driver strikes a second match and they bend and peer at the lock, and it is shiny like a new lock, and the match dies and the young man lights another, and in the light of the match he sees Vachel's face, and there is a look of pain on the face. The young man has never seen a face in so much pain, and he is afraid and uncertain, and Vachel says please light another match, and the young man hesitates and does not light one because he does not want to see the face again. "Never mind. Take me back to the train."

"It's gone by now."

"There's a second section," and the young man bends at the knees and hoists Vachel's bags and carries them to the car, and they drive back through the quiet streets to the railroad station.

The Illinois Central. The Monongahela. The Lackawanna. The Chicago Milwaukee St. Paul & Pacific. The New York New Haven

& Hartford. Atlanta & West Point. Western of Alabama. The Wabash. Central of Georgia. The Lehigh Valley. The Louisville & Nashville. Norfolk & Western. Delaware & Hudson. Southern. Union Pacific. Missouri Pacific. Erie. Central Vermont. D & R G W. The Atchison Topeka & Santa Fé.

The Twentieth Century. The Northwestern Limited. The Capitol Limited. Pioneer Limited. The Orange Blossom Special. The Floridan. The Pan-American. The Oriental Limited. Gotham Limited. The Mark Twain. The Patriot. The Abe Lincoln.

A timetable please. I gave you one. Well then give me another and can you tell me please what does this asterisk mean?

*Will not run Christmas and New Year Day.

*Will not run Decoration Day and the Fourth of July.

*Will not run Labor Day and Thanksgiving.

*Will not run General Lee's Birthday.

*Eastern Standard Time.

*Central Time.

*Mountain Time.

*Pacific Time.

*South Station Only.

*North Station Only.

*No Baggage Car.

*No Dining Car.

*No Sleepers.

*The railroad is not responsible for inconveniences occasioned by the necessity to alter schedules above.

Late one evening, in the hotel in Chicago, he has a visitor, a face forty and prosperous charging at him out of the past. Desperately he tries to attach a name to the face.

"I'm Crimmins. Remember Crimmins?" and they clasp hands, and Vachel closes the door behind his visitor, remembering Crimmins vividly now. "Kenwood Avenue," says Crimmins.

"We saw *Hamlet,* you and I and somebody else. Sit down sit down."

"We pushed toys in Fieldses basement."

"E. H. Sothern in *Hamlet.*"

"I'm proud that you remember. I really am. I didn't know if you'd remember. I guess you know so many people by now."

"But you walked out on *Hamlet,*" and they laugh, remembering together Kenwood Avenue as a street in another age, recalling it fondly as if that other age had been a happy time, each studying each now, each silently observing that between Kenwood Avenue and the Loop, between that other age and this the path has been straight, true, direct. Crimmins is part-owner of a broomstick factory. The child is father to the man. At midnight, sandwiches and coffee between them, they are still remembering, laughing.

"You'll laugh. I know you'll laugh. Officially what I am—officially on the letterhead what I am I am Tri-State District Supervisor. What it means I train them, hire them and fire them."

"Broomsticks and mop handles you say. Need a good man?"

"It's honest."

"Of course it's honest." Vachel laughs. "Do you remember we wound up the toys and turned them loose?"

"I remember Vachel Lindsay wound them up, not me," remembering indeed and having told the story five hundred times to five hundred housewives in whom he detected an interest in poetry. He always looks at bookshelves, knowing as a lesson of the years that habit and taste in literature, strangely enough, are at least loosely related to habits and tastes in broomsticks and mop handles. He is a good salesman, and honest, and forty and flourishing and wise in the ways of his limited world, sharp, acute, a good listener though not dedicated to silence, an accurate observer of as much of this earth as he cares to include in his study of life. He is still the Crimmins for whom the problem of Hamlet was really no problem except that thinking made it so.

"Thinking confuses things," he says, pondering with Vachel Vachel's problem. "Stop thinking and do. Take an idea and sleep on it and then do it or don't but one way or another never think about a thing two days in a row. I would say either cancel it or don't."

"I need a rest, a year. Two years."

"I couldn't rest that long. Can't rest at all if you want to know the truth. Never took a vacation and never sick a day in my life. I get to resting and my head aches."

"I'm a machine and I can't be a machine any more. Sometimes I think that's what's wrong with the country. Machines. We pile them to the skies. We think everything runs in jeweled sockets. We're building a tin heaven and a tin earth."

"That's right," says Crimmins. "That's what I always say. I

always say you're either cut out for a thing or not. Personally it probably goes against your grain. If a fellow is a quiet fellow likes to sit pretty much in one place he is naturally going to let it get him down steaming around like you been."

"I have this thing I feel I must say. It's strong in me like broomsticks are strong in you."

"That's the truth."

"Then too, I must eat."

"I know it. I remember," and Crimmins laughs the great laugh that Vachel first heard in the partitioned room on Kenwood Avenue. Hearing it now he sees, again, clearly, the crumbling house in the fading neighborhood, the dim hallway, warning signs upon the walls, a fretful landlady, a girl up from somewhere south, Tennessee or somewhere.

"Trouble is it's like my old man used to say. I told you many times about my old man. He was seventy Tuesday, never sick a day in his life, every tooth in his head his own. Like with the farm. Like he would say, if you wanta be a farmer you have got to farm it all the way up. You got to work the ground hard and not worry about how you treat it, just worry about making it last your time and let the far time take care of itself. Did anybody worry about us in the olden days? Like with hogs he would say, you got to feed hogs all the way up and saltem and half killem with thirst and then waterem and runnem over the scale and close your ears when they squeal. Because it's either you or the hog. You have got to feed a hog all the way up and milk a cow all the way down. It's like the old man used to say."

And it is true, and Vachel knows that it is true, and the wise Crimmins is wiser than wise in his way, forty and flourishing and playing one game only and acknowledging no debt to the far time and knowing nothing of the older time and never sick a day in his life.

"Like in the beginning I remember I would walk in a house and they needed no broomsticks, and out I would walk again. Then this fellow he took me in hand and he said naturally nobody buys a thing if you *ask* them. You have got to tell them that they *need* this goddam broomstick. So I would tell them, and nine times in ten they would buy, and some of them were these here people that needed ten thousand things worse. Then I would feel pretty punk and low and go around wishing I was in another line. Yet I got over that. If I did not sell them the next fellow would, so no need to feel punk but go ahead and sell them notwithstanding, and you must not let your conscience interfere."

Crimmins puts it before him in the squarest, frankest way: be one thing or the other because you cannot be both, be tougher than hell or quit the farm, sell or turn in your sample bag; be poet or platform artist, but be one and not both because you cannot be both. Perhaps it is true. Witter Bynner has said it, and Armstrong. Perhaps this is Crimmins' generation, Crimmins' customer.

"Take an average man I can tell you talking with him fifteen minutes is he the type of a man I want or not. Even if I didn't know you I would say no. You ain't the type. You think too much."

"Too reflective?" Vachel says. He laughs. "I need a long rest in a quiet place."

"That is exactly what I was going to say. Too reflective. Cancel it. Don't think about it, just cancel it."

And there and then it ends at least for now, suddenly and abruptly in a hotel room in Chicago, four thousand dollars and twenty cities short of completion, the third Transcontinental, conceived and executed by two gentlemen who believed and still believe that the cleansing properties of poetry are surely as useful as broomsticks and mop handles. But the territory seems to belong to Crimmins. He is apparently the type.

Book V—THE HAPPY ENDING

CHAPTER ONE

1

THE YOUNG GIRL-CHILDREN are not quite ladies, although it is suggested that they be referred to as young ladies, and they are not quite children either, for they are full at calf and thigh, and luscious of hip, and beneath the blouse the flesh is full and white and untouched and presumably untouchable, and the flesh quivers when the body is in motion, and the woman-child is unaware, or only in the first dim stages of awareness, of the power that is in her at calf and thigh and hip and breast.

Beneath the tree called Friendship Oak Vachel stands looking upward uncertainly, knowing he must climb into the tree, yet hesitating. With his free hand (in the other he carries a copy of Harriet Monroe's anthology, *The New Poetry*) he reaches out and tests the strength of the ladder leading upward. "There was nothing to this effect in my contract," he says, and the young ladies laugh. "Well, if I must I must," and he tucks the book under his arm and climbs hand over hand onto the platform fixed among the branches, and he sits with legs outstretched, his back against the trunk of the tree. The young ladies climb more swiftly and surely than he. They sit in a semicircle before him, their legs tucked under them.

He does not speak. He is the slightest bit winded from the exertion of climbing, and for a full minute he sits looking out upon the young ladies, and they are variously brown-eyed and blue-eyed and black-eyed and green-eyed, and their hair is brown and gold and black, and in another time he would have looked upon them as fifteen or twenty separate and individual intellects whom for a brief time he holds captive, and holding them captive thus he would, in a past time, have lectured them upon the wickedness of finishing schools, and he might have inspired one or two of the twenty to be another Harriet Stowe another Julia Howe another Margaret Fuller or another Jane Addams, but, as of this moment, they are not vessels to be filled to overpouring with heretical notions. They are children, and like all children they are born democrats, and in a past time he might have labored against the corruption of their natural democracy, but he does not labor now, in this time of his life, or have the strength to care much or the strength to make the effort to put weapons in their hands, to make them indignant, to make them question, to urge revolt and rebellion upon them. They are variously brown-eyed and green-eyed and black-eyed, and variously golden-haired and brown-haired and black-haired and altogether beautiful as all that is young is fragrant and clean and unspoiled and beautiful because it is the world's hope. But they are nothing more, at least for now, than children in a tree, enrolled in a course entitled American Poetry, and they have not read much American poetry or poetry of any sort, but it is all very poetic here in the tree, and Mr. Lindsay is poetic as a poet should be.

And Vachel, feeling that his wind is regained, opens the anthology across his thighs, and he has a sad tired look about his eyes as a poet should have, and his voice is very low, as if speaking is an effort, and he is altogether a very queer creature, never taking the roll and never assigning themes to be written and never really saying anything that can be taken down upon a note pad.

He begins at the beginning, reading softly, almost inaudibly, and those who wish to listen must be silent enough to listen, and those who do not wish to listen, he announces, are now and forever excused from further attendance. It does not matter to him, he says, and he is a little sarcastic and a little bit bitter as a poet ought to be. He begins with Conrad Aiken, who comes first in the book, announcing the name of the poet and the title of the poem and flatly refusing to supply information relating to the date of the poem or the dates of the poet since these are facts, says he, which the interested student may gather for herself on her own time by her own effort. And the young ladies laugh and look at one another, and after the first week they do not bring their note pads because Mr. Lindsay never says anything that can be written down, later to be committed hurriedly to memory and rewritten a final time upon an examination paper and then forever forgotten.

He reads very slowly in a tired voice that has the pleasant quality of breathlessness about it, and he pauses a long pause between poems, and sometimes he looks up into the foliage of the tree in an absent-minded way as all poets look absent-mindedly at trees, obviously thinking up new poems. He reads from fifteen minutes after eleven until the dot of noon, and at noon he marks with a green leaf his place in the book, and he tucks the book under his arm again and goes backward down the ladder from the platform of Friendship Oak, and four days a week this happens, his coming, his reading, his going, his disappearance, and he is shadowy and mysterious and lonesome and sad with a mighty poetic sadness.

And afterward they talk of him and speculate upon the reasons for his sadness. Surely there is somewhere a lost love in his life, and it is sad and romantic and unquestionably the most poetic event of the young lives of the ladies who are not quite women, and it would be futile if not deliberately unkind to disenchant them by suggesting to them the true, unpoetic and unromantic reasons for Vachel's presence among them.

Permanent address: Gulf Park College, Gulfport Mississippi. A Junior College for Young Women.

I hereby make application for the admission of my daughter for the school year beginning . . . Tuition meals and room with adjoining bath one thousand and forty-five dollars per academic year. If father has title as Judge Doctor Major please give same. Nationality of parents? Religious faith of parents? References (please write names and addresses plainly): Clergyman? Banker? Family Physician? Splendid training in Music Art Speech and Theater Arts Home Economics and Secretarial Science. A semitropical campus.

Top: Everyone basks in the health-giving sunshine on our white sand beaches.

Center: You can golf on well-kept and sporty golf courses for moderate green fees. Beautiful live oaks, pines and magnolias line the fairways.

Below: Pleasure craft of many kinds anchored in the protected small-craft harbor.

Romantic notions persist. He is seen on sun-swept afternoons sitting barefoot on the white sands, far from the crowds, in lyrical solitude. And he sits staring at the sea in a state of semi-idiocy and the waves break and wash the beach and the cool water laps his bare toes, flooding and ebbing with a restful rhythm contrasting sharply with the clatter and the rattle and applause of recent years.

And when the sun begins to lower he rises stiffly and works his wet feet into his shoes and goes slowly, sleepily, the laces of his shoes trailing behind him, up the beach to the Great Southern Hotel where a room has been provided as rooms are frequently provided for the old, the ill, the insane, or for a person who is a guest and yet not quite a guest because he is a professor, although not quite a professor but, rather, a friend of the president of the school, a college chum of long ago. Dr. Cox, the president of Gulf Park, has come to the rescue, and Vachel is grateful for Cox and grateful to the people here and there in the country who, hearing that he is somehow without strength and somehow without a home and in need of a home, offer him a room and a task involving very little effort, and a token payment.

And coming to Gulfport was a compromise, and all in all a good move, although a room, even in the Great Southern Hotel (On the Beach at the Center of Gulfport, Offering Hospitality in an Atmosphere of Beauty, Comfort and Charm) is not quite a home. But at least the room is quiet, and he can sleep, and in the late afternoon, still smelling of the salt sea, he lowers the window shades and strips to his shorts, and in the cool dark between the cool sheets he sleeps as he has not slept for a long, long time, through evening and night, to morning.

On each succeeding day, a minute or five minutes or a quarter hour later than the day before, he submits at last to his weariness and seeks in sleep to restore himself and be again the Vachel who in a place like Gulfport Mississippi could make an anti-Chamber of Commerce speech before the Chamber, and make the boys love it, and make them ask for more, and divert Mr. George F. Babbitt for an hour of his life from his contract bridge and his crossword puzzles.

And soon it is not until night that he must draw his shades and seek his sleep. Yet now he does not go quickly to bed. Instead, he opens a suitcase containing a thousand scraps of paper, and meditatively, with fond hands, he goes slowly through the thousand notes, destroying some because in the long interval their meanings have been lost, studying others, head tilted and brows furrowed in an attitude of doubt, discarding, retaining, his lips spelling out lines which were good lines when he wrote them and are still good lines, there on the scraps of paper, and all he needs now is a poem to go with the lines. He feels—he knows, he is certain—that he will write his great poems yet. He is almost confident, and with the returning strength of returning confidence he becomes interested again in the game, or the business, or the problem, or the whatever it is of living.

In Friendship Oak he reads Aiken and Akins and Aldington and Aldis, taking them as they come in the book, reading in a toneless listless way, devotionlessly, and the beautiful exciting children in the semicircle about him lean back to back and head upon shoulder and know because they are young and romantic that this is the way a poet reads after he has seen the world and been bruised in love and fallen upon thorns. And suddenly one day, at twenty minutes of noon, the listless voice becomes for a moment another voice, and he discovers for the first time lines he should have discovered before. Or perhaps he has read them before, but never with the feeling of personal discovery, as now he reads them and for an instant, for the first time in a long time, finds in a line of poetry a kind of power. "Let me read that again," he says, and the girl-children straighten and become alert. He speaks, and he has not bothered to speak before. "Sherwood Anderson," he says, and he reads: "Pshaw, I'm steady enough—let me alone. Keokuk, Tennessee, Michigan, Chicago, Kalamazoo—don't the names in this country make you fairly drunk? We'll stand by this brown stream for hours. I'll not be swept away—watch my hand, how steady it is. To catch this song and sing it would do much, make much clear."

He reads the hour out, reading hard for twenty minutes, the rest of Anderson, then Arensberg, Austin, Barrett, Beach, and on the dot of noon he dismisses his class and lowers himself to the ground, and on this day he walks not alone but in the company of two maidens, from Friendship Oak to the dining hall.

"Poisons," says the surgeon. "Most people aren't aware how much poisons they have in their system."

"And you think I'd feel better . . ."

"Think? Know!"

"I saw a Dr. Zadek in Biloxi and he said . . ."

"Ha! Zadek! What I know about Zadek! I wouldn't say it. Who knows? Maybe he knows what he's doing. I wouldn't say he doesn't."

"But you'd say . . ."

"I'd say operate. Look!" The Mobile surgeon, with the impatience of a man unalterably convinced of his own cause, swings about in his chair and opens his file case and steers Vachel to a bright light, and he holds against the light an X-ray negative. "See," says he, "that's what you look like inside. That's your skull, my friend. Read it and weep," and Vachel squints reluctantly into the light, unable to read what he has had no practice in reading.

"For all I can tell it's Yorick's skull," he says.

"It's not. It's yours. See the poisons," and he traces with a finger the rivers and the valleys of poison, and Vachel has not the vaguest idea what he is looking at, or whether they are bad things or good things, and he says so. "Well anyone can see," says the surgeon. "You're a smart man. You can see," and Vachel looks again, and he is convinced because he has tried the sea and tried the sun, and he has slept and rested, and still he is not the young Vachel again, and he supposes it must be the poisons.

Three times he goes under the knife, twice for the sinuses and once for the cheekbone, and each time, afterward, he sits bareheaded in the sun for a week, and he is never certain there were poisons, but something happens to something inside his skull, and between the knife and the sun and the sea and the sleep and the rest he begins almost to enjoy the sessions in the tree.

The little girls, at second glance, are subtly different. They have grown. They look like women and talk like women.

He warned them at the outset that if any were poets they need not think he would read their poems because he is not paid to read anything except poetry that has been printed and therefore merits his professional attention. Having issued the order he was immediately ashamed, and at length he rescinds it, and four girls bring him poetry to read, handwritten and strangely familiar: it is poetry of the sort he wrote when he was sixteen and Bryan came. He keeps each poem for several days before offering comment upon it. I must say it right, he thinks, for one must be gentleman and diplomat in such matters, honest and yet not discouraging, frank but not unkind.

In a way, he looks forward to the five private minutes he will have with the individual poet. Such consultations must always be private, for young poets are sensitive. He knows. He remembers.

And the young poets are women, too. ("I'm just so afraid because I don't understand method." "Method!" says he. "Pooh! Technical discussions rage because most poets are twenty-five. That's the technical age. You're too full of art-school questions. So were we all. We feel we must settle them or be unhappy. Forget it, lady, and write your own poetry according to your own method.") They are women, and if they be poets or understand poetry or hope to understand it so much the better. But they are first of all women, and beautiful, and quite without warning—the sun? the knife? the sea?—he is seized with a strange and unsettling desire: he will make away with a girl-child, ride away in the night, flee, go home, and take with him the child of beauty and batter down the door of the old house, and enter, and whoever is living there now he will drive them away and live again in the ancestral home in the magical city, and a home will be a home and not a room, and he will not be a stranger as here he is a stranger living on a charity that is not quite charity by grace of the fact that he is a friend of Dr. Cox and therefore a sort of a guest although not quite a guest. He will go home to the place where every street is familiar and every name is the name of someone who in some way is a part of his life or was a part of Mama's and Papa's or with whom he went to school, where all names are related in some way to the City of Springfield.

In the night, now, he flirts for an hour with his poetry, and it stirs him and works like a stimulant upon his system, and he is full of plans again, and a further line from Anderson sounding like Whitman pulses within him, and not for a long time has the tired body been strong enough to retain and vibrate to a line of poetry: *Great projects arise within me.*

By day the projects seem neither great nor possible of fulfillment. By day, as it happens, he is a man of near fifty, and however exciting or miraculous the milestone may appear to him, it is, to the young ladies of Friendship Oak, an almost grandfatherly age. Then too, as it happens, he is a poor man, and young ladies instructed in the virtues of wealth are likely to look upon near-poverty as excusable in a poet but nevertheless a prohibitive obstacle, for though they may be in love with true love their mothers and their fathers are frequently not.

And the strange unsettling desire grips him, and he reads, with a quickening interest now, lines that have for him new meaning. "I don't know what anybody else is getting out of this course," says he, lifting his eyes from the book, "but I'm learning things every day. The course picks up as it goes along," and as a matter of fact it does, for the young ladies as well as for him. The new meanings give a new depth to Vachel's plans for his new poetry, and when he is strong and completely well again he will write the best songs of his years. He will live to be one hundred and five. The chapter is not yet half-completed. The best is yet to be.

He buys a new L. C. Smith to replace his old Underwood.

The business of convalescence is at best an extremely slow process which Vachel in his impatience tries too quickly to accomplish. He has a brief bout with the flu, with the result that between the expense of the new typewriter and the high cost of influenza he finds his budget as well as his body overtaxed.

Against the advice of his doctor he makes two trips, going once to the University of Alabama and once to Princeton. This time the doctor is wrong. The trips do him good.

They are easy, leisurely journeys, and his pocketbook is replenished and he is none the worse for the flu. He regains the lost ground and passes the point at which he fell ill, and in time he passes the point or the phase, however brought about, at which he had silly dreams of stealing away a girl-child. The old, wide love, which narrowed for a time, now widens again, and the love of person tends to become once more the love of persons and people, and great projects arise within him, and they are real projects, based on old ambitions now refined, and he will tour the country again, but in a wiser way, and he will keep ten months of each year for himself and his writing, and pay the piper as well.

("What are the dates of the new poetry?" the young lady interrupts to ask. "Dates?" says he. "Roughly, nineteen-twelve to question mark. We ain't dead yet.")

The director of an English theater company—one of those directors who doubles as ticket taker and master electrician and understudies actors suddenly called away to paying roles in better parts of London—writes to Vachel for six copies of the War Bulletins. With Vachel's permission he would like to stage the Village Improvement Parade.

Vachel immediately grants the permission, but, as to the magazines, he has none; attempts to locate copies in Springfield uncover only three, and some of the letters to Springfield are returned unopened because old friends are dead, and three more copies are eventually forthcoming from New York dealers in rare books and manuscripts, at five dollars apiece, a sum which Vachel gladly pays.

They come tattered and yellow and thick with dust, and before reshipping them he reads them again, wincing at clumsy passages and thinking old thoughts and reminded again of old dead days when he was indiscreet and undiplomatic, although quite accurate in some of his prophecy. The issues of The Twenties are not far different from those of nineteen-and-ten, and when he is strong again he will begin again at nineteen-ten, right back in Springfield where he wrote peppery things about the Country Club and Christ the Socialist and beggary the noblest of professions. He will begin again, and he will be wiser the next fifty years.

He grows stronger, and the stronger he grows the faster his plans multiply. They are sound plans. He is, if anything, stronger than he was in nineteen-ten, because he is wiser, and because his hand is more skillful, and mistakes once made will not be made again. He will not be so quick to give away the labor of his days, the Bulletins, permissions to reprint his poetry, things he gave away in the interest of the holy war to people who were never interested in holy wars. He is an old bear, and he knows where the pit traps are dug. He will give himself no longer to crowds, and he will play pet poodle no more for the women's clubs. He will be free again, and wiser in his freedom, and when grasshoppers eat holes in his shirt he will squash them with the flat of his hand.

He is full of plans, and the big over-all plan is as it always was— the saving of the world—and he has slipped a long way and lost sight of the goal, but he is reascending the position and coming back again to the time of his youth when he wrote heavily with a broad-pointed pen in the black notebook: *the man who is not a fanatic is as useless as a tombstone.*

He reads aloud in Friendship Oak: Benét, Bodenheim, Cather, Colum, Corbin, Eastman, Ficke, Fletcher, Frost, Garland, Hardy, Kreymborg, Lindsay, Long, Mackaye, Masters, Millay, Monroe, Reed, Robinson, Rosenberg, Sandburg, Tagore, Teasdale, Tietjens, Torrence, Untermeyer, Williams, Wood, Yeats, and the poetry is many things, not protest alone, but the main thread is protest and revolt. It is in the lines. And the man who is not somewhere in some way or other printing out new lines is prodigal son to the mother necessity.

An old restlessness is upon him. The white sea beach has lost, for him, its power to cure, for there is no sickness now to cure. The sun no longer heals, for the wounds are closed. The young ladies of the tree, having been first the elements of a chore and next the fancy of a temporary seizure, resume their natural size and place, and Vachel sees them anew with a corrected vision. He is well.

Gulfport was only a temporary thing in the first place, and he came like a ship to the port, to be moored to the wharf until repairs could be made. He was happy enough at the time to sign a piece of paper assuring him a certain permanence, and he was happy enough to sign the paper again when requested to do so, and that was when he was sick. Now he is well, and Vachel in good health and good sense has never subscribed to what seems to him the unreasonable proposition that a human being can be bound by contract to any city, state, nation or other subdivision. Nobody has ever told him when or where to come or go, and nobody is going to start telling him now, and the more the contract is waved in his face the more obstinate he becomes, and he asserts to the consternation of the assembled committee that if everybody packed his bags and took off from wherever he was at least once in every two years the whole world would benefit from the interfusion. It is a theory arrived at upon the spur of the moment, but he states it as if it comes down from the prophets, and the contract is again waved in his face, and again waved away, and he leaves feeling more than ever recovered, and righteous, and bumptious, and altogether like the Vachel of nineteen-and-ten.

2

East and west on 36 and north and south on 66 on singing rubber at 45 mph to the limits of the city, and the theory is that if somehow they are slowed they can then be stopped, and once stopped they will eat a meal or buy a souvenir or a tank of gasoline or a quart of oil or spend a few nickels at a telephone or maybe only buy a quart of milk or a wax-paper sandwich, but it all adds up.

The theory is that a few dollars well spent in full-stop signs and two-minute red lights will slow them down and shift them out of high gear into low, and once they have slowed and gone to the trouble of shifting the gears they might as well get out and stretch the legs and let the kids pee like they been pestering to do ever since Decatur or St. Louis or wherever it was.

And the theory is that it is well worth the cost to paint a few signs against the sky from here halfway to Bloomington so's people won't forget this is Lincoln land, so even if the kids don't need to pee they might stop to see the Tomb because it is educational for the kids and patriotic for the grownups, and it makes no difference how they get stopped just so long as they do, because once stopped they will drop a dollar or a fiver or maybe even ten, and it all adds up.

Or if they saw the Tomb last year they might stop this time to see the Lindsay home where the poet was brought up in a Christian way and where he got the inspiration for his famous poems although all that one remembers offhand is Booth and The Congo, but never mind the details, nobody is interested in the details. The idea is to stop them some way or other because once they're stopped and up on their feet they'll drop a fiver or maybe ten, and you hit them with whatever is handy to hit them with: you hit them in the belly or you hit them in the gas tank or you hit them in the patriotic plexus, or you poke your head in through the window and ask "What! You aint seen the Lindsay place! You want the kids to grow up uneducated?"

One way or another you full-stop them and get them on their feet. It adds up.

3

Permanent address: Room 1129, Davenport Hotel, Spokane Washington. *My dear A.J., I am here for all time so far as I know. I haven't the least notion of lecturing or traveling.*

The word is Hospitality, and Vachel buys it because he is forever taking people at their word and buying by the peck when he ought to be asking for a trial sample. The Chamber of Commerce offers him a room and all the food he can eat, and he need not make a spectacle of himself as poor old Bryan was a spectacle, floating on the lagoon endorsing Florida land. All he need do, he is told, is be a resident of Spokane and an advocate of Hospitality, and he is so grateful that he goes forth now and then in the city to lecture free, and he gives free a few new poems to the *Chronicle*, and when he is hungry he lifts the phone and says *food,* and food is brought.

"Heigh-ho," says Lorenzo, bursting into Vachel's room. "Oh. Excuse me."

"Perfectly all right," says Vachel, slipping quickly into a pair of trousers.

"How's the scholar?" says Lorenzo. His name is not really Lorenzo, but Vachel calls him that because he puts Vachel in mind of one of the craftier of the Medici. Vachel admires him in the way all openhanded men, despite themselves, admire schemers and promoters. "I was in the neighborhood and I thought I'd pop up."

"Any time," says Vachel.

"I got a question."

"Shoot."

"You've heard of Edgar Guest."

"Oh yes."

"Mighty fine poet."

"Mighty fine."

"Cigar?" says Lorenzo. He unwraps his cigar and bites off the end and feels in his pocket for a match.

"Trouble with Guest he's a bookworm," says Vachel.

"Hell, a little scholarly influence don't hurt. He's comin to town."

"Permanently?"

"No. Just to sign a few books. What we wanta do is work up a little hospitality. Might have a sort of poet day. Know what I mean?" He touches flame to his cigar and withdraws the cigar from his mouth and studies the wet end. "How's it strike ya?"

"What day?"

"Friday."

"Now that's unfortunate because I won't be able to make it."

"Oh man, ya *got* to make it. How would it be a poet day without our number one?"

"I just have something else on. I've got to go over to Seattle. Something I've neglected and can't neglect any longer."

"What?" says Lorenzo.

"Something personal."

"Well okay. If that's the way you feel. Hell of a note, though. What's so personal?"

"Just something personal."

"Hell of a note. Well, I gotta run. I'll tell the boys," and he swings the door open and then turns, pausing in his exit. "Ya know," he says, "you're supposed to be talking up the old hospitality and as far as I can see ya ain't done much but stick right here."

"I'll try to do better."

"Okay, man. Didn't mean to barge in. I was in the neighborhood and I thought I'd pop up."

"Pop up any time," says Vachel. "Good-by, Lorenzo," and Lorenzo makes his way chuckling down the hall, and he chuckles because Vachel is always calling him Lorenzo and that is not his name at all.

Vachel, having bought a peck and made a promise, becomes a citizen of Spokane, thinking that in this far corner of the land there are somehow new frontiers, and he thinks the land might be rewon, working east from Spokane and rewinning the Valley of the Mississippi for Huckleberry Finn, and rewinning Virginia and Massachusetts for Jefferson and the sassy side of Adams, and rewinning Illinois for Abraham Lincoln, and he will do it by praising and celebrating the new-adopted city and making it by precept and example the model upon which all reformed cities shall be patterned. And the streets of Spokane are called Adams and Jefferson and Madison and Washington and Lincoln and Sherman and Grant, and the names still enchant him as the same names obsessed him in Springfield, and he clings yet to the hope that there is somewhere in the United States, perhaps here in the far corner, a lingering allegiance that makes each name meaningful, and he darkly suspects that Jefferson died with the birth of the combustible engine, and he will not admit it because to admit it would mean that the holy war is lost.

He stands at his window, looking down eleven floors at Post Street, and it might be eleven floors and a street in Pittsburgh or Buffalo or Milwaukee or Dallas, and he knows it, and he cannot admit it because admission would be admission that he is old and past the age of usefulness in a land where the issues are different from the issues of his generation. There are no island cities any more, and the day of the great individual wonder worker is past, and the dream of Springfield is interrupted by the cold light of a new morning, and he is as dead as Bryan and Altgeld and Wilson.

And Spokane is not the frontier West. Rather, it is neighbor to New York, reading the same syndicated newspaper writer, the same Edgar Guest, staring at the same motion-picture screen and gulping the same latest editorial by Mr. George Horace Lorimer in The Saturday Evening Post. Vachel is old, and the times have passed him by. He is a Jefferson Lincoln Democrat in a Coolidge Republican time.

He would be young. He would go down the eleven floors and dash into the street and begin again, and go wandering with his poems in an oilcloth rainproof folder, and if he does the swift trains and swift trucks will pass him by, freighted with the gospel according to Lorimer. He is near fifty, and old, a village man in a city time, a man writing poems by hand in a factory time. He is Vachel Lindsay in the year of Eddie Guest.

"Heigh-ho," says Lorenzo, re-entering in a shroud of blue smoke.

"Hello again," says Vachel, turning from the window.

"Another thing occurred to me," Lorenzo says, withdrawing his cigar and contemplating the soggy end. "I been reading in a book about Astor. Wonderful man, wouldn't you say?"

"Wonderful man. The kind of man who always galloped into hotel rooms and never knocked."

"Sorry old man."

"I'm not an old man."

Lorenzo reinserts his cigar and puffs hard to revive it. "Ya oughta write a poem on Astor."

"I'm writing one on Jackson."

"Great man, Jackson. Well anyhow, one a the Astors is comin to town and the greeters kinda felt it would be a nice touch if ya had a poem right ready."

There is a knock, and Vachel shouts *enter*, and a young man in a starched white suit wheels a tray into the room. Vachel comes forward from the window and removes the heat retainers from the plates, and he sniffs the food. "Coffee?" says he to Lorenzo.

"Don't mind if I do," says Lorenzo, and he draws a chair to the table upon which the starched young man is placing the dishes.

"But I've got the Jackson poem," says Vachel.

"Well, it's your business. I guess you know what you're doin."

"Let's hope so."

"Still and all, an Astor is an Astor."

"And Jackson is Jackson." Vachel wishes the food had been brought another time.

"How they feedin ya?"

"Very well," says Vachel, and he studies Lorenzo's face above the coffee cup, but he can detect no deeper meaning behind the question. Nevertheless, Vachel is uncomfortable. "You must understand," he says, "Astor just isn't my type of material."

"I ain't pressin the point."

"I've got nothing against him in a personal way."

"I ain't insisting. I guess you know your business. It's like with me. I got my line and you wouldn't tell me how to sell it. Good coffee." Lorenzo tilts his head and drinks and relights his cigar. "Got to get moving," he says.

"If I get the Jackson poem done . . ."

"Listen old man. If ya get to it ya get to it. We'd appreciate it."

"I might at that," says Vachel.

"I don't want ya ta think me or anybody else is tellin ya what kind a poems ta write. That ain't square."

"Sometime when you're in the neighborhood why don't you bring me that book about Astor and let me take a look at it?"

"Sure will," says Lorenzo. "Well, heigh-ho," and Lorenzo goes, and Vachel hopes he will forget to bring the book, but he will not. He never forgets. He never forgets anything, and Vachel, if he can help it, will not quite get to the Astor poem, and Lorenzo will never mention it, but he will remember; and Vachel will not be a Greeter, and Lorenzo will not insist but he will not forget, and Vachel will take his stand for Al Smith and try to laugh it off, saying he has always been a Democrat and it's a kind of a habit, and Lorenzo will say nothing, but will blow smoke-rings across the room and look from Vachel to the good coffee on the well-spread table, and say, "I don't want ya ta think me or anybody else is telling ya what kind a politics ta have."

Nobody will ever say anything. Nobody tells anybody what to write about in the free country, and everybody chooses his own way and his own subjects, and one may choose his own heroes, as Vachel chooses now, above all others, Andrew Jackson the agrarian, and the three meals a day are his, and the rent-free room, and it will last until Lorenzo putting two and two painfully together adds Vachel up to four, and there will be a further journey to a further city.

Sometimes he thinks: what harm could there be in just one poem to the memory of William Waldorf Astor, and what harm if I were to shake the hand of Eddie Guest and call him brother poet? Life would be pleasanter, and I would not be so uneasy and insecure, and what would Jesus do, would he be a whore just once or twice for the cup of good coffee and live to fight another day? What would

Johnny Appleseed do? Did they not, perhaps, in some unrecorded chapter of their lives, just once, with crisis upon them, play the whore?

Vachel decides that they did not. He will fight it through and let happen what happens, and stick to his own kind of writing and choose his own subjects, and in his lonely room, neglecting the Life of Astor which Lorenzo brings him, he voyages in the books of the heroes. Dear Witter Bynner you must read John Adams he at least took nothing lying down and was ready to sass anyone from Washington to Hamilton looking up his facts afterward because after a tiff or two with these foxy high-class constipated lawyers representing foxy high-class constipated trust companies you are just about ready to seat dear old John Adams at the head of the class he would thoroughly goddam most any sbx and look up his facts afterward. What a sassy boy I am on a hot day.

CHAPTER TWO

1

IT WAS NOT really a lie he had told Lorenzo, at least not entirely a lie; Vachel had, indeed, been planning a trip, not to Seattle, to be sure, but to Mills College down in Oakland.

He thinks he will go down to see Reinhardt, the president of Mills, telling himself that it is Reinhardt he goes to see, telling himself a small lie, yet in no way deceiving himself—deceiving himself no more than he deceived Mama when he told her he could be reached at the Christian Publishing Company in St. Louis when all the time he would be at Sara's; as now, down in Oakland, if he sees his old friend Reinhardt at all it will be coincidence. Not that he would *mind* seeing Reinhardt. He thinks of Reinhardt as one of those men who not only calls himself an educator but actually educates people, a kind of Statue of Liberty on the western side. Once a student has come within his range that student is forever different.

Yet he is not riding down on the overnight sleeper to Oakland to see Reinhardt at all and there is no use fooling himself or lying to himself or pretending that things are one way when they are another. He is riding down to Oakland in search of a dear friend whom he deeply loves, and her name is not Reinhardt; he is traveling, too, however unaware he may be of the fact, in search of his own completeness.

Elisabeth is twenty-three years old. Vachel wonders, alighting from the train, exactly where one would locate a twenty-three-year-old lady on a sunny Friday morning in the city of Oakland. It would, of course, depend on the lady.

He could call Reinhardt, he supposes. But he wants to be romantic, and it would be most unromantic, locating a lady by telephone, even though Reinhardt would know exactly how to track her down. But I do not want to track her down, he thinks, like a Hearst reporter. He wants to seek her as Tom Sawyer would seek her, the romantic way, not as Huck Finn would do it because Huck was

331

never romantic and he was frequently being hurt, and Tom was never hurt. (There have been ladies before—there was Sara—and they wanted him to be romantic and always, he suspected, they wanted most of all to have him dress better, and they wanted him to trade his pen for a Ford, and he wants to find Elisabeth now as if by accident, coming upon her as she is, not as she might pretend to be if she knew he were coming. It is better to be hurt beforehand than to be hurt afterward.)

He turns off Hearst Avenue, onto the University of California campus. She says in her letters that there is a better library here than across town at Mills, and she said if ever perchance he was passing through town he might find her here, and of course they were only letters and maybe just talk to be talking maybe just saying things she thinks he would like to hear knowing that he is a poet and all and fond of books and libraries and all such things that a lady when she is twenty-three has no business being fond of at all. (There was a young lady once, and she told Vachel she was in love with books but she never entered a library because it was bad for her complexion, and it seemed to him, afterward, that she was neither in love with books nor with him, although she was in love with something she thought he was, discovering later that he never made as much money on a lecture tour as she thought he made and he never received for a published poem quite what she thought he received, and she ultimately married a gentleman from Cleveland who, Vachel hopes, owns as big a factory as she thinks he owns.)

He walks slowly between the library tables, half-hoping that she will not be here because if he does not find her she can never hurt him. And, if he does not find her, he might never be forced to drive himself onward toward his own completeness.

"May I help you?" a librarian asks.

"Thank you," he says. "No, I think I can manage," thinking he ought to tell her that he has spent the best years of his life in libraries and he knows his way around, but not telling her because she is only trying to be helpful and because of the sudden, senseless memory of the little girl in the library at Hiram, and how they always met at the library, and how it always seemed a safe and neutral place where there could be no more between them than the heavy books and the light touching of hands. "You might tell me," says he, "where someone would be if she were working on Catullus."

"Latin poets," says the librarian. "Follow me. That's the second request this morning."

"Undoubtedly a revival," says he. "Do you suppose Catullus will ever replace Eddie Guest?"

"It was a young lady," the librarian says, and he follows her.

She said she was doing some work in Catullus. She did not say why. She seemed to assume that Catullus was at least as exciting as contract bridge, and she sent him, in the mail, not a photograph showing him a face he had already seen and remembered well, but a few lines out of Catullus.

"Down to the end. The alcove on your left."

"Much obliged," says he, going on alone and knowing that it might just be that down at the end, in the alcove to his left, she will be there as she said she would if perchance he is passing through town sometime. There are some things in life, said Helen Curtis (that was her name—back at Hiram—Helen Curtis), some things in life which a man or a woman can count upon. There is such a thing in life as constancy. It is a rare thing, and perhaps because it is rare it is the reason Vachel writes so many poems on the moon, the constant moon. It is rare, but it exists, and it is as real as the old house in Springfield, waiting, constant, real, as Mama was real, constant to the last (she asked for him at the very last), as real and as enduring as the light in the Statehouse dome, something existing in Nature and in inanimate things but only rarely existing in human beings which is why, he supposes, they hang a lighted wick above the altar in the synagogue because they can count on a wick as they cannot count on any human being, Hebrew or Latin or otherwise, and maybe that is why she does her work in Catullus because Catullus is faithful and unchanging day to day because he is not like fashions in poetry that change from one decade to the next and the sweet singer of one year is the hotel poet the next, because Catullus does not die, as even Mama dies. It is barely possible that she will be there in the alcove to the left, and, turning the corner down at the end he sees her, and she sits with her back to him, and he goes silently to her and touches her shoulder, saying softly, "Women, like poetry, should be taken out of the libraries into the fresh air."

They walk, directing their steps by silent, mutual consent toward Mills College across town, where first they met and walked together two years before, and from time to time since, passing the quiet hour preceding the noisy platform hour. She had been selected, as at all schools someone was always selected, to be Guide to the Distinguished Visitor, to point out the buildings and to name them for him, to show him the landmarks of the triangular route from railroad to lecture hall and back to the railroad, and he had told her, as he told all the young ladies and young men who served that function in all the places he had been, that he had already guessed the names of the buildings, and he had already seen the Busts of the Worthy Donors for whom the buildings were named, and he had seen a railroad depot and a hotel and a lecture hall before, and that he wanted more than anything a chance to stretch his legs and breathe some fresh air and rest his eyes. "And they always laughed," he says, "because they always thought I was joking, and they always ran my legs off and stretched my neck to the limit showing me the highest building in town, and it was never very high, and certainly it was never in the best taste."

"But it was the highest," she says. "That's what counts. They'll build a new tower of Babel someday."

"With an elevator. But my question is: can you really get to God in an elevator?" and they agree, somewhere between the two campuses in Oakland, that God cannot be reached by elevator, not even by the fastest elevator in the highest building. He had suspected that she would agree to that. He had never been absolutely sure because there had been only brief meetings before, and then there had been the lecture, and he had gone swiftly from the lecture to the hotel, or to the train, and he had not seen her again until the next time. He had only remembered, between times, that there had been that girl in Oakland introduced to him by Dr. Reinhardt, and he supposes he might have known that Reinhardt would select a girl like her.

They talk of Reinhardt, arriving at him by way of high buildings and Catullus and Lorenzo and Edgar Guest and Andrew Jackson, and she agrees that Reinhardt is a sort of Statue of Liberty because from him she has learned, as Vachel, from Susan, learned, that man has erected monuments to himself, and that the monuments are not high buildings or the Busts of Worthy Donors but the mind of man recorded in the books which have long survived and will long survive mere stone.

Thus, when he came in the past, she showed him a quiet twilight hour, an hour of rest before the exertion of the recital. For this he had been grateful, and he had remembered, afterward, with the faintest guilt, not only the good quiet talk together but the handshake of greeting and, again, the clasp of their hands at parting, and her hand had been warm in his.

He takes her hand, and it is warm, and she makes no effort to remove it, no protest, understanding that his gesture is an act of honesty, his declaration that he has traveled far in search of someone who will hold his hand, and by this simple exchange of honest confidence they reduce in themselves the terrible fear arising from the knowledge that they, and their kind, are vastly outnumbered by people who steadfastly believe (or act as if they believed) that God and love are at the top of the highest building. It is an agreement to agree, an admission of the loneliness of each in an age ("the iron age," she calls it) when most people are much too busy transacting business ("the business of America is business," says Mr. Coolidge) to seek in their own hearts the large answer that is love.

It seems to him that in his hand he holds an answer. It does not seem possible that as recently as two days ago he stood at the hotel window thinking I am old and past the age of usefulness when now he is young, as all young men in love are young. He is not at the end of a trail but at his beginnings, and his mind races forward in time and he sees himself a young man growing older on the streets of Springfield, returning at last, whole, complete, he and this maiden, and the old house alive with light and noise, and there will be children, and that which is he will go forward after him, after he, at one hundred and five, is gone. He will not die an old man in a lonely room in an alien city. "If I got very firm with them I could get it back," he says. "It's only a bank and they'd have to give it back. But first—just for a little while—we'd live in the hotel. We'd start life clean, no debts, at least no heavy debts, and a hotel can be spiritual enough as long as it's only on a temporary basis," and he releases her hand and swings her around, and they stand face to face, she insisting that this is all very sudden, and equally vague, and he admitting to being both sudden and vague and at the same time so intensely and crucially involved within himself that his mind runs away with his tongue, and that he is asking her to marry him and that however she answers, whether yes or no, that she do it in a way that will not hurt him because such speech, however confused, has been a brave and painful rescue of his own manhood, a tortuous break with the ghost of that woman who doomed him for a certain term to walk the night half-complete, half-man.

2

They are married on a May day in Vachel's room in the Davenport Hotel. The room is trimmed with gold brocade, and Vachel wears a black flannel shirt, and neither Lorenzo nor any of his tribe is invited.

Lorenzo (afterward) affirms his belief in a man's right to invite whoever he pleases to his wedding, but at the same time, says he, it was a hell of a note because it could of been a big thing wrote up in all the papers with a Spokane date. "I'm sorry," says Vachel to Lorenzo, "but I'm sick of publicity and having my heart poked into by dirty fingers."

Lorenzo nevertheless belatedly summons a reporter, and the reporter asks, "What's her name?" and Vachel tells him Locust-Blossom because, the day after they were married, they went walking and found the locust trees in bloom, and he christened her then and there Locust-Blossom. Hesitantly the reporter puts pencil to paper. "You can say," says Vachel, "that we were married by spontaneous combustion the instant we got acquainted," and the reporter wets the end of his pencil and looks questioningly from Elisabeth to Vachel and back to Elisabeth.

"Not literally," she says.

"We'd met a good many times before," Vachel amends.

"Where were you married?"

"Here. Right in this room," says Vachel.

"Not at a church?"

"We belong to the Universal Church, but there seems to be none in this town. So this room was as good."

"Did you try the yellow pages?" says Lorenzo. "Got to get people in the habit of the yellow pages. . . ."

"We tried them. We looked all through the yellow pages and there was no Universal Church or Church Universal. Didn't we, Locust-Blossom?"

"Would you tell me—what are your plans?" the man from the *Chronicle* asks.

"Plans," says Vachel. "Let me see. Locust-Blossom, what are our plans? We'll paint sidewalks and blow bubbles for a living?" and she smiles, and when she smiles her dimpled chin is deeper dimpled and the humorous eyes laugh, and the eyes signal that the game is Vachel's, and he plays on. "My wife will read further in the flaming love poetry of Catullus, and I, not understanding Latin, will try to write some poems in English, and she will be critic and censor, my young governor, my ruler, in all ways head of the firm and boss at this end of the state."

"Could you tell me—could you describe—yourself—what you wore?" The reporter turns to Elisabeth.

"We forget," says Vachel. "She was Juliet. She was Rosalind. Then there are some nice poems of Milton. She was like the heroine in some of Milton's nicest poems. Go read some Milton," and the *Chronicle* man stares glumly at his note paper, upon which the single word *Locust-Blossom* is written, and he says that he must go, and Lorenzo halts him.

"One other thing," says Lorenzo. "I got it all figured. Spokane is the jumping-off point to Mount Rainier. Right?"

"Right," says Vachel, agreeably.

"Right," says Elisabeth.

"Now get this. Put this down. Towering fifteen thousand feet. Volcanic eruptions of the ages past. Built by Mother Nature herself. It's the greatest single glacial-peak system in the United States. So! Poems by Vachel Lindsay written on his wedding trip in Mount Rainier National Park, mentioning of course Spokane."

"Right," says Vachel.

But the bridal couple spends the honeymoon days tramping instead in Glacier National Park, Montana, weighting their packs on their backs in the manner prescribed by a Blackfoot Indian elder who seems to appreciate the fact that Elisabeth and Vachel neither gape at him nor order him to pose for a snapshot but shake his hand when they meet in the wood. Elisabeth finds two feathers on the trail, one from a blue bird and one from a red bird, and Vachel wears the feathers in his hat, and the Blackfoot Indian assures them that two such feathers in combination are a sign of very deep loyalty and devotion.

Here, in the silent wood, by running streams and splashing falls, beneath the sun which seems so near and beneath the winking stars infinitely more plenteous than the stars above the lighted city, the world that is the world most people know is distant and unreal. Here, except for a chance meeting with an Indian unseduced by the white world, they are alone, and the Indian, much preferring his own company to that of these pale people, stops, shakes hands, speaks briefly and passes on, so that even then they are alone. Once, at the crest of a rise, they look down upon two crouching middle-aged men struggling to open tinned fish with a stone; one of the men carries, in a rear pocket, a rolled newspaper, and with each movement the newspaper wags behind him, like a tail. At length, suspecting the hopelessness of the project, one of the men hurls the tin of fish into the near-by stream where, crashing upon the rocks, the tin bursts, spraying its contents into the running water. The men do not see what has happened. Only Vachel and Elisabeth see, and they watch as the water swallows both tin and food, and they laugh and return the way they came.

Here, alone, they come to know each other.

At twenty-three she is, in many ways, wiser than he, both wiser and older. In many ways she understands better the forces at work in the world about them. They spend an hour upon a sun-beaten rock, drawing pictures with long sticks in the sand below, and he talks for most of the hour on the dilemma of art in the modern world, and all that he says in the hour she says in five seconds: "What does the world care for poets in these iron days?"

He has been flattered by crowds, and she does not flatter him. He has been fed cake, and she will show him the way to bread. He was compared in the daily press to Homer chanting to the Greeks, and she does not compare him thus: she knows Homer; she knows, also, that to sell Vachel to the public it was necessary to advertise him extravagantly, and Vachel half-believed his own advertisements, and so he was confused by a besieging public that confused the man and his poetry, and he was flattered by the newspapers. But he is never really loved. And she will love him.

She is neither impressed by his Greatness nor deceived by his Distinction, and she learns to find him in his own lines, not always where others find him in the rhapsodic, pulsating rhythms, not in the well-turned phrases, not in singing stanzas but in the two lines in which, speaking of John Altgeld, he speaks of himself: "To live in mankind is far more than to live in a name, to live in mankind, far, far more than to live in a name."

In the dawn, beneath the fading stars, she lies wakeful beside him, knowing that her first feeling for him, her early suspicion, has been confirmed: he is a man of heart in an iron age, not caring if his name is a name in a classroom text one thousand years from now, caring only that Man will be richer in himself, fuller and broader and deeper in the thousand years to come ("Man *and* Woman," he says, and this, too, she loves in him), and it becomes important now, the only truly important thing in her life, that he live and grow in his earth-time, not because he is Homer or Milton or Shakespeare or anyone of the sort, but only because he is Vachel. She will expend the strength of her youth showing him the way to bread and escape from flattery because he is Man at his civic and humane and responsible best, and he may yet be something else; he may yet be Homer. He has written great lines, a few fine poems, but the best have yet to be written, for his greatness as a poet is not in the social, political poems, compelling as they are, because Vachel is not an analyst, a Veblen, a George, a Marx, a Shaw (he prefers to look up his facts after he has cooled off) but a prophet, a mystic, and Utopia, to him, is more than universal bread, more than a tin heaven and a tin earth; it is the human spirit in full flower, and he has approached it in his poetry from many directions and many times almost struck the note and defined the undefinable, but he has not yet hit it square so that all generations may read, and pause, and say *this is it! this is the word!* He must live long, as Milton and Goethe lived long. All this she knows though she be half his age.

And afterward, after the chapter is done, distinguished scholars will seek in his lines the answer to something they will describe as his failure, some seeking the answer in him, some seeking it in her, and they will find it nowhere, because the failure does not exist. All men and all women of heart are only seeming failures in the iron age.

This she cannot now know. She knows only that she must rescue him from Lorenzo and guide toward port the ship that has long been compassless, battered and fired upon in the iron sea. If Vachel is to fail of long life, and of greatness, it is not that Elisabeth comes with too little, but that she comes too late. He has been gnawed by sharks in heavy seas, and he has been captained by mutineers, and the mutiny is inspired by Mammon the Soul of the Spider. It is this aspect of failure which the distinguished scholar and the distinguished scientist cannot hope to understand; it is a thing they do not dare to examine in the comfortable shadow of the Bust of the Worthy Donor.

CHAPTER THREE

1

"HEIGH-HO," says Lorenzo, "how goes the Astor poem?" and Vachel says it goes indeed, and Elisabeth rises from the table at which she and Vachel have been working, and Vachel, first gathering the littered papers together and putting them out of sight, then rises and follows Elisabeth to the coffee table. She turns the switch of the burner, and she brings cream and sugar, and as an afterthought she gives the burner switch a further turn to the high position, for the sooner Lorenzo has his coffee the sooner he will depart. "I'll have your monkey suit for you this afternoon," says Lorenzo, and Vachel says fine. He will wear what is required. Up to a certain point he will do what he must to please Lorenzo. Lorenzo is forever on the point of unloading Vachel as a bad investment, and then Vachel in one way or another does a small thing to please, and Lorenzo never quite unloads. "It'll really be a blowout," says Lorenzo.

Elisabeth decides, early in the afternoon, that she cannot attend the dinner, and Vachel, with the total reliance of the nonscientific man upon the answers only science can give, hastily turns pages in the book to which he has had frequent cause to refer in recent weeks. "What symptoms?" he says.

"No symptoms," says she, and she laughs.

"That makes it difficult. You've got to have symptoms or I can't diagnose."

None, she repeats. She says she feels neither ill nor well, neither bad nor good. She feels only a general, over-all placidity. "Contentment," she says, and he looks in the index under Contentment. But there is no entry. "No ambitious physician can put up with contentment," he observes. "And certainly Klunck is ambitious." (He is reading Klunck's *Mother and Infant*.) "Twenty printings of this thing. I'm in the wrong racket. I'll stay home if you want me to. I don't much look forward to it."

"No," Elisabeth says. "You go."

He reads at random in the book. It is a kind of literature with which he has had little previous acquaintance. He is fascinated by it, the second section in particular—Infant—which concerns the baby rather than the mother. Dr. Klunck seems to have thought of everything, and surely there is a multitude of things to think of, more things to know about, more things to have on hand and more things to worry about not having than anyone would imagine. He wonders how people dared to have babies prior to the publication of Dr. Klunck's book. "Yet there's something missing," he says, and he sets the book aside.

Elisabeth agrees that there is something missing from the book. They have always agreed to that much, and they have always understood together, as Vachel, quite alone, understood a long time ago at Hiram, that science ends where belief begins. "In a way it would give me a good excuse not to go, your not feeling well. Even Lorenzo would understand that." He immediately regrets giving voice to the thought. They have covered the ground before, and they have made their decision.

"Sooner or later we'll have to face it," she says.

"It might as well be sooner. It might as well be tonight." For a moment he is silent, and then, almost angrily, he adds, "And I think I know what's wrong with the book. With Klunck."

He does not speak further. They know, together, what is wrong with the book—that the baby of the book is ounces and pounds and so much milk and so many dozen diapers and so many safety pins, that at one age it will sit and at another stand and at another walk, and in time it will be a happy healthy robust child (Klunck is fond of the word robust) and at another age it will be a happy healthy adult nicely adjusted to the whole happy universe.

But what if the baby, in the afteryears, has a generous heart and a perceptive brain and a code of belief which holds that the soul is beyond purchase? Will it learn happily that its father sold his soul for so much milk and so many diapers and so many dozen safety pins?

The boy comes with the dress suit for Vachel and a corsage of sweet peas for Elisabeth.

"If I'm not going tonight I should really send the flowers back," she says.

"Keep them," says Vachel. "The florist is a millionaire."

Republican and Democrat, in Spokane as elsewhere, now, in the prosperous time, are fingers of the same hand.

It was not always thus between the parties. In the beginning, in the body of Jefferson, the party of the people was born, and after Jefferson the hold of the people was loosened, and then Andrew Jackson came and renewed it and gave it a second youth, and after Jackson there was no one. And the people in search of a party found themselves in Lincoln, and for a time there was again a party of the people, and it was again lost and then again found, in Bryan and in Wilson, and now, tonight, in Spokane, Democrats in finery gather in the names of Jefferson and Jackson.

Lorenzo is among them. He is a Republican, and the singular irony is amusing to those Democrats who can still amuse themselves with ironies. There are still, among Spokane Democrats, those who were launched into politics by the force of Bryan's silver tongue, and they were sustained over time by the idealism of Wilson and the surge of the union movement, and they wear finery union-made, but still, in secret hearts, the symbol of their politics is the coonskin of Andrew Jackson.

And the presence of Lorenzo, to most, is in the nature of things, not an irony at all, for they are Democrats only because they live in a Democratic precinct, and they heigh-ho Lorenzo as he moves from cluster to cluster among them, and they laugh with mock surprise what-are-*you*-doing-here? But they are not really surprised. They have been to Republican Lincoln Day dinners here in the same hall, and it is a political nicety to laugh with mock surprise at the presence of friendly enemies.

Lorenzo pays his money and takes his place at table under the big portraits of Jefferson and Jackson, and he laughs at Coolidge jokes and offers anti-Democrat jokes, joke for joke, and behind hands Democrat and Republican alike swap the sort of joke that crosses party lines, and the waiters in a confidential way pour just a spot of this or that, and the spot is quite enough to dissolve all party difference.

Lorenzo, in a state of mellow heartiness, applauds the speakers and at length, called upon, he rises. His special duty, he notes, is to introduce the poet of the evening, but he must first say a word concerning his own deep feeling, and how we are all gathered here in friendship, and how it does not matter if we are this party or that because we are all Americans and proud to be, and it is all in fun, and he must say a word now about the great poet and the great poem. The music of the phrase fascinates Lorenzo, and he expands: "A great poet," says he, "with a poem about a great man, here for the people of two great parties, meeting in a great little city in a great state in the greatest country in the world." He tells of the Astor poem, and how it came to him—Lorenzo—like lightning from the blue, and how Vachel grabbed up the idea when Lorenzo brought it to him and worked up a mighty great little poem, and now you will hear it for yourself, and Lorenzo brings an arm about in a wide arc, and he rests his glance upon Vachel, and heads turn, and Vachel stands.

The irony is not lost upon Vachel. Ironies are not so funny as they used to be, but he retains a taste for them. Scattered at the tables there are some, like him, conscious of the ironies. That he should come to this! That he is the Vachel of the Altgeld poem! That he is the Vachel of the Bryan lines! And they remember when, at Democratic dinners, someone would read the Altgeld aloud, and it was like a prayer. And it comes to this, that he is at last the purchase of Lorenzo, the bard of William Waldorf Astor!

He lifts a hand, and there is humming silence, and the first words cut through the blue smoke, through the hum, sharp, clear, strong, a plea for attention, a rifle report on a midnight: *I will speak of your deeds, Andrew Jackson, when I take the free road again,* and the humming ceases and Lorenzo's smile freezes on his lips, and he turns sharply in his chair to face Vachel. *Old turkey cock on a forest rock, old faithful heart who could boast and strut; I will think of you when the woods are cut—old, old Andrew Jackson.* And the red blood rises in the head of Lorenzo, and he is first shamed and then angry, as the lines are angry: *Some are born to be bullied and chidden, some to be bridled and ridden, born to be harried or whipped or hidden; others born booted and spurred to ride. I dreamed as a boy of Andrew Jackson, booted and spurred to ride.*

The words are not lost upon Lorenzo. He has never read poetry, and therefore never understood it, and so he has always dreaded it, but these lines he understands, and he will fix Vachel oh he will fix him, and his brain throbs with the image of himself confronting Vachel, and telling him oh he will tell him. Ungrateful! Ungrateful!

And the lines are not lost upon those who remember the Altgeld and the Bryan and who have a cultivated taste for the ironies, for it was to be an Astor poem and it comes a Jackson poem, and Vachel will catch hell from Lorenzo, and there is a time of life when a large decision must be made, and such a time has come now to Vachel as it comes in some year of life to all of them: a time to decide whether or not to be purchased. *And he thinks of Van Buren and all such men, then stands up and laughs, and laughs again. For he thinks what all lions think of all jackals. . . .*

And I lift my eyes from my all-night camp fire, and I see him ride the high clouds of desire, for he was born booted and spurred to ride—booted and spurred to ride! My darlings, born booted and spurred to ride!

And this is the night of decision for Vachel and for Elisabeth, and together they make the decision, and together, somehow, they will get along without Lorenzo or the rent-free room or the tray of food three times daily, traveling the line of least resistance, doing the practical thing, singing the practical song, singing of Andrew Jackson in the year of William Waldorf Astor.

"Heigh-ho," says Lorenzo, as always, and after a decent interval he explains how the budget has been cut and how decisions have been made at high levels, and how he, Lorenzo, is not responsible for decisions, and how he is sorry what with the blessed event and all but that is the way it is, and yes, yes, as a matter of fact, yes, in Spokane, or not only Spokane, it ain't only Spokane it's whatever city you're in, there's somebody at high levels, and he is the master of the dance, and you play the tune. Or you don't play the tune. It's up to you. It's a free country.

2

She is named Susan Doniphan. No one, Vachel thinks, has a right to be so wrinkled, or so small, or so young that her age can be measured in minutes, and he never knew, until this hour immediately following her birth, that no act of creation (no, not even the creation of a poem) is comparable. "But so wrinkled," says he.

"They're almost always wrinkled," says the nurse.

"So small," he says.

"And always small."

"But beautiful. Quite beautiful. Not that I care. It comes naturally. From her mother, that is. I don't suppose I could hold her, or even touch her, on account of the germs, although it seems unfair. You'll pardon me if I seem excited. It—that is, she—she's my first, you know. I suppose it's not exciting for you. But it is for me. I suppose you go through it so much."

"About every hour," says the nurse.

She becomes unwrinkled. Even before leaving the hospital she has lost her wrinkles, and such progress, Vachel thinks, must certainly be a sign of genius. Not that he cares, of course, although (secretly) considering her mother and her father it might very well be.

Before leaving the hospital he thanks the doctor and the nurses, and, grudgingly, feeling that in some small way he is being false to principle, he admits to a certain respect for scientific wizardry.

Klunck, in the second section—Infant—asserts that it is preferable that baby sleep in his own room. (The use of the pronouns—he, him, his—is a source of constant irritation to Vachel.) But there is only one room, and Dr. Klunck apparently assumed that he was writing for two-room families.

Whenever possible Vachel and Elisabeth are willing to go along with Klunck. Klunck suggests that the sudden, sharp noise of a ringing telephone is likely to disturb the baby. He suggests that the baby and the telephone be kept in separate rooms. This is obviously impossible. "It appears," says Vachel, "that either Susan or the telephone must go," and he yanks the cords from the wall, an act which the telephone company later describes as a serious breach of faith.

She grows. He can see, almost from day to day, how she grows, how, in a miraculous instant of transition, the eyes that do not focus suddenly focus and follow his finger, and how, on another magic day, she smiles the smile that Vachel claims has always been a smile, but which Klunck says is nothing more emotive than gas, but which is unmistakably a smile, quite unlike any smile he has ever seen. Even the knowledge that she will smile at anyone—at the grocer's boy, the mailman—does not in the least diminish the supreme pleasure he derives from her smile. There is, he claims, a special smile for him, different from all the others, and he tells her so, and she smiles again. Then, soon, she laughs outright at almost any reasonable provocation—at the snap of his fingers, at a gurgling sound in his throat, at the clap of hands, the clucking of the tongue, the whistling of an absolutely tuneless tune, the humming of a song.

The objects of her world become meaningful: in the beginning there are only hunger and food, weariness and sleep, indistinct faces above her crib, animal realities, felt, not understood; and soon there is the first experiential act, the first conquest of the brain: a cry will bring to the cribside one or the other indistinct face, faces now becoming, day by day, distinct, faces remotely but definitely associated in her awakening brain with enveloping arms, and it is for these arms she learns to cry, loudly, plaintively.

Her cry is answered. He rises in the night and goes feeling his way across the dark room, locating at last the undersized bulb which he has painted green, like a night light, and he twists it in its socket, and he and she are green, and she cries a cry unlike any he has heard from her before. With one hand he strokes her cheek, and her cry is reduced to an unhappy whimper, and with the other hand, awkwardly, he turns pages in Dr. Klunck's book, hopeful that somewhere in the book there will be a most explicit explanation of the particular cry she cries at this most unusual hour. There seems to be none. Perhaps two hands are better than one, and with both hands now he resumes his search among the pages of the book, and Susan redoubles the volume of her cry, and he drops the book to the floor and lifts her from the crib, and the crying not only ceases but becomes, instantly, a laugh, deep, rejoicing, victorious laughter.

Of this laughter the book does not speak. His arms envelop her, and their cheeks touch, and the two heads are great shadows on the far wall, and she becomes, for him, for the first time, the human figure complete, the single link between himself and the endless future. She is himself plunged into eternity.

It says nothing of that in the book. It says nothing of love. The book says that he—she, Susan—must have milk, water, warmth, food, and yet she cries in the night for none of these, but for love, and the book is wrong, and he is right and has always been right.

She is asleep. First smoothing the crumpled sheet he then returns her to her crib, and he covers her, and suddenly, inexplicably, he weeps above her bed, weeping as only strong men weep, not for her or for himself or for any single person, but for her and for the endless future and the eternal family of men, not weeping upon the occasion of tragedy but at the bedside of all tragedy, looking down upon her and upon all that she has been and will be over the centuries, knowing that between birth and death, between crib and coffin, between the unwrinkling of infancy and the wrinkling of age man loses the power to love and to cry for love, learning in a few short years to be murderer, thief, pillager, sacker of cities, learning to deny love and to deny all that has been good, noble and truly brave in man. Or learning, if not cruelty, a criminal indifference to cruelty, seeking always milk, warmth, water and food, uninspired by loves and loyalties that are warmer than all warmth and whiter than all milk.

What happens to him? Who is his teacher, and why is the evil lesson so easily learned?

He should not weep. It would frighten her if she woke and looked up and saw green tears upon the cheek of him who comes to her with love when she cries in the night. He should not unsettle her. He twists the green bulb, and it is dark again. He should not unsettle her because, in all life, if she is the child of his spirit as well as the child of his body, there will be little enough of love, little enough sweet peaceful sleep.

3

The thing in The Saturday Evening Post comes out in November. Every week since summer he has gone to the newsstand down the street and flipped the pages of the Post to see if his piece were in it, and it never was until now, and he holds a nickel between two fingers, and the vendor takes it. Don't tell me, the vendor thinks, pocketing the nickel.

Vachel worked hard at it, and the check that came was the biggest and fattest he had ever seen, and he thought they would live forever on the check, although now the money is gone God knows where. Sometimes he thinks they ought to keep books and see where the money goes.

"We're in the Post," says he, and Elisabeth comes and looks over his shoulder, and after supper, just for fun, she reads the article aloud, and he follows along, reading from the carbon copy. "They ran it word for word," he says when they have read it through, and he thinks that if he could write two or three things a year for the Post . . .

It had been a chore. They got themselves into a sly mood, Elisabeth and he, planning it, making an outline, and then, when they restudied the outline, it seemed too bold, and they shoved the sharper attitudes somewhere down in the middle, and they began with pleasant excursions into Springfield history. He had wanted to jump right in with both feet and lash the newspapers and the boards of education for the way they handle poets and poetry, and then they decided to soft-pedal it and hide it somewhere down below because after all the important thing at the time was to sell it and never mind the propaganda.

Then, after it was outlined, he went to work at the writing, and it was hard work because it was difficult to be sly and subtle after all the years of plain talk. He had never pulled punches before, and now he was pulling them, as an old fighter, fighting for cash, not glory, pulls them, and when the writing was done he went over the thing line by line and word by word, and with the soft lead pencil he softened word by word and phrase by phrase, that it would sell and the big fat check would come, and they would pay the stork and all that the stork would make necessary.

Elisabeth proofed the pages, transposing *i* and *e* where necessary, lower-casing the word *poetry* as it is lower-cased in the American language, and Vachel sat with elbow on table and chin in hand, trying to think up a title, and it was her suggestion that they finally agreed upon, and he typed in capital letters, WHAT IT MEANS TO BE A POET IN AMERICA. Then they rounded up stamps and a suitable envelope and sent the thing off to Philadelphia, and after it was mailed he thought of things he might have hit a little harder without risking a rejection from the Post.

He had written: "All poets do two men's work and cheerfully expect to. Most of the wives do their own washing and the poet cheerfully hangs it out to dry." And the sentences dissatisfied him, and he had half a mind to wire the Post and have the lines killed, or at least have the word *cheerfully* knocked out where it twice appeared because as a matter of fact the doing of two men's work is not something done cheerfully, and it seemed at the time, and it still seems, a gross injustice that his wife who is reader and writer and who has things to say should not somehow be freed from the time-consuming labor of keeping house, and as a matter of fact he has never hung the wash cheerfully it has always been a bore and a nuisance and it has always taken time from his work and why should he do two jobs when the real-estate man and the banker and the newspaper editor have but one to do, and why should his literate wife be partner to mop and broom when the illiterate wives or at best the involuntarily literate wives of the Spokane Babbittry never lift a hand about the house.

He had written: "I must admit that I have in certain very ener-

getic years made money speaking from platforms. I now hate platforms of all kinds with all my heart and soul, and will so continue
till I have years of rest. The railroads and the hotels have taken my
money and they are welcome. I do not owe anybody much and am
not likely to do so." And it seemed wrong, the whole paragraph
seemed wrong and inexact, and he thought he would wire and have
it killed. But he never did.

The lady at the desk is the lady from the time before. He remembers her because, last time, she was so pleased and so amazed that
he paid in advance, endorsing to the hospital the check from the
Post, and so delighted to meet someone who actually wrote for the
Post that her hands trembled a little as she counted out his change.

This time he has no check. But his credit, she assures him, is good.

"I suppose," he says, "that practically the noblest thing a person
can do in life is have good credit."

She is not certain that it is the noblest, she says, but surely it is
mighty fine, and, with all the efficiency of a master of institutional
procedure, she completes the necessary papers and rings for the
nurse who will attend Elisabeth, and Vachel and Elisabeth embrace,
and then she is gone, and he roams down the corridor, past little
rooms where the sick lie, down the long stairway to the bright place
where expectant fathers, as useless as mourners at a wake, keep
their unique vigil.

There are, besides Vachel, two men, and as he enters they turn
their heads as one, then return to their own pursuits, one man to
his solitaire, the other to his magazine, and Vachel settles for his
wait in a deep chair by a far window, and he sits and waits and
watches, and a first doctor comes, and then a second, and after a
time a third, the third bringing news for Vachel of the mother and
the new-arrived boy, and then departing, and Vachel remains alone
and thoughtful in the now empty room.

Then he lifts himself and moves from his chair to the table upon
which the Father's Book lies open. He takes his pen from his pocket,
uncaps it. He does not sit. He stands bending over the table, and
behind him the door opens, and the new arrival takes up the new
watch, even as the new boys and the new girls coming this moment
head-foremost into the mysterious universe will keep the new
watch, the unique vigil. Then, quickly, because all this is too much
to say, he writes only the name of the infant—Nicholas Cave Lind-

say—and the name of the mother and of the father, and the date, and below, as a parenthetical afterthought, *Guest of Spokane, citizen of Springfield, Illinois.*

4

Susan, finding in a big gray book a drawing that fascinates her, asks Elisabeth what is this picture, and Elisabeth explains that it is a spider, and you will see spiders come summer.

And the book? The book is daddy's. See his name, these golden letters on the cover. Yes, all the books are his—and mine and yours and the baby's—but this book is his in a special way that you will understand sometime; in a way it is not only his book—it is *he.*

He? I have told you. He is far away on a train.

The words? You are too young to understand, but I will read the words all the same, and she reads the words below the picture that Susan likes so well: "The thing that eats the rotting stars on the black sea-beach of shame is a giant spider's deathless soul, and Mammon is its name."

CHAPTER FOUR

1

AGAIN.

And he thought it would not come to this again. He thought that he was through with it as the old, young fighter, through with it, unlaces his gloves and removes them and saves them, souvenirs. After Gulfport he thought he was through with it, but he is not, and he thought he had a home at last, but he has not, and he thought that in Elisabeth he had again lover and mother, and, for the first time, companion and colleague, and in the children he had again himself, but he does not, for they are not his and he is not theirs: there are miles and miles between, and Denver is one sun-hour removed from Spokane. In Denver he rises and breakfasts, and an hour afterward, in Spokane, they are rising and breakfasting, the three of them, and he looks at the clock upon the lobby wall, and he thinks of them.

Hotels.

There is something evil in hotels. He does not know what. Just something evil, and the prices are high because everything is high, and everyone is gay and laughing in hotels and the jolly men are free and glad to be away, and the bellboy comes to them with the forbidden bottle, and the jolly men are gay, and they feel young and free, and doors open and close in the night, and the trip will soon be over for them and they will sober and go home and resume their accustomed places, and someday they will go no more with sample case in hand; someday they will settle themselves in the home office. They never sinned. They owe no atonement.

And Vachel sinned, and now he is paying, and the sin was sinned long ago, and Papa warned him to be a proper boy, and he was not he studied art when he should have studied medicine wrote poetry when he should have been writing leases and contracts and now he is paying and the hotels are crowded with jolly men new-arrived at the jolly secure time of life, and at fifty they have rings on their fingers and neckties from Scotland and money in the bank and a

home and a car and a fifty-fifty chance of clearing liens and mort-
gages, and Vachel is just beginning because, long ago, he would not
adjust as the jolly men adjusted, and he thought it was a free country, and he served his country, and his sin was that he served it
according to his own lights, in his own way. But he served Christ
when he should have served Mammon, and he served Dante and
Milton and Shakespeare, and now he must pay because he served
the wrong gods. He must pay.

Again the figure eight, Spokane to Denver to Miami to New York,
and he starts strong because there was a long, restful, happy, creative, productive time between the last time and now, and on the
first leg of the journey he sings as he sang in the times gone by, and
the remembering people remember that he sounds as he sounded
before, and the new poems are better than the old poems. The new
Jackson poem is something to remember, and the new Babbitt poem
is a poem to remember, and the people file from the halls mulling a
tune and asking themselves what it is that beats in the feet over and
over again, and then they know suddenly that it is not a tune at
all, that it is words, and the words are somehow strung together so
that they are music. *Babbitt, your tribe is passing away. This is the
end of your infamous day. The Virginians are coming again.* And
somebody asks from the floor, what does he mean, Virginians, and
he says that if they would take the trouble to read what he writes
they would know what he means, and there is an uncomfortable
silence, and he goes on to explain what he means, Virginians, that it
has nothing to do with whether you come from Virginia or not; it
means Jefferson and Randolph and Patrick Henry, Washington and
Lee, Virginia when she was words and deeds, and somebody says
but Lee hanged John Brown and Virginia was slave country, and
Vachel says it does not matter, it matters only that in good causes
and bad tell them yes they would tell you no, tell them the sky was
blue they would fight you for the greenness of the sky, just to be
different, just to be themselves and live by their own rules and
assert their right to be individuals. "Martin Arrowsmith gave himself to science rather than be a slick and successful doctor. He was
a Virginian. Read that book. It'll do you good. I mean people with
the grand gesture of soul and body," and in part it sounds confused.
It sounds like history according to someone who was never really
a historian, and yet it sounds right and true, and he chants tight-

lipped *With your neat little safety-vault boxes, with your faces like geese and foxes, you short-legged, short-armed, short-minded men, your short-sighted days are over, your habits of strutting through clover, your movie-thugs, killing off souls and dreams, your magazines drying up healing streams, your newspapers blasting· truth and splendor, Babbitt, your story is passing away. The Virginians are coming again,* and he says it with so much conviction that it seems the saying alone will make it come true, and he looks right down across the lights and right into everybody's eyes, or so it seems, and afterward when the people leave the hall the rhythm keeps pumping and pumping in the head, and it is like the time years and years ago and The Congo and Booth did the same thing in the head, and after the first time there were no more poets until Vachel came again.

And it was so long betweentimes. It was long, and the contest for the mind and the time and the attention of the people was lost by the poets because they did not come every day on every train, and Vachel thought they would come, but they did not, and they lost by default as the good is ever losing to the evil by default, and this, too, it seems, was his sin, that he spent himself wooing the people when he should have retired to health and long life in secluded places where poets sing only to poets.

And yet, now, in Denver, on the first leg of the new journey, in the first sun-hour out of Spokane, it seems that he is truly strong, as he was strong before, and it seems again that the people might be won. There is a new generation of poets in the land. They are young enough to be his sons and daughters, and maybe they have learned from the mistakes of their fathers, and maybe they will come pouring through the breach which Vachel widened and is now again widening in Salt Lake and Denver on the first jagged side of the newest cross-continental figure eight.

He is strong again. *I see them, the next generation, gentlemen, hard-riding, long-legged men, with horse-whip, dog-whip, gauntlet and braid, mutineers, musketeers, in command unafraid,* the Virginians, and he is strong and hopeful clear down the slope of the figure, out of the shadow of the mountains and into Oklahoma, a second sun-hour out of Spokane, and still he is strong, and still he thinks he will beat the game and gather in the bread and butter, and complete the figure.

It is, to begin with, a bread-and-butter journey, and he tells himself he will go for the money, not the glory. But the habit of a lifetime is not easily unlearned, and welcome and listening silence and applause are still, as always, meat and drink, and he is again embroiled in the war against Babbitt, and the bread-and-butter journey becomes something more. (Stevens left and hid away in Paris, and when the exchange rates dropped he came home again and resumed his place at the University, and he broke with Turner over Wordsworth, and Turner broke with Knott, for Knott insists that Milton did indeed meet Galileo, yet Knott hates Wordsworth as Turner hates Stevens, and their wives and their children one another hate, and none of the three has spoken to the others these fifteen years. At meetings of the faculty they sit far apart, as cats and dogs crouch snarling in opposite corners of a garden. Vachel says he will not recite three times, as he has always recited three times at the University, once for Stevens and his clique, once for Turner and his, and once for Knott and the fierce band of anti-Wordsworthians. They must all come together and listen, if they care to listen, and they come and sit and scowl. They think all the world is divided over Wordsworth. They think the world cares whether Milton met Galileo. Vachel recites only once at the University. It is a small victory, the bringing of the dissidents together, or maybe it is no victory at all, yet maybe some among the factions will learn, or begin to learn, afterward, thinking back to this night and the last sight of Vachel, that nonsense is nonsense, and poets and poetry and all that is substantial in the world will be blasted as one in the final minutes of the final hour when the world's fate is decided by the men and the women who never heard of Milton and who never knew there was the question of Wordsworth.)

Maybe it is not victory, really, but it is battle, and Vachel is aroused again, hearing the noise of battle, and for a month he is Johnny Appleseed planting the seeds, and the seeds will be trees and he will never see the trees, as Johnny Appleseed never saw the trees, but the seeds will grow in the young. They are already growing and flowering in places he visited long ago and has since forgotten as anyone who sings for a million people in a thousand cities in forty-eight states must leave something of himself everywhere and be himself unforgotten though the face of the place is by him forgotten. It is this thought that sustains him now and gives him strength, and there will be bread and butter at the end of the trail besides, and Elisabeth and Susan and Nicholas Cave. This will be the last time. After him the young new poets of the new generation will water the seed and care for the young tree, and planting and watering and caring-for must produce, in time, a fruit-bearing tree. He sings: *Babbitt sold Judas. Babbitt sold Christ. Babbitt sold everything under the sun. So, Babbitt, your racket is passing away. Your sons will be changelings and burn down your world.*

There is something evil about the railroads. Evil. Evil. Evil. I am a man, Vachel thinks, and a machine must wait for a man. But no. The machine will not wait. The man must chase the machine. Run. Run. Run. Sometimes it seems he is always running after railroads. And the machine when it is hungry it is fed and when it is thirsty it is watered and when it is tired it is rested and a machine lives better than a man, and the evil is in the machine, he thinks. "In the machine."

"Well," says the conductor, recrossing his legs and relighting his pipe, "suppose there wasn't no machine?"

"Then there would be no evil."

"Bahh," says the conductor, spitting expertly leeward through the open window.

Railroad and hotel are evil.

Evil. Evil.

Run. Run.

Singing, reciting, he goes, a man full-aware of the possibilities, a man in love with a country as always and ever he has loved it and sought the consummation of the love, and he moves across it as a bird across the face of the sky, for an instant big, and then, out of sight, seemingly forgotten, and yet remembered in the eye of the beholder, leaving upon the mind the suggestion of possibility, as the bird, not the sky, leaves upon the mind the suggestion of grace and motion and freedom and victory.

And the people watch and listen, and the point is made, and the only thing that Vachel ever hoped to do he does: he makes the suggestion. He suggests that life is not buying and selling, but that life is beauty of spirit and health of mind, and the fields are abundant, and life is comradeship and books and poetry and peace, and possibilities beyond imagining.

And the crowds come as they have always come, and his name

is lettered on banners stretched across the avenue, and printed on billboards and cardboard posters in shop windows, and it pains him now and then that the crowds are never as large as those which can be drawn to a Legion fireworks display or a church, and the moving picture outdraws him night after night.

He comforts himself: he came for the bread and butter, and this will be the last time, and after this journey he will withdraw to write.

And on the nights of the days of doubt he does not sing as he once sang. If it is noticeable it is not mentioned, and the money is cheerfully paid, and he travels on to the next city, rounding the upper bulb of the figure. Singing, reciting, he goes.

The United States of America. The Twenties.
Addendum.
Postscript.
"A bump in the road."
Call it by any name. Call it depression, recession.

Shibe Park, Philadelphia. Connie Mack has brought home a winner after fifteen years. President Hoover, taking his box seat, is booed by the people. They chant: "We want beer. We want beer." It is early October, 1929. They are chanting the wrong chant. The house is afire and they are out at the ball game shouting for beer, and Connie Mack has come back after all these years and it seems that America is America again.

Generally it is called crash, but it is not crash. Three million men unemployed by the end of 1929 wander into the streets not all at once, but one by one, separately and individually, for it is not sudden crash, not the burst of a bubble but the slow escape of air from a mammoth balloon that in bursting floats clumsily downward and settles to the ground in a state of leisurely collapse.

It has happened before, and in the past when it happened the workless men moved westward to new lands, and they laughed and sang as they went, and the patched balloon was soon again aloft. But now there are no new lands to the West.

The land is alive with medicine men: the depression is caused by sunspots, by Republicans, by Jews, by aliens, by God, by fast living, by Prohibition. Depressions come in cycles.

The Lynds report of Muncie Indiana: "Middletown does not regard the depression as in any sense 'its own fault,' or even the fault of the economy by which it lives." Middletown thinks of the depression as "just a bad bump in the road."

We must pray, says the preacher. We must build an army, says the general. We must go naked, says the nudist. Back to the Farm. Paper Money. Annex Canada. Birth Control. Meditation. Rejuvenation. Change Through Change. "If I Tell Myself It Is Not So It Cannot Be So."

There are no answers. There is no such thing as an airproof balloon. But it occurs to precious few to let the balloon lie where it has fallen and to build a green and pleasant land of sturdier stuff.

It occurs to Vachel. It occurred to him long ago, and he had written of it and given away his writings free in the place he called home, and he had written books which nobody bought. The collapsed balloon, lying leaking on the ground, he eyes now as a forgiving soldier eyes a fallen foe, not with enmity but with compassion. The balloon is the United States of America, and the United States of America is people one by one, and it is they who are tortured now; not that they seek tortuously for the large and everlasting answers, not that they are hungry, not that they are cold, not that they are jobless, but that they are afraid. Fear changes the face as no bodily pain can disfigure it, for pain sooner or later passes away, while fear remains, and the fear of pain is worse than pain for it attacks not body but spirit, and fear fosters fear and fuels hate and causes division among men and sends them thickly and madly in haste with straining grasping hands to the gold or the green or whatever it is that represents safety. And in the scramble the larger goals are forgotten.

The depression, in retrospect, was indeed a crash. It is only a few short years, a chapter in a book, as the glory of Greece or the time of Caesar or the years of Napoleon or the reign of Victoria or this war or that war are merely chapters in a book. Except when one lives in the years: then the years are three hundred and sixty-five individual and memorable days, and a famous battle that is a paragraph of a chapter is only a paragraph of a chapter unless one lies six or eight hours or however long wounded on a battlefield. Then it is more.

The depression is a crash, in retrospect, and a crash is something heard and then silent almost before it is heard, except if one lives in the time of depression and is hungry and cold and shoeless and fearful. Then it is not a crash but a protracted condition of existence, as the blindness of Milton was, for Milton, a violent disruption of existence though to all but him it is only a stray fact of history.

The depression, to some, is personal suffering, and to others a time of the impersonal suffering of neighbors, and some, though they do not themselves suffer, suffer for the suffering, and these are few, for men do not easily suffer for one another.

For Vachel, it is the time of suffering for a loved one, and the loved one is weak and helpless because health, for her, has apparently meant not a vigor of spirit but a set of figures charted on a graph.

Vachel is shaken: he thought the United States of America was words and deeds, not graphs upon the wall; he thought she was heroes and heroines, and she has proved herself but accountants and bookkeepers; he thought she was Lady Liberty in the harbor, and she is but a lady tending store; he thought she was Plymouth Rock and the Wilderness Road, but she is Wall Street and La Salle Street; he thought she was Huckleberry Finn, but she is a pimply-faced messenger boy with an armful of ticker tape.

It is inconceivable to him that the mother of Jackson and Bryan and Wilson, of Jefferson, Lincoln and Whitman, should collapse now and lie moaning and sinking, felled by something as unsubstantial as the deflation of printed figures and the downward curve of a penciled line on charts and graphs on the walls of offices in imposing but rather tasteless buildings at the frantic intersection of Wall Street and Broad Street in the City of New York.

The change within Vachel, like the changing temper of the country itself, is not immediately apparent. It is not, from day to day, noticeable. It is only apparent to one who sees him now in Tulsa, and then, losing sight of him, sees him again in a matter of months in Baltimore, and then, weeks later, in Chicago.

It is not a sudden thing. It is not the work of months or weeks, but the work of years, accelerated now in the time of national fear and disillusion.

He is a fighter, and he climbs once too often between the ropes into the ring, and he raises his hands in defense of himself, but the blows rain upon him before the hands are high, and the blows that once he would have rolled with now fall with penetrating violence, and the answering blows with which, in better days, he might have demolished an opponent, now fall harmless or fail to reach their mark at all.

He is day by day Vachel, the same Vachel, but all in all not Vachel of the olden time when he could bawl like Billy Sunday and stare for hours across the stagelights and recite from memory every poem he ever wrote. He is a tired man. But weariness is not a thing seen by an audience at a distance of feet and yards. Weariness is a subtle ailment of mind and body, and one does not perceive it unless, taking a man by the shoulder, as now Frost, now Masters, now Untermeyer, now an old and close friend in a private moment takes Vachel by the shoulder, one swings him about and sees him at a distance of inches, and the bright eyes are red and swollen, and there is a breathiness in the voice that can be simple weariness or may also be the outward warning sign of a faltering heart, and the hair of the head is suddenly gray, and the lines of the face are not lines that will be pressed away in sleep: they are permanent lines.

And he must have coffee, and he must have cigarettes (last time he waved away the cigarettes) and he must take pictures from his pocket and show them again, forgetting that he showed them yesterday, as if he were the only father and the only husband, and the pictures must be extravagantly praised by all to whom he shows them.

And he must have people, and they must attend his lectures, and if they do not attend they are guilty of betrayal, and no matter that Percy Grainger is out of town when Vachel recites in White Plains, why was he not there does nobody care nobody has everyone deserted, and there are people indeed, crowding his room heigh-ho hello backslapping, and why are they here why do they intrude is a tired man not entitled to some decent privacy?

Singly the signs mean nothing, for a man may smoke a cigarette or drink a cup of coffee, and a man's hair at fifty need not be the color of thirty, and a breathiness of voice can be simply weariness at the end of a day's hard work, and tired lines may be simply tired lines, and a man is entitled to be proud of a pretty wife and robust children, and a man is entitled to be irritable once in a while, or discouraged or fault-finding, and singly the signs add up to nothing, and now he is here, and it will be recalled that the night he was here he was a little bit down in the mouth, and everybody is down in the mouth sometimes, and a little unreasonable, and a good night's sleep sets a man up in the other alley come morning.

But in the morning, after the troubled night's half-sleep, there is nobody there, and Vachel is alone, and he departs alone as he arrived and all that anyone remembers in the aftertime is that when he came here he was blue, and it is a long time before notes are compared and the history is woven together and dates are checked against dates and city against city, and the items taken singly are taken together, whole, and added up, jointed like the meaningless pieces of a cardboard puzzle.

Or in an aftertime the several documents are gathered together, and there are letters and then again letters, the earlier written in a bold familiar hand and decorated lavishly with daisies and doves and caricatures, and spiced with lively language, and ten or twelve pages were never enough to say what he had to say; the early letters are held against the later, and the later letters are Vachel's undecorated and unadorned, cramped and ungenerous, erratic, as if written on a moving train, and it was assumed upon receipt that they were written thus, on a train, or perhaps the letter was not so closely studied but merely filed away to be answered at a later date, and then, at the later date, removed from the files, not to be answered but to be reread a last time before the closing of the file, and in the rereading to be compared to the early letters. And then it is seen. And one wonders why it was not apparent at the time, and why nobody noticed and nobody knew, and why, seemingly, nobody cared when there were hundreds who cared.

They are evil. He knows them, and they are evil, and everybody says they are evil. The salesmen on the trains say they are evil, and the man behind the cage in the bank, he says so, and the policeman on the corner and the man at the cigarette counter, and the hotel manager and the railroad conductor.

And he knows it is not so. It is not they. But it must be someone, and everyone says so, and maybe it is they, after all, and they press his clothes in Baltimore and cash his check in Newark charge a quarter for cashing the check drive big black cars smoke big cigars swarm all over the trains, and their names are high on neon signs in New York and even in Yankee Boston and on all the mastheads of the magazines, and he fights it, and there are many things to fight, and there must be someone to blame for the weariness and somebody must have all the money because he does not. And they are on the campuses working quietly on scholarly things, and they have time and strength to write. Why not he? Who are they to have when he has not?

It is a part of the sickness and a part of the chaos that overtakes him. It infects him as it infects the whole body of the people, as in all times of distress it is a signal of distress and fear.

He forgets. He forgets lines of his poetry and times of trains and the number of his house in Spokane; he forgets, too, his own history and the people of his days: Rabbi Tedesche of Springfield and how he sat in the circle at Maydie Lee's, Rabbi Ezekiel's heretical synagogue in *The Golden Book of Springfield*, Levinson who poured his money into Poetry, Louis Untermeyer who was always kind to him, students of the Chicago days, students of the New York days, the Zionist poem and the time he called Yahweh as good a God as any.

But it is not they. It is no one. It is everyone and no one, and everything and no single thing, but he seeks evil and names it as a man in a dark chamber, having barked his legs on a concealed object, curses the object and calls it evil, forgetting the thousand thousand coincidences of history that bring him in this moment into contact with the painful object. Thus Vachel, in the darkness of failing health, in the darkness of fear, in the darkness of depression, in the darkness of weariness, strikes blindly at a near and vulnerable object. It is like the time of boyhood when all the West blamed trouble upon the East; it is like the earlier time of his life when he thought evil was the saloon. And then he grew and saw the picture whole, and he knew the issue was not East against West nor whisky against temperance nor black against white nor Jew against Gentile: it was Mammon the soul of the spider, and it was every man against Mammon, and now, in the darkness, the wide view narrows again. It is a sickness.

The Wednesday at Hiram is a good day. It is Hiram College Ohio as he remembers it, and The Haven still smells of sweet-hot chocolate (it is not called The Haven any more, but he calls it that) and the old faces are gone and old names but faintly remembered if remembered at all, and the grass is greener with a new special grass seed and a new ultrafertile fertilizer, and the dusty approaches are hard-topped now, but it is not essentially different from the Hiram he remembers.

Vachel's books are shelved in the Hiram library in a special section all their own; he is considered a great poet because he is a Hiram poet, as President Garfield was a Hiram graduate and therefore a great President. Vachel did not exactly graduate from Hiram, but everyone seems to have forgotten that, and that which three decades ago was a jolly circumstance is on this October day a celebrated page out of the past.

There is to be the formal installation of a new president today, and the students file into chapel as they filed into chapel in Vachel's time, some eager, some indifferent, and they hear the prayer and seat themselves with the rustle and buzz that he remembers, and Vachel, on the platform before them, is glad that he came although there is no fee, only railroad fare. He is introduced, and he rises, and he speaks the appropriate speech, flavored with thirty-plus-year-old reminiscences. He rolls the honorary degree between his palms, plucking absently at the red ribbon, and he concludes by reciting the new Ezekiel poem, slowly, solemnly, the slow, solemn quatrains, the late effort that he wrote for this day, remembering with what hope, what zeal, he wrote his first songs here thirty-plus-years ago, and he read them aloud on Hiram Hill (only they do not call it the Hill any more) and he concludes and sits, having, for three decades, planned what fiery thing he would

say upon such an occasion, and then, the occasion at hand, not saying it, being somehow too tired to say it.

And suppose he had said it? Suppose he had told them how it
really is, how these were for him the years of innocence, the years
of the jolly circumstance, and how there are a few each year who
come, as he came, and inspect the prescribed books but turn, at
last, to other books, and leave at length in humorous disgrace and
plunge into the world, not to heal the body of the single ailing man,
but to heal the ailing body of men, and to ask no fee, and then to
find that the world is not a pleasant and innocent place, not a jolly
circumstance. Suppose he had told them? Then what? Would they
believe him? And he thinks no, they would not believe him, for
they have read it in the books, and in the books it tells how all
questions may be answered by the simple application of correct
formulas, and science not love conquers all.

But he could at least have been kind. He could at least have
warned the ambitious, errant few to read the texts and leave the
poetry alone, and not to lay siege to whoredoms and abominations
but to go home to Cleveland Akron and Columbus and be a proper
man, the end result of the proper boy, and live a long and private
life and eat well and let the bankbook be the only book worth the
work. And suppose he had warned them? Would they have listened?
They would have dismissed him as a cranky, cynical old man, and
gone forth, the few, with faces set against the wicked city, and in
twenty years or forty years they would remember what he said,
that unless you are a proper boy you will live unrewarded and die
unforgiven as he is dying because he will not be a proper boy.

And so, first reminiscing pleasantly and speaking nothings amus-
ingly, he then resumes his seat, and afterward he stands alone on the
green grass. He tamps a cigarette on the back of his hand and lights
it, and he breathes deep and brings the smoke upward from his lungs
and pushes it outward before him, and then he walks in the shadow
of familiar buildings, and long-forgotten faces and events present
themselves to mind there was a girl where is she now a Spider Web
gang where are they now what doing and how many died in the
war and how many died in childbirth and how many are rich and
how many poor and how many have thought of him over the years
and why and when. Most of them, he supposes, went home to their
towns and villages and live there now in brick houses electrically

refrigerated gasoline stoves motorcars hot and cold running and they sit in rocking chairs of an evening and look out across the future maybe twenty years ahead because they remembered twenty years ago to insure themselves against old age by putting a little by and they worked for themselves and themselves only and at thirty they were not stranded in New Mexico with General Booth on their mind they were working their way to the top in George Babbitt's real-estate office in Columbus Akron Cleveland and they sit rocking and looking out across the new-seeded lawn at the pleasant future.

Behind him someone calls his name. He sucks deep on his cigarette and drops it to the walk and steps on it. A young man comes running. "You forgot this," the young man says, and he hands Vachel the rolled degree tied with red ribbon.

"Oh? Thank you," says Vachel.

"That was a very inspiring speech," the young man says.

"I'm glad."

"Are you—are you in a big hurry?"

"I'm just killing time till the train."

"I thought maybe you'd like to—maybe—maybe if you have time you'd like a bite." The young man is nervous and eager, and his lips tremble. "I know you're probably busy."

"No," says Vachel, "I have time," and they walk together, and the young man can think of nothing to say because Vachel is a very great poet and the young man has never been in such a presence before. And Vachel knows that he is ten thousand young nervous men on every college campus in every state of the union, and no doubt he writes stories and poetry, and no doubt he will state, if queried in the matter, that his modest hope is that in the time of his life he will make the world a better place than he found it. "So you write poetry," says Vachel.

"Why—yes," the young man says. "Some. How . . . ?"

"I just guessed. Smoke?"

"No. But thank you. Up this path. I guess maybe they've changed it since you were here. I thought I would like to ask you about poetry—how is the best way to go about writing it do you think?" and the young man walks stiffly and expectantly beside Vachel, quite certain that after the next puff of his cigarette Vachel will answer the question.

"Learn to live on a dollar a day," says Vachel.

The young man holds the door of the shop that was in Vachel's time The Haven but which is now called by another name, and they find seats at a table. The table top is carved with names, dates, hearts, initials. Vachel studies the table top, and the young man keeps his hands upon his lap so that Vachel will not see that they tremble.

"Then what?"

"How do you mean?"

"Live on a dollar a day and then what?"

"Live on a dollar a day and belong to nobody. Be responsible to yourself only. Just coffee for me," says Vachel to the waitress.

"Same," the young man says.

"Do good. Fight against evil. Do you know good from evil?"

"I used to think so," the young man says. "Then I took philosophy."

"Good is good and evil is evil. Tell that to your philosophy professor. All that is brutal is evil. Hating is evil. War is evil. Lynching is evil. The waste of life is evil. Don't waste your life."

"No," the young man says, "I am determined not to waste my life."

"Write your poems and live on a dollar a day. Sell yourself to nobody. Slavery is evil. Prostitution is evil."

"Ten cents," says the waitress.

"Sugar?" the young man says.

Vachel stirs sugar in his coffee, and he thinks he ought to tell the young man go home to Dayton or Youngstown or Mansfield where you come from because you cannot live on a dollar a day and sooner or later you will find it necessary to sell yourself your spirit your art in the market place. But he does not tell the young man that he and the ten thousand like him are alive before their time or maybe after their time, and that the land is lost. He will let the young man learn himself, and maybe enough young men, representing the new generations, will learn, and they will set their faces against the land and do as Vachel has done and as now he is too tired longer to do.

2

Outside the window the moving land is flat prairie, and the corn waves in the fields. It crackles in the sun, and Vachel hears it as surely as if he is thigh-high in the lane between the rows. The air is misty and smoky and he remembers that last night was Chicago, and it had occurred to him dimly that Springfield would be somewhere in the early morning and he would rise and press his nose to the window, and this he does. And again, as once before, unreasoning, with clumsy fingers, he dresses swiftly and gathers up his belongings and stands excitedly at the head of the car and waits hearing hissing brakes and the reverse grind of steel wheel upon steel track, and then the earth is still, and he alights.

He walks swiftly. Senselessly, he carries his bags instead of checking them, and after the second block he sets them down and straightens and stretches his fingers and blows cool air on his red palms, and then he lifts the bags again, and at Capitol Avenue he turns the corner, and his eyes are flooded with sunlight, and he sets the bags down again and turns away from the low sun and reinspects his hands and blows again on his palms, and then he sits on one of the bags and lights a cigarette. The smoke is dry in his throat. He puffs twice and flips his cigarette away. He struggles with his bags east up Capitol.

In front of the Sangamon County Trust Company he stands the bags upon the walk and tugs at the iron-handled door. It does not open, and he presses his face against the glass, employing his hands as blinders beside his eyes. Within, a watchman comes stiffly toward the door. The watchman takes a large watch from his pocket and points to it, and Vachel cannot see the face of the watch, but he understands, and he sits again on one of the bags, leaning back against the smooth-stone building, and he waits.

Before him the morning crowd moves eastward, workward, into the heart of the city. It is an interesting sound they make, heel-and-toe-heel-and-toe upon the pavement, leather heels and rubber heels and the faint, nearly inaudible sound of sole upon cement in the almost uncapturable instant between successive strikes of the heel. He sits, head bent, listening, and at length he straightens and studies the faces. The faces are puffed and fresh from sleep, and the eyes stare straight ahead or now and then glance mechanically down at watch upon wrist and mechanically the pace quickens, or mechanically, after consultation with the watch, the pace slows and coffee suggests itself as a possibility, and consulting the watch the mind subtracts nine from twelve and adds six to the three and knows there will be nine hours less the hour for lunch, and mechanically the feet shuffle stop at the red light at the corner and then move ahead on green and mechanically feet turn from the pavement enter smoke-stained buildings or mechanically mechanical feet pause before coffee shop and the eyes check the wrist again and the head shakes slightly no and the feet resume the course and whistle blows nine and all feet together now quicken and the coffee shops empty themselves upon the signal and the watchman from within unlocks the door of the bank and swings the door open and fastens it and steals a breath of air before re-entering the bank. The hands of his watch are right-angled at nine, as the hands of all clocks and watches are thus-angled, and the watchman's shift is finally over and his eyes burn, anticipating sleep.

In the bank, before the vault, men stand waiting for the automatic springing of the lock. Before the telephone switchboard the wide-bottomed girl sits waiting, knowing that in an instant lights will flash.

Vachel loses courage. He is not certain in the first place what action he is about to take, but whatever it is he will need courage. He lifts his bags, but instead of entering the bank he goes up the street to the coffee shop. He changes a dime into nickels, dropping one nickel into a pocket and the other into the coin slot of the wall telephone. He calls Susan Wilcox at the high school, wondering why he should be calling Susan at all, knowing only that when the door of the bank was flung open and his courage suddenly failed he saw a vivid Susan who was always the equal of all necessities, seeing her then, as always, as a great granite figure of courage.

She is summoned to the telephone by a little girl who, like little girls of a previous generation, like little boys, like Vachel himself, dares only to whisper in her presence, not knowing, until a later time, that when some morning brings crisis it will be to this granite figure that they will turn for courage. It happens again and again, if not every day then every week, whispering children returning to her in times of crisis.

"You may speak to Miss Wilcox," the little girl whispers.

"Susan? I'm at the bank."

"Who? Who is at what bank?"

"Vachel. I'm at the Sangamon. I wonder if you could get down here."

"Yes," she says. "I think I can. I will."

He knew she would.

It would have something to do with the house. Vachel would not be likely to have any other sort of business with the bank. She knew that sooner or later he would come home to reclaim the house which, in a confused moment, in the first hour after his mother's death, he signed away in lieu of taxes and charges which he did not understand and could not be expected to understand because, as she remembers (and well remembers), he was always so busy trying to save Springfield from merchandising itself to death that he overestimated all along the proportion of people who appreciate his efforts because, poor Vachel, he seems to forget sometimes that Springfield is not now and never was the least bit worried about its soul. So he signed the house away, firmly believing that he could regain it for the asking, and he complained to her (those were long letters) when the city made a museum of the house that it was like cutting off the leg of a perfectly well man and bottling it in alcohol, expecting her to do something, as if she could unsign what he had foolishly signed when, looking at it from the merchandising side, he is so much more valuable as a museum piece bottled in alcohol than as a flesh-and-blood entity going about trying to save a city that has very little soul and does not want it saved because having a soul is as bad for business as, say, closing shop on Saturdays or building, say, an art museum somewhere where you might otherwise have a nice smoking factory.

Confound the house! It is an old house. And a strange house. Yet it has become something more than another old house. It has assumed a certain value far surpassing the value any sensible realtor will place upon it.

Well if he wants it she will try to help him get it. It seems to be what he wants. Not that she can do a thing. Maybe he ought to see a lawyer instead of a schoolteacher because if there is anyone who can understand a banker it is probably a lawyer. She will do what she can. Not much, probably, but anything she can. Because he is one of her children, one of the few faces she can never forget and never desert, one of the few who have proved, in the world beyond the classroom, that she teaches the useful lesson.

She sees him, the knickerbockered boy come home, the lad who wrote the speech she could not sponsor, and coming toward her now he takes her hands in his and tells her that what he *really* wants is someone to carry his suitcases, and he knew she would not mind, but then, on second thought, he will carry them himself, and they go together into the bank, laughing as if at some perfect joke.

Vachel sets his bags in the middle of the floor. The young man with the fresh flower nods and smiles at him, asking if he can be of service. Vachel's eyes search the desks behind the low barrier separating the officers of the bank from the lobby. "I'm looking for a face," he says, remembering but vaguely the face which sat with him and the three ladies from Via Christi and pushed under his nose onionskin papers to sign which he thereupon signed because he was anxious to read over the shoulders of the three good ladies the letter from Olive in China and the letter from Woodrow Wilson and Mama's unfinished dissertation on the relationship of God and civics.

"Would you happen to know the name?" asks the young man with the fresh flower.

"No. But I'd remember the face."

"He might not still be here," Susan suggests.

"Then his equivalent will be here." And then he sees the face for which he has been searching, and he takes Susan by the arm, and they go together to the low swinging gate which will not open until someone in a secret place buzzes a buzzer, and Vachel turns and orders the young man to go press the buzzer, and the young man insists that it is not his duty to press it, and Vachel insists that if the buzzer is not soon pressed it will become necessary to kick the gate down with the heel of his shoe, and the fresh flower bobs on the excited breast of the indignant young man, but he walks swiftly nevertheless to the place where the buzzer is.

Beyond the barrier Vachel confronts that man whose face he remembers. "You remember me," says Vachel, and the man rises.

"I seem to remember," he says. "Good morning, Miss Wilcox."

"You remember me better than that."

"I believe I do. We hold a parcel. We absorbed . . ."

"I want it," says Vachel.

"I remember your mother." The man brings two chairs, one for Susan and one for Vachel, and then he sits at his own chair behind the desk, and Susan sits, and Vachel continues to stand, leaning forward, resting his weight on his palms on the banker's desk, and he sees that the eyes of the man are wide, and that his lips are bloodless, and that they tremble.

"The house is mine."

"I'd have to check. I don't know whose it is. Maybe it's yours."

"Whose else can it be? It was mine in the beginning and it's mine now. I was born in it. The best things I ever wrote I wrote in it. My Mama and my Papa died in it. I have the right to go back where I belong. Have I or haven't I? Susan! Have I the right?"

"Has he the right?" says the banker to Susan.

"I'll give you a month," Vachel says.

"A month is very quick. The agreement . . ."

"There was no agreement. If there was I did not agree to it."

"You signed it."

"May I speak?" says Susan.

"I don't care if I signed it. I didn't sign it. If I signed it with both hands in blood it still means nothing to me. I never signed anything giving anybody the right to steal my house."

"There's too much heat," says Susan, "and not enough light. Vachel, sit down. Even if there were an agreement, and there may be, I know that the bank would want to be reasonable. The bank has always been reasonable. Vachel, sit down."

"We've never been unreasonable. There was a man in here yesterday told me—he said . . ."

She interrupts. "I must be getting back. I'm impatient of tomfoolery. You can be sure of that. Possibly you remember."

(He remembers. It seemed like years and years, although it could have been no more than a quarter hour, and it was as if he were a stranger in a land where a strange speech was spoken, and she gave him—could he ever forget?—eight lines of poetry beginning *Oh, to be in England now that April's there,* and she bade him stand in the aisle and read the lines, and he read, pausing at the end of each short line, and she explained to him that one did not pause at the end of each line, and he began again, and again, at each line's end, he paused. Then she read it aloud and they went over it together, word by word, and she implored him to feel as the poet, to pretend that he was an Englishman in a land far from home thinking about flowers in bloom and a chaffinch in song. But he could not understand, and he could not feel. He could not imagine himself an Englishman, and he could not imagine April— it was December then—and he could not see birds or flowers in the absence of birds and flowers, and she allowed him to sit, and gratefully he sat, and she never called upon him again or demanded of him impossible feats of the mind. And afterward, like his father before him, he went into the bank, and he has since observed with some satisfaction that his house is bigger and his automobile newer and his wife and his children better dressed than most of the boys and girls, now men and women, who were able, as he was not, to pretend that things existed when they obviously did not.)

In the chair before his desk she sits again, the hated figure, leaning slightly forward toward him, her voice soft, her aged face calm, intent, and she is telling him again that things exist beyond himself and beyond this bank, and that all that is written on onionskin agreements is not binding beyond the power of men to unbind.

And then they rise, the two of them, and then they are gone, the aged woman who had tried to urge upon him April in December, the middle-aged man in whose glazed and tired and swollen eyes the banker had seen something more fearful than anything he had yet seen in that quiet marble place.

Within a month the bank relinquishes the house to Vachel. It is the first event in a series of struggles for custody, the unabating struggle that has begun between friends of the poet and foes of the poet, between those who maintain that he sees Springfield with the eye of truth and those who claim that what he sees has never existed.

By what right the house is now his nobody seems to know.

Was there not an onionskin agreement? What happened to it? Nobody seems to know. In the aftertime a friend, curious, sits a summer week turning pages in the office of the recorder of deeds and transactions. The task is singularly unrewarding, and the friend then goes, out of whetted curiosity, from banker to lawyer, from friend to friend, and he hears from men and women, whose memories are faint and fading, tales that only deepen the darkness of the dark mystery.

Nothing is explainable, either now or in the time to come. In time to come, long after Vachel and Susan Wilcox have been succeeded in Springfield by young men and young women who will be heirs to their unenvied role—even then the old house will be contended for. It will be a house of mystery, valued though valueless, and there will be a continuing struggle for custody, a continuing mystery concerning its title, a bitter, desperate and unabating contest between those who would enshrine it and those who prefer that all be forgotten, between those who will remember and those who would like to forget.

But there is really no mystery. There is only the thing unseen, bright April in dark December which the man from the bank and his friends and the friends of his friends cannot see, cannot feel, cannot know. But it works upon them and causes them to perform certain acts they would not otherwise perform, reaching downward and becoming a part of their being from a height they cannot see and cannot even imagine.

It is like conscience which one cannot see or feel but which exists because of course it exists and nobody would deny it, and yet it is nowhere, neither on paper nor in a shop window, and yet it exists and nobody would dare to deny it, and it makes a man in Springfield perform the unexplainable act which he would not otherwise perform, because even if it is not visible it exists because some people say it exists and must be honored.

Like conscience exists. Like Vachel exists and must be honored because he is like conscience, because he speaks a speech which, like certain speeches of Lincoln, we would just as soon lose, but which we cannot lose because certain other Springfield people will not allow them to be lost, and because these certain people, though we do not always like them, are a vocal part of our city, and therefore of us, and we are inconveniently obliged to honor our conscience. These people—they teach in our schools, and sometimes they get into our politics and our unions and even our businesses, sometimes even into our pulpits, and they write so many of our books and so much of our poetry, and they haunt us which is what he said once in a poem, *I'll haunt this town, though gone the maids and men, and in December when the leaves are dead and the first snow has carpeted the street my pen shall cut in winter's snowy floor cries that in channeled glory leap and shine,* which is how the house becomes his, because he haunts this town and because he shall haunt it ever, he and the rest.

Because Hamlet, still alive, threatens to become ghost, and ghost is conscience, and the house becomes his because, in part, certain superstitious folk believe that to burn or to hide or to bury or otherwise destroy an onionskin agreement is to lay the threatening ghost while the ghost is still man, alive, while he can be pacified, before he becomes ghost.

CHAPTER FIVE

1

EVERY AFTERNOON, all through the hot July, sunsuited the children sit on the green grass, and the green grass-blades grow brown day by day at the tips, and Susan sees how they grow browner and browner every day, and Vachel in the shade of the house reads in a big book that Susan has examined and found to be only words and no pictures except one in the front where the man and the lady with no clothes on are standing by a tree eating apples from the tree.

She must sit with Nicholas beside her and wait for the five minutes to warm the water in the tub, and sometimes the five minutes seem long and sometimes short, but always after a time Papa lifts his eyes from the book and observes that the five minutes have at last come, and they run to the tub and lift themselves over and into the sun-warmed water. They splash themselves and each other and sometimes hold their noses and dip their heads beneath the water. In commotion, the water laps the tubside and spills out upon the grass. About the tub the green grass is green, not brown at the tips of the blades, and he who sits there shaded by the house reading in the book with only one picture would know why the grass is somewhere green and everywhere brown, because he knows everything.

"Is grass green?" says Susan.

"Yes," he replies.

"Brown," she says.

"Green," says he, turning pages and finding the passage he seeks, and reading to Susan from the seventh book of *Paradise Lost:* "Brought forth the tender grass—that is, God brought it forth— brought forth the tender grass whose verdure clad her universal face with pleasant green," and she does not understand, but she supposes if he says so it must be so, for he knows all things (as many things as God, she supposes), and yet the grass looks brown to her, and she studies it, and the more she studies it the more certain she is that it is brown. "It is brown," she says.

"Very well," says Vachel, returning to his place in the book, and reading, and the garden of the book is his own garden, for he has always read all books as if they were written in the present, about him, about his city, about persons and places he knows, and the garden of Milton's lost paradise is situated on Fifth Street in Springfield Illinois, and man and woman prior to their corruption are before him now in a big tin tub, and the garden is green.

"It is *brown,*" insists Susan.

"Green." He smiles at her. "Things are not what they are. They are only what they *can* be."

Yet Susan does not understand, for things explained are never understood as well as things learned, and only now is she learning that she will know all things in time, for once Papa himself was a boy in this house, and he was no bigger than she, and he no more knew how long five minutes were than she, or why the grass grows somewhere green and somewhere brown, or how to read in books that are all writing and only one picture.

But she must ask things because she must know. "Is today Saturday?" she asks, and he smiles again at her and says no, not today, today is not Saturday, tomorrow is Saturday, and the day after tomorrow is Sunday, and Sunday we will go for a ride with Duncan and Nell in their car. "That's a good idea," she says.

For a moment he watches the children in the tub, and then his eyes return to his book, and in so doing they see for the first time the green-brown grass, how the grass is dead a full inch from the top of the blade. He leans from his chair and plucks a blade. It is green and moist near the root, and green but less moist as he runs his finger upward toward the brown tip, and it is brown and dead and it crumbles between his fingers at the extremity of the blade. He shrugs and tosses away the blade of grass and resumes his place in the shade. He begins to read again, and then, on second thought, he calls to Elisabeth will she call Willis Spaulding at City Hall, or if Willis is not there will she tell somebody in the Water Department that the grass is dying may he water his lawn. He would call himself, he tells her, but he must stay and keep an eye on the children, and Elisabeth answers through the open window, yes, she will call.

And then it is Saturday as, yesterday, he said it would be, and the day is hot like every other day, and even the children now are conscious of the heat, and weary of it, and comfortable only during the time the tub is full and they are in it. It is Saturday, indeed, and Susan knows because they come, as every Saturday they come, the two men Duncan and Willis, and they will have somewhere on their persons a gift, and Susan has been told that little girls if they are nice little girls greet guests how-do-you-do and offer them a chair and ask politely after their health, and she wants to be a nice little girl, but she forgets, and she runs barefooted and sunsuited to Willis and Duncan, across the dry grass and onto the burning sidewalk, and she flies at them breathless, asking what did they bring today. Once they brought a nozzle for the garden hose, and it was gold and shiny, and once they came and they talked with Vachel and she did not understand the nature of their talk, as she does not understand the mysterious talk of the old, but she remembers that it was the day after the night when the lights were broken, when Vachel turned on the lights and they were broken and he read for a time by candlelight, and then they all went to bed early, and then in the day Willis and Duncan came and Vachel told them about the lights and Duncan and Willis looked one to the other and scowled and said they would fix the lights, and Vachel said no, he would not let them do it, he would read by daylight and candlelight, but they said they would fix the lights all the same, and afterward they went away and fixed them.

Up the street they come, Susan between them, and Vachel closes his book and sets it upon his chair and moves the chair three feet into the shade, beside two waiting chairs, and he walks slowly across the garden and waits, and they come, two men of middle age, as he is of middle age, Duncan with a necktie draped untied about his neck, for it is hot, and Duncan will sit in one of the three shaded chairs and pick silently at the loose threads of the union-made necktie as he has picked at loose threads in ties, and loose leaves of union-made cigars, and loose bindings of union-made books these thirty years, and long ago in Springfield it ceased to be a joke that his ties and cigars and books are ill-made because it is a part of Duncan's Socialist religion, and he answers, when goaded, it is more important that a worker go home by daylight than that he make a perfect tie, a perfect cigar, a perfect book. Vachel had forgotten, in the long absence, the habits formed by the single-minded dedication of Duncan McDonald, and now, returning, he is reminded again of that dedication by the sight of the necktie removed from about the neck and draped, because of the heat, across the shoulders.

Beside Duncan, with Susan between, Willis talks to his friend over the head of the child. He is shorter than Duncan, and seemingly he is sprier, or perhaps, Vachel thinks, it is because his legs are shorter that he appears to move more quickly than Duncan. His necktie is tied close to the skin of his neck, as for thirty years he has tied the tie thus and thereby proved that he, the single-minded Willis Spaulding, is an honest reliable trustworthy upstanding sound and proper man whom the believing Mr. Babbitt may safely vote for, and on November days in many years Mr. Babbitt has voted one vote for Willis Spaulding, Democrat, not knowing that, in point of fact, Willis is not a safe man at all: for he has wrought change in his time, as Duncan has wrought change, and as Vachel has wrought change, and they meet now at the edge of the garden, the three.

They do not shake hands. Vachel has only twice in his life shaken their hands, only the first time, and none can remember the first time except that it was sometime long ago, maybe nineteen-and-ten, when in Maydie Lee's cottage they met and argued many things though in most things they were agreed, each with each, and then again the second time, the recent time, when Vachel returned from the long journey and reunited himself with them and with Springfield, as in all romantic stories the lover returns to the loved one. Then, returning, it was as if he had never gone, for in the mind he had never traveled beyond the limits of the city, as they, in body, had never for any extended time departed the city. Returning, he found them waiting, and they came to him a dedicated Socialist and an honest servant of the people, offering to be of use if possible, for their only pride now, as ever, is in their usefulness. It is the passion of their lives, a part of them, and all their habits and all their ways are part and parcel of their method. Thus Duncan's tie is union-made and Willis' tie tied tight because the voter voting considers the necktie. And thus, when Vachel returns they are waiting on his doorstep because Vachel, too, is a man whose passion is usefulness, and men and women who wish to be useful cling to one another and assist and love and inform one another. They are few, and they are often lonely, and it is as if he had never gone away and traveled the figure eights and lived a stranger and a paying guest in faraway cities. Always he has been here in the old house on Fifth Street, and he has been here because they have been here, and they have supported and encouraged each other and eased each other's lonesomeness. All the years and all the distance have not separated them, for each has known that the others were somewhere in their singular ways proving their usefulness, as each knows now that he is not alone, that in all cities men and women, socialists, democrats, radicals, poets, meet of a humid Saturday afternoon to plot change, to be úseful.

Stooping, Willis feels of the grass, of its dryness, and then, as if the second act were complementary to the first, he straightens and takes from a pocket a large sheet of paper upon which, for the thousandth time in his life, he has sketched roughly The Plan. And he believes The Plan will someday be a Lake, and Vachel in all the years has seen The Plan numberless times, and in truth, at this moment of his life, he has quite dismissed The Plan. He is almost tired of hearing of the Lake. It will never be a Lake it will always be a Plan. Vachel would like to see his garden green again, and it will not be green again, and it will not be green this year or next year or any year if there must first be a Lake. The Lake is a delusion. It is a thing in Willis' mind, and it will never be more than a thing in Willis' mind, as minimum-wage laws and forty-two-hour work weeks and social security are but things in Duncan's mind, and Vachel is weary of Plans however noble. "I got some revised facts and figures here," says Willis, "and I been thinking that maybe what we need is something more than facts and figures. I'm getting up a little folder," and he is always getting up little folders, little throwaways, and people are always throwing them away indeed, and he will ask Vachel to write a few words of description not facts and figures. "Description. But poetic," Willis is saying, and Vachel nods and takes the offered paper and promises to write something poetic to go with the facts and figures. "Maybe it'll be the difference when it comes to the vote," says Willis.

"Yes. The vote. Will it ever come to a vote?" Vachel slips the paper between the pages of his book. He sits on the chair in the shade, placing the paper-bulging book upon his lap, and Willis and Duncan sit, and Susan asks are five minutes yet, and Vachel says yes he thinks five minutes have passed, and Susan and Nicholas enter the water, and Duncan reaches and takes the book from

Vachel's lap. It is an old book and he looks for the union label, and not finding it he contents himself with the thought that old books such as this were published before the printers were organized. *"Paradise Lost,"* he says. "Did you ever read Milton on the freedom of the press?"

"I think of Milton more as poet," says Vachel, thinking of Milton as poet, seeing Milton a middle-aged man, blind in the old house, blind and writing *Paradise Lost.*

"It's by no means a dead issue," says Willis.

"A free press," says Duncan.

"The lake," says Willis, thinking of the lake and the autumn rains captured and the winter snows captured and the spring rains captured and held in the lake and released in the dry, hot, burning summer, and the lake owned by the public (the masses of the people, Duncan would say), by the public, Willis thinks, for he has tried always to think in terms of a vocabulary that nobody can tag with the Socialist label because the word makes a difference as the necktie makes a difference, and call it by any name it remains a Plan for a Lake that the people or the public or the masses will own and operate and regulate, and the captured waters will benefit the many, not belong, as at present, to the few (the corporate interests, Duncan would say), to the few, Willis thinks. "The lake," says Willis, "I was thinking of the lake."

"About how long?" Vachel asks.

"Hundred and fifty, two hundred words."

"Nickel a word?" Vachel laughs.

"Afraid not," says Willis. He, too, laughs.

"Any deadline?"

"Get it to me when you can."

"Things seem high," says Vachel.

"I know. I'm sorry," Willis says.

"I didn't mean it that way. I mean in general. The nozzle doesn't come with the hose any more."

"It never did," says Duncan. "Prices are always high. They're rigged that way."

"Maybe so."

But it is too hot for talk. Tilted in shaded chairs they lean against the house, not talking, sitting, motionless, catching upon the cheek the breeze that is almost no breeze at all, doubting the reality of the breeze, yet seeing in the browned and dying grass a motion confirming the motion of the air.

2

The day of home-coming had been cold. The train windows had been frosted all the way down from Chicago and he had picked at the window with a thumbnail and made two small spaces through which Susan and Nicholas could see Illinois, for a train ride is no ride at all unless one can see through the windows, and Susan and Nicholas had sat squinting through the two small spaces until the spaces froze over again, and then Vachel cleared them anew with his thumbnail. And then they all slept, all four of them, and then it was Springfield and it was snowing, and Vachel went alone through the cold and the snow to the bank for the key, and the man was gruff and discourteous at the bank, but Vachel did not care. Indeed, he scarcely noticed. He returned in a cab and picked them up at the depot, and they took only the bags with the few things they would need for the night, the first night, and the key turned in the lock and the house was cold and they did not take their coats off for a long time because it was a full hour before the heat came up and spread itself into all corners.

And Vachel was in a terrible hurry to "really be home" as he called it, as if somehow he was not really home yet and would not be home until all the evidence of home-coming was removed, until the heat was in all corners and the hot water came up through the pipes without rattling hot against cold and the snow was removed from the walk and all the bags were unpacked and closeted and the telephone was connected and the mailman informed and the iceman and the milkman negotiated with. And Elisabeth fell in love with the big room that was Mama's and Papa's as Vachel knew she would, and the first supper was helter-skelter odds and ends of a few canned things in the cupboard and milk that Vachel dashed out for because it was too late for deliveries and coffee sandy with grounds because the coffeemaker was packed and down at the depot, and after the children were in bed Elisabeth and he sat for a long time in the kitchen smoking cigarettes and straining coffee back and forth through a strainer a hundred times, and drinking it and laughing.

And then he had gone upstairs into the little room that had been his room all the years, and it was as if he had not been gone a day: the file cabinets slid open in exactly the way he remembered, the top drawer clicking an old familiar click-click like a small boy playing a hickory stick on a picket fence, and shadows on the ceilings and on the walls patterned according to old laws involving the glow of the bulb in the table lamp and the intervention of the ribs of the shade and the shadow of Vachel's head upon the ceiling and the long, irregular watermark on the ceiling and the old chair with one foreshortened leg. And in the cabinet drawers the notes lay thick and faded and fast fading, in ink, in lead, lying, waiting, placed there ten twenty thirty years ago sometime, as now, to be re-approached and reconsidered, perhaps to be great poems as John Milton the public man came back to the long-waiting notes after the long time away from his table, full-prepared in his later time to write the greater greatest poems because in the later time, in the middle years, back in the old house, he was a greater self. Yet many of the notes meant nothing now, and these he crumpled into balls and pitched into the basket in a long arc, and sometimes they dropped short of the basket or bounced too long and spread themselves in a half-moon upon the floor as always in past times he had fashioned the paper arc and known dimly by the sound that the balls fell square or wide or long or short, and the sound was the same, and tomorrow, as always on tomorrow, he will clear the floor before proceeding to the business of the day.

And the faraway noises are the same: rubber tires upon pavement, hooves upon pavement, leather heels upon pavement, and silence now in winter, and there will be, in warmer months, voices beneath the open window and moths beating on the screen and the chuffing of trains in the railroad yard and laughter and bass voices in the Governor's mansion.

And he rose and went to the window and scratched upon the frosted pane, and he peered through the cleared square and saw the pin point of light that had always glittered in the dome of the capitol building, and it glittered still as he knew, of course, it would, because the light and the noises and the shadows of the little room and all the details of its furnishings were the permanence he came to rediscover after the years as a public man.

And the sound of Elisabeth's steps on the stairway was the sound of Mama's steps, and the distance from the top of the landing to the doorway of the little room is just so many steps, never more and never less, and she stood there on the night of home-coming and he did not turn to her but he knew she was there as he seldom turned to Mama yet always knew she was there looking fondly with love before turning and twisting the knob of her own bedroom door and entering and closing the door behind her, as Elisabeth stood looking and loving and then turned and twisted the same knob of the same bedroom door, and entered, and he waited for the sound of the closing door, but it did not close. *Of course. Of course.*

Under *G* in the file cabinet there was a two-word note, *Mentor Graham,* and he had once planned a Mentor Graham poem in honor of the man who was tutor to Lincoln. He rolled the note into the carriage of his typewriter and yawned and depressed the light switch and paused an instant and knew that in a second instant the dark room would fill with the lesser light from without, and it did, as it always did and as it always would, and happily on the midnight of home-coming he made his way through the dark familiar passage to the room where Mama and Papa had slept, where he was born, where he and Elisabeth now would sleep, now and in all the years.

And he thought it would happen, as it had always happened, that for a day or a week or two weeks or a month or a longer or shorter time he would sit before naked white paper and with pencil or pen whichever came handy make six or a dozen or six dozen or a dozen dozen false starts upon new poems, and in time the lines would be stanzas and in time the stanzas would be poems, as it had always happened and thus would always happen.

As in the writing of every poem there were first the hours and days of sitting still somewhere before the first false starts that would become truer starts that would become in the end the true poems that people sang and read and would sing and read still after Vachel at one hundred and five is buried in the earth because they were love poems as he was a lover and unashamed to love the public (as Willis would say) or the masses (as Duncan would say).

As here in this very room he wrote the Altgeld poem, so he would write again new poems, and he thought it would happen as it had always happened here in this room: he would write falsely and hurl the crumpled false paper in a more or less accurate arc toward the basket, and he would explain to Papa that it will not be long now before the false starts are done with, and after that, Papa, I will go off to a job, or maybe just go off upon the road and let the farmers' wives feed me or go out to Uncle Olan and let Uncle Olan feed me, or go to a bigtown somewhere and live on fignewtons and sodawater and own one pair of trousers that the girl down the hall will press, or George Richards and I will paint the walls of the Pig and the Goose and the Pig and the Goose will feed us and in time I shall write great poems.

And then he was brought back to the present, and in the winter of the present he was fifty or close upon fifty and he had not the time to be making the basketful of false starts, and the special prize of five hundred dollars that Poetry gave him was melting in coal and coffee and cigarettes and grocery bills and taxes on the house and the milkman addressed a note to him this morning and the iceman bringing ice in the icy dead of winter left a printed note upon the icebox signed Your Friendly Iceman reading *Your ice company, like you, has pressing obligations to meet. Will you not help it to do so by paying charges promptly? Many housewives find that a simple and convenient way to* and he did not read the rest because he fully intended to pay the iceman and everyman in the course of time. Now, however, he was budgeting somewhat because he seemed to be getting a slow start on the writing. But he knew he would get started again the way he had sat in the sun at Gulf Park and taken things easy and then started in as good as new.

But the sitting in the little room did not seem to help, and he knew that the trouble was he was sitting too much and not getting out in the air enough, and it seemed to him the room was too small, that somehow he had outgrown the room, and he wrapped himself often now in a sweater and scarf and coat and hat and went prowling as always he had in the past gone prowling when things were a little bit bottled up inside him.

Winter in final fury sent a last cold snow, and March froze the snow solid underfoot, and fields and roofs were white, and the sidewalks and streets were packed tight with heel-marked, tire-marked snow, and the snow blackened underfoot and seemed to be one with the cement beneath. The sun, in an hour of warmth each day, softened the snow a trifle and then departed and left the snow hanging frozen from the trees and the roofs and the steeples of churches and the dome of the Statehouse, and it seemed that winter would never end and spring never come, and Vachel wished spring would come because in the spring, he knew, he would find himself again.

He tried for a time to shape the Mentor Graham poem, ruffling through his notes and leaning back in his chair, closing his eyes and conjuring up the image of the man of books who in a place called Salem Illinois, not far from Springfield, struck up a friendship with a kid named Lincoln and taught young Lincoln a little grammar and a little surveying and a little philosophy and a little history and a little of anything that might turn out to be useful in life. And then the young man Lincoln went away and set up to practice the law in Springfield. Graham was a strange man, never quite right in his head, nor ever quite proper in manner or dress, and when he was an old man sitting pondering life and old age on the curbstone on the square in Petersburg (for he had wandered down to Petersburg) he was fair game for the young men; they taunted him, calling him Old Philosopher, and when this failed to rouse him they stoned him, for they had nothing better to do and they never really meant any harm. They never hurt him. The stoning saddened him, but it never hurt him, and he died as old men die, of a disease called Neglect, and he was buried somewhere, and he had been useful in his way and taught a young man whose name he soon forgot a smattering of things that no doubt turned out to be useful in life.

And Vachel wanted to write a Mentor Graham poem, and in the end he wrote it more or less, and it was the last poem he wrote, even as the lingering snow was the last snow he ever saw, and spring the last spring.

Spring came unannounced and unpredicted. The mercury, said the *Journal,* zoomed, breaking records for the date, for the *Journal* was still, as always, interested in records of this or that, the more trivial the better.

The unfrozen snows slid from the roofs. The snows in the bare trees, washed from the branches, coursed in trickling streams down the gray trunks, and all the earth was mud and waste, and the walks and the streets were under an inch of water, and the water poured over shoetops, delighting or disgusting, depending on whether one was a child or an adult, and the gutters ran heavy with water and carried in their streams snow-broken twigs and refuse of all sorts, and paper boats that children made and set to sail upon gutters that for a day were oceans that land-bound children had read about but never seen.

Roofs leaked and sewers overflowed and trains were late and the cellars of homes were submerged, and rats in the cellars drifted dead and bloated upon the waters, and mine pits were flooded and a day of pay was lost, and somehow it was almost like a holiday, like a parade, and people stood at the windows of offices to gaze upon the streets and to remark how the streets looked like canals that they had seen in picture books. Wells and cesspools crumbled and were ruined. Small trees were uprooted by the rushing waters. Roofs collapsed. Horses were mired, and there were pictures in the paper of horses in the mud and a cat trapped atop a chicken house.

On the second day of spring the sun shone strong again, but the streets and the walks were dry and the rats were shoveled dead from the cellars and the cat came down from the roof of the chicken house and the impromptu holiday was over.

The sun drank the water, and that which it did not drink settled into the earth, and beneath the earth the plentiful waters gathered and propelled themselves in self-widening, ever-widening rivers. The waters joined, river with river, and they spilled themselves into the Illinois, into the Spoon, thence into the Mississippi, thence to be swallowed by the sea and lost in the sea.

Yet even the spring did not restore him, and he sat with his hands upon his knees, confronting his typewriter, knowing that soon the barrier would somehow be removed. Had not the hard, fast snow on a single day melted and vanished?

And he thought that perhaps if he read poetry his faculties would sharpen, for steel is honed upon steel and diamonds are cut with diamonds, and he went to the books that no one had disturbed in his absence, and he knelt at the poetry shelf. He focused his eyes upon the close, small print on the backs of old volumes. The titles were old friends, and they would restore him, and he wondered who now would be best company, whether Browning or Swinburne, Whitman or Poe, the Elizabethans or the Americans, and at length he chose Milton and took him from the shelf—the collected—and afterward he decided he would concentrate on *Paradise Lost* instead of Milton collected, and he took *Paradise Lost* from its place on the shelf, and it fell open to the drawing (a rather poor drawing, Vachel thought) of Adam and Eve in the garden.

After supper he went again to his room and cleared his worktable and adjusted his chair, and sat, and he put his feet upon the table and leaned back prepared to savor the magnificent roll of the first lines of the poem, the address to the Muse, *Of man's first disobedi-*

ence, and the fruit of that forbidden tree, whose mortal taste brought death into the world, and all our woe, with loss of Eden, till one greater man restore us, and regain the blissful seat, Sing, heavenly muse. Thus Milton, in the old house in middle age after the public life was over, addressed his Muse and launched the great work of his life, and Vachel, thinking that if he drank of Milton he might restore himself, prepared to read.

But daylight was fading, and before beginning his reading he removed his feet from the table and leaned forward toward the lamp and pressed the switch and the lamp did not light, and he knew it was the bulb. The bulb was dead. He could see that it was dead. He unscrewed it and shook it at his ear and it made a rattling sound, and he went downstairs and threw the bulb into the garbage can in the kitchen, and he unscrewed a bulb from a hall lamp and shook it at his ear, and it made a rattling sound, and he took it upstairs to his room and inserted it, and the lamp did not light. He knew that what must have happened was that the plug had somehow been loosened from its socket, and he traced the lamp wire from the lamp to the socket in the wall, but it had not been loosened, and he went to the lamp to test it, to see if he had screwed the bulb tight, and then he pressed the switch twice, and then he knew it must be that a fuse had blown. But he did not go to the fuse box. Instead, he took his book downstairs and set it upon the dining-room table, and he took a candelabra from the mantel, and he found a candle in the utility drawer in the kitchen, and he lighted the candle and set it in the candleholder and read by candlelight at the dining-room table.

Elisabeth and Susan, on either side of him, read in their own books by the light of the candle, and Susan thought it was fun and she hoped they could read like this every night, and Vachel read Book One through the description of Mammon, and he said softly, "Lord!" and Elisabeth said, "What, dear?" and he read to her Milton on Mammon, *the least erected spirit that fell from heaven, for even in heaven his looks and thoughts were always downward bent, admiring more the riches of heaven's pavement, trodden gold, than aught divine or holy else enjoyed in vision beatific: by him first Men also, and by his suggestion taught, ransacked the center, and with impious hands rifled the bowels of their mother earth,* reading softly and following the lines with his index finger because candlelight is not good light.

And afterward they all went up to bed, and the next day was

Saturday and Duncan and Willis came and Vachel told them about the lights and they looked one to the other and scowled and said they would fix the lights, and Vachel said no he could read by daylight and candlelight. But they insisted, and he went into the house and found in one place and another the poetry the electric people had sent, signed Doody Evryway. Doody was a little man shaped like a light bulb. *I'm in your home at your command, conveniently on every hand, to do your bidding with swift strokes, I'm your electric servant, folks,* and that was the first poem, and the poems were stronger in tone each succeeding time, first a reminder, then a stronger reminder, then mild demand and then a stronger demand, and at length a sad farewell from Doody Evryway *I have remained quite faithfully, but now have other chores to fill, I will be back per usual, upon the payment of your bill,* and Duncan and Willis went away at the end of the afternoon, and in the evening the lights came suddenly on and Vachel went from Book One to Book Two of *Paradise Lost,* and on Sunday they all went for a ride with Nell and Duncan McDonald.

There was one heavy rain in May. It washed the city clean of the results of the thaw, and then the sun became warmer and gardens grew and grass turned almost overnight a rich green, and the parks were full and the fire companies hosed the children on appointed days on appointed streets, and in June the tourists came, and nobody knew it but it was to be, for quite some time, the last summer of travel in a big way because by next summer there would not be, somehow, the willingness to pay tourist rates on gasoline and food and hotel rooms. But, beginning in June, they came, and they climbed the hill to see the Lincoln tomb, and then they came down the hill and went across town to see the Lincoln home, and they stood behind the ropes that were looped from post to post and stared and tried to believe that on that very chair, in that very bed, through that very window, the great man sat or slept or looked out upon the street, and some of them went up to New Salem to see the little place where Lincoln had kept store and where Mentor Graham had taught him useful things.

A few, mostly schoolteachers and students, found their way to Fifth Street, and they knocked on the door of the old house and asked to see Vachel, and he came, and they saw him, and they told him how they remembered hearing him and seeing him, and he said it was very kind of them to remember.

And after a time, on account of the heat, he became weary of coming to the door. He carried a kitchen chair into the garden where he could not hear the knocking. He set it in the shade of the house, and here he read slowly in *Paradise Lost* and knew that after a little time, after a few weeks more, he would be ready again to write his own new poems.

On the green grass, in the sun, Nicholas and Susan amused themselves, running barefoot on the soft carpet of grass, seemingly unconscious of the heat. But in July even they, even children, became aware of the heat's oppression, and one day they were strangely still and silent, and he raised his eyes from the speech of the faithful Abdiel in the fifth book of *Paradise Lost,* and he saw them sitting motionless with parted lips, near him in the shade. There were beads of perspiration on their foreheads, and he marked his place in the book and told them he had a grand idea. They went slowly into the house with him, and he took a coffee can and emptied it and rinsed it and punched holes in its bottom with the ice pick, and he mixed warm water with cold and filled the can and went with them into the garden and stood with the dripping can held above their heads. It cooled them, and they demanded that he shower them many times, and this he did before returning in an hour's time to the speech of Abdiel the faithful.

Every day they demanded to be showered, and he complied until at length he had a still better idea, and he went downtown and bought a washtub and fifty feet of garden hose and nozzle, and he paid for them with a five-dollar bill and counted his change as of late he had taken to counting his change, and then he looked questioningly at the hardware man. "It seems to be short," Vachel said, and the hardware man told him crisply exactly the price of each item, and in the telling it developed that the nozzle was extra, and Vachel said he thought he could do without the nozzle for the present, and the hardware man, considerably vexed, unscrewed the nozzle from the hose and returned the additional change to Vachel. Vachel put the hose into the tub and carried the tub home.

Every day he set the tub in the sun to warm, and after it warmed he filled it with water, and after the water was warm he gave the signal to Susan and Nicholas, and then for five minutes, plugging the hose end with a finger and making a spray, he watered the lawn, and once Duncan and Willis brought a nozzle for the hose, but Vachel never bothered to attach it because soon afterward the Water Commission strongly urged that water not be wasted on garden grass, and the green grass browned and died in the garden in the rainless summer.

And every day seemed hotter than the day before. His hands were wet upon his book. The dye of the old book stained his hands blue, and to move was to sweat, and the sweat came down his forehead and into his eyes. But he read because he knew that when the cool autumn came he would be ready again for his writing, and Willis asked him periodically if he had written the poetic paragraph for the throwaway, and he said no but he was coming around to it, and Willis said no hurry no hurry, and Vachel read through Book Seven the creation of the earth according to Milton, how the earth in the beginning and in Milton's time and in all times was abundantly lighted and watered, and God said to Adam in the eighth book *This Paradise I give thee; count it thine to till and keep,* and Adam and Eve were naked and unashamed and thankful in the garden.

And it was as if Milton were there in the garden in Springfield, saying here is my vision. And it was Vachel's vision and the vision of thoughtful poets in all times from Socrates to Sandburg, and it was Willis' and Duncan's, the vision of useful men in all ages: the abundant earth and the peaceful garden.

And Vachel knew that autumn, when it came, might fail to strengthen him and return to his mind and hand the power that had once been his. And he knew that if autumn came empty he would do that which was still in his power to do, for he had created in his lifetime a vision, and the vision lay printed and bound black upon white in his books, and having created the vision he would not undo it by writing, in his later time, bad poetry, or tales with dishonest happy endings, for the bills would be paid but the vision would be erased. He would not sell himself in any autumn to support any vision but his own, and he reread John Milton on the faithful Abdiel: *Among the faithless, faithful. Among innumerable false, unmoved, unshaken, unseduced, unterrified his loyalty he kept, his love, his zeal; nor number, nor example with him wrought to swerve from truth, or change his constant mind though single. From amidst them forth he passed, long way through hostile scorn, which he sustained superior, nor of violence feared aught; and with retorted scorn his back he turned on those proud towers to swift destruction doomed.*

CHAPTER SIX

1

A FEW LINES for Willis because Willis is an old and dear and trusted friend and he stuck by Vachel in the old days when Vachel was nobody and maybe would always be nobody, as Susan Wilcox gave of herself to him though he was only another child and maybe always would be but a child putting words upon paper, as Duncan takes them for rides in the car on Sunday because it is all they can afford and the children love to ride in a car, for Willis, an old friend, a few lines advocating a Plan that will always be a plan and never a Lake.

At his table, writing, and the rain drips from the eaves and where was the rain in the summertime when everybody needed it and the grass and the farmers, and even now the rain is lost in the ground as the snow will be lost in the ground as the rain next spring will be lost in the ground because nobody thinks to put the rain away for a sunny day except Willis and the Public Ownership League and what good are they they have a bad name all up and down Illinois. The rain darkens the afternoon and he reaches for the light and presses the switch and the light does not light *I am Doody Evryway with little troubles just like you Please try to remember me when-e'er your bill comes due* Your Friendly Iceman grocer butcher baker candlestick tax collector, and he thinks he will light the candles but then he thinks no he will go somewhere and write it out for Willis and get it done once and for all. He folds four sheets of manuscript paper and puts them into his pocket and he takes two sharp-pointed pencils and puts them pointside upside into his pocket promising himself to remember to be careful when he·goes to his pocket for them, and he leaves the house saying not good-by nor when he will return and he goes through the rain down Fifth Street to Capitol and downtown on Capitol, and the lights reflect themselves on the wet cement blinking on and off and on and off and he wishes he had remembered his hat because surely he will catch cold and when old men catch cold it is harder for older people. Yet he is not old. He

390

only feels old. He is young, and to show that he is young he walks very briskly and spryly in a straight line down Capitol Avenue through puddles and up and down curbs, and water overruns his shoes, and the cuffs of his trousers slap-slap-slap against his ankles and his hair is plastered flat across his forehead like Charlie Chaplin in the moving pictures will Chaplin play in the speakies it would be a shame if Chaplin dies out up the steps of the Lincoln library and over to the table where he always sits and his cigarettes are wet if he lights one it will dry as it burns, and he lights it, lighting the match upon the dry corner of the box and the assistant librarian horrified, and yet what to say to a famous poet for smoking in the library, and anyway closing time in a very few minutes, and he plunges his hand into his pocket pricking his fingers on the sharp-pointed pencil, and he writes one sentence for Willis and the Lake on a piece of paper that was folded on the inside and did not get wet, and the lights go off and on and off and on signifying closing time in five minutes. He writes one further sentence in the five allotted minutes thinking whatsisname in Boston writes a sonnet a day. We are closing, she says.

Down the steps into the street the rain on Seventh Street as in the seventh book of Milton God saying *Let the waters generate,* generating down upon his head his hair his body spilling into his shoes down Seventh Street in the supper hour, and on this very street first looking into Dante when he was a small boy Miss Gloria Fisk they called her Miss Glorious Fits but she is a good lady and it is a wonder with so many good ladies and good men in one city up the steps of City Hall out of the rain an unlocked door he enters and pulls a lightstring and the light lights and he sits at a desk and pulls forth pencils paper and reads what he wrote in the library. He writes further for Willis: "It will surely provide in tremendous quantities one of the City's most vital practical necessities WATER. But it will also provide . . ."

Before him scowling puzzled the watchman watches. "What goes on here?"

"I am Vachel Lindsay."

"That's nice," the watchman says. "Now get out," adding and explaining how he would lose his job how the night is bad and he is sorry but they did need the rain and he hates to be inhospitable suppose everybody came and used City Hall he would lose his job and jobs are hard to find.

On the corner of Seventh and Monroe in the history books at high school the Monroe Doctrine we owe it therefore to candor it is the system says Mr. Wilson he would lose his job and jobs are hard to find, and he thinks he will go to the high school and sit at his desk and write the lesson for Willis. Down Monroe and over past the *Journal* office he could use a typewriter in the *Journal* upstairs and into the city room. "I'd like to," says the desk man, "but I'd only catch hell." "Of course," says Vachel and down the stairs in the *Journal* window downstairs the wire news the latest bulletin as if there were anything new since John Milton stated it once and forever *this paradise I give you count it thine to till and keep* and Cleveland running ahead in this very window and afterward Papa will march with the Democrats in the torchlight parade and Vachel will ride along half-asleep in the buggy down Capitol to the Abraham Lincoln Hotel no Negroes no poets except in proper dress but not wet like this dripping all over the carpets into the rain again and down Capitol and over to Adams via Monroe and Adams dear Witter Bynner perfectly willing to sass anyone from G. Wash to A. Hamilton out Adams to the high school and the doors are locked and if Miss Susan Wilcox were here she would admit him he would enter sit before her and start again and not make the same mistakes again it is cold and Mama will have it warm and dry for him and Papa will give him two pills to be swallowed with rainwater and they will turn on all the lights in the house and write out the lesson for Willis Wilcox grow old along with me the best is yet to be the last of life for which the first was made

O Mama

O Papa

Thence through the rain the way he had always walked from the high school to home down Monroe to the Statehouse and across the Statehouse lawn swinging his lunchpail in one hand and his books strapped in leather in the other and Olive beside him and thou beside me singing in the wilderness as in Omar Khayyám when he read it on the train the Anti-Saloon League dropped him he forgot to pass the hat.

Through the rain and home and into the dark house and Elisabeth frightened and wordless brings him dry clothes and hot soup and coffee Lotus-Blossom he calls her, and he sits by candlelight at the dining-room table and writes very quickly the two hundred words for Willis.

It is not very good writing. But Willis will print it in his throw-away, and it will be read, and because of what Vachel has written, and because Willis every year takes people to see his imaginary lake, and because the voter is not so dumb as some people think, the imaginary lake will become Lake Springfield, and there will never again be a Springfield summer like the summer just ended, evil-dry and barren, when the gardens of the city withered, browned and died in the waterless earth.

In the morning the sun shines. The day smells of autumn. Last night was confused, but today all things are clear. All things are seen aright.

At his table in his room he edits what he has written for Willis. It is not a very convincing piece of writing. It is rhetorical rather than logical, sounding too much like a newspaper editorial. But it is the sort of thing Willis will be able to use to advantage.

It is rather sloppily punctuated. Vachel has never mastered the fine points of punctuation, particularly with relation to the comma, but he has usually known, more or less by instinct, when to use the comma, and he now inserts commas according to the rules of instinct. At points where there seems to be a necessity for punctuation of some sort, yet where the comma seems somehow too formal, he uses the dash. He reads: "It will surely provide in tremendous quantities one of the City's most vital practical necessities WATER," feeling that a comma ought to be introduced between *necessities* and *water.* He seems to remember something Susan Wilcox once said about something in apposition to something, and he wonders if the rule would apply here. It seems to him on afterthought that a comma is not bold enough, and so he rounds out the comma, making it a period, and places another dot above it, making the figure a colon. It seems more logical.

Then he leaves the house, standing on the porch a moment to test the weather, then returning for a topcoat, then proceeding downtown to City Hall. He leaves the written matter with Willis' secretary, and he returns home the way he came, through the autumn, which, in Springfield, is usually a clear, cool, vigorous time of year. He has always loved autumn in Springfield.

And today, he thinks, will be the day. Today is autumn, and autumn is really the beginning of the year, not spring, as some suppose. Spring is prelude to summer, and he could not write during the summer because of the heat, but autumn and winter are good seasons for writing. Now he will write.

There is a telephone message from Willis. He received the material, and thank you.

Vachel goes to his room and closes his door behind him and sits at his table and prepares to write, setting out clean paper and sharpened pencils, the tools of his trade, and somehow no first word or sentence comes, as always the first words have come and precipitated the flow, and while waiting he thinks he will retype the Mentor Graham poem, thinking first he will change the ribbon on his typewriter because the new heavy-black print is good to see. There is a certain strength in black type. He changes the ribbon. To test it he types, *the quick brown fox jumps over the lazy dog,* which is the only sentence he knows containing all the letters of the alphabet, and then he types the sentence in capital letters, and then with a split matchstick he cleans the lower-case *e* which is clogged, and then he is prepared to write.

Yet he thinks he ought to let the retyping go for a while, and he pushes the typewriter to one side and studies the clean paper, and he taps his pencil on the table until, at length, the sound irritates him, and he lays the pencil down and it rolls to the edge of his table and falls to the floor. He pushes back his chair to see where the pencil has rolled, and he sees it beneath the table, and he brings it toward him with his foot, rolling it to a point within reach of his hand, and he rescues it and sets it in its place on the table, and then he picks it up again and scratches idly on the clean paper, the quick brown fox jumps over the lazy dog, thinking one might write a poem each line of which contains every letter of the alphabet once for a single sentence praising Singleton Stanley typewriters the Singleton Stanley people offered him one hundred dollars back in the good old days before the war when he was young in the lyric year and he threw away whole poems because they did not suit him, back when poetry came profuse to his hand.

Undoubtedly it will be that way soon again. It is early in the day and his head is clear and all things are focused in sharp outline, and the wind is in the trees outside his window. The Governor's mansion throws its shadow east, black against the sunlit lawn.

And he sits a long time with his hands upon his knees, staring down at the white paper the quick brown fox jumping over the lazy dog the cross-eyed yellow dog when he sat in Washington Park writing of Utopia in Springfield which saw him sitting round-shouldered in the park and believed that he was cheating them because they did not understand and do not yet understand having no arithmetic machine that can possibly compute the cost it cost him and still costs to dream of Utopia in Springfield. It has cost aplenty, and now he pays, having spent himself and given himself away free with both hands at zero-per-cent interest not a loan but a gift a little colt, bronco, loaned to the farm and they whipped it until it was dead and it danced till it died was never a proper bronco Papa warned it to be proper left black notebooks full of Springfield names that died owing money to the house of Lindsay, and he should have gone and made them pay I am Doody Vachel and you owe so much and so much and you must pay or I will absorb your kilowatt.

The shadow of the mansion reaches the walk. On Fifth Street, on the doorsteps, children play, waiting for the return of the father, and the fathers come and the children run to greet them. The air is filled with evening sounds. The days are growing shorter. Vachel will be asked by Susan soon why the days grow shorter is the sun going out will the sun ever burn up will the world ever end what makes shadows, and the day's end stirs a mild panic within him, for early in the day he knew that today would be the day, and the day has come and gone and today after all was not the day, and he sat all day useless.

Thus tonight must be the night, and he always wrote his best at night wrote Bryan at night in the mountains at Empire one night when his debts were paid and Woodrow Wilson was riding the trains and peace was to be tomorrow saw Tom Dines' name in the Denver paper *Oh, Tom Dines and Art Fitzgerald and the gangs that they could get,* the Democratic crowds they got and always got, and the work was easy for them when Bryan came, and Tom Dines went to Denver and put behind him his radical ways and became a big wheel in the business machine should have gone to Denver or somewhere and become a big man in a big business of America is business *Calvin Coolidge here Herbert Hoover here* why Herbert how interesting you are the first President born west of the Mississippi yes ma'am but all the frontiers are closed and all the pioneers are dead all the Boones and Appleseeds dead or presidents of corporations like Abe Lincoln's boy the president of the Pullman Car Company, wrote the Bryan at night and will write tonight.

And at night he sits again at his table, and the night is soundless. The long night is ahead, and surely by night's end he will have written something worth reading come morning, and the panic rises within him like a fever Papa says fever always rises at night, and he strains for the word that will loose all other words and lines and stanzas and poems as first lines always led to others *It is portentous and a thing of state in a nation of one hundred million relenting repenting millions Booth led boldly with his big bass little colt bronco loaned to the farm the thing that eats the rotting stars would we were blind with Milton I'll haunt this town though gone the maids and men sometimes I dip my pen and find the bottle full of fire* might write a poem nothing but first lines containing all the letters of the quick brown cross-eyed fox, and the fever rises.

He prepares to write, concentrating, fastening his thinking cap as Susan Wilcox told them blasts of the engine whistle beneath the schoolhouse window might write a Susan Wilcox poem after the Mentor Graham poem Susan Wilcox with a *u* and an *x* a good start on all the letters of the concentrate not let the mind wander away in long sentences without commas in apposition to the most practical vital necessity water everywhere but not a drop to Coleridge it is said wrote in a trance would be nice to fall in a trance and wake up a new poem there on the paper not let the mind drift away as in dreams as in sleep perchance without commas but concentrate concentrate concentrate as at Hiram where he got the football scar now faded across his chin.

Thinking, resting his chin upon his hand, he thinks the first line will surely come by dawn. He must concentrate. He must give of himself, clear-headed, bringing out of himself the genius of his later days, the later years, and morning comes on forever said the Chinese nightingale dedicated to Sara wore a green hat with a white Paradise lost by John Milton in the old house after the years as a public man.

Concentrate!

And the black night is silver, and it is filled with dawn sounds and the coming-awake of the City after the night of sleep, and the sun comes out of the east creating shade on the western side of the Governor's mansion, and the clean paper sits before him, and the sun having circled the world (or, to be more exact, since it will be necessary to explain it sometime to Susan, the earth having rotated upon its axis one full turn) now lights his table and the papers thereon upon which the labor of twenty hours is typewritten with a new ribbon upper-cased and lower-cased THE QUICK BROWN FOX JUMPS OVER THE LAZY DOG the quick brown fox jumps over the lazy dog.

Unrelieved day and unrelieved night, and a rising fever that is unrelieved panic and weariness, and the panic is not a morning panic now, for it is the length of a day and a night, and end meets end until, like a circle, it has no end and no beginning, as days and nights for Vachel have now neither end nor beginning.

And he sits knowing that there are wells within him yet to be tapped, and yet he knows that there are none, that he is weary and barren, that he gave too much of himself and went too far too often and scattered his seed as Johnny Appleseed scattered his seed and in the end walked alone and unremembered.

2

John Milton, in the old house, lamenting the lost cause and the squandered paradise, had yet one song to sing, and it was the Samson song.

And the song of Samson was the song of himself, of him, John Milton, like Samson, eyeless in Gaza, fallen upon evil days, prisoner of the Philistines in the old house.

And if there is now no song to sing, if now he is shorn and helpless, unmanned by the Philistines, there is yet the deed to do, the final duty, the final cry to cry here in the dark house where, in the room above, he cried the first cry, drew the first breath, sucked first upon the wine of life, drinking then the first drink as now he will drink the drink that will be his last, that will halt the breath, silence the cry.

Because if there is now no song to sing there is then no reason to be. Death by the poisoned cup will be swift.

And what would life be without the song? What use the wine of life and the breath of life if there be no song, no cry upon the lip? Life was a song, and all the joy of life was in singing the song that mirrored the spirit. Life was creation, first the painting of pictures, and then the singing of his own songs, and the two were joined, and the song was the portrait of the promise of the possibilities he saw from these windows, the promise of Springfield and the United States of the World.

And he sang the wrong song.

He sang the wrong song in Athens Illinois and his friend Plato, writing in the aftertime, said that he drank from the stained cup and lay down to die, guilty of speculating about the heaven above and the earth below and of making the worse appear the better cause.

And the Hebrew sang the wrong song, singing put up thy sword into his place, for all they that take the sword shall perish with the sword, and they affixed him to the cross near the trough where Papa's horses drank on the square in Springfield Illinois.

And if he drink of the cup he might yet live. But if he live without song he will surely die because in Illinois, as in Jerusalem, as in Athens, he who makes song dies young and therefore remains forever young. Later, when the times are equal to the man, when the city discovers the gentleman from Fifth Street, when at last his books are read and the attempt is made to understand, there will be only young songs in the book. He will be forever young, forever the Hebrew in Gaza, forever the boy who could not carry the tune, the wanderer, the soldier singing of Jerusalem on the streets of Babylon, the bird in the hedge by the side of the road. He will be forever the young man bearing upon his coat of arms a bronco, rampant.

There will be myth and memory, and the books will go unread. But in the long pull there will be so much of myth and so little of memory that the books will be reopened, and he will be alive again, and he will be as young as he was when he wrote Altgeld in the room above, Booth at Uncle Olan's, Bryan in the Colorado mountains. The dead stay young.

He pours from the skullandcrossbones bottle, into the cup, and in the poison cup is life, and he closes his eyes, and then, swiftly, he drinks of the cup of life clear to the bottom drinks scalding lips mouth inners empty cup falling floorward great noise upon the floor as of a man falling floorward must rise and seek the bed and die where he was born Oh I die Horatio the potent poison quite o'ercrows my spirit I cannot live to hear the news from England on hands and knees to the stairway hand over hand over hand stepward upward Locust-Blossom at stairway do not scream Locust-Blossom you will wake the children lifts him softly crying not to wake the children up the stairway to the bed lights now a candle because the lights again are broken goes now through the night because the telephone too is sadly broken dying now at midnight it is portentous and a thing of state that here at midnight in our little town the doctor comes looks down into his face and sees and opens not even satchel. "Why why why WHY?" the doctor cries.

I will tell you through heat through mouth afire with the last strength of my burning body as well as I am able lean close, closer, closer: "They tried to get me. I got them first."

Those are the last words.

The rest is silence.

Springfield Illinois. December 7, 1931. Weather: sunshine.

Oak Ridge Cemetery
Eight citizens bear a coffin.
Willis Spaulding, straining at a coffin corner, is weeping. Duncan Mc-Donald, his face contorted, straining, also weeps. It is embarrassing to see strong men weep. They are strong men. One is building, almost singlehanded, a lake. Five summers hence, on Lake Springfield, near Spaulding Dam, near Vachel Lindsay Bridge, white-sailed boats will glide before the breeze.
The Salvation Army lays a wreath upon the grave.
A workman plants a small sign beside the plot: Perpetual Care.
A choir prepares to sing Hark, Ten Thousand Harps and Voices.

Newsroom
I have five faithful servingmen, their names are who, what, why, where, when. Vachel Lindsay, died, of heart disease, at his home, early this morning. The press accepts, unquestioningly, the stated cause. It was, indeed, heart disease. The press lists the titles of poems and books. It mangles the titles. It calls books by the name of poems and poems by the name of books. It refers to the poems as fantastic. It looked hurriedly into the poems this morning. They looked fantastic.
The news of the day is crisply written in a later time by the poet Edgar Lee Masters, easily the best reporter on the Illinois beat. "His funeral was as distinguished as sorrow could make it and desire to erase past neglect could contrive."

Western Union
Clerk with a green eyeshade. Messages of condolence. The names are familiar. I have heard the names: Sinclair Lewis, Edgar Lee Masters, Harriet Monroe, Sara Teasdale.
Hiram Ohio.
London.
Residence of the Governor, Springfield Illinois.

Bookstore
A run on the Lindsay books. We will raise the price a little.

Knife and Fork
Rotary stands one minute in silence.
The Chamber of Commerce unanimously agrees to mourn his passing, approves the report of the national-affairs committee regarding a proposal to survey business conditions, discusses the effect of deep-waterways transportation on inland cities.

400

Advertisement in the Local Newspaper
Photograph of a tombstone: "A simple Colonial Tablet of White Crystalline Georgia Marble fabricated and inscribed as only the true artists would prefer. The Springfield Monument Company (exclusive distributor of Georgia Marble) are pleased to have been selected as the designers and builders of the correct memorial to Springfield's famous troubadour."

*Reflections of a Friend Preparatory to the
Delivery of a Funeral Oration*
High tragedy in the Greek sense. Will they understand the allusion? I will explain the allusion: Aristotle described high tragedy as the fall of someone highborn, noble. There is also some reference to a tragic flaw —an internal thing—that makes the tragedy inevitable.

Vachel was highborn. He was the free son of free people in a free land. That is as highborn as any man has ever been in the history of the world.

He was noble, as all men are potentially noble, whether they be poets or firemen, miners or farmers, good shoemakers or poor fish peddlers. We know more about nobility than Aristotle did in his time.

He was highborn and noble, and he lived among us, and the tragedy need not have been tragedy. For he did not die because of that inner thing in the Greek sense. He died because of outward things. We—all of us—understand these things better now than the Greeks did—this outward relation between a man and his time, a man and his place. Vachel died because he was that part of us—of time and place—that dies in our land, our clean conscience, our poetic self, the lone man who breaks with the present, thinking he might suggest to us a fuller future. The man of responsibility.

He was a great man. I do not know if he was a great poet. I will not touch upon that. I will say: that is a problem I leave with the scholars.

He was a great citizen of our town, our country, and the world. He was a great patriot and a great lover. Goethe said—I will quote Goethe: "What is meant by love of one's country? What is meant by patriotic deeds? If the poet has employed a life in battling with pernicious prejudices, in setting aside narrow views, in enlightening the minds, purifying the tastes, ennobling the feelings and thoughts of his countrymen, what better could he have done? How could he have acted more patriotically?" I think that is a good definition of both love and patriotism.

Another element of tragedy is waste. Tragic waste. Vachel might have lived twenty, thirty, forty more years. He used to say—jokingly, I think —that he planned to live to be one hundred and five. 1984. But he is dead before his time. And we have lost a half-century. We have wasted fifty years. We could have saved him. We in Springfield could have saved him for the price of one mile of concrete roadway. Illinois could have saved him twice over for the price of upkeep on the Governor's house. The United States could have saved him at a cost so small that not the tiniest item of Government service would have been sacrificed. Perhaps these are not the best ways. But there are ways. A country that can build a Panama Canal and submarines and battleships can surely devise ways. If we want to.

But the tragedy—his death—is not truly tragedy if we leave this scene knowing something new about ourselves. About our world. He said himself—I heard him—there is a time to die and there are noble ways to die. And he will have died in his own good time in a noble way if we leave here knowing anew that there are thousands upon thousands of Vachels in the land, in our factories, in our shops, on our farms, in our schools, on our open roads, and they are young and old and white and black and we must give them voice. We must give them long life. The time to save them is when they are young men and women.

I remember some lines that Vachel once wrote. I will recite them. He wrote: "Who can pass a district school without the hope that there may wait some baby heart the books may flame with zeal to make his playmates great . . . ?"

Who can, indeed? But we must give the baby hearts—as Vachel put it—time to grow to greatness. We must see that they do not die. On battlefields. We must see that they are not crushed here at home in our own—our own—for lack of a better word—system. As he was crushed. You will say: but we do not know who the great ones are. I say: then we must be careful to crush no one, not the least among us. For we never know where greatness lives. We do not know how much we have already killed. We almost killed Vachel before he was fairly begun. He emerged despite us. But that does not prove that the genius that is in us will always refuse to be denied. It proves only that here and there among us are a few stronger than the rest. Stronger stomachs. Greater wills. You will say: oil will rise and float on water. I say: men are not oil and water.

Undoubtedly he was mistaken in many things. Perhaps he should not have taken the romantic view of history. I heard him say often that he took the romantic view of history. Perhaps he should have allied himself with some political group—Socialists, say, or pacifists or anarchists—and he would have received strength from them as he would, in exchange, have given them strength. Perhaps he should have saved himself first, and lived to fight another day. Who is to say? If he had lived another sort of life he would not have been Vachel as you and I knew him. He would not have been before us now in the—the condition—the condition he is, as the reminder, the proof, the terrible warning that we in Springfield are still not entitled to call ourselves true Christians, true patriots, the rightful heirs to the kind of city Vachel envisioned. The kind of city we will sooner or later have. Yes. We will have such a city. I will say it affirmatively: yes, we will have such a city. Because it is necessary to believe. Because it is a matter of faith as well as a matter of action.

I think they will understand the allusions. This is, after all, a funeral, not a political occasion.

They are lowering it.

Breathe deep.

Keep the voice steady.

When I am finished I will ask the choir to sing Hark, Ten Thousand Harps and Voices.

House Resolution

"Whereas Nicholas Vachel Lindsay has passed to that World of Beauty of which he sang; and

"Whereas his literary genius and his ability to see beauty where the world ignored it, established him as a world-famed poet, and created an entire new style in utter disregard of the stilted and conventional; and

"Whereas he won not only the affection but that which is proverbially far more difficult, the acclamation and recognition of his own people, and was proclaimed as their first citizen; and

"Whereas he was beloved by those in all walks of life and of every faith and creed; now, therefore, be it

"Resolved by the House of Representatives of the 57th General Assembly of the State of Illinois at the first special session thereof, and That we recognize the loss to the State and the Nation, and to all his fellow men, in the passing of this great man of broad understanding and sincere human sympathy, and express to the members of his family, our deepest sympathy; and be it further

"Resolved, That this preamble and resolution be spread upon the Journal of the House; that a suitably engrossed copy thereof be forwarded to his family; and, as a further tribute to his memory, that the House do now adjourn."